British Government and Politics

A Comparative Guide

Duncan Watts

Edinburgh University Press

Edinburgh University Press Ltd
22 George Square, Edinburgh

Typeset in 11/13pt Monotype Baskerville by
Servis Filmsetting Ltd, Manchester, and
printed and bound in Great Britain by
Antony Rowe Ltd, Chippenham, Wilts

A CIP record for this book is available from the British Library

ISBN-10 0 7486 2323 X (paperback)
ISBN-13 978 0 7486 2323 5 (paperback)

The right of Duncan Watts to be identified as author of this work has been
asserted in accordance with the Copyright, Designs and Patents Act 1988.

Published with the support of the Edinburgh University Scholarly Publishing Initiatives Fund.

British Government
and Politics

Books in the Politics Study Guides series

British Government and Politics: A Comparative Guide
Duncan Watts

International Politics: An Introductory Guide
Alasdair Blair, Steven Curtis and Sean McGough

US Government and Politics: An Introductory Guide
Will Storey

Britain and the European Union
Alistair Jones

The Changing Constitution
Kevin Harrison and Tony Boyd

Democracy in Britain
Matt Cole

Devolution in the United Kingdom
Russell Deacon and Alan Sandry

Elections and Voting in the UK
Chris Robinson

The Judiciary, Civil Liberties and Human Rights
Steven Foster

Political Communication
Steven Foster

Political Parties in Britain
Matt Cole

The Politics of Northern Ireland
Joanne McEvoy

Pressure Groups
Duncan Watts

The Prime Minister and Cabinet
Stephen Buckley

The UK Parliament
Moyra Grant

Contents

Boxes

Tables

Leaders of the two main parties in Britain since 1945

Conservatives	Period as Conservative leader	Labour	Period as Labour leader
Winston Churchill	1940–1955 *1940–1945; 1951–1955	Clement Attlee	1935–1955 *1945–1951
Anthony Eden	1955–1957 *1955–1957	Hugh Gaitskell	1955–1963
Harold Macmillan	1957–1963 *1957–1963	Harold Wilson	1963–1976 *1964–1970; 1974–1976
Alec Douglas Home	1963–1965 *1963–1964	James Callaghan	1976–1981 *1976–1979
Edward Heath	1965–1975 *1970–1974	Michael Foot	1981–1983
Margaret Thatcher	1975–1990 *1979–1990	Neil Kinnock	1983–1992
John Major	1990–1997 *1990–1997	John Smith	1992–1994
William Hague	1997–2001	Tony Blair	1994– *1997–
Iain Duncan Smith	2001–2003		
Michael Howard	2003–2005		
David Cameron	2005–		

* denotes period in office as prime minister

US Presidents since 1945

President	Party	Term in White House
Franklin D. Roosevelt	Democrat	1945
Harry S Truman	Democrat	1945–1953
Dwight Eisenhower	Republican	1953–1961
John F. Kennedy	Democrat	1961–1963
Lyndon Johnson	Democrat	1963–1969
Richard Nixon	Republican	1969–1974
Gerald Ford	Republican	1974–1977
James Carter	Democrat	1977–1981
Ronald Reagan	Republican	1981–1989
George H. Bush	Republican	1989–1993
William Clinton	Democrat	1993–2001
George W. Bush	Republican	2001–

Votes and seats in British general elections since 1945

Year	Party	% Votes	No. of Seats	% Seats
1945	Con	39.8	213	33.3
	Lib	9.0	12	1.9
	Lab	47.8	393	61.4
1950	Con	43.5	298	47.7
	Lib	9.1	9	1.4
	Lab	46.1	315	50.4
1951	Con	48.0	321	51.4
	Lib	2.5	6	1.0
	Lab	48.8	295	47.2
1955	Con	49.7	344	54.6
	Lib	2.7	6	1.0
	Lab	46.4	277	44.0
1959	Con	49.4	365	57.9
	Lib	5.9	6	1.0
	Lab	43.8	258	41.0
1964	Con	43.4	304	48.3
	Lib	11.2	9	1.4
	Lab	44.1	317	50.3
1966	Con	41.9	253	40.2
	Lib	8.5	12	1.9
	Lab	47.9	363	57.6
1970	Con	46.4	330	52.4
	Lib	7.5	6	1.0
	Lab	43.0	287	45.6
1974 (Feb)	Con	37.9	297	46.8
	Lib	19.3	14	2.2
	Lab	37.1	301	47.4

Year	Party	% Votes	No. of Seats	% Seats
1974	Con	35.0	277	43.6
(Oct)	Lib	18.3	13	2.1
	Lab	39.2	319	50.2
1979	Con	43.9	339	53.4
	Lib	13.8	11	1.7
	Lab	36.9	268	42.4
1983	Con	42.4	397	61.0
	All	25.4	23	3.5
	Lab	27.6	209	32.0
1987	Con	42.3	376	57.8
	All	22.6	22	3.4
	Lab	30.9	229	35.2
1992	Con	41.9	336	51.6
	Lib Dem	17.9	20	3.1
	Lab	34.3	271	41.6
1997	Con	30.7	165	25.0
	Lib Dem	16.8	46	7.0
	Lab	43.2	419	63.4
2001	Con	31.7	166	25.2
	Lib Dem	18.3	52	7.9
	Lab	40.7	412	62.5
2005	Con	32.4	198	30.7
	Lib Dem	22.0	62	9.6
	Lab	35.2	356	55.1

CHAPTER 1

The Setting of British Politics: British Society and the British People

Contents

Overview

In this opening chapter, we examine the background against which the British political system operates. By understanding the nature of British political development and society, and the values shared by many of the island's peoples, we can better appreciate key institutions and practices in British politics, and the attitudes and behaviour of British citizens.

Key issues to be covered in this chapter

- Aspects of the historical development of Britain, in particular national unity and the preference for peaceful change
- The traditional cohesion of British society and the absence of divisions based on ethnicity, language or religion
- The forces that have contributed to its growing diversity, including the rise of nationalism in Scotland and Wales, immigration and the impact of growing support for Islamic religious beliefs
- The meaning of the term 'political culture'
- Characteristic British political attitudes and habits, and the changes affecting them in recent decades

Introduction

Our study of British politics is primarily concerned with the way in which our representative democracy functions. But political systems do not operate in a vacuum. They are shaped by the society in which we live and reflect the assumptions, habits and values of our people. This is as true of Britain as any other country, so that some analysis of the social basis of our political life, and of the history and outlook of the British people, seems to be an appropriate place to begin our study of British government and politics.

The historical background

Most of the 192 countries in the world today are relatively recent creations, brought about by a struggle for independence in wars or revolutions from those powers which previously controlled their destiny. However, Britain has a very long tradition of independent nationhood, free from successful invasion for nearly a thousand years. Our institutions have evolved gradually over centuries, change usually coming about not as a result of civil upheaval or warfare, but by a process of adaptation. Generally speaking, they have maintained their name and much of their original form, but the way in which they operate has been modified in response to particular circumstances. For this reason, two writers were able to describe the situation as one of 'new wine in old bottles'.[1]

Our largely unbroken history of political independence has been matched by a long history of national unity. Wales was conquered in Tudor times and has since the Act of Union (1535) been governed via decisions taken at Westminster. Scotland, an independent country until the Act of Union (1707), was governed in the same way until it gained its Parliament in 1999. Scots have long been aware of their sense of nationality and proud of their different administrative and legal systems, but over recent centuries the relationship between the two countries has been a good one, their fortunes interwoven.

Ireland is a different case. Relations with our neighbouring island have been turbulent and often unhappy; 26 counties gained their independence from the rest of the UK in 1922, but the majority of inhabitants in the six counties of Northern Ireland have been keen to retain their allegiance to Great Britain. The province of Northern Ireland has had a troubled history. It had its own Parliament until the era of prolonged disturbance and political violence that culminated in the imposition of Direct Rule from Westminster in 1969 and the creation of an elected assembly (currently suspended) since 1998.

There have at times been tensions between the component countries of the United Kingdom, but – leaving aside the substantial problems surrounding Ireland – for most of the time it has been a cohesive political unit, marked by a lack of serious conflict. As we shall see, such a portrayal of British political development may seem complacent and inaccurate in the light of some changes in recent decades. But if this book had been written thirty or forty years ago, few would have questioned the essential accuracy of the description.

The traditions of national independence and broad political unity owe much to the facts of geography. Britain is an island, the Channel offering protection from invasion and insulating the country from any revolutionary movements of the continent. Indeed, one of the other important characteristics of British political development has been a preference for peaceful change. Britain has evolved primarily by non-revolutionary means and has enjoyed a remarkable historical continuity. There has been no major break or upheaval, such as the American, French and Russian revolutions, nor much in the way of civil war or conflict. Certainly, riots and rebellions were common in both the sixteenth and seventeenth centuries. Moreover, the latter provided disruption to the traditional pattern of constitutional evolution, witnessing as it did 'a civil war, a royal decapitation, an abdication and an Interregnum generally regarded by our European neighbours as a radical horror, much as the Bolshevist regime in Russia was regarded by the other European powers in the 1920s and 1930s'.[2] But over the following centuries, the British reputation for peace and stability was restored. Although there has been violence at times in British history, nonetheless the point about continuity remains relatively true compared to most other countries. As a result, there has been institutional continuity. Britain has made fewer efforts than most countries to erase the political past and start again. The essential structure of our constitutional arrangements has been bent and bruised, but not broken.

Since the late 1960s, the picture of Britain as a united nation has been under threat as a result of the continuing troubles in Northern

Ireland (see pp. 204–6), and the developing strength of the nationalist movement in Scotland and Wales. In Scotland, the impetus to intensified national feeling has come from a variety of factors, including its distinctive historical traditions and institutions, the economic potential of 'Scotland's oil' and a feeling of remoteness from and neglect by Westminster. The resurgence of nationalism has led to strong support for the Scottish National Party, which is committed to national independence from England. In Wales, the desire for separatism is much weaker and the growth of nationalism has a stronger cultural and linguistic dimension. Support for Plaid Cymru, the nationalist party, has been largely concentrated in five constituencies in rural mid-north Wales, where Welsh is commonly spoken.

Today, the picture of national unity has to be qualified. Political diversity is now a feature of the United Kingdom. So too the **homogeneity** of British society has come under challenge. There is greater social diversity than in the Britain of fifty years ago.

British society and the British way of life

It was until a few decades ago a common-place in books relating to British society for writers to point out that Britain has been relatively free from much of the internal disorder that occurs when different sections of the community are pitted against each other. In a description of the social fabric of British politics, Blondel[3] described Britain as a relatively homogeneous society. Society was seen as cohesive, there being none of the important divisions of **ethnicity**, religion, language and culture to be found in other European states and the USA. We were portrayed as an integrated community in which values did not differ radically between different social groups.

In the absence of such distinctions, social class is the phenomenon that attracted particular attention. Continentals have long portrayed the British as unduly obsessed by **social class** and seen this as the explanation for an assortment of our economic and political problems. By comparison with countries such as Australia and the United States, considerations of class have been important and the British have been conscious of their social status in relation to others. But although at times this has led to feelings of envy and resentment, it has not usually provoked substantial tensions between different sections of the community of the type that threaten social harmony and cohesion.

Neither has that overall homogeneity been challenged by any town and country divide. Britain is a highly urbanised and industrialised country in which almost 40 per cent of the people live in seven large conurbations, rather more in towns of over 10,000 inhabitants and only 20 per cent living in the rural areas, in small towns and villages. There have never been the strong clashes of interest between town and country that characterise countries such as France with its powerful agrarian lobby.

The changing nature of British society in recent decades

Over the last three or four decades, British society has been transformed in several respects. Social class is less important and there is greater social mobility than ever before. Whereas in the 1960s, two-thirds of the population were categorised as working class and a third middle class (based on such considerations as occupation, income, location, housing, accent, spending habits and general lifestyle), today the two categories are broadly equal. Education has been a great leveller, providing new opportunities for vast numbers of young people born into relatively poor circumstances, allowing them to acquire qualifications and improve their job prospects and earning capacity.

If divisions based on class have become less significant, in other respects Britain is now much more socially diverse. Britain has always had minority populations and successive bouts of immigration have modified the national character and shaped our national development. But until fifty years ago, this did not significantly challenge broad social cohesion or ethnic unity. Since the early 1950s, the situation has changed considerably. In spite of the early introduction of controls, the onset of Commonwealth immigration led to a substantial increase in numbers of Afro-Caribbean, Asian and other immigrants. More recently, the entry of asylum seekers (whether as genuine seekers after political freedom or economic migrants in search of a better way of life) has further added to the diversity of the British population, which is illustrated in Table 1.1. The distinctive feature of entrants from the New Commonwealth was that in many cases they were highly visible, because of a different skin colour. Migrants from Ireland or Central and Eastern Europe could blend in

Table 1.1 The ethnic mix of the United Kingdom, 2001

Nation	Total population	Asian and black	Percentage Asian and black
England	49,138,931	4,459,470	9.1
Northern Ireland	1,685,167	12,569	.7
Scotland	5,062,011	101,677	2.0
Wales	2,903,085	61,580	2.1
Total	58,789,194	4,635,296	7.9

Figures provided by the Office for National Statistics and based on the 2001 Census

NB The proportion of minority ethnic groups in England rose from 6% to 9% between 1991 and 2001, partly as a result of the addition of a new category, mixed ethnic groups.

more easily with the way of life of the native population, whereas the negative attitudes and sometimes evident hostility experienced by new black immigrants made it more difficult for them to adapt to Britain's traditional culture.

Overall, the million or so non-white population of 1970 has become 4.5m (almost 8 per cent) today. More than half of the present non-white population was born in Britain. Four out of five Afro-Caribbeans under 35 began their life here and there are as many Afro-Caribbean Britons under 30 with a white parent as there are with two black parents. But immigration has had a particular impact upon some towns and cities. **Multiculturalism** and **multi-ethnicity** have arrived and are here to stay.

Immigration and race relations have been subjects of political controversy for several decades. At times there have been serious tensions between the white and non-white populations, on occasion disturbances and rioting. Immigration has provoked a sharp reaction from the political far right, which has gained in electoral support in a number of northern towns and cities and itself been involved in civil conflict. The issue of asylum seekers arriving in large numbers arouses particular anxiety when it seems that the controls in place can be evaded.

Within ethnic minority groups, there are some more radical members who are alienated from the rest of society (see Box 1.1). Others feel disaffected, perhaps conscious of the discrimination they still experience. But many have enriched the British culture and lifestyle, by the contributions they can make to the economy and society. When they can gain acceptance, many are reasonably contented with their lot and as integrated as they wish to be into the British way of life. They may well in different degrees wish to retain their heritage and identity, but still consider themselves as British.

Box 1.1 The diversity of Muslim attitudes

As we have seen, British Muslims derive from many different countries. They cannot be lumped together as a homogeneous group. They number some 1.6 million, many of whom were born in this country. Like everyone else, they have different personalities, different interests and different opinions. In religious matters, some are strict and devout, others less so.

Muslims have been in Britain since the 1950s. Specific Muslim groups originally settled in specific British cities. Those from Kashmir settled in Birmingham and Bradford, to be joined by others from the Punjab and north-western Pakistan. Indians Muslims from Gujarat settled in northern cities such as Huddersfield, Bangladeshis flocked to east London whilst North Africans and other Arabs went to live in west London. Many of these immigrants belonged to groups of Sunni Islam, but Britain also received small Shia groups from countries such as Iraq. In other words, Muslims from different places often had religious leanings which reflected different shades of Islamic belief.

The first generation of Muslims to arrive in Britain were often victims of racist attitudes and could do little but accept them. The second generation was more willing to challenge them and sometimes this led to fierce confrontations with the police and other authorities. But many members of Muslim communities still wanted to find and share a common set of values, hopes and aspirations that united whites and non-whites, and not to separate themselves from the rest of society. In the last decade, a more radical Islam has found a hearing in Britain.

Reactions to the London bombings

The response to the London attacks (see pp. 9–10) of the overwhelming majority of British Muslims of whatever background was one of shock, horror and near disbelief that any of their number could have committed or been associated with such appalling actions. Some victims of the explosions were Muslims and so were many of those involved in the rescue exercises and the medical teams. Yet the London terrorism provoked anti-Muslims feeling among a section of the white population. As after September 11th, there were examples of Muslim communities suffering from mindless and irrational attacks, involving verbal and physical abuse.

There is a small section of the Muslim community that has some sympathy with those who engage in armed struggle against the West whether in Afghanistan, Iraq or anywhere else. It is strongly anti-American and disapproves of British governmental support for American attitudes and policies. A very much smaller contingent among them has shown itself willing to engage in terrorist action.

The terrorist suspects were an element within the Muslim population, radical Islamic militants. They tend to be between 18 and 30 years of age, are more likely to be male and are often members of a small cell that contains perhaps a few dozen active members. They are led or inspired by an older individual, with more experience and motivation. They are sometimes bound by friendship or family ties, perhaps having spent time in Afghanistan, Iraq or some other theatre of jihad or armed struggle. In the words of a former Metropolitan police commissioner,[4] they do not fit into the caricature of fanatics from some distant village overseas, but were people who seemed to their neighbours to be 'apparently ordinary British citizens, young men conservatively and cleanly dressed, and probably with some higher education. Highly computer literate, they will have used the internet to research explosives, chemicals and electronics.'

For many of the new generation of Muslims, the common denominator is not their ethnic origin – whether they derive from India, Pakistan or one of the Arab countries – but their religion. Ties of faith are becoming more important than ties of culture. As a writer in *The Economist*[5] put it: 'They are less concerned with their shades of difference and more interested in finding a common Muslim identity. They tend to view world events through an Islamic prism and identify with their co-religionists in any place where conflict is raging.'

At best, the relations between the different communities have been generally harmonious and problems that arise are ones that can be accommodated. Discrimination and sometimes intimidation do occur and such wrongs pose a challenge to white society. The majority of white people, particularly those whose routine brings them into contact with others of all ethnic backgrounds, have been tolerant and fairly comfortably embraced change. There has not been anything like the recurrent ethnic and racial problems that beset some other countries. Politicians – with a few prominent exceptions – are keen to promote good race relations and do or say nothing to endanger social cohesion.

Religion has been a greater source of division than in the past. Religious rivalry has not been a traditional feature of the United Kingdom, except as part of the complex of problems associated with Northern Ireland. In countries ranging from Canada to France, religion has been an important factor in political life, but in Britain tolerance of religious differences – often based on indifference to the topic – has been the norm. But again, religion has been a cause of diversity in recent years.

In particular, immigration has been a key factor associated with religion, leading to a rapid increase in support for Islamic beliefs (see Table 1.2 for an indication of the multi-faith society that Britain has become). This has had political repercussions. On the one hand, there have been demands from some Muslims for their own schools, raising issues about the desirability of allowing or encouraging separatist tendencies. On the other, the events of 11 September 2001 have had an impact, at the very least alerting us to changes that had already taken place in British society. A few months before, disturbances in the north of England had laid bare the grievances of British Muslims, forcing recognition of the fact that community relations were no longer just about race relations, but about faith as well. The post-Iraq war situation has led to developing antagonism among some Muslims for the actions taken by Britain and America against their fellow believers in that troubled country. In 2005, some Muslim associations advised their followers not to support the Blair government that took Britain into war.

The position of Muslims in Britain has been the subject of much discussion since the outbreak of **terrorism** in London on 7 July 2005: 52 were killed and some 700 injured in the explosions. A fortnight later, further attacks again brought the capital to a halt, but this time

Table 1.2 The religious mix of the United Kingdom, 2001

Religion	England	Scotland	Wales	Northern Ireland	UK Total	UK (%)
Buddhist	139,046	6,830	5,407	533	151,816	0.3
Christian	35,251,244	3,294,545	2,087,242	1,446,386	42,079,417	71.6
Hindu	546,982	5,564	5,439	825	558,810	1.0
Jewish	257,671	6,448	2,256	365	266,740	0.5
Muslim	1,524,887	42,557	21,739	1,943	1,591,126	2.7
Sikh	327,343	6,572	2,015	219	336,149	0.6
Other religions	143,811	26,974	6,909	1,143	178,837	0.3
Total of all religions	38,190,984	3,389,490	2,131,007	1,451,414	45,162,895	76.8
No religion	7,171,332	1,394,460	537,935		9,103,727	15.5
Not stated	3,776,515	278,061	234,143		4,288,719	7.3
Total of no religion/ not stated	10,947,847	1,672,521	772,078	233,853	13,626,299	23.2

Figures provided by the Office for National Statistics and based on the 2001 Census; the no religion/not stated figures are not listed for N. Ireland and this accounts for the slight discrepancy in the final percentages.

they were bungled and no casualties resulted (see Box 1.2 for a further discussion of the growth and nature of terrorism in Britain). The attacks were not the activities of foreign extremists brought up in oppressive states abroad and suffering from severe deprivation. They were the work of people brought up in multiracial Britain and thus posed a challenge not just for ministers, but for **civil society** too.

In recent years, diversity and tension have characterised aspects of the social scene. There has also been political change. We have seen that in response to growing national feeling the Scots have gained

Box 1.2 The threat of terrorism

Terrorism is not a new phenomenon, but the terror of the past was of a different order to the variety being experienced in Britain in the new millennium. It was traditionally a means to the attainment of some political or strategic end. Those charged with dealing with it could either seek to defeat it, submit to it or negotiate with it.

Whatever their reservations, many British politicians and members of the general public came to accept the inevitability and indeed necessity of opening up dialogue with Irish republican extremists. Ultimately, such discussions were arguably worthwhile. Members of the IRA were fighting for something that many in Northern Ireland believed was a legitimate goal, the unity of the island of Ireland. Talks might open up a political route which would allow for the possibility of that goal eventually being realised.

The terrorism experienced by Londoners in 2005 was very different. It was the worst terrorist attack in British history. Today's Islamic-inspired terrorism recognises no limits, makes no demands concerning grievances that can be addressed and seems to represent no one other than the fanatics themselves. As with previous attacks in Madrid, Bali and New York, in the eyes of many people this was arbitrary and nihilistic brutality. Terror was an end in itself, not a means to a strategic end. In addition, there is another distinctive feature. The attacks in London were the work of suicide bombers, the first such attacks on British soil. The suicide bomber represents a unique kind of threat, an enemy that does not fear being captured or killed is always bound to be more potent.

That the terrorists involved were prepared to kill and die may seem enough. That some of them at least were born and raised in this country is for many people even worse. If they had hailed from some foreign cell, the violence could have been viewed as an external phenomenon, an alien intrusion. There is no such comfort if some of the perpetrators of terrorism were alienated British citizens.

their own parliament. So too has Wales gained a National Assembly. Such moves have been part of a developing interest in **devolution**, the decentralisation of power from Westminster. Some who opposed devolution feared a Balkanisation of the United Kingdom, believing that it would inevitably lead to eventual separatism. Devolution has raised the issue of the nature and values of Britishness.

Of late, there has been renewed discussion of national identity and what it means to be British. There is no prescribed list of qualities or characteristics that make up 'Britishness', but a recent Commission for Racial Equality (CRE) poll found that 86 per cent of those interviewed agreed that you do not have to be white to be British.[6] We now live in a very much more diverse society than that of our ancestors.

The debate about identity has been given another twist by a further development of the last three decades or so, British membership of the European Community, now Union (see Box 1.3). Since the signing of the Maastricht Treaty, British people have become citizens of the European Union, although surveys suggest that the overwhelming majority do not consider themselves to be European in the way that inhabitants of France or Holland might do. The issue of Britain in Europe has posed challenges for politicians of all parties, for as yet there is little sign that the British feel enthusiastic about being part of the Union. They may perceive some advantages for the country in membership, but perhaps because of their proud traditions as an island race, and differences of language and culture, they are not yet convinced of the merits of closer **integration** with our European partners.

Box 1.3 British membership of the European Union and popular attitudes to it

The European Union was originally established as the European Economic Community (EEC), by the Treaty of Rome (1957). The name was later shortened to European Community (EC). Following ratification by all member states of the Maastricht Treaty, the European Union (EU) was created in November 1993. For the sake of simplicity, we use European Community to cover the pre-Maastricht era and European Union when referring to the years since ratification.

After the ending of the Second World War, six Western European nations (Belgium, France, Holland, Italy, Luxembourg and West Germany) decided to work towards greater union on the continent in economic, military and political policy. At first, they created a

European Coal and Steel Community (ECSC), before later signing the Rome Treaty that created a 'common market', a tariff-free area designed to 'promote . . . a harmonious development of economic activities'. If that was the tangible objective in the short term, the goal set out in the Preamble was bolder and more far-reaching in its long-term implications – to establish 'an ever closer union' between European peoples.

Britain did not join the ECSC, nor did it sign the Treaty of Rome in 1957. Europe was not a priority at a time when Britain was considered to be a 'world power', with important Commonwealth and American ties. Also, the British were wary of the continental approach, for it involved **supranationalism** and was seen as a step on the road to the creation of a European **federation**.

As British ministers came to realise that the European Community was becoming an economic success story, they reconsidered their attitudes to the EC. By the early 1960s, Britain was having to adjust to a decline in its world status. At home, it was beset by periodic economic problems. At the third attempt, it joined the Community in 1973, during the lifetime of the Conservative government led by Edward Heath.

There was no widespread popular enthusiasm for entry. However, there was a fairly general feeling – evident in the 1975 referendum – that it was probably wise and necessary for Britain to work with its new European partners, for the alternatives did not look very promising. The point was well made by Northedge[7]:

> The important thing about British entry into Europe was that it had almost every appearance of being a policy of last resort, adopted . . . when all other expedients had failed . . . it was brought about in humiliating circumstances, and when other options in foreign policy had lost their convincingness.

For many years, Eurobarometer, the EU's polling organisation, regularly found that a majority of British respondents favoured closer cooperation in Europe in some form and recognised the inevitability of further steps along the route to unity, on the right terms. But since the implementation of the Maastricht Treaty, the public mood has become more Eurosceptic. There has been increased anxiety about the nature and extent of the British commitment. This has come about in part because the full implications of British membership were not for many years fully appreciated. British political parties have increasingly found the issue of Europe divisive and governments have found European policy difficult to handle.

Underlying British ideas and values

We use the term culture in referring to the way of life that people experience, to describe the sum of their inherited and cherished ideas, knowledge and values. Their beliefs and values, and the things that they care about, are based on the experiences to which they are exposed throughout their lives. They may also derive from their class, ethnic group, language, gender or religion.

Political culture refers to culture in its political aspect. Political culture is the term given to those widely shared political beliefs, values and norms most citizens share concerning the relationship of citizens to government and to one another. These long-term attitudes, ideas and traditions are passed on from one generation to the next. Usually, we think of the political culture of a country such as Britain, France or the United States, but it may be the citizens of an ethnic or religious community who are under consideration – perhaps the people living in a geographic community such as Londoners or Europeans, or those with a shared identity such as French Canadians or Sikhs in the subcontinent.

Political culture is different from public opinion. The term **public opinion** refers to the cluster of attitudes and beliefs held by people about a variety of issues, in our case those concerning politics and policy issues. It will vary on and across the issues of the day. By contrast, political culture – in Heywood's term[8] – 'is fashioned out of long-term values rather than simply people's reactions to specific policies and problems'.

In attempting to understand and categorise the political culture of any country or group, we often fall back upon references to national character and come out with generalised, impressionistic observations such as the observation that Italian politics are unstable, because of the volatile Mediterranean temperament of the Italian people. However, attempts have been made in several surveys to investigate the idea of political culture more closely. By taking a selected sample of the electorate and questioning those chosen about their political actions and beliefs, and aggregating the findings, researchers have been able to search for patterns and produce a profile of the political culture of the sample. By inference, because the sample was a representative one, then the survey can inform us about the political culture of the entire population.

Research findings in a particularly country cannot be regarded as applicable for all of the people for all of the time. They inevitably focus on what the majority of the people appear to think and feel. However, some of the surveys carried out since the 1960s have pointed to the differences in the political beliefs of individuals within the same society. It has also shown that political culture is not an unchanging landscape, a fixed background against which the political process operates. Attitudes can evolve and change over time, for there are in society often a number of forces at work which serve to modify popular attitudes, among them migration and the emergence in a number of liberal democracies of a substantial underclass. Both can be a cause of greater diversity in popular attitudes, for immigrants and those alienated from majority lifestyles may have a looser attachment with prevailing cultural norms.

Survey work is geared to improving our understanding of the political values of citizens in democratic countries. It enables us to make comparisons about the attitudes that characterise their inhabitants. Some surveys have pointed to the similarity of people's concerns across the globe. In 1965, an American, Hadley Cantril[9], found that they want a happy family life, a decent standard of living and good health and – in politics – they like conditions of stability and fear warfare. More recently, Ron Inglehart[10] in research published in 1989 and 1997, has separately detected a shift of emphasis. Whereas older citizens emphasise materialist attitudes and values, preferring economic growth, a stable society based on respect for law and order and strong national defence, members of younger generations are more **post-materialist** in their thinking. They are concerned about the importance of ensuring a healthy environment, freedom of expression and more personal power in their social and political life. Writing in 2000, Russell Dalton[11] noted that whereas the proportion of citizens with post-materialist attitudes in Britain and the United States has been around 20 per cent over the last couple of decades, it has grown rapidly in other countries, notably Germany and the Netherlands where it is 36 per cent and 39 per cent respectively.

Almond and Verba: *The Civic Culture,* 1963[12]

In writing of the British political culture, commentators have often pointed to longstanding features such as the commitment to the democratic process, majority rule and the rule of law. They note the preference for strong and effective government, which is equated in the minds of many voters with single-party administrations. Yet alongside the importance attached to strong government based on a parliamentary majority, there is also a broad tolerance for the expression of alternative and minority opinions. There is in addition a deep regard for personal liberty and the rights of the citizen, inroads into which are regarded with considerable mistrust. Excessive regulations, the use of speed cameras and the abandonment of trial by jury in some types of criminal cases make people uneasy, although at a time when the threat of terrorism is widely recognised, greater airport vigilance and more searches of personal possessions are widely accepted as inevitable and necessary.

Two American political scientists, Almond and Verba, attempted to probe more deeply into the attitudes and values that underpin the British political system in a landmark study published in 1963. They drew their sample survey evidence from interviews with approximately a thousand people in each of five countries. The survey work was completed in 1959–60. The researchers pointed to considerable variations in the political beliefs of the societies they explored. Their comparative results, taken from their book, *The Civic Culture*, can be seen in Table 1.3.

Almond and Verba found that the British people were proud of and attached to their political institutions, were generally satisfied with what government did for them and combined deference (respect) towards the system with confidence and competence in participating and using it. As a result of the good fortune of historical development, they had reached an ideal mix of active and participant citizen and deferential and passive subject. This made Britain a distinctly manageable country to govern.

More recent survey evidence

In their 1980 update, Almond and Verba[13] noted that some of the attitudes and problems of the 1960s and 1970s had left their mark on the political cultures. Britons had become less deferential and more sceptical of government, their trust in its essential benevolence having seriously declined. According to Parry et al.,[14] writing in the early 1990s, the British were less trusting and more cynical than Austrians,

Table 1.3 Variations in political beliefs, 1959–60

Attitude	US	UK	Germany	Italy	Mexico
% who say they are proud of:					
i. government, political institutions	85	46	7	3	30
ii. position in international affairs	5	11	5	2	3
iii. economic system	23	10	33	3	24
% who say national government improves conditions	76	77	61	66	58
% who expect serious consideration of their point of view from:					
i. bureaucracy	48	59	53	35	14
ii. police	56	74	59	35	12
% who say ordinary man should be active in his local community	51	39	22	10	26

Germans and the Swiss, but more trusting and less cynical than the Italians or the Americans. Yet more recent research by Curtice and Jowell[15] suggests that the number of British people who trust government to put the needs of the nation above the interests of party 'just about always/most of the time' has steadily fallen from 39 per cent in 1974 to 22 per cent in 1996, and 75 per cent now trust the government 'only some of the time/almost never'.

The original Almond and Verba view of British attitudes has been under challenge over recent decades. As we have seen, they themselves later detected signs of a growing distrust of government that has characterised recent decades. More seriously, the emphasis on the peaceful nature of British society and agreement about what needs to be done can no longer be taken for granted. There have been increasing levels of recorded crime, sectarian street violence in Northern Ireland, and urban rioting in several large towns and cities. The 'moderate' political culture, with its support of parliamentary government and preference for the rule of law, does not command universal consent (see Box 1.4 for further discussion on the erosion of three traditional characteristics of British society).

Box 1.4 British society and its values

Homogeneity, consensus and deference, 1970–2005: a changing scene

Writing back in the early 1970s, writers such as Blondel and Punnett[16] detected three particular characteristics that were long-established features of the British way of life, homogeneity (sameness), consensus (broad agreement) and deference (social respect for one's superiors). Since they set out their analysis, all three characteristics have been under strain.

Ethnic homogeneity is no longer the force that it was, for British society is now more culturally diverse than ever before. It has been – sometimes painfully – transformed into a multicultural society, with London and several towns and cities being areas of high-density immigration. It still lacks the problems that characterise many other countries where linguistic, religious or racial cleavages are more apparent. However, conflicts based on such divisions are often difficult to resolve, more so than those based on class and economic disparities. People have a chance of escaping from a depressed region, poor living conditions or a particular social class. It is more difficult to escape from a group into which you were born – even should you wish so to do – especially if your skin colour is distinctive.

Consensus in society about shared ideas and values has been shaken in recent years, as well. Broad agreement on policy goals was a feature of government in the 1950s to 1970s. It was replaced after

1979 by the more ideological approach of the Thatcher years, when the Prime Minister provided a distinctive and, many would say, harsher approach to social and economic policy. Consensus on procedural matters has also been under strain. The vast majority still accept that grievances can be addressed through peaceful, parliamentary channels, but a minority has been more willing to employ direct action to achieve its ends. Strikes have been much less common than they were in the 1960s and 1970s, but (sometimes politically motivated) protests and riots have been more in evidence in recent decades. The rise of the Countryside Alliance points to the danger of a town versus country divide, focusing on different approaches to issues such as fox-hunting and support for the rural way of life.

Deference too has been a declining feature of British life. Walter Bagehot[17] drew attention to deference in his classic study of *The English Constitution*, written in 1867, noting the respect of the people for law and order and their liking, near-reverence for the monarchy. It is a rather out-of-date concept that dates back to the social respect with which some members of the working class looked up to those above them on the class ladder. They regarded the traditional rulers of the country as people 'born to rule', having had the right background, education and upbringing. Working-class Conservatism was often explained in terms of deference, voters seeing the sort of people who once led the party as superior in their governing abilities. Those days have long disappeared. In a more educated age, people are likely to value others according to their contribution rather than their social status, and journalistic attitudes to figures of authority have also served to undermine respect. In any case, it is less easy to look up to Conservative leaders who – in several recent cases – have had a similar background to one's own.

The information here presented is based on that set out in *Understanding US/UK government and politics*, Manchester University Press, 2003, written by the author of this volume.

Public dissatisfaction with political institutions and the unwritten constitution has increased and more people seem willing to break the law when their consciences tell them that it is wrong. Support for unconventional forms of protest such as strikes, sit-ins and motorway protests has been on the increase. The activities of animal rights and fuel protesters and the support for Countryside marches and anti-war demonstrations suggest a greater willingness to resort to **direct action**, made all the easier in today's society with its ease of communication via new means of technology such as mobile phones.

Box 1.5 Forces that have shaped British society and popular attitudes: a summary

Traditional features pointing to a 'moderate' political culture

- The long history of national independence and unity
- The absence of successful invasion of the British Isles
- Broad historical continuity, the absence of upheaval, the preference for gradualism and peaceful change
- Traditional pride in and respect for governing institutions
- The absence of fundamental social divisions
- Strong attachment to democratic values, the rule of law and personal freedom.

The challenge to traditional attitudes and modes of behaviour in recent years

- Increased dissatisfaction with governing institutions
- Decline of deference: less trust in government and of politicians
- Less commitment to peaceful change
- Greater willingness to resort to forms of direct action – including violence – to register protest
- Developing nationalism in parts of the UK
- Doubts about national identity, made more apparent by growing social diversity and EU involvement
- The development of a multiracial society, but increased tension between different communities
- The bombings of 7 July 2005 and the terrorist threat.

Broadly, there is still a preference for orderly, peaceful protest and little sympathy for methods that involve violence against people or property. But some of the long-held and generalised comments on British attitudes need to be updated as some traditional features have lost their former relevance.

• •

 ## What you should have learnt from reading this chapter

- A description of British history, society and attitudes written a few decades ago would have probably read something like this. Continuity and tradition have been significant elements of British political development. Change has come about gradually, by evolutionary rather than revolutionary means. There has been a high degree of national unity in the United Kingdom. British society has been cohesive, not marked by conspicuous ethnic, linguistic or religious differences. It has been characterised by consensual attitudes, citizens generally showing a preference for agreement rather than division, and being willing to defer to and trust those who rule over them.

- Today, this picture seems unduly complacent and in some respects distinctly inaccurate. The preference for moderation and peaceful change has been challenged by some groups willing to resort to direct action to achieve their goals. Many people are much less trusting of government and more cynical about politicians. The unity of the United Kingdom cannot be taken for granted, under pressure as it has been from the forces of nationalism in Scotland and Wales. British society has become markedly more diverse, as a result of the impact of Commonwealth and other immigration. This has had a profound impact on some communities, not least in terms of religious belief.

- In the new millennium, the threat of terrorism has become a reality. There are some people, born in Britain, who deride Western values. A very much smaller number are willing to translate their rejection of American and British attitudes and policies into a willingness to oppose them through the use of violence and mass killing.

Glossary of key terms

Civil society That arena of social life 'above' the personal realm of the family but 'beneath' the state. It comprises mainly voluntary organisations and civil associations that allow individuals to work together in groups, freely and independently of state regulation.

Deference Respect. In this case, the willingness of many people to accept the views of their political and social superiors.

Devolution The process of transferring significant power from a higher authority to a lower one – e.g. from a central government to subordinate regional forms. The transfer stops short of any cession of sovereignty, so that powers devolved can always be taken back by the higher authority.

Direct action Political action outside the constitutional and legal framework, covering a huge variety of activities, many of which are militant but legal, although some of them are illegal and/or may be violent. It is essentially an attempt to coerce those in authority into doing something that otherwise they would not do.

Ethnicity A mixture of different social characteristics that may include common origin, culture, geography, history, language and religion that give a social group a common consciousness and separates them from other social groups.

Federation A form of government in which power is divided between one central, federal government and several several provinces/states or countries: a federal union.

Homogeneity Made up of similar elements, sameness.

Integration The process of absorbing people belonging to different ethnic, religious or other groups into an existing community.

Multiculturalism Refers to the diverse range of ethnic groups and cultures that make up society. Multiculturalists argue that all people of goodwill – whatever their background – can live together, celebrate diversity, each community preserving its culture whilst respecting that of others.

Multi-ethnicity Refers to the diverse range of ethnic groups that make up society.

Political culture The collective expression of the fundamental attitudes, beliefs, values and ideas that dispose people to react in a particular way in their approach to political issues. All societies have a political culture that gives form and substance to political processes.

Post-materialism A theory that explains the nature of political concerns and values in terms of levels of economic development. Whereas conditions of material scarcity mean that politics is dominated by economic issues, conditions of relative affluence and prosperity make people more concerned with the search for a better quality of life. This includes interest in issues such as animal rights, environmentalism, feminism, racial harmony and world peace.

Public opinion The opinion of the majority of the population on a particular issue, at a particular time and place. There can be no single public opinion. Rather, there are several opinions held by members of the public.

Social class The division of the population into categories on the basis of their economic and social status, determined by their background, occupation, income and other aspects of their lifestyle. The usual distinction is into manual (working-class) and non-manual (middle- and upper-class) groups, although there are many substrata within these categories.

Supranationalism This implies the transfer of some national sovereignty to a multi-national organisation that acts on behalf of all the countries involved (e.g. from Britain to the EU).

Terrorism The use of methods such as bombing, hijacking, kidnapping, murder and torture to spread fear and horror in the service of political ends. Those who practise it tend to see themselves as freedom fighters for a particular cause.

Likely examination questions

As this is essentially a background chapter, few questions are likely to be asked on the material here presented. But it is useful in informing your understanding of government and politics in Britain and elsewhere. A possible question might be:

What do you understand by the term 'political culture'? What are the characteristics of the British political culture?

Helpful websites

www.data-archive.ac.uk   UK Data Archive (University of Essex). Evidence on British social attitudes and public opinion.

www.natcen.ac.uk   National Centre for Social Research.

www.statistics.gov.uk   Useful source of up-to-date information on economic and social features of British life.

Suggestions for further reading

The *British Social Attitudes* surveys produced every year over the last two decades or so, provide valuable insights into the nature of national identity and analyses of changes in the British political culture. See especially J. Curtice and R. Jowell, 'The Sceptical Electorate', in R. Jowell, J. Curtice, A. Park et al. (eds), *British Social Attitudes: The 12th Report*, Dartmouth Publishing, 1995.

Great Britain 2005, the handbook produced by the Government Information Service, provides a fund of statistical information and comment on policy developments and institutional changes, covering the whole range of social, economic and political issues.

R. Inglehart, *Modernisation and Postmodernisation: Cultural, Economic and Social Change in 43 Societies*, Princeton University Press, 1997.

B. Jones (ed.), *Politics UK*, Prentice Hall, 2004. Chapters 2–4 provide introductory but useful coverage of the historical, social and economic contexts of British politics and Chapter 5 covers political culture and political participation.

CHAPTER 2

The Constitution and the Protection of Rights

Contents

Overview

The constitution is at the heart of most political systems, describing the fundamental rules by which they operate. Usually, these rules are contained in a single written document, although in rare examples they may be located in major pronouncements, writings, statutes, precedents and legal decisions. Such constitutions may be an imperfect and incomplete guide to what actually happens in any country, but they help to shape the way in which governmental systems function, setting out the most important procedural rules, giving legitimacy to those who rule and providing individuals with a set of basic rights and freedoms.

In this chapter, we examine the nature and characteristics of constitutions, noting in particular the distinctiveness of the British Constitution about which there has been much debate in recent years. We also examine the ways in which rights may be protected and the early effectiveness or otherwise of the British Human Rights Act.

Key issues to be covered in this chapter

- General characteristics of constitutions
- The benefits and disadvantages of written constitutions
- The evolution and sources of the British Constitution
- Constitutional change under the Blair government and its impact
- The widespread existence of Bills of Rights around the world
- The protection of rights in Britain, past and present
- The constitutions and protection of rights in France, South Africa and USA

The Constitution

Every country has a constitution of some kind. There are many definitions of the term, such as that provided by the *Oxford English Dictionary*: 'the system or body of fundamental principles according to which a nation state or body politic is constituted and governed'. When we think of constitutions, we normally have in mind the documents of countries such as France and the United States, which also embody a statement of the rights of the individual. But countries that do not possess such a single, authoritative statement still possess a constitution.

Constitutions declare the existence of the state and express the most important principles, rules and procedures of the political system. Specifically, they set out:

- the allocation of governmental activities, outlining which structures will perform which tasks
- the power relationships between the various institutions, showing how each is dependent upon or independent of the operations of the others
- the limitations upon the powers of rulers and guarantees of the rights of the ruled: an explanation of the constraints on the state's authority and a listing of the freedoms of the individual citizen and the benefits to which he or she is entitled from the state.

Article 1 of the Italian Constitution of 1948 clearly establishes some important information about the nature of the country and the way in which its system of government operates, by declaring:

> Italy is a democratic republic based on work. Sovereignty belongs to the people, who will exercise it in the forms and within the limits prescribed by the constitution.

A *constitutional regime* is one that operates within the rule of law and ensures that there are effective restraints on those who exercise power, as laid out in the constitution. Constitutional regimes are associated with the provision of a generally democratic and humane political order.

An *unconstitutional regime* operates on the basis of unchecked political power, so that the structural arrangements set out in the constitution are not put into practice. There is persistent neglect or non-enforcement of limitations upon rulers and the rights of the governed, as is the case in authoritarian states. In some countries, the rule of law is not upheld and there is a complete disregard of constitutional arrangements, perhaps because of a state of civil unrest – (e.g. Somalia).

The growth of interest in constitutional revision

Constitutions are solemn and binding documents meant to last. They have a certain timeless quality about them, as seemingly eternal features of the political scene. Yet they are in fact liable to undergo change of a fundamental nature. Indeed, most European constitutions are twentieth-century creations. The Swiss version is now the oldest on the continent, dating as it does from 1874.

In recent decades, there has been a developing interest in constitutions and constitutional matters in many parts of the world. Some constitutions have been rewritten, others revised. More than two-thirds of those now in existence have been enacted since the end of the Second World War. In several cases, they were produced for states that gained their independence in the post-colonial period (India or Nigeria). In Portugal and Spain, they resulted from the collapse of fascist-type dictatorships in the 1970s. More recently, there has been a need to write a constitution for more than twenty states once part of the Soviet Union and its Central and Eastern European satellites, where peoples who once lived under communist tyranny have been attempting to establish new institutions and principles for their political lives.

The purpose of this burst of writing and revising constitutions has been the same in most cases. Countries have seen a need to revamp their constitutions to bring their formal documents up-to-date and make them more in tune with the actuality of their governing arrangements. Andrew Heywood[1] makes the point that:

> In general, it can be said that political conflicts assume a constitutional dimension only when those demanding change seek to redraw, and not merely re-adjust, the rules of the political game. Constitutional change is therefore about the re-apportionment of both power and political authority.

The purpose and content of constitutions

Constitutions are primarily concerned with outlining the arrangements for operating the key institutions of government, and setting out the rules by which they operate and the roles of the people who work within them. Most also include declarations of rights, which are usually listed near the beginning of the document. They tend to come about as a result of some major internal dissension or upheaval over a period of years, be it civil war or revolution, or defeat in war. Following the dismantling of a governmental structure, those charged with writing a new one have to think about the way in which the political system should be organised.

Constitutions have several functions, among them to:

- provide legitimacy to those in power, which is probably why even non-democratic states have them; their existence is reassuring to the people, for they suggest the appearance of legality.
- protect freedom, restraining the behaviour of those in office, for they set out what those in authority can do and define the limits of their power. Writing more than four decades ago, the Austrian liberal Friedrich Hayek[2] described a constitution as a means of limiting the power of government.
- encourage governmental stability, by introducing a degree of order and predictability into governmental arrangements. Every one knows the rules of the game, and this means that actions are rarely purely arbitrary or random.
- draw attention to the goals and values that characterise a particular state. They proclaim a commitment, which may be to democracy, but may equally be to Islam or socialism. Thus the 1977 Soviet Constitution defined the USSR as a 'developed socialist society'.
- delineate the respective spheres of influence of the central and regional/provincial tiers in **federal** countries, such as the United States. In addition, the American states each have their own constitutions.
- usher a new beginning, as in the cases of Portugal and Spain in the 1970s. They are especially important in states subjected to internal dissension and long-term upheaval. The US Constitution

followed the War of Independence, just as the Japanese and West German documents followed defeat in the Second World War.

The importance of constitutions was recognised by the Spanish historian Julian Marais[3], at the time when Spain acquired a new constitution: 'If the constitution does not inspire respect, admiration and enthusiasm, democracy is not assured.' In other words, the document acts as a kind of moral yard-stick against which the performance of the political system can be judged. It acts as a reminder of the high ideals that inspired its creation.

Heywood[4] makes the point that 'there is an imperfect relationship between the content of a constitution and political practice'. Constitutions 'work' in certain conditions, 'notably when they correspond to, and are supported by, the political culture, when they are respected by rulers and accord with the interests and values of dominant groups, and when they are adaptable and can remain relevant in changing political circumstances'.

The characteristics of constitutions

Constitutions are often classified according to their characteristics. They may be:

Written or unwritten constitutions

The terms are unclear, for most of the British Constitution is written down somewhere, so that it is not technically unwritten. In 1963, Wheare[5] stressed that rather than having an unwritten constitution, Britain lacked a written one. Given the confusion of terms, it is probably more useful to distinguish between:

- *codified constitutions*, in which all the main provisions are brought together in a single document and
- *uncodified constitutions*, which exist where there are constitutional rules, many of which are written down, but have not been gathered together.

Flexible or rigid constitutions

Flexible constitutions are rare. They can be altered via the law-making process (i.e., by a simple majority in the legislature) without much difficulty, as in New Zealand and the United Kingdom. In other words, no laws are regarded as fundamental and there is no formal process for constitutional amendment. In rigid constitutions, the principles and institutions assume the character of fundamental law. The procedure for amendment is deliberately made difficult, so that no change can be made without due consideration and discussion. Flexibility and rigidity are relative, not absolute terms. For instance, the American Constitution possesses a degree of flexibility that allows it to adapt to changing needs. Parties and pressure groups have developed, although they have no formal constitutional status. Moreover, all written constitutions depend upon interpretation and judges.

Unitary or federal constitutions

Unitary systems are to be found in countries ranging from Britain to Israel, from France to Ireland. They tend to be especially suitable in smaller countries and in those where there are no significant ethnic, linguistic or religious differences. In unitary systems, all power is concentrated in the hands of the central government. As the constitution of the Fifth French Republic states: 'France is a republic, indivisible.' Federal systems are characterised by a division between a federal (central) government and various regional units that may be called states (in the USA), *Länder* (in Germany) or provinces (as in Belgium) have often developed in countries where the people are reluctant to surrender all power to a central government. In each case, the powers and functions of the central authority and the regional unit are clearly defined in a written constitution. Each authority is independent in its own sphere, although there may be concurrent powers shared between the two levels.

The distinction between the two forms can be exaggerated. In most democratic states, power is to some extent decentralised. Sometimes, as in Britain or Spain today, the degree of decentralisation to some areas may be extensive. When such autonomy has been granted to a regional authority, it is highly unlikely that it would in practice ever be taken away. Similarly, in countries that are federal, there has often been in recent decades a trend towards growing central power, so that back in the 1970s examiners could sometimes ask whether the United States was in reality becoming a centralised, unitary state. (In the recent phase of **devolutionary federalism**, the pendulum has swung back towards the states – see pp. 218–19.)

Other characteristics of constitutions:

- *some are monarchical, others republican.* This is not today a key distinction, for monarchy in democratic states takes the constitutional form. In Britain, Belgium, Denmark, Holland, Norway and Sweden, the monarch reigns by hereditary right; absolute monarchies are very rare. Republics have no hereditary head of state, but rather someone who is either elected by the people or their elected representatives.

- *some are presidential, others parliamentary*, a distinction that informs us about the relationship between the **executive** and **legislature**. In presidential constitutions, the two branches of government function independently on the basis of the **separation of powers** – e.g. in the USA, the President is elected separately from Congress'. In parliamentary systems, the executive is chosen from and accountable to the legislature (see also pp. 112–13).

- *some are based on the sovereignty of Parliament, others on the sovereignty of the people.* Britain provides an example of the former (see Box 2.1), with Parliament formally possessing supreme power. America provides an example of the latter, its constitution opening with the words: 'We the people of the United States . . . do ordain and establish this Constitution,' an idea which echoes **Rousseau**'s belief that government should reflect the general will of the people.

The Constitution of the United Kingdom

As we have seen, the UK does not have a written constitution in the sense of a single written document, though substantial elements of it are written in various places. It is largely because of its ancient origins that the British Constitution is so unsystematic. No attempt has been made to collate it together, and codify the various rules and conventions that are part of it. Yet those who work the Constitution generally understand the key issues involved.

The nearest the British came to having a written constitution was during the protectorate of Oliver Cromwell when an *Instrument of*

Box 2.1 Parliamentary sovereignty

Parliamentary sovereignty has traditionally been viewed as a key element of the British Constitution. Constitutional experts such as A.V. Dicey[6] have proclaimed that Parliament has legal sovereignty (absolute and unlimited authority), in that it is the supreme law-making body in Great Britain. Only Parliament can make, amend and unmake law, and no other institution can override its decisions. No one Parliament can bind its successor.

In reality, the doctrine has been undermined by various considerations in recent years, most notably by adherence to the European Convention and membership of the European Union (see Box 2.2). Both imply that any British government must modify its law to take account of European wishes. European law ultimately prevails over British law. Yet even before these European limitations, parliamentary sovereignty was a questionable notion. It implies that Parliament is supreme and all-powerful, yet in the twentieth century it is widely agreed that power has passed from Parliament to the Executive both because of the growing scale and complexity of government (and the consequent difficulties of achieving effective parliamentary control), and because of the extent of party discipline. Any government armed with a large majority has a good chance of pushing its programme through. Sceptics argue that if the doctrine implies that Parliament has real power, the truth is that it usually acts as a rubber-stamp for governmental action.

In reality, then, there are *political constraints* on Parliament's legal sovereignty. These include membership of the EU, the demands of the International Monetary Fund (where a government is seeking to borrow money from the IMF, it may impose stringent conditions on policy to be followed in the future), the activities of pressure groups, the City and other economic bodies, the powerful media and the electorate which has ultimate political sovereignty in that it can vote a government out of office. The need to gain and maintain public support is a crucial limitation on any group of ministers, especially in the run-up to an election.

Parliamentary sovereignty is in practice modified by the nature of the political system. In the last resort, the people are sovereign. In a democracy, their wishes must ultimately prevail. Government and Parliament need popular acquiescence and consent for their actions.

Box 2.2 How the European Union impacts upon parliamentary sovereignty

When Britain joined the European Community as it then was, it accepted 43 volumes of existing legislation, so that many directives and regulations passed before we became a member were suddenly binding upon us. Since then, in several areas, British law-making has been influenced by the decisions of the European Court of Justice, most notably in the *Factortame* dispute concerning Spanish fishermen operating in British-registered vessels. The Conservatives passed the Merchant Shipping Act (1988) to define what was meant by a British-registered vessel. The statute was overturned by the Court, which found the legislation to be discriminatory and unfair, and a breach of Community law. It was clear that in future national law could be made to bow to Community law, and that British courts had the right to review and suspend any British law which seemed to infringe that of the EC. This was not the first case to make this clear, for the supremacy of European law was recognised in earlier judgements concerning the need for equal treatment of men and women.

Government was drawn up, making a decisive break with past habits. But for some 900 years the country has not undergone invasion, nor has it experienced sudden, dramatic upheavals in the system of government since 1688. Given these circumstances, and the fact that the country is small enough to enable all people in all areas to feel at least some contact with Westminster, there has been little demand until the last couple of decades for the protection offered by a written constitution.

If Britain seems to be at some disadvantage in not possessing a written constitution, the long constitutional history of the country does not point to any special urgency about creating one. Constitutions may be a safeguard against arbitrary seizures of power, but there is no history of dictatorships in our islands. Rights and liberties have developed organically, based not so much on law but on traditional freedoms and traditional practices.

The British Constitution has been a model followed by many other countries, and peoples in other countries who have long been denied their rights have seen Britain as an inspiration. As Wade and Philips[7] put it, the Constitution 'embraces laws, customs and conventions hammered out, as it were, on the anvil of experience'. The British approach has been empirical, no attempt having been made to bring together the various constitutional laws and rulings. However, many of the basic principles and rules in Britain are recorded. As it has such a long history, much has been written about the British system of government.

Sources of the British Constitution

Because of the way in which our political system has evolved over time, there are many sources that can be consulted in order to locate the elusive British Constitution. These include:

Major constitutional documents that express important constitutional principles
For example, Magna Carta (1215) asserted the view that a monarch could and should be controlled by his subjects: the Act of Settlement (1701) strengthened Parliament's control over the sovereign, by determining the succession to the throne.

Major texts and commentaries by eminent experts on the Constitution
These have been so influential in their interpretation of the Constitution that they are seen as part of the Constitution itself: for example, Bagehot's *The English Constitution* (1867) and the introduction to it in its reproduced form (1963) which has come to be accepted as a major commentary on the state of the Constitution (Bagehot is most noted for distinguishing between its outward form and its working reality, or as he put the contrast, between its 'dignified' and 'efficient' parts: A. V. Dicey's *The Law of the Constitution* (1885) is similarly regarded as a classic analysis of the evolution and operation of British governing arrangements at the time.

Major statutes
There are some major statutes that have an impact on the constitutional structure, in that they have changed the way we are governed or the relationships within the state: e.g. the Parliament Acts (1911 and 1949), both of which trimmed the powers of the House of Lords; the Scotland Act (1998) that established the Scottish Parliament. The nature and operation of UK electoral systems and the structures and

powers of local government are both matters covered primarily in statutes.

The prerogative powers of the Crown

The Royal Prerogative comprises a number of powers or privileges performed in the past by the monarch, but now performed in his or her name by ministers. Their authority derives from the Crown, rather than from Parliament, so that parliamentary authority is not required by the Executive as it conducts these tasks. Prerogative powers are exercised by ministers individually or collectively. They include the rights to exercise mercy (a prerogative of the Home Secretary); declare war and make treaties; give orders to the armed forces; appoint ministers; and dispense honours (all duties performed by the Prime Minister and his or her colleagues). Because of the opportunity to act in this way, the Thatcher government was able to deploy troops in the Falklands conflict (1982). So too was Tony Blair able to commit British troops to a military invasion of Iraq, in 2003. In neither case, was it legally essential to have parliamentary approval, although over Iraq in particular MPs felt entitled to – and were given – an early debate on the controversial decision. This has probably created a precedent, for it is unlikely that in future any British government would send forces into action without allowing MPs a chance to express their opinion.

The law and customs of Parliament

The rules relating to the procedures of the House and the privileges of its members are set out in the book consulted by the Speaker, Erskine May's *Law, Privileges, Proceedings and Usages of Parliament*, regarded as the authoritative commentary on the interpretation of parliamentary rules.

Common and case (judge-made) law

Common law is the immemorial law of the people (such as the claim to the right of free speech and free assembly), which in practice has been determined and implemented by judges. Court decisions affect the Constitution by interpreting statutes that might be unclear or establishing individual rights in relation to those in authority: e.g. the decision by the law lords in the Lemon case (1978) that the law of blasphemous libel was still operable, after the publication in *Gay News* of a poem expressing longing for the body of Christ. Judges have for centuries been an important source of rules on issues of constitutional significance. Their importance has been enhanced by the passage of the Human Rights Act (1998).

Constitutional conventions
These are unwritten rules of constitutional behaviour, customs of political practice that are usually accepted and observed: for example, that the choice of prime minister should be made from the House of Commons; the concepts of individual and collective cabinet responsibility, both of which have been modified in recent years. It is a convention rather than a formal requirement that the sovereign will always give consent to any bill that has passed through its parliamentary stages; no bill has been rejected by the monarch since 1707.

European Union law
European Union law comprises primary legislation, as is to be found in the Treaty of Rome and the other treaties, and secondary law, as is to be found in EU **regulations** and **directives**. European law takes precedence over UK law, is binding on the UK and applicable by UK courts. In several cases, pieces of European economic and social legislation have conferred important rights on British workers, as in the area of equal pay. The impact of membership was made very apparent in the Factortame case (see p. 32), which illustrated how the courts can overrule parliamentary legislation which conflicts with Community law. As Gillian Peele[8] has pointed out: 'The incremental strengthening of EU law and the erosion of the doctrine of parliamentary sovereignty as traditionally understood, has important implications for the constitutional balance of the British political system.'

The British Constitution comprises an accumulation over many centuries of traditions, customs, conventions, precedents and Acts of Parliament that serve as a complex framework within which those who wield power must operate. It is old by any standards, for its origins can be traced back at least to the period after the Norman Conquest. Constitutional developments have come about gradually. Although many of the institutions have a long history, the role they

Box 2.3 Aspects of the British Constitution: a summary

The British Constitution is:

- *uncodified*, there being no single document in which most of the rules concerning the government of the country are brought together.
- *unitary* rather than a federal. Parliament at Westminster makes laws for all parts of the United Kingdom. Parts of the UK may have powers devolved to them, nonetheless all parts of the kingdom are subject to the legislative supremacy of Parliament.
- *flexible*. Being unwritten, in a formal sense, it can be easily amended, and even drastic changes can be made by passing an Act of Parliament, though there is a developing custom that fundamental changes would probably require a referendum if they have not already been submitted to the electorate in a general election.

The basic elements of the Constitution rest on three major constitutional principles:

1. *The sovereignty of Parliament* – the idea that Parliament theoretically possesses and exercises unlimited authority
2. *The rule of law* – the principle that no one is above the law, that ministers, public authorities and individuals are subject to it
3. *The fusion (rather than the complete separation) of powers* – government ministers who head executive departments sit as members of the legislature and are responsible to it.

play is constantly changing, which is why Hanson and Walles[9] were able to refer to the British habit of placing 'new wine in old bottles'.

The British Constitution in flux: the case for constitutional renewal

From the 1960s, many thinkers and writers began to urge the cause of 'constitutional reform', which became a fashionable topic for discussion among the chattering classes. It has been on the political agenda ever since. There were specific concerns such as the case for devolution of power to Scotland and Wales in the 1970s and 1980s, but subsequent concern was more wide-ranging.

Those who favoured constitutional change suggested that:

- whereas in the past the flexibility of the British Constitution had been regarded as an asset, the basis of good government, from the 1970s there were increasing doubts about the effectiveness of some institutions. The political system seemed less successful in 'delivering the goods' than it had been and, in particular, there were serious problems at the periphery with the rise of nationalism in Scotland and Wales, serious disruption in Northern Ireland, a stagnant economy and poor industrial relations, and other signs of political discontent. Commentators began to wonder if constitutional malaise was at the root of many problems.
- Britain's Constitution was undergoing change. By signing up to the European Convention (especially by allowing individuals to appeal to Strasbourg), ministers were acknowledging that European decisions could override those in British courts. Membership of the European Community/Union made this more of an issue, for European law takes precedence over British law, thus undermining the traditional doctrine of the sovereignty of Parliament.
- government in Britain was becoming increasingly centralised, powerful and undemocratic. There were too few checks and balances. Some pointed to the steady erosion of the functions and powers of local government, the increased number of **quangos** and the limitations on human rights. Given such dangers, if a fully-fledged written constitution was not a priority, we certainly needed measures to reform the second chamber, increase personal rights, bring in freedom of information legislation and other things which might shift power from Whitehall in favour of the citizen.

Box 2.4 Radical and moderate constitutional reformers: the academic debate

Radical reformers took the view that fundamental surgery was required. In their view, the balance of the constitution had been undermined in the long era of Conservative rule. Howard Elcock[10] felt that there were important issues of centralisation, accountability and human rights to address:

Again and again, Mrs Thatcher swung her handbag and institutions which we fondly thought were part of the checks and balances of the British Constitution disappeared or were maimed beyond easy repair . . . [the problems] can only be satisfactorily resolved by Britain adopting a written Constitution.

Charter 88, a pressure group set up to campaign for major constitutional renewal at the time of the 300th anniversary of the **Glorious Revolution** of 1688, wanted to see the introduction of a package of constitutional measures ranging from a written constitution to a reformed, democratic second chamber, from a Bill of Rights to an independent, reformed judiciary.

In *The Observer*, the academic and writer Andrew Adonis,[11] now employed as a key adviser in 10 Downing Street, outlined the case for more moderate change:

Ardent reformers claim that Britain is appallingly governed and barely democratic . . . In reality, Britain is seriously democratic and comparatively well governed. For all its shortcomings, I am hard put to name countries of a similar size or larger which on any long view have been better, more democratically governed. Germany is the only contender, though for less than fifty years . . . The case for reform is not that Britain's governance is chronically bad, but that it could be so much better. It could be so if Westminster revived its once proud tradition of incremental reform to adapt Britain's governing institutions to the times . . . since the First World War, inflexibility has been the rule.

Philip Norton[12] also adopted the moderate perspective. Conceding that there was a need for change, he argued for the strengthening of Parliament, the abolition or reduction of quangos and the devolving of more power to citizens at the local level. The emphasis was 'to strengthen the existing framework, not destroy it'. He rejected the alarmist Elcockian view that a dangerous centralisation of power had occurred and that checks and balances had been eroded. He accepted that in some areas there had been centralisation, as in other countries, but stressed that there had in some respects been a growing fragmentation of power, with power passing to bodies such as pressure groups.

The Blair government and the Constitution

Labour was not always committed to constitutional reform. Prime Minister Callaghan once told Peter Hennessy[13] that the British political system really worked rather well: 'I think that's the answer, even if it's on the back of an envelope and doesn't have a written constitution with every comma and every semicolon in place. Because sometimes they can make for difficulties common sense can overcome.' Similar caution prevailed in the 1980s on some constitutional issues, though there was a growing acceptance of the need for reform in particular areas. It was during the late Kinnock and Smith eras, that Labour came to embrace the idea of substantial change, for several reasons:

- A genuine belief among some members of the case for constitutional reform, as being appropriate to a party committed to political and social change.
- A belief that the present system was not serving the Labour Party well (it seemed unable to win elections, have the opportunity to implement its own programme or effectively prevent aspects of the Conservative government's programme from being implemented).
- The need to win support from the Liberal Democrats, who were long-standing advocates of constitutional renewal and whose support might be essential if Labour was to attain office in a **hung Parliament**.

Tony Blair[14] had the opportunity to make the idea a reality. He signified his interest in constitutional renewal before the 1997 election, although some enthusiasts for the subject doubted the urgency of his commitment. He reminded such sceptics of the need to ensure that they did not get so far ahead of where the public was positioned that changes would not be backed by public opinion (see Box 2.5). He reaffirmed his belief that 'building a proper modern constitution for Britain is a very important part of what we are about'.

In its 1997 manifesto, Labour criticised British government as 'centralised, inefficient and bureaucratic'. It wanted 'measured and sensible reform' to open up government, improve the quality of our democracy and decentralise power. To remedy this situation, it outlined a series of proposed reforms along the lines of a pre-election package agreed with the Liberal Democrats. The Conservatives saw little scope for substantial improvement in our constitutional arrangements and stressed the importance of the 'strength and stability of our Constitution – the institutions, laws and traditions that bind us together as a nation'. They feared that 'radical changes' might endanger 'the

Box 2.5 The public mood on constitutional reform

There was no indication of widespread interest in constitutional reform, a topic that in the mid-1990s featured low in popular priorities for an incoming administration. Nonetheless, a State of the Nation poll conducted for the Rowntree Trust in 1995 found that little more than 20 per cent of the voters thought that government was working well. Many of those interviewed felt that the political system was out-of-date and in need of overhaul (50 per cent). There was strong support for the wider use of referendums and many people wanted a Freedom of Information Act (81 per cent) and a Bill of Rights (79 per cent).

whole character of our constitutional balance' and 'unravel what generations of our predecessors have created'. In other words, the Constitution is a delicate flower and to tamper with something that has grown so organically could imperil the whole.

By 2001, the programme of constitutional renewal was well underway. Among the changes made during the lifetime of the Blair governments are the following:

- the incorporation of the European Convention into British law, via the Human Rights Act
- the introduction of a new electoral system for European elections
- the establishment of the Jenkins Commission on the electoral system for Westminster (and an initially cautious welcome for its recommendations, although these have been subsequently ignored)
- the near-abolition of the hereditary system in the second chamber (Phase One): the establishment of a Royal Commission and then discussion of plans for a new, body to replace the existing House of Lords (Phase Two – as yet, still to follow)
- the introduction of devolution for Scotland and Wales (following the outcome of the referendums of September 1997), via the Scotland Act and the Wales Act
- the passage of a Freedom of Information Act
- the creation of a new authority for London, including an elected mayor – along with provision for the adoption of elected mayors in other parts of the country

- talks leading to the Good Friday Agreement in Northern Ireland, with the intention of creating an assembly and power-sharing executive.
- the wider use of referendums to establish support for constitutional change.

Other changes are in the process of delivery, notably that relating to reform of the office of Lord Chancellor and the creation of a supreme court, as part of the Constitutional Reform Bill.

A defence of the Government's record on constitutional reform

The Government's performance on constitutional renewal can be defended in two ways. There is a general defence of what ministers have done, as well as a specific defence relating to individual changes.

The general case is that the Constitution was in need of repair, the subject having been neglected over the years. What the Government has done to tackle the situation amounts to a major and unprecedented instalment of constitutional change, with several key bills placed on the statute book. They had been agreed with the Liberal Democrats and set out in the manifesto, and much of their programme was achieved. Of course, there are deficiencies in the package and things that might have been done differently, but nonetheless little or none of it would have been achieved if Labour had not been in power. No twentieth-century government has attempted so much in the constitutional arena. This is in marked contrast to constitutional change in the past, which has always evolved slowly and over a long period of time.

Such a package was – in the words of Tony Blair[15] – 'the biggest programme of change to democracy ever proposed'. A more interesting defence has been offered by Lord Irvine[16], the former Lord Chancellor, who has pointed out that in addition to addressing universal programmes, the Labour solutions were 'tailored to the particular needs of the British Constitution'. What did he mean by this?

1. The proposals in the package were about issues on which the British Constitution needed updating, such as devolution and Lords reform, among several others. Each reform deals with a specific

issue as necessary. The changes are not part of an overall plan, as would be the case if we were writing a new constitution.

2. What was being proposed was important, but gradual reform, in line with a very British evolutionary approach to change. Ours is an old constitution that has developed over centuries, the essence being retained but new developments being introduced from time to time.

3. The reforms were incremental, in the sense that an initially modest change can be developed, as becomes desirable. In several cases, the powers granted under new legislation have not been extensive, as with the Welsh National Assembly and the Freedom of Information Act. But they can be expanded, according to experience and demand. We have a Human Rights Act, which was described by the then Home Secretary, Jack Straw, on its introduction, as being 'a floor, but not a ceiling'. In the same way, Ron Davies, in introducing the legislation for the Welsh devolved body, spoke of devolution as 'a process, but not an event'. So too Phase One of Lords reform dealt with one issue (removing the hereditary peers), but there is scope for a Phase Two to develop the composition and powers of a second chamber in a more wide-ranging way.

The overall approach is distinctively British, an exercise in practical repair work. These reforms came about without too much controversy, partly because of Labour's majority but also because Labour has learned from the difficulties of earlier administrations, e.g. it has held referendums prior to the parliamentary passage of devolution, thereby allowing the public to already settle the substantive issue and Parliament to fill in the details. Similarly, over the House of Lords, it has adopted a gradualist approach, getting rid of the hereditaries before embarking upon discussion of the alternatives, a much more contentious matter. As we have seen, Tony Blair[17] had written of the need to carry people with him: 'there is a very great danger that groups like Charter 88 and other constitutional enthusiasts get so far ahead of where the public is that you fail to take them along'.

Specifically, individual measures can be defended, for instance:

- *Devolution.* It is arguable that by establishing devolved machinery in Edinburgh and Cardiff, ministers have staved off a threat to the very existence of the UK. Without reform, nationalist demands

north of the border may have intensified. It needed some concession such as devolution to take the sting out of this national feeling.
In addition, following on the work of the previous administration,
much has been done to secure a settlement in Northern Ireland;
new machinery is in place, including a power-sharing executive
and assembly, though it is currently suspended.

- *Human rights.* The incorporation of the European Convention for
  the first time gives British people a form of Bill of Rights that can
  be used in the British courts. It isn't a home grown one, tailored to
  British needs, but it does offer useful redress.
- *The House of Lords.* It may be that we only have the first phase, but
  the hereditary principle had offended many democrats for years
  and the removal of most of the hereditaries has modernised the
  House and brought it more in line with modern thinking. Also, the
  Government set up the Royal Commission, headed by Lord
  Wakeham, to look at the next stage of reform. Although the shape
  of Phase Two is still uncertain, the removal of the remaining
  hereditaries is under consideration.

An attack on the Labour record

Again, the case advanced can be both general and specific. From the
political *right*, the general attack might be that a package of change
was unnecessary, unwanted and undesirable. There is little interest
among the public on constitutional matters, for it is a subject of
concern only to political anoraks and groups like Charter 88. There
are dangers in interfering with a structure that has evolved over the
years, for in tackling one problem you may cause another to rear its
head. Some Conservatives also point out that for all the talk of decentralisation, Tony Blair has been acquiring more personal power, as is
indicated by his dictatorial attitude over the issue of the Labour candidates for the leadership of the Welsh National Assembly and his
rejection (first time round) of Ken Livingstone as the Labour candidate for the London mayoralty.

From the *centre-left*, the attack (or rather, the sense of disappointment) is twofold. Some writers have criticised the programme for its
overall lack of vision. Gillian Peele[18] takes the view that the implications of individual reforms have not always been thought through and

they do not in some cases harmonise with each other: 'They are ill thought out, not joined up, with dissimilar patterns of solution introduced in the face of similar problems – different electoral systems for the devolved assemblies and Europe, indeed different degrees of devolution within the United Kingdom.' Moreover, some changes have not gone far enough. As Labour got nearer to power, so it became more timid. Ministers tend to be more so than shadow ministers, knowing that constitutional changes can create difficulties for themselves.

This general view can be illustrated by reference to the limitations of individual changes such as the legislation on devolution and the House of Lords:

- Over *devolution*, the attack from the Tories is that it is a threat to the unity of the UK. The demands for separation will be increased, if devolution proves difficult to work. The Scottish Executive could find itself locked into conflict with Westminster, especially if a different party has control in London and Edinburgh. Also, as a result of the complexity of devolution, Scottish MPs at Westminster can vote on purely English matters, whereas English MPs can no longer vote on matters affecting Scotland – fuelling a sense of English injustice that has stirred English nationalism.

- On the *House of Lords*, Conservatives felt that if there had to be reform it should have been in one instalment, though they would not have opted for change anyway. Other critics fear that Phase Two, if and when it comes, will not lead to the predominantly elected chamber that they favour. The Prime Minister prefers an appointed body; many MPs in all parties want a wholly/substantially elected one.

The protection of rights

Bills of Rights have been written into the majority of constitutions that have been created in recent decades. The ideas of those who helped to formulate the American Constitution were taken up by the French revolutionaries at the end of the eighteenth century. The principles they laid down in the *Declaration of the Rights of Man and Citizens* in 1789 were to inspire and divide the continent, and few European countries remained unaffected by them. Some states incorporated

Box 2.6 The difference between liberties and rights

Freedom of worship and freedom of expression are sometimes referred to as examples of *civil liberties* or *negative rights*, in that they mark out areas of social life which the constitution restricts or prohibits governmental intrusion on the free choice of individuals. They restrain the interference of government, marking out a sphere of governmental inactivity.

Social and economic rights are often described as positive rights. They extend the role and responsibilities of government into areas such as education, health provision and the right to work. They are more controversial because they expand the activities of government and are also dependent on the availability of resources.

statements of human rights into their own constitutions, as did the Swedes in 1809 and Holland in 1815. In the twentieth century, and especially in the years since 1945, most constitutions have made some provision for the protection of basic rights, the South African constitution being a notable example (see p. 54).

British ministers did not follow continental examples. However, some Dependent Territories and many newly independent Commonwealth countries had entrenched Bills of Rights in their constitutions. In several cases, these were based on the **European Convention** or the **International Covenant**. They conferred fundamental freedoms and provided for the protection of rights. In Canada, India and Zimbabwe, the Supreme Courts were given wide duties and powers in protecting human rights.

More recent statements of rights have been bold in their extension of rights into the social arena, with promised entitlements covering areas from employment to medical care. Hague and Harrop[19] note how several post-communist regimes have referred to the right to a healthy environment.

The protection of rights in Britain

Britain traditionally had a negative approach to rights. Few were guaranteed, even free speech, which British citizens took for granted. The position was that they could do or say anything, provided that there was no specific law against it. Unlike the situation in other Western democracies, there was no Bill of Rights or document setting out our basic entitlements.

In the late nineteenth century, A.V. Dicey[20] wrote of the 'three pillars of liberty' and the rule of law as our main protection. The pillars were Parliament, public opinion and the courts. The good sense and vigilance of the MP, the 'culture of liberty' which people had come to expect and the justice available in the courts would afford us protection, set against – as they were – a background in which there was equality before the law to which all were subjected.

In the twentieth century, there were other ways in which freedoms could be protected. An aggrieved individual might write to the news-papers, seek the attention of radio/television or work through a pres-sure group such as Liberty. Some sought to defend their freedoms by taking to direct action. For others, they saw the advantage to be gained from exploiting the new European machinery available, either via the European Community/Union (see below) or via the European Convention (described on pp. 48–9).

Box 2.7 The European Union and the protection of rights

The treaties involved in the development of the EU confer important rights. Certain categories of people benefit from aspects of Union policy, such as French agricultural workers whose standard of living has been protected by the Common Agricultural Policy. Again, the Treaty of Rome (1957) – many of the objectives of which are being fulfilled by the Single European Act (1986) – ensures freedom of movement and the transferability of professional qualifications throughout the EU. But many problems have arisen such as the non-recognition of qualifications, the unequal treatment of men and women, or disagreements over pensions and social security where the claimant has worked in more than one state. These and a multi-plicity of similar issues can be brought to the attention of the Commission, the European Parliament or end up in the Court of Justice in Luxembourg. Important gains affecting women's rights, especially in areas of equal pay, have derived from the Court's deci-sions. Other rights have been conferred by the Social Chapter, such as paternity rights, the maximum 48-hour week for many workers and the right of workers to be represented in works councils.

Anxieties about freedoms and rights

Towards the end of the century, some academics, commentators and parliamentarians doubted if the means of protection for rights were adequate. They noted that Parliament, supposed to be our protector, had sometimes been the cause of lapses in our record on freedom. Bills pushed through by use of a governmental majority sometimes trampled on rights, as with the Commonwealth Immigrants Act of 1968 or the Criminal Justice and Public Order Act of 1994. Several laws introduced during the Thatcher years helped to persuade many people that traditional rights were in danger. Whereas defenders of the Tory governments of 1979–97 could point to the increase in economic freedoms brought about by the selling of council houses, privatisation and the reduction of income tax, critics were more concerned about what Charter 88 called an 'intensification of authoritarian rule'. They pointed to many examples of the erosion of civil liberties which significantly altered the relationship between the individual and the state. Areas of particular concern included:

- Police powers
- The prevention of terrorism
- Obsessive secrecy and action against those who exposed it
- Restrictions on assembly and other rights connected with protest
- Discriminatory legislation on immigration and citizenship.

Some of these concerns were highlighted in a series of reports by the UN Human Rights Committee, which found that Britain was failing to meet the standards laid down by its Covenant. Klug et al.[21] used this Covenant and the European Convention to develop a Human Rights Index in a survey known as *The Democratic Audit*, first published in 1996. This was the first thorough analysis of British compliance with international human rights standards. It provided a snapshot of standards in the mid-1990s. It found 42 violations and 22 near-violations or causes for anxiety. The breaches occurred across the whole spectrum of issues examined, rather than being just examples of statues too narrowly drawn or protections patchy in their operation. They concluded that there was a 'weakness at the very heart of Britain's political and constitutional system'. They saw some merit in aggrieved individuals taking the journey to Strasbourg (see pp. 48–9) to gain their rights, but concluded by speaking of the 'grudging and unsystematic attitude' of ministers, which means that 'the protection of political rights and freedoms in the UK generally moves forward in a slow, crab-like progression, by small increments, directed by the haphazard nature of individual applications and driven by the stick of Strasbourg'.

The Strasbourg route

In 1966, British citizens had been given the right to take a grievance against those in authority to the European Court on Human Rights in Strasbourg, where several cases were lost by British governments. For many campaigners, this was not enough. There was no effective protection of liberties available in Britain. With this in mind, some called for the incorporation of the European Convention into British law. Others wanted a home-grown Bill of Rights. From the late 1960s onwards, lone voices had begun to speak of the merits of some such declaration. By the end of the century, they were joined by several prominent judges and some MPs.

Labour: the Human Rights Act

The case for incorporation of the Convention was accepted by Labour back in the early 1990s, under the Smith leadership. Along with many centre-left politicians, he and his successor, Tony Blair, recognised that the status of the Convention was anomalous. Britain was bound by it, but yet citizens had difficulty in using it. Ultimately, it was binding on the British government but ministers were tempted to play for time and not give way when infringements of rights were alleged. This was because they knew that Strasbourg justice was slow (five to six years to get a Court decision). Many people were tempted to give up the struggle, rather than wait for a European verdict.

In October 1997, New Labour produced a White Paper showing how for the first time a declaration of fundamental human rights would be enshrined into British law. The detail of the proposals showed that the courts were not being empowered to strike down offending Acts of Parliament, as happens in Canada. Instead, judges would be able to declare a particular law incompatible with the Convention, enabling government and Parliament to change it if they so wished, and providing a fast-track procedure for them to so do. In

Box 2.8 The European Convention on Human Rights (ECHR)

The European Convention was drawn up mainly by British lawyers in the Home Office. It began its work in 1953. Britain was an early signatory and its citizens had the right of access to the European machinery. This meant that although the Convention was not part of British law, citizens who felt that their rights had been infringed could take the long road to Strasbourg to gain redress and possibly compensation.

Via the broad phrases of the 66 Articles and several Protocols, the Convention sets out a list of basic freedoms such as:

Article 2:	The right to life
Article 3:	Prohibition of torture
Article 5:	Right to liberty and security
Article 6:	Right to a fair trial
Article10:	Freedom of expression
Article 12:	Right to marry
Article 14:	Prohibition of discrimination
Protocol 1:	Article 1 – Protection of property
	Article 2 – Right to education
	Article 3 – Right to free elections

For each right, the basic statement is followed by a series of qualifications which list the exceptions to it. For example, although Article 10 guarantees freedom of expression, this is limited by considerations such as those 'necessary in a democratic society, in the interests of national security, for the prevention of disorder or crime, or for the protection of health or morals, for the protection of the rights of others'. The Strasbourg Court has the task of interpreting the Convention in a particular case. Now, with the incorporation of the Convention into British law via the Human Rights Act, British courts have similar scope.

There have always been some doubts about the content of the Convention, not surprisingly given that it is now more than fifty years old. Written in a very different climate of opinion, it has some contentious features, such as Article 5 which qualifies 'the right to liberty and security of person' by allowing 'the lawful detention of persons for the prevention of the spreading of infectious diseases, of persons of unsound mind, alcoholics or drug addicts or vagrants'. This may seem an arbitrary power in the hands of the authorities to detain people who have not committed a specific offence, but who have chosen to adopt an unconventional lifestyle.

this way, the proposed Act would not pose a threat to the principle of parliamentary sovereignty.

The resulting Human Rights Act (passed in 1998) became operative from October 2000. It provides the first written statement of people's rights and obligations by enshrining most – but not all – of the European Convention on Human Rights into British law. It allows them to use the Convention as a means of securing justice in the British courts. Judges are now able to apply human rights law in their rulings.

Box 2.9 Britain and anti-terrorist legislation: judicial review and the European Convention

Britain, alone in Europe, has withdrawn or derogated from Article 5 of the Convention. This guarantees the right to a fair trial and allows only limited circumstances under which a person may be deprived of liberty. Under part four of the Anti-Terrorism Crime and Security Act (2001), ministers were empowered to detain those considered a security threat, without trial. As a result, foreign nationals were held for three years in Britain's highest security prisons, Belmarsh and Woodhill.

In December 2004, the law lords decided that the detention of foreign terror suspects without trial was unlawful. There was no legal obligation for ministers to abide by the opinion of the senior judges, but the fact that they sat as a panel of nine rather than five was an indication of how seriously they viewed the threat to British liberties. In the words of Lord Scott: 'Indefinite imprisonment ... on grounds not disclosed is the stuff of nightmares.' The punishment was considered disproportionate to the threat posed and discriminatory in that it applied only to foreign nationals.

Charles Clarke, the Home Secretary who had to deal with the ruling, accepted that there was a breach of human rights law. He acted to allay the concerns by proposing a new control order which would involve release of the detainees who would be placed under conditions of strict surveillance, including a ban on use of the Internet or mobile phones and possibly house arrest. He also removed the discriminatory aspect of the 2001 Act, by allowing British – as well as foreign – suspects to be treated in the same way. It remains to be seen whether house arrest would require a further derogation. If used, it too is liable to be challenged in the courts by critics who see it as detention by another name. Article 5 allows only limited circumstances under which a person may be deprived of liberty. When a member of the Italian mafia was required to live on a tiny island for 18 months while awaiting trial, the European Court in Strasbourg held that he had been denied his human rights.

The development of the practice of **judicial review** by the higher courts since the late 1960s has become a recognised feature of our constitutional arrangements. The effect of the passage of the Human Rights Act was to systematise the process and to elevate the law lords in particular into a de facto constitutional court, charged with deciding whether particular legislative Acts or executive actions were consistent with the obligations under the Convention which the Act codified.

The development of human rights law is becoming a feature of the work of all the higher courts, not merely the law lords. Around the same time as the Belmarsh judgement above, the high court ruled that human rights law applied to the actions of British troops in Iraq and the law lords ruled against the government on its **Roma** immigration control policies. Both cases involved human rights principles.

The effect of incorporation of the Convention is to introduce a new human rights culture into British politics. In general, decisions by Parliament, a local authority or other public body must not infringe the rights guaranteed under the Act. Where rights conflict, such as privacy versus freedom of information, the courts will decide where the balance should lie. Judges have to ask of deciding cases as they come before them, in effect creating new law. If courts decide that a statute breaches the Act, they can declare it 'incompatible', but they cannot strike it down. They cannot overrule Parliament. It will be for Parliament to amend the law, thus preserving the idea of parliamentary sovereignty. The ultimate decision in any conflict lies with Parliament, not the courts.

There were some concerns that the Act would clog up the courts (particularly in the early stages) and that the chief beneficiaries would be lawyers. It was expected that the courts would be deluged with all kinds of cases, some of them extreme. In Scotland, where the European Convention was already in force, 98 per cent of the cases in the first year failed. In the event, there was no legal free-for-all. Between 2000 and 2002, of 431 cases involving human rights heard in the high courts, the claims were upheld in 94. Keir Starmer[22], a barrister much involved in such cases, has concluded that 'hand on heart, the Human Rights Act has changed the outcome of only a very few cases'. This is partly because the common law has turned out to be more accommodating than many reformers feared. Faced with a potential clash between the two traditions (common law and the Convention), judges have simply declared them to be complementary or even argued that the ECHR reveals ambient human rights principles in common law. In any individual case, they still have to weigh individual rights against the common good.

The Act has important implications, not just for the improved protection of rights in Britain. Although Parliament still has the final say over legislation, some commentators feel that a turning point has been reached. Bogdanor[23] suggests that the measure 'alters considerably the balance between Parliament and the **judiciary**' and enables judges 'to interpret parliamentary legislation in terms of a higher law, the European Convention'. Others suggest that important social change will continue to be brought about by elected politicians rather than judges, this having been the case in other countries that incorporated the Convention many years ago.

British judges are unlikely to deliver judgements that involve a radically different interpretation of rights from that of the European Court, not least because British citizens retain a right of ultimate appeal to Strasbourg once domestic remedies have been exhausted. The likelihood is that over a period of time, British courts will establish substantial new protections for aggrieved individuals.

See *especially* pp. 174–6 and 178–81 for further discussion of growing judicial power and consideration of whether judges are the best persons to decide issues of civil rights. Note how judicial review is being used to safeguard British liberties.

Does Britain need its own home-grown Bill of Rights?

Advocates of a discrete, home-grown British bill are likely to take the ECHR and rights conferred in other international treaties as the starting point for any discussion of further development of the protection required. But some libertarian groups are dissatisfied with the Convention in its present form, as embodied in the Human Rights Act, and would like to see:

- the phraseology of some existing rights amended
- additional rights included

- and a statement of rights which was more attuned to the British situation today than one drawn up a half-century ago.

The case of France

The Declaration of the Rights of Man was proclaimed in the early days of the French Revolution. It asserted the rights of all men (not women) to liberty, property, security and resistance to oppression; that the law was equally applicable to everyone; that all citizens were entitled to its protection and liable to its sanctions; that there should be freedom of speech and publication, as well as of religious belief. This was an announcement of fundamental importance, both for France, Europe and several other parts of the world that were inspired by its bold message and implications.

The Declaration has formed an integral part of all subsequent constitutions. The preamble to the 1946 Constitution included a statement of economic, social and political principles, some of which concerned civic rights: equal rights for women 'in all spheres'; the rights to belong to a trade union, to undertake free collective bargaining and to strike; and (among others) the right to strike. The rights listed in the Declaration and the 1946 statement are entrenched and – although the means of their enforcement are not clearly stated – are capable of being enforced as the need arises.

In the Constitution of the Fifth Republic, the Preamble 'solemnly proclaims its attachment to the Rights of Man . . . as defined by the Declaration of 1789, confirmed and completed by the preamble to the Constitution of 1946'. Article 2 'assures equality before the law to all citizens without distinction of origin, race or religion. She [France] respects all beliefs.' Stevens[24] shows how in 1982 the Constitutional Council used the principles of the 1789 Declaration to defend the rights of shareholders in companies that were to be nationalised, to receive adequate compensation and eleven years later to insist on proportionality between the gravity of an offence and the penalty prescribed.

France has had seventeen constitutions since 1787, including two since 1945 (the Fourth and Fifth Republics). The Fourth Republic was a byword for political instability, there being twenty-two governments in which at least a dozen parties at some time participated during its twelve-year existence. When Charles de Gaulle came to power in 1958, he wanted to provide France with firm leadership. He had long favoured a presidential form of government similar to that of the United States. Soon after his accession, a constitution was devised for the new Fifth Republic. As previously, there is a president and a premier, but whereas the premier had been the main source of authority and the president was a figure head, after 1958 the president emerged with much increased powers. The document carefully defined the powers of the legislature and restricted its opportunities for defeating a government.

The case of South Africa

After enduring years of systematic oppression of individual and group rights under the apartheid regime, the transformation in the position of the individual in South Africa has been remarkable. The Preamble to the 1996 Constitution states that its object is 'to create a new order in which all South Africans will be entitled to a common South African citizenship in a state in which there is equality between men and women of all races, so that all citizens shall be able to enjoy and exercise their fundamental rights and freedoms'. These rights are guarded by a Constitutional Court which determines whether state actions are in accordance with constitutional provisions.

Suspicion of parliamentary as well as executive power is reflected in the Constitution, for in the apartheid era both branches of government were involved in support for 'objectionable' measures. Not surprisingly, in view of past history, there is a strong emphasis in the new version on anti-discriminatory provision, and an innovation is the guarantee of rights in the area of sexual orientation. Under Article 9 (iii) on Equality, 'the state may not unfairly discriminate directly or indirectly against anyone on one or more grounds, including race, gender, sex, pregnancy, marital status, ethnic or social origin, colour, sexual orientation, age, disability, religion, conscience, belief, culture, language and birth'. Specific social and economic rights are not spelt out, but the inclusion of the wide-ranging Article 10 is potentially significant in its implications: 'Everyone has inherent dignity and the right to have their dignity respected and protected.'

The case of the USA

The American Constitution has survived for more than 200 years, making it the world's oldest written constitution. It is considerably less detailed than European ones such as those of France and Germany. It deals mainly with broad principles which lay down a loose framework in which government operates. It has stood the test of time, although it has been subject to twenty-seven amendments. Of these, the first ten became a key issue in the ratification process following the conclusion of the Convention which devised the document. These form the Bill of Rights, which originally applied to the federal government only, but today most of them also apply at state and local level.

There is a difference between constitutional theory and everyday reality. In spite of the provisions of the 14th Amendment providing equal protection of the law and the 15th extending the right to vote to African-American males, there were constant denials of constitutional rights to black people. Such constitutional guarantees were not effected until the 1950s and 1960s and in some respects are still open to evasion. This suggests that rights do not depend on the existence of a written constitution alone. The tradition of liberty in a country and the nature of its political culture are more important than any constitutional document.

Nonetheless, Americans view their constitution with considerable awe and reverence, leading Louis Hartz[25] to write in 1955 of 'the cult of constitution worship'. The issue of constitutional reform rarely surfaces. Those who want to argue the case for change tend to talk in terms of restoring the original to its former glory, rather than of carrying out a radical overhaul. When innovations have been proposed – as with the suggestion of 'term limits' to curtail the length of time a congressman may spend in office – they have failed to command the necessary support in the House of Representatives and the Senate.

• •

✓ What you should have learnt from reading this chapter

- Constitutions are important, in that they proclaim the basic principles according to which people should be governed. In almost all cases, they exist in the form of single, authoritative documents that are often difficult to amend. Where there is no such constitutional statement, the country can still be regarded as having a constitution. The 'unwritten' British one is flexible and has survived well, even if in recent years there have been regular calls for constitutional reform of the type introduced by the Blair government.

- The strength of a constitution is to be measured not by the text or format, but in the extent to which it operates successfully with reasonable stability, continuity and durability. Many 'written' ones do not prove to be long lasting, whatever the good intentions of those who draft them.

- Most constitutions contain a declaration of rights, as in the case of the American and French ones. Early ones placed more emphasis on civil and political rights, but some of those devised in the last few decades such as the South African one have also included economic and social rights. The existence of a constitution and Bill of Rights is no guarantee that essential liberties and rights will be respected. Liberty ultimately depends more on the political culture of any country than on any written proclamation.

Glossary of key terms

Bills of Rights Formal statements of the rights and privileges to which citizens are entitled, usually embodied in a constitution.

Devolutionary federalism The devolving of responsibility for once federally run programmes to the states which – being closer to the people – are thought to be better placed to respond to local needs.

Directives A type of EU secondary law which is binding on member states as to the result to be achieved, but can be implemented as best suits the needs of the individual country.

European Convention on Human Rights (ECHR) The statement of basic liberties and rights devised by the Council of Europe in 1950 and enforced by the Strasbourg Court of Justice, whose verdict is binding. Britain has now incorporated the Convention into UK law, as have most other signatories.

Executive One of the three branches of government, along with the legislature and judiciary. The part of government concerned with making governmental decisions and policies, rather than passing laws. The political executive in Britain comprises the Prime Minister and the Cabinet.

Factortame In a European Court of Justice verdict (1991) judges upheld the claim of the owners of a Spanish fishing vessel that the Merchant Shipping Act (1988) was invalid, as it conflicted with the Common Fisheries Policy of the European Union. This was the first time that a British law was effectively set aside by the Court. The judgement indicated that EU law takes precedence over British law.

Federal system A constitutionally defined structure in which a central (federal) authority shares power with smaller territorial areas, in the USA known as states.

Glorious Revolution The enforced abdication of the centralising Catholic King James II from the throne in 1688, brought about by the revolt of the Protestant nobility who invited William III of the Netherlands to replace him. It established the dependence of the monarch on Parliament and is seen as an important step on the route to parliamentary government.

Hung Parliament A post-election situation in which no party possesses an overall majority in the House of Commons.

International Covenant The International Covenant on Civil and Political Rights (ICCPR) agreed by members of the United Nations in 1966. In theory binding, it lacks effective enforcement machinery. Signatories have to report periodically on their record of compliance with its provisions to a human rights committee.

Judicial review The constitutional function exercised by the judiciary of reviewing the laws, decrees and actions of the Executive and legislature, to ensure that they are compatible with the Constitution and established rights.

Judiciary The branch of government concerned with the administration of justice.

Legislature The branch of government that makes law through the formal enactment of legislation.

Parliamentary sovereignty The absolute and unlimited authority of Parliament to make, repeal or amend any law.

Quangos An acronym for quasi-autonomous non-governmental organisations that carry out public service functions. Although funded by government, they do not operate under direct governmental control.

Regulations A type of EU secondary law that is binding on all member states, without the need for any national legislation.

Roma Commonly known as gypsies, a traditionally nomadic people who originated in northern India but today are particularly concentrated in parts of Europe. They are easily identifiable because of their clothing and their darker skin and hair.

Rousseau Eighteenth-century French philosopher and writer who favoured the idea of democracy, but viewed majority rule as potentially unjust. He argued that government should be based on recognition of the collective will of the people, 'the general will'.

Separation of powers The principle that executive, legislative and judicial power should be separated through the creation of three independent branches of government.

Unitary system A structure in which there is a single sovereign body, central government, that does not share power with devolved or local institutions, although it may choose to grant power to them. Legal sovereignty lies entirely at the centre.

Likely examination questions

To what extent do constitutions shape political practice?

Discuss the merits and disadvantages of Britain's uncodified constitution?

Discuss the view that the measures in Labour's programme of constitutional change have been considered in isolation and that the package lacks any overall vision.

Is it true to say that constitutions are meaningless without recognition of basic civil liberties and rights?

Discuss the view that the passage of the Human Rights Act represents the first step towards the introduction of a written constitution in Britain.

 Helpful websites

For details of bodies concerned with specific changes/proposals, see the appropriate chapter.

The following more general sites are likely to be of interest and value:

Charter 88 offers a pro-reform look at constitutional issues at www.charter88.org.uk

The Constitution Unit provides an academic analysis of the changes made and contemplated at www.ucl.ac.uk/constitution-unit

The Guardian covers constitutional issues at www.politics.guardian.co.uk/constitutions

Suggestions for further reading

Useful articles

Two short articles provide a brief, but useful assessment or recent developments:

A. Granath, 'Constitutional Reform: A Work in Progress', *Talking Politics*, April 2002.

N. Smith, 'New Labour and Constitutional Reform', *Talking Politics*, September 2001.

Two more detailed, analytical studies are offered by:

D. Beetham, I. Byrne, P. Ngan et al., 'Democratic Audit: Labour's Record so far', *Parliamentary Affairs*, 54, 2001.

R. Hazell, 'The Constitution: Coming in from the Cold', *Parliamentary Affairs*, 54, 2002.

Useful books

R. Blackburn and R. Plant (eds), *Constitutional Reform: The Labour Government's Constitutional Reform Agenda*, Longman, 1999.

N. Forman, *Constitutional Change in the UK*, Routledge, 2002.

A. King, *Does the UK Still Have a Constitution?*, Sweet and Maxwell, 2001.

A. Lansley and R. Wilson, *Conservatives and the Constitution*, Conservative 2000 Foundation, 1997.

J. Morrison, *Reforming Britain: New Labour, New Constitution?*, Reuters/Pearson Educational, 2001.

The Legislature

Contents

Overview

Legislatures are representative bodies that reflect the sentiments and opinions of the public. Their members consider public issues and pass laws on them. In Britain, there are various views of the role of Parliament within the political system. Some portray it mainly as a forum for the discussion of important issues and in which grievances are aired. Others believe that Parliament should be equipped with a range of powers in order that it can provide an effective check upon the Executive.

In this chapter, we examine the power and influence of Parliament as a whole and of its individual members, asking what purposes Parliament serves and how effective it is in carrying out its tasks.

Key issues to be covered in this chapter

- The structure of legislatures
- The functions of legislatures in general
- The role of the British House of Lords, its changing character and proposals for its future
- The work of the House of Commons
- The role and significance of MPs
- The social composition of legislatures: how representative are they?
- The pay and conditions of legislators
- The decline of legislatures and the need for parliamentary reform
- The legislatures of Denmark, the European Parliament and the United States

Introduction

Most countries have a legislature as part of their institutions of government. The names employed for legislatures vary around the world. The term Congress is used in some countries; Parliament is employed in Britain and the Commonwealth; on the continent, it is more common to speak of the National Assembly (as in France) or the Chamber of Deputies (as in Italy). The individual chambers are variously named, with titles ranging from the House of Representatives and Senate in the USA to the Knesset in Israel.

The exact number of legislatures varies from year to year. Blondel[1] notes that in the 1970s and early 1980s there were often some twenty to thirty (mainly in Africa and Latin America) that were not allowed to function. Since then, the number of military regimes has diminished, as countries have returned to democratic rule. In addition, new states have been established in parts of former communist-controlled Eastern Europe, again increasing the number of parliaments. As a result of these changes, 178 are currently in existence.[2]

What is the legislature?

Legislatures have always been structures in which policy issues are discussed and assessed. The roots of the name of the first modern legislature, the British Parliament, suggest this crucial function – 'parler', to talk. Most early legislatures were created to provide advice to the political executive, often a monarch, and to represent relevant political groups. Many legislatures have also been responsible for introducing public policies. The roots of the word 'legislature' are the Latin terms *legis* (law) and *latio* (bringing, carrying or proposing). Legislatures are then the branch of government empowered to make law. Whether known as assemblies or parliaments, they are forums for debate and deliberation.

The word 'assembly' is sometimes distinguished from 'parliament'. Its literal meaning is a gathering. Some writers portray an assembly as being a weaker body, more of a talking shop. In contrast, parliaments have law-making powers. Here, we are not making much of the distinction, for the labels employed vary according to countries and traditions. 'Assembly' can be used to describe either house and can be used interchangeably with 'legislature' and 'parliament'.

The main functions of legislatures

Most elected legislatures perform three broad roles:

- *Enactment of legislation.* In fact, in most countries the dominant role in policy-making has passed to the Executive, but legislatures still have an active and significant role. The essence of their power is that in most systems a majority of the members of the legislature need to vote to authorise the passage of any law. The power to enact laws that raise revenue and to authorise expenditure on public policies (the 'power of the purse') has been a central responsibility of the legislative majority. In some systems, legislatures have a system of special committees that thoroughly assess and can amend all proposed legislation. In others, many laws are initiated by members of the legislature.
- *Representation.* Elected representatives represent public opinions and the public interests within the governing process and therefore play an important role in providing a link between government and the people. The 'interests' that may be represented include those of a particular social group, a political party, the country as a whole and the legislator's own conscience and inclinations.
- *Oversight of the Executive.* Legislatures normally oversee the actions of the political executive. This scrutiny means that there are regular procedures by which the legislature can question and even investigate whether the executive has acted properly in its implementation of public policies. At minimum, the legislature is a discussion/debating chamber and this provides modest scrutiny. Many legislatures allow for questioning of specific plans and actions of particular members of the executive. In Britain, Italy and Germany, ministers in the Cabinet appear before the legislature and respond to questions and criticisms concerning the work of their department.

Most legislatures have formal investigatory powers on a continuing basis. The investigation of Bill Clinton in the **impeachment** process was a dramatic American example of powerful scrutiny.

Strong scrutiny can also be provided by specialist committees, such
as the departmental ones in Britain and the Congressional committees in the USA that conduct powerful investigations in televised proceedings. Of course, a particularly powerful form of
making the executive accountable is provided by the ability to over-
turn the government. In a parliamentary system, the legislature
can oblige or pressure the executive to resign. In Italy, for instance,
the legislature has forced the executive to resign regularly since the
Second World War.

Sometimes oversight includes the right to approve the selection
of key appointments. In the USA, the Senate possesses the right
to 'advise and consent' on presidential appointments such as
cabinet members and Supreme Court justices.

- A further function of legislatures is that they act as *major channels of
  recruitment*, providing a good pool of talent. In parliamentary
  systems, service in the assembly is the required career path for
  ministers and premiers. Assemblies recruit and train the next generation of political leaders.
- On the floor of the chamber, apart from involvement in law-
  making, which takes up much of the time available, members also
  take part in other activities such as *discussion of financial provisions,
  participating in general debates and asking questions*, the latter an activity
  more common in Britain and Commonwealth countries than it is
  elsewhere. The habit has been extended to some continental countries and to the European Parliament, but the process is often more
  formal and sedate than at Westminster, and has nothing like the
  adversarial and pugnacious character of Question Time in the
  House of Commons.

General policy debates are uncommon in several countries, partly
because governments may not wish to allow such an opportunity to
voice hostile opinions. They are rare on the African continent. Most of
the debates in Western European legislatures, the Commonwealth
countries and in South America are about legislation, usually
government-inspired bills. Often the final outcome of the discussion is
not in doubt, although in the United States bills deriving from the
administration are more likely to run into difficulties. In several countries of the developing world, debates occur but often on matters of

limited significance. In authoritarian ones where representative assemblies are allowed to function, legislation does not result in debates that are meaningful in a Western sense. Governmental policy is set out from 'on high', and the legislature is only asked to give its approval.

The structures of legislatures

The obvious distinction in the structural arrangements of different legislatures concerns whether they are unicameral or bicameral:

- *Unicameral legislatures* have one chamber, examples ranging from Bulgaria to Hungary
- *Bicameral chambers* have two chambers, examples ranging from Australia to Great Britain. Bicameral legislatures are more common in federal states than in unitary ones.

Bicameralism now operates in just over sixty countries. Second chambers are more common in federal countries and those that are geographically extensive. In the USA, the two chambers are of formally equal status, but the Senate is the dominant one. It alone has all the responsibilities of confirming appointments, and is particularly significant in the area of foreign policy. In federal countries, the second chamber is often more powerful (for instance in Canada and Germany). In such examples, the size of the country, the need for regional representation and the sometimes sharp geographical cleavages make a second chamber seem desirable.

Broadly, apart from whether a country has a federal or unitary system, the factor which determines the likelihood of a second chamber is the size of the population in any country. Larger countries tend to have two chambers, the fear being that a single chamber would find itself overwhelmed by its legislative and other tasks.

Most non-federal second chambers are constitutionally and politically subordinate to first chambers, especially in parliamentary systems. Many have lost much of their power, so that in Britain, France and Norway they retain only the right to revise or delay (but not veto) legislation. Weaker versions of bicameralism (with one house much less powerful than the other) often reflect the composition of the second chamber. Until 1999, the House of Lords had a predominant hereditary element. In early 2006, 92 hereditaries remain, although ministers have indicated the possibility of legislation to remove them. The Lords only has the power to delay non-financial legislation for one session. Canada has a wholly nominated upper house and, as in Britain, all money bills must be introduced in the lower chamber.

Unicameralism has been on the increase in recent years and nearly two-thirds of the world's legislatures now have only one chamber. Over time, some bicameral systems have evolved into unicameral ones. This has usually happened where the problems of conflict and stalemate between the two houses have increased; where there has been little need for extensive checks and balances; or where representation in the popularly elected chamber has been thought adequate. Countries that have abolished the second chamber include Costa Rica, Denmark, Sweden and New Zealand. Significantly, they have mostly been small in size and/or population. In such countries, the pressure of legislation is much less than in a country the size of Britain.

Bicameralism has certain benefits. Second chambers:

- act as a check upon first chambers, the more important if one party has a landslide majority
- more effectively check the executive;
- broaden the basis of representation, especially in federal states giving representation to the region;
- allow for thorough scrutiny of legislation, providing more time for careful examination of bills;
- act as a constitutional long stop, delaying the passage of bills and allowing time for debate.

Critics allege that second chambers:

- can be needlessly costly
- perform no useful role not capable of being covered by a streamlined lower house
- slow down the task of government, sometimes delaying much-needed legislation
- (sometimes) do not represent the electorate and are often of conservative leanings
- are a recipe for constitutional stalemate or 'gridlock'. They institutionalise conflict.

Lower houses range in size from the large (Britain 646 members, Italy 630 and India 545) to the very small (Iceland (73) and Costa Rica (57)). Unsurprisingly, size is related to population, though the proportions vary considerably in various states. India has on average one representative for every two million people; the USA one per 420,000: Britain, France and Germany around one for 100,000; Ireland and Norway one for 20,000–30,000.

From such figures it can be seen that countries with less inhabitants are at an advantage. The legislatures are smaller, giving members more chance to participate in the proceedings, Moreover, since they represent fewer constituents, the bonds between people and representatives are close. For these reasons, legislatures in smaller countries are more likely to function effectively than those in much larger ones.

The British House of Lords

For much of the nineteenth century, the membership of the House of Lords was based on heredity and the chamber enjoyed equality of status with the House of Commons. However, its position became increasingly inappropriate when the franchise was extended and the lower house became more representative of the people. The Lords was able to survive the transition into a democratic age on the basis that its powers were trimmed and its membership modified.

In the twentieth century, there were several changes to the composition and powers of the second chamber. The main changes concerning *membership* were all introduced by the Macmillan (Conservative) government:

* *Payment of an attendance allowance* to peers to encourage a better turnout, 1957.
* The introduction of life peers by the *Life Peerages Act 1958*. This permitted men and women to be created as peers for the duration of their lives, on the advice of the Prime Minister (who usually consults with the Leader of the Opposition). The purpose was to diversify membership of the chamber, bringing in people from various walks of life who had something to contribute to the deliberations of the upper house. By being used to boost Labour membership, the Act could be seen as a skilful way of deflecting criticism of the House of Lords as one-sided and unfair.

- *The Peerage Act 1963* allowed hereditary peers to renounce their title for the duration of their lifetime.

The main changes affecting the *powers* of the House of Lords were:

- *The Parliament Act 1911* (introduced by the pre-First World War Liberal government). This removed the power of absolute delay over legislation. In future, any bill which passed the Commons in three successive sessions would automatically become law. In other words, the House of Lords had lost its permanent veto.
- *The Parliament Act 1949* (introduced by the post-1945 Labour government). This further limited the delaying power of the Lords, so that any bill that passed in two successive sessions now became law. This effectively curtailed the delaying power to eight to nine months and made it harder for the upper house to frustrate the wishes of the elected one. It has been used on four occasions, most recently for the passage of the bill that abolished fox-hunting.

It seemed difficult to achieve a fundamental reform of the second chamber that tackled functions, powers and composition. Party agreement was hard to establish and the subject was not viewed as a priority. The Conservatives lacked any real incentive to bring about major change, for the Lords had an overwhelmingly conservative membership and was generally more accommodating to Conservative ministers. Labour had no reason to approve of the Lords, disliking its overwhelmingly hereditary composition and finding it a bulwark that blocked any proposals for radical reform. But it was a convenient target for an easy attack on unfair privilege and could conveniently be blamed for the lack of action by a Labour administration. As a result, major change was not forthcoming, although it had been envisaged in the Preamble to the 1911 Act:

> Whereas it is intended to substitute for the House of Lords as it at present exists, a Second Chamber constituted on a popular instead of an hereditary basis, but such substitution cannot be immediately be brought into operation . . .

Labour's 1998 changes: Phase One of Lords reform
Before the 1997 election, Labour and the Liberal Democrats agreed on a first phase of Lords reform. The 1997 Labour manifesto committed

the party to action to end by statute 'the right of hereditary peers to sit and vote in the House of Lords'. *Phase One* was to provide for the abolition of the hereditary peerage, which was effectively carried out in October 1998. The House voted to remove all but ninety-two of the hereditaries who were elected by party groupings to serve in the revised chamber.

The House of Lords Act left the judicial and spiritual membership of the chamber untouched. The Lords Spiritual comprise the two Archbishops (Canterbury and York), as well as the twenty-four next most senior bishops. They retain their membership only for as long as they hold office within the Church. The law lords are members by virtue of their high judicial positions. They retain their seats until their death, so that there are at any one time more law lords than are necessary to enable the Lords to fulfil its judicial functions (see below).

Membership of the chamber now fluctuates. In November 2005, the 736 peers (of whom 135 were female) included:

    588 Life peers
    92 Elected hereditaries
    28 Law lords
    25 Bishops

As a result of the 1998 changes, the overwhelming Conservative bias vanished. Of the above, 208 were proclaimed Conservatives, 210 Labour and 74 Liberal Democrats. In the rare event of members of the two opposition parties all voting together, they can easily outvote ministers. The votes of the 192 crossbenchers often determine the fate of ministerial policy. Since gaining power, Labour has been defeated on numerous issues, ranging from modification of the jury system to freedom of information, from the privatisation of the National Air Traffic Service to fox-hunting.

The Wakeham proposals for Phase Two
As for the future, Lord Wakeham headed a Royal Commission established by Tony Blair to examine options for *Phase Two*. He reported in January 2000 and came up with a fixer's solution, one likely to find favour with the Prime Minister wary of having a substantially or fully elected house. Wakeham recommended a smaller chamber of

around 550, although the number would fluctuate to get the party
balance right. An Appointments Commission would be required:

- to secure an overall political balance matching the political
  opinion of the country in the last election – no party is to have an
  overall majority
- to ensure that about 20 per cent of the total membership is made
  up of independents and
- to achieve the intention of ensuring that diverse faiths be
  represented.

As for the elected element, a 'significant number' of the new second
chamber should be regional members. Three models were outlined:

- 65 regional members, with one-third of the regions choosing them
  at each general election
- 87 regional members, directly elected at the time of each
  European election, again one-third of the regions involved
- 195 chosen on the same basis as phase two, using a 'partially open'
  list system.

Within the Wakeham team there were some members who
favoured a fully elected chamber and others who wanted to see an
appointed one. Hence his proposals were a compromise, based on
what might be achievable. They pleased few commentators and were
particularly disappointing for those who felt that it was time to move
towards a more democratic means of choosing the membership. *The
Economist*[3] found the proposals too timid, observing:

> It is not beyond the wit of the reformers through staggered elections
> and longer terms of office, to produce an elected Lords with a
> different complexion from the Commons. An elected Upper House
> would, at last, enjoy the democratic legitimacy it needs in order to
> make full use of these powers.

The work performed by the House of Lords

Countries with second chambers have them for several reasons.
Sometimes, their role is to provide continuity and stability in
Parliament and law-making; sometimes, to act as a constitutional long
stop (preventing or delaying the passage of radical innovations);
sometimes, to act as a revising body. (In federal states, the upper house

can be used to provide for regional representation.) The House of Lords fulfils all three roles. It spends around 60 per cent of its time examining legislation and 35 per cent or so on scrutinising the work of government.

Back in 1918, Lord Bryce distinguished four roles for the British second chamber:

1. *The consideration and revision of bills from the House of Commons.* The House of Lords has the power to examine legislation in detail and may pass, amend or reject bills. Ministers may accept or reject amendments, rejection leading to a process of negotiation between the two chambers. The Commons can use the 1949 Parliament Act to insist on getting its way. Revision is the key function today and the House spends nearly half of its time on scrutiny of Public Bills (see p. 78), some of which have been badly drafted or inadequately discussed in the lower house; many amendments are actually put down by the government.

2. *The initiation of non-controversial legislation.* About a quarter of bills begin their parliamentary life in the upper house, although these are mainly those which are non-controversial and on which there is no strong party disagreement. Backbench peers can also introduce Private Peers' Bills. Few are passed, but they provide a chance to air topics ranging from social reform to a Bill of Rights.

3. *The power of delay.* The Lords can hold up legislation under the Parliament Act, the extra time being designed to provide a pause for reflection and reconsideration. (In the past, this power has been used to frustrate the wishes of more radical governments; Labour has traditionally been wary of it.)

4. *The holding of general debates.* Peers – under less pressure of time than MPs – can conduct useful discussions on matters such as leisure and the environment. There are many life peers who have expertise to contribute on issues ranging from education to race, health to policing. Such debates usually take up more than 25 per cent of the time of the Lords and are less rancorous than those in the Commons.

Finally, the Lords does valuable work in scrutinising European legislation (see Box 3.1), investigating some topics in great detail and

Box 3.1 Scrutinising European legislation

In 1974, the House of Lords established the Lords' Committee on the European Community, in order to scrutinise Commission proposals and to draw the attention of the House to those that raise important issues of policy or principle. It can suggest a debate on those matters it considers to be of sufficient significance.

The Committee examines the merits of proposals for legislation and undertakes wide-ranging investigations of EU policy. Its wide terms of reference even permit it to make freestanding enquiries into EU issues in the absence of specific proposals. Its remit is much wider than that of its Commons' counterpart and its prestige is higher. Although some debates are held in the Lords, it is more common for reports to be communicated to ministers by letter.

The Committee has 19 members and an elaborate system of sub-committees covering the principal areas of EU competence. There is a total working membership of around 55 peers. The main Committee reflects the broad political balance within the House, but the sub-committee members are chosen for their political expertise. The Committee examines proposals that are considered important by the Chairman.

The Committee is widely acknowledged for performing a valuable role in scrutiny of EU legislation. Membership of the main and sub-committees is often very distinguished and the reports of high quality. They are useful as a source of information and of informed opinion. Although aimed in the first instance at the House and through the House at ministers, they are taken seriously by the institutions of the EU, including the European Parliament.

producing authoritative, well-written reports. It also – in its judicial capacity – acts as the final court of appeal, a role performed by law lords who deal with cases that raise important points of law. This role is eventually to be transferred to a new supreme court. The judges will be the current law lords, housed in a different building. They will no longer be peers

The case for the House of Lords

Defence of the House of Lords has in the past been made more difficult because of its largely hereditary composition. This was widely regarded as inappropriate for a democratic age. Now that the hereditary element has gone (see Phase One above), it is easier to concentrate on the merits of the House. Points for the defence are that:

- Most sizeable countries are bicameral rather than unicameral. Although Denmark, Israel, New Zealand and Sweden manage well with one chamber, neither of those countries has the volume of work and particularly of legislation that characterise the British system. Unicameralism would be impossible without major streamlining of the House of Commons.
- Many writers still feel that a second chamber produces a valuable opportunity for careful scrutiny of government work. For all of its anomalies, past and present, the House actually performs this role rather well. As former prime minister John Major used to say: 'If it ain't broke, don't fix it.' It has been fixed to some extent, in a way that has lessened the anomaly of heredity that was an affront to many people in a democratic era. The removal of the hereditaries means that members now are mostly life peers, chosen because they have something special to contribute.
- The diversity of membership among the life peers means that there is normally someone who can speak with authority on even the most obscure subject. Relatively free from the constraints of time and able to speak in a less partisan atmosphere, debates do produce some interesting contributions from members with specialist knowledge and expertise, be it on education, the economy, welfare or a host of other topics. There is an impressive array of experience and talent. Many successful industrialists and businessmen and women become life peers, as do some trade unionists (especially after their retirement). Senior academics, people active in local government and in the charitable and voluntary fields, and people from the arts have also been given peerages.
- An appointed house provides an opportunity to bring in more women and members of minority groups, especially if appointment is placed in the hands of an independent appointments commission.
- The chamber has done useful work of revision and also shown a spirit of independence in the last couple of decades or so. The so-called resurgence of the Lords in that period has been attributed to the large number of life peers with their particular

specialisms to feed into debates, the arrival of television, which created a little more interest in its proceedings, and the greater willingness of party members to defy the whips and vote with the crossbenchers. Governments of both parties have been frequently defeated. Tony Blair's first phase of reform has left a more justifiable house willing to use its muscle.

Two interesting defences of the Lords have been expressed by present peers. The first is from Lord Howe[4], a Conservative Chancellor of the Exchequer in the early Thatcher years and later Deputy Prime Minister. It notes the independence shown by the present chamber:

> The dramatic change in composition since 1997 has greatly increased the practical, day-to-day confidence of the Lords. 'Ministers', proclaimed *The Independent* the other day, 'have failed to intimidate Parliament'. The paper was rightly applauding the repulse of David Blunkett's attack upon the jury system.
>
> But which House was being applauded? The record speaks for itself. In the five sessions between 1997–2001, there were 1,640 divisions in the House of Commons, without a single Government defeat. In the same period, in the House of Lords there were 639 whipped divisions, of which the Government lost no less than 164 (25%).

A rather different case for the Lords has been expressed by Melvyn Bragg[5], the author and presenter of the *South Bank Show* as well as many other television programmes. Once a traditional left-wing opponent of the House of Lords, he was made a Labour peer, with the title of Lord Bragg of Wigton. Since his elevation to the peerage, he has undergone a change of heart on the value of the chamber, in particular noting the quality of debate and the value of the work of revision, whilst remaining aware of its essentially conservative, gentlemanly character.

> Even when – as happens more often than is generally reported – it engages in good debates in a serious and well-informed way, there is something in the Gilbert and Sullivan appearance and superficial reputation of the Upper House which condemns it to the margins or the giggle factor . . . [Yet] the debates on statements from the Commons – on Kosovo, for instance – are often of high quality, as are the Wednesday debates initiated by the different parties in rotation. But it is in the scrutinising of legislation that the House makes

its true mark. In the first few years, I took several people to the place and often at night, say about 10, we would go into the debating chamber and find a score of mostly lawyers carefully clarifying Bills which had been whipped out hot and perhaps too hastily from the scrummage of the Commons . . .

There is a gorgeousness in some of the rooms, a sense of tradition even though the building itself is mere C19. Those who work there are exceptionally pleasant and helpful. It would be easy to be seduced by this place. Barbara Castle [a now-deceased Labour ex-minister and member] advised me: 'Don't inhale' on the day of my induction.

The case against the present House of Lords

The major criticism still concerns the basis of membership. Phase One of the Blair package may have removed the hereditaries, but the House still lacks a democratic basis. Tony Benn has often remarked that when considering those who occupy positions of power, the key question is: 'Can they be removed?' In the present chamber, the answer is 'no'. Peers are there for a long period, be they bishops, law lords or life peers.

Specifically, it is argued that:

- (from a government point of view) the task of Lords reform is unfinished. A Phase Two was always intended, for although the major anomaly has been removed, the present membership is still able to inflict damage on an elected centre-left government, by virtue of its Conservative dominance. On issues such as fox-hunting, the chamber has been only too willing to frustrate the wishes of the lower chamber. On three occasions since 1997 the Commons voted overwhelmingly to abolish blood sports, but the Lords proved obstructive. (Hence the need to use the Parliament Act in 2004 to get the measure on to the statute book.)
- (by critics) the present situation is not significantly better than it was previously. Heredity may be an unacceptable basis for membership of a legislature today, but so too is appointment. At the present time, it is the Prime Minister who makes nominations and those appointed – several of them Labour, to boost the party's representation – are said to be 'Tony's cronies'. Given the method of appointment, the House of Lords does not have the legitimacy to flex its muscle, whereas with a democratic chamber, real power

could be exercised. Those who oppose an elected House of Lords are said to fear a second chamber that could delay legislation, hold ministers to account, scrutinise treaties and public appointments. Yet these are powers exercised by second chambers in most liberal democracies.

- the current House of Lords should reflect Britain as it is today. Of the appointments made in 2001 only 17 per cent were women and 3.5 per cent were from an ethnic minority. Continuing to appoint members would ensure an upper house of ageing white men, whereas an election – particularly one conducted under a 'fair voting' system – would yield an assembly that represents the people and in which women and minorities would have a chance of election.

Charter 88 has from its inception campaigned for a fully elected chamber. Its director[6] complains of the failure to embrace fully the democratic idea:

Only Britain could lay claim to be the mother of all parliamentary democracies, but refuse to allow voters to elect those that govern them. The only other wholly, or majority, appointed second chambers exist in small numbers in countries like Lesotho and Swaziland. It seems strange that we should wish to follow those examples rather than the elected chambers of Western Europe, the USA and Australia . . . ultimately only election confers legitimacy in modern government.

The future of the House of Lords under Phase Two: differing ideas

The difficulty of having a fully elected second chamber is that it may prove to be a rival to the lower house, a danger which is increased in Britain if the upper body is elected by some scheme of proportional representation and can therefore claim to be more representative of the people. (Such dangers could be mitigated to some extent by staggering the election process and allowing members to sit for a long term of perhaps ten or fifteen years.) There is a good case for an elected chamber in a federal country, for there it can serve the purpose of safeguarding the individual states against encroachment by the federal government.

Box 3.2 The method of appointment to second chambers in other countries

The manner of determining membership of second chambers varies between countries. There are four main ways of choosing members of an upper house:

1. *Direct election* is the most common and according to Hague and Harrop[7] is used in 27 out of 66 chambers, e.g. Australia, the Czech Republic and the United States (see pp. 103–4). Partial election is a possible variation, as considered for the British Phase Two (see pp. 75–7).

2. *Indirect election* is the second most common. Sometimes, indirectly elected houses are selected by members of local authorities (the now non-existent Swedish body was composed entirely of members elected by local councillors), sometimes by members of the lower house (Norway). The French Senate is elected by electoral colleges of councillors and deputies in each department, so that it provides for a combination of election by local authorities and election by the lower house. Norway has an upper house elected by the lower house.

3. *Appointment for life* Members are nominated for life by the government of the day. Canada has a second chamber, the Senate, whose members are nominated for life by the Governor-General in theory, but by the government of the day in practice. Nominations tend to be made on the basis of a candidate's support for the party in power. The Italian Senate has a handful of senators-for-life, in a powerful chamber that has equal status with the lower house.

4. *Vocational representation* Ireland's unique Senate has members elected by graduates of Irish universities, others nominated by the Prime Minister and 43 elected from five vocational panels (Cultural and Educational, Agricultural, Labour, Industrial and Commercial, and Administrative).

The Prime Minister seems to be opposed to a fully elected chamber, seeing it as a rival to the lower chamber. Many MPs dislike the idea of an appointed House, fearing that this would represent a boost to prime ministerial power. Part-elected, part-appointed alternatives have failed to command majority support in the Commons. Ministers are said to be thinking about creating some form of indirectly elected Lords, with party strength being determined by performance in the previous general election. In the meantime, the removal of the remaining ninety-two hereditaries has been contemplated. Lords reform has always been controversial and for this reason, it tends to lose its priority the longer a government remains in office. It wins few votes in a general election. Yet speculation continues as to whether Labour will embrace the cause of reform in a third term. The Secretary of State for Constitutional Affairs reluctantly accepted an amendment passed by the 2004 Labour annual conference proposing that a reformed chamber be 'as democratic as possible'. However, in addition to suggesting direct or indirect election, the amendment mentioned that 'appointment by a democratic body' could be a means of achieving his end. This might mean support for the 'secondary mandate' proposal urged by singer-songwriter Billy Bragg which would link membership of the second chamber with votes cast in a general election, with members being chosen from party lists at a regional level. The disadvantages would be that voters would have no say in determining the chosen individuals and would be unable to support different parties for the first and second chamber. The Bragg plan remains an option under discussion.

The main functions of the House of Commons

The main functions of the House of Commons are:

- *Law-making.* The Commons has a significant role in the legislative process, not in the sense of 'making the law' but rather in reacting to the initiatives of government. Most public bills (see Box 3.3) come from the government of the day, although some are introduced by backbench MPs (private members' bills). Legislation takes up much of the time of the House; in 1999–2000, 560 hours were spent on government legislation and 83 more on that deriving from MPs. In Parliament, bills pass through eleven stages, five of which are in the lower house – First Reading, Second Reading (debate on principles), Third Reading (debate on details), Committee Stage (taken in **standing committees**) and finally the Report Stage (amended bill, reported back to whole House).

Governments normally get their way on legislation, because of the majority. Just occasionally a bill may be withdrawn in response to parliamentary pressure (i.e. the Post Office privatisation plans of the Major government were dropped before they reached the Commons). Very rarely is a government bill defeated, though the Shops Bill (to liberalise Sunday trading) was lost on a free vote in 1986 and the Blair government suffered a serious defeat over its proposed powers of detention in the Terrorism Bill (November 2005). Similarly, if few bills are unsuccessful, so too are few hostile amendments passed. Around 90 per cent of those carried are introduced by ministers.

There is potential for amendment of legislation, but few changes are made against the wishes of ministers. In other words, even though it is the most time-consuming area of the work of the House, the impact of Parliament on legislation is modest. The conclusion is that Parliament is inefficient in its legislative role, a conclusion born out by the recent report of the Modernisation Committee[8] which wanted more consultation and more pre-legislative study by departmental select committees, among other things.

- *Raising and spending public money.* Parliament's permission is needed for raising and spending money, but this is virtually automatic. The government takes key decisions and although the House has the ultimate deterrent of rejecting proposals this did not happen in the twentieth century. The Commons plays a scrutinising role, mainly carried out in Departmental Select Committees and via the Public Accounts Committee. But, as Graham Thomas[9] writes: 'Parliament has largely given up its role in financial matters to the executive.'

Box 3.3 Types of bill

Public Bills alter the general law of the land and affect public policy. They concern the whole community. Most public bills are *Government bills* and are brought in by the relevant departmental minister who pilots them through the House. *Private Members' Bills* are introduced by MPs and private peers' bills by members of the upper house.

By contrast, *private bills* affect a section of the community or some particular interest such as a local authority or business. The procedure differs from that for public bills.

- *Acting as a watchdog over the government.* Probably the most important function of the contemporary House of Commons is the scrutinising and influencing of government. This role is exercised by MPs individually and by the House as a whole. The work of scrutiny and influence goes on all the time and finds expression in everything the House does. Parliamentary scrutiny is carried out in several ways, such as via questions, debates, committees and of course by the opposition parties – especially Her Majesty's Opposition. Often, the most significant criticism is that from goverment backbenchers, because ministers know that they need the votes of their MPs and so they may make concessions to them.

A watchdog over government

Scrutiny via Her Majesty's Opposition

The existence of an official opposition party is regarded as one of the litmus tests of a democracy. In Britain, the importance of HM Opposition is recognised by the payment of an official salary to the Leader of the Opposition and opposition Chief Whip. The Opposition also gets a share of the 'Short money', the grant payable to opposition parties to help them carry out their parliamentary business, fund their travel and associated expenses and finance the running costs of the Leader of the Opposition's office.

The Opposition plays an essential role in the day-to-day affairs of Parliament. It has three main functions:

1. The Opposition opposes the government. Ministers stood at the last election on the basis of distinctive principles and policies, and their 'shadow' counterparts naturally oppose them when they do things differently.
2. It supports the government where appropriate, not opposing for the sake of so doing. This is the concept of responsible, constructive opposition. Careful scrutiny is given, but if ministers do things broadly seen as in the national interest (e.g. over policy matters in Northern Ireland) then the Opposition will try to be bi-partisan.
3. The Opposition is also an alternative government. If its criticisms are not responsible and well thought out, it will lack credibility and be seen as obstructive. The Opposition will need to review its

policies as circumstances change and produce a coherent and convincing range of alternative courses for action.

Problems for the Opposition

- The Opposition lacks the information available to the government. Ministers have civil servants/political advisers to brief them and are in a position to 'know the state of the books'. Oppositions lack 'official' help and detailed knowledge.
- Governments set the political agenda and the Opposition normally has to respond to it. Ministers can take over the best opposition policies and the Prime Minister sets the election date.
- There is pressure from dispirited activists to push the party back to an 'extreme' position with which they are more content, e.g. the Conservatives on Europe. Activists like to see clear water between themselves and ministerial policies, but shedding the middle of the road may put off more centrist voters.
- Morale can be low, especially after a massive election defeat – as experienced by Labour in the early–mid-1980s and the Conservatives post-1997. There seems little point in turning up to be defeated by a massive majority. Division and in-fighting often set in, as some shadow ministers turn on the work of ministers in their party's previous spell in government.
- Prospects for re-election can seem dismal, when the majority is vast. It seems like a long heave before the public forget the errors committed when the opposition was in office.
- If the Opposition tries to reverse party policy too quickly in order to expose governmental weakness, voters may ask why it didn't get things right when it was in government.

Scrutiny via Question Time

Question Time is a very British practice, though Canada has a similar system. The practice of MPs asking questions of ministers in the House developed substantially in the twentieth century. Oral questions are asked to departments on a rota basis. Some are asked to find out information, but others are often vehicles for making a party point – perhaps by raising a constituency problem. Those not answered in the House get a written reply. In addition to those raised orally, some 35,000 written questions are asked.

Prime Minister's Question Time used to be held for fifteen minutes twice a week. Originally introduced by Harold Macmillan, it was modified by Tony Blair in 1997 to its present once weekly half-hour Wednesday session. He wanted a less confrontational system and – so critics would allege – to spare himself the extra session of an encounter for which he has little enthusiasm. For many politically interested television viewers, Question Time – as portrayed in news extracts or live on the Parliamentary Channel – is the high point of the parliamentary week, a regular joust between the party leaders.

The arrival of the television cameras and the use of extracts on news bulletins have served to personalise politics even more. Television likes Question Time, an entertaining spectacle that often generates little light but considerable drama. The institution began to degenerate in the Kinnock–Thatcher era and despite the changed format it is still a knockabout, rough contest. Though it is often viewed as an ordeal by the Prime Minister, he or she has the advantage of being well briefed and able to speak last.

Scrutiny via select committees

A system of departmental select committees began to function in 1980, after years of *ad hoc* arrangements for committees. Fourteen committees were set up, each to monitor the work, of one government department – (e.g. one for foreign affairs, one for home affairs). Membership of the eighteen current committees varies from eleven to seventeen, and reflects party strengths in the House. The Committee of Selection appoints members, for the lifetime of a Parliament. Often MPs are re-appointed in the next Parliament, if they are re-elected – this longevity enables them to acquire a real expertise on their subject.

Select Committees have powers to send for persons, papers and records, and receive evidence from ministers and civil servants. They can use the services of outside experts. They are each empowered to establish a subcommittee, two in the case of the Departmental committees on the Environment, Food and Rural Affairs and the Transport, Local Government and the Regions.

The advantages claimed for select committees are that:

- members work in a less partisan way than is possible in the whole House; they try to produce an agreed report

- members are often well informed, developing a real specialism on the subjects within their orbit
- members can feed their knowledge back into House of Commons debates and so help to inform others
- they have made government more open, evidence being taken in public and ministers being examined in a thorough way.

But:

- in recent years, the whips have tried to keep more independent MPs off committees and not re-appoint those who are critical (the worst example occurred in 2001, when the Labour leadership made an abortive attempt to keep two committee chairpersons off the committees, when Parliament resumed – such was the reaction against this executive interference that Gwynneth Dunwoody, the very independently minded chair of the Transport Committee, and Donald Anderson, of the Foreign Affairs Committee, were re-instated).
- on occasion, there have been other allegations of ministerial intervention. During the Hutton Inquiry, the Chairman of the Foreign Affairs Committee declared that a request had been made by the Defence Secretary to his committee members, suggesting that they avoid asking awkward questions about the issue of Iraqi weapons of mass destruction.
- committees need more resources: they have too small a budget
- they generate much paperwork, but their reports may or may not be debated – then they are put on a shelf and forgotten
- they need more powers: ministers are sometimes evasive or decline to answer clearly.

Elected representatives: the duties and responsibilities of British MPs

The proper role of an MP has been much debated. The classic case for allowing an MP to act as an individual, once elected, was set out in 1774 by a well-known political theorist of the day, Edmund Burke, who had just been elected for Bristol. In a letter to his new constituents, he informed them that MPs should not be considered to be merely delegates or agents of the voters in the area for which they had been elected. Rather, they should be considered first as members of Parliament, representing the one interest of the nation. They must define this according to their own judgement of the issues to be decided by Parliament:

> Your representative owes you, not his industry only, but his judgement: and he betrays, instead of serving you, if he sacrifices it to your opinion.

Burke was of course writing before the advent of party and before the massive increase in constituency work of recent years. But many members would still argue that on issues of private morality, they have a duty to seek out information, listen to the speeches in the House and then make up their mind in the light of what they hear and not under the pressure of their constituency postbag.

Members of Parliament have several obligations that may on occasion conflict with each other. The four main spheres of responsibility are to:

1. *The Party*. It was because of the party label that the MP got elected. It is entitled to demand loyalty in return. Both parties well understand that lack of unity and discipline damaged Labour's position in the period 1979–87, just as they helped bring about the Conservative defeat in recent elections. He or she is expected to toe the party line in debates and votes, attend party committees and promote the party's outlook and policies – keeping the national leadership and local association satisfied with his or her performance. Austin Mitchell[10], a long-serving Labour MP, has written disparagingly of the baleful influence of party, describing it as 'a career ladder to climb, a substitute for thought and a whirl of the obsessive. In Parliament, the party is a framework of control, ensuring that MPs tramp through the lobbies, feeding party points every day, providing yah-boo fun, and trundling them to every by-election as unpaid door knockers.'

2. *The constituency*. MPs are careful to nurse their constituencies, by holding regular surgeries, promoting any constituency interests (such as fishing or the motor industry), attending political meetings and various social functions, and receiving any constituents who visit Westminster. Much of the work of MPs today is taken up with welfare-type work on behalf of constituents. They are

expected to handle grievances and problems, and ensure that they are dealt with at the appropriate level – perhaps by asking a question, speaking in an **adjournment debate** in the House or seeing/writing to the relevant minister. The prospect of bad publicity in the media makes it likely that organisations will be responsive to MPs' activities.

3. *The Nation.* MPs have an obligation to the whole country. They serve in the national legislature and can be expected to attend regularly and make a contribution by taking part in debates, asking questions, playing a part in select and standing committees, and scrutinising the Executive and making ministers accountable. They should inform themselves about the various problems on which they are called to vote and ensure that they bear in mind the national interest as well as party and constituency interests..

4. *His or her conscience.* MPs have their own ideas and preferences. They may wish to introduce private members' legislation on some area of concern. Otherwise, they have their own conscience to consider and cannot be reasonably expected to speak and act in defiance of what they know is right or wrong.

Of course, there are *conflicting responsibilities* outlined above. MPs will be expected by their constituents to present the local viewpoint when there is a problem such as an industry in decline or the threat of closure of a car plant. But MPs need to see the problem in its national setting. It may be that economic reality dictates that particular goods can no longer be economically manufactured locally.

Personal and party interests may conflict. Left-wing Labour MPs may be unable to accept their government's pursuit of a nuclear defence policy, just as pro-European Conservatives may feel they have to support British membership of the European Union in spite of the leadership's approach. Personal and constituency interests may also differ. Pro-abortion MPs may find themselves out of step with their largely Roman Catholic constituents, just as 'liberals' on capital punishment may find their views create local difficulties. So too might pro-European members have difficulty in representing a fishing port where there is a backlash against the EU Common Fisheries Policy.

According to a survey in 1996[11], MPs spend on average just over 50 per cent of their working week on parliamentary as opposed to constituency work.

Factors influencing the effectiveness of MPs

The ability of MPs to act effectively and independently as free agents has been restricted by the demands of party loyalty and by increasing domination of the House of Commons by the government of the day.

MPs know that their parties expect them to show support in the lobbies and that opportunities for independent thought and action are few. Those who have been dissidents have often fallen foul of the party, so that the number of mavericks are relatively small. For those MPs who have no hopes of future promotion or whose parliamentary career is coming to an end, party discipline may not be a problem and some on the Labour benches are prone to rebellion (see Box 3.4). For most, it is an obvious constraint.

An MP's ability to do his or her job well is also limited by:

- *Poor facilities.* These may have improved over the last generation, but MPs who have had experience of the worlds of commerce and industry will probably find the lack of office space and equipment, and constituency help, a real impediment (see also p. 101).
- *The immense amount and complexity of government business.* Government was probably always complex to those involved and there never was a 'golden age' in which MPs knew everything about every aspect of policy. In the twentieth century, the role of government has dramatically expanded and we now live in the age of the managed economy and welfare state. The voters expect more from their governments at home and the demands of global interests and responsibilities (such as involvement in the European Union) create additional areas of ministerial activity.
- *The growing burden of constituency work.* Constituents assume that their member will be active in taking up their problems, on anything from consumerism to welfarism because these are the sorts of issue with which government is now concerned. Faced by this situation, MPs find it best to specialise in selected areas, for it is unlikely that they can be informed about the whole range of policy issues. Their problem is not so much a lack of information

but rather a lack of time in which to master it – the responsibilities of constituency work have now become so much more demanding.

All MPs now have a very large postbag. Letters, faxes and e-mails are sent to them in ever-increasing numbers. Most MPs are dealing with correspondence for two or three hours daily. But they also have other representative duties, ranging from taking part in meetings with ministers and pressure groups to being available for interviews with journalists. These tasks are very time-consuming.

Box 3.4 MPs and party loyalty

Critics often lament the strength of party discipline and see MPs as 'lobby fodder', lacking in independent judgement. Michael Foot[12] once claimed that: 'two well-whipped forces confront one another in formal, pre-arranged combat. Speeches of Gladstonian power or Disraeli-ite wit are unlikely to shift a single vote'.

Unity is essential for any party, because:

- splits can mean the loss of the governing party's majority; the survival of both the Callaghan and Major governments was often in jeopardy.
- governments wish to legislate on programmes on which they have fought the election and need to count on translating ideas into action.
- divisions are harmful to parties, for they provide opportunities for other parties and journalists to expose and exploit their differences.
- parties which do face three ways in a division cause difficulty for the public and commentators who are unsure what party policy actually is.

Parties, then, like to avoid divisions, aware as they are that they can damage their credibility, in the way that the splits under John Major over Europe, taxation and other issues contributed to the Conservative defeat in 1997. They realise that there are inevitably internal differences, for parties are broad coalitions of sometimes quite widely differing viewpoints. But they expect that MPs will not often question party policy in public or be disloyal when crucial parliamentary votes are counted.

Most MPs can accept these constraints. *Why do they normally toe the party line?*

- However much they doubt their own side's policy, the last thing they wish to do is to endanger the government's survival and see the Opposition occupy the ministerial seats.
- They know that in the privacy of a backbench meeting (in the 1922 Committee or in the Parliamentary Labour Party) they can argue for a concession from the Minister and – especially if it seems that their doubts are widely held – probably get one. The Minister may well be flexible in order to ensure that his Bill gets safely through: several were made during the passage of the bill providing for tuition fees for students in higher education, 2003–2004, in order to ensure that the Government got the measure on the statute book.
- Finally, there is the 'carrot and the stick'. For some young MPs who hope to climb the ministerial ladder, the prospect of early promotion keeps them in line. Persistent rebellion may lead to formal sanctions being applied, as happened to eight Eurosceptics under the Major government.

MPs were more assertive in Labour's second term. In 2003, the year when the invasion of Iraq was launched, its own members were in rebellious mood. At the beginning of the year, the largest-ever rebellions occurred were recorded (121 and 137, both over Iraq), but on fox-hunting, foundation hospitals and hunting high levels of dissent were recorded. Furthermore, many members abstained rather than vote with the Government. The habit of rebellion seemed to become well established, with many Labour MPs keen to inflict a 'bloody nose' on a Prime Minister whose leadership style and policies they disliked.

In the third term, ministers have had to come to terms with governing on a reduced majority. However, Tony Blair has been reluctant to compromise on issues ranging from anti-terrorist legislation to public service reform. Since he announced his plan to retire before the next election, some Labour MPs – ex-ministers among them – seem keen to undermine his leadership and expedite his departure by regularly displaying their opposition.

MPs can also express their individual attitudes in free votes – primarily held on socio-moral issues – in which no party whip is applied. Over the abolition of fox-hunting, Labour members rejected the option of a system of licensed hunts in favour of a total ban. The Prime Minister found himself using the Parliament Act to enforce a measure about which he had grave doubts.

The significance of the average backbench MP

We have seen that there never was a 'golden age' in which MPs were well informed about all aspects of government and were free to exercise judgement free of party pressures. But certainly 150 years ago, the demands upon members were much less than they are now and they additionally enjoyed much social standing within the community. Today, MPs are often derided by the voters, many of whom are cynical about their ideas, performance and integrity.

The capacity of individual MPs to influence national events is limited. They may ask questions, speak in debates, be active in standing or select committees and be well known as a crusader for good causes. Maybe a private members, bill will be for ever associated with their name. Most MPs do not have a high profile, but some are often seen on the media and can make an impact via broadcasting. Otherwise, much depends on what they regard as their primary tasks. There are different routes that they may follow, as described by Professor Richards some years ago in *Honourable Members*[13]:

- *Useful party members.* Such members tend to specialise in particular areas of policy and serve on the relevant committees and appear on the media to discuss issues on which they can contribute their expertise. They are useful to the party, often loyal in the lobbies and may become a Parliamentary Private Secretary or advance further.
- *Good constituency members.* Such MPs devote much of their time to constituency work, taking up personal cases and earning themselves a well-deserved reputation for diligence and effectiveness on behalf of those they seek to serve.
- *Individualists: independents within the system.* These MPs are sometimes members of the 'awkward squad', often colourful characters who are not easily contained within the party system. Genuine Independents are few (e.g. ex-broadcaster Martin Bell, the member for Tatton, 1997–2001), but MPs in this category often take a distinctive line and worry little about advancement – perhaps knowing it is unlikely to come their way. Tam Dalyell (Lab) was noted for taking up issues such as the sinking of the *General Belgrano* in the Falklands war or the details of the Locherbie plane crash. Richard Shepherd (Con) is active in the areas of freedom of information/

state secrecy and abuse of executive power. Both have been persistent, diligent and courageous members.

- *Part-timers.* Some MPs still seek to combine their parliamentary activity with an outside occupation, perhaps serving in journalism, the law or business. The number of part-timers has diminished, following Labour's landslide wins in 1997 and 2001, for in the past many have been Conservatives.

MPs can of course fit into more than one grouping. A hard-working part-timer can still be a good constituency MP. So too can an independent. Similarly, a long-term party loyalist can mature into a sturdy individualist.

Parliamentary reform in recent years

Parliamentary reformers argue that there is a growing imbalance between the government and Parliament. The trend of recent years has been towards the growth in executive power at the expense of legislatures, a trend not confined to Great Britain. Writers such as Philip Norton[14] feel that it can be over-stressed and point out that in recent years Parliament has become more effective, with MPs becoming better-informed and professional, and the House more effective. But even if MPs doubt some aspects of the diagnosis, they still see a need for further reforms to make Parliament work better.

Interest in the subject of parliamentary reform has increased in recent years as part of a general concern about the health and vitality of British political institutions. Surveys have shown that many people now question the way in which Parliament does its work. Some of the concern voiced by academic commentators and journalists is about the House of Commons as a collective entity, whilst at the popular level there is more scepticism about the conduct, performance and work of individual MPs. Such public disquiet has encouraged some people to seek to achieve their goals by extra-parliamentary action, rather than via traditional democratic channels.

Differing approaches to reform

There are differing approaches to the issue of Parliament's main role. For some writers, it is there mainly to sustain the government and provide a forum via which it can mobilise public opinion and in which the opposition parties can offer their criticisms of government policy. In other words, it is a debating chamber in which grievances are aired and the party struggle conducted day-to-day. If this view is taken, then it is unlikely serious reform will be undertaken.

On the other hand, there are others who believe that Parliament must be a strong body, wielding power and influence. They think that it should hold the government of the day to account for its actions, acting as a vigilant watchdog. This is an idealistic view of what Parliament should be like, rather than a description of how it operates for much of the time. Those who want to see Parliament reformed in such a way that MPs have greater influence are talking the language of criticism. They lament the reduction of Parliament's influence in the twentieth century and want to see it act more effectively.

Academics and commentators advocate a range of ideas, some of which may be found in the following list:

- *More powerful select committees.* Critics say that more resources are needed, with a better budget, more staffing by experts, stronger powers to make ministers and officials answer, more attention to and debate of committee reports and less influence by the whips over selection of membership. The House did introduce payment for Select Committee chairs to come into force for the 2003–4 session, £12,500 on top of their standard MP's pay.
- *Better pay and facilities for MPs.* Pay and facilities are much better than they were a few decades ago, but many MPs still find that they cannot get all the secretarial and research help they need. Many point to the need for more constituency help and better computer links with their local base.
- *Full-time MPs.* Given the size of Labour's majority, many MPs are full-time, for it is the Conservatives who tend to have second jobs. Critics say that no MP can do two jobs well and that anyway some previous occupations (e.g. mining) cannot be combined with par-liamentary duties. Pay and facilities should be such that all MPs can be full-time; they can get experience of life outside Westminster in their holidays.
- *Less MPs.* Philip Norton, Michael Howard and others have called for a cut in number to around 450. This would reduce the current

payroll and by so doing enable more to be spent on better resourcing fewer MPs to enable them to operate effectively. As there are now more full-time MPs, pressure on the existing institution is considerable; for instance, MPs ask far more questions today, hoping that this will win them constituency approval. Norton wants a smaller, more professional house and makes the point that the present one, organised for the days of the gifted amateur, is one of the largest elected chambers in the world.

- *More free votes.* Strong party discipline seems to worry MPs much less than critics outside. They like free votes on social and moral topics, but accept that if governments are to push through their legislative programme then whipping is essential. Also, they know that there are other ways of influencing events.

Reforms have been introduced in recent years, including:

- *Changes to working hours.* In 2002, the House narrowly voted to end its antiquated sittings designed for a bygone age and work more family-friendly hours. Members decided that the House should not be remote and alien in its working practices. Rather, it should work hours that made it more accessible and intelligent to the voters who would receive a better explanation of key debates and divisions on the television. In 2005, following a revolt by a cross-party coalition of MPs and claims that the revised hours had 'sucked the very essence out of Commons debate', a compromise was reached, reverting to late sittings on Tuesdays.

  Since May 2005 the working hours of the House of Commons have been:

Monday	2.30 p.m.–10.00 p.m.
Tuesday	2.30 p.m.–10.00 p.m.
Wednesday	11.30 a.m.–7.00 p.m.
Thursday	10.30 a.m.–6.00 p.m.
Friday (selected dates only)	9.30 a.m.–2.30 p.m.

N.b. The hours given show the usual finishing times, but on rare occasions the House may conclude its proceedings earlier or – more likely – continue beyond them. The Friday sessions only apply when private members' bills are being considered.

- *Improvements to the legislative process.* This has long been called for, to allow for more effective consultation and scrutiny. A Select Committee on Modernisation was set up after the 1997 election, and its first report – on the legislative process – urged more consultation on draft bills, more pre-legislative scrutiny by Select Committees, better use of Standing Committees and that bills should be carried over from one session to the next (thus curtailing the use of the guillotine).

Various changes have been introduced as a result of the report of the recent Committee. They have been cautious, but have potential for development. In particular, the use of pre-legislative scrutiny and the introduction of debates (and occasionally Questions sessions) in Westminster Hall, a specially converted room off the main hall, have been useful incremental steps. But procedural changes only go so far. Many critics feel that there needs to be a cultural change at Westminster about the role of the legislature in relation to the Executive.

The social composition of elected legislators

In general, legislatures tend to be overwhelmingly male, middle-aged, middle class, and in North America and Europe, white; in fact, European parliaments are notoriously unrepresentative of ethnic minorities.

Berrington[15] has noted that 'almost every study of legislators in Western democracies shows that they come from more well-to-do backgrounds, are drawn from more prestigious and intellectually satisfying backgrounds and are much better educated than their electors'. As a general guide, right-wing parties have a heavy preponderance of legislators who have made their careers in business and commerce, whereas left-wing parties have a strong professional (particularly educational) representation. Law tends to be well represented in both parties, particularly in the United States. A growing number of people from the communications industry, newspapers, television and public relations, are now to be found in most legislatures.

The fate of women in national parliaments varies considerably across the world (see Table 3.1). They have fared badly in the United States and in some European countries such as France, Greece, Ireland and Italy (all Catholic or Orthodox in religion) representation

Table 3.1 Regional averages in female representation (%), November 2005

Region	Female representation in lower chamber	Female representation in both houses combined
Scandinavia	40.0	40.0
Americas	18.8	18.9
Europe (excluding Scandinavia)	16.9	16.8
Asia	15.7	15.5
Sub-Saharan Africa	16.0	16.0
Pacific	12.0	13.9
Arab states	8.2	7.7

Figures based on those provided on the Inter-Parliamentary Union website, which is constantly updated (www.ipu.org). Altogether, IPU counts nearly 7,000 women serving in the upper and lower houses of national parliaments around the world (16.1%).

has traditionally been low. Scandinavia has high levels of female representation, exceeding 40 per cent in Sweden, its impressive record perhaps being explained by:

- a cultural and legal framework which is generally sympathetic to female advancement
- a strong commitment on the part of political parties to promoting women as candidates and
- the use of a proportional voting system, by which parties present lists of candidates to voters, rather than individual candidates.

Membership of Parliament, in particular the House of Commons

The House of Lords is unrepresentative of the nation. Few members belong to ethnic minorities or have a working-class background.

There is a preponderance of middle-aged to elderly people, many peers having been appointed in middle age, and having achieved distinction in their chosen field. The average age is currently around 68 years. Women are under-represented, although at 18.4 per cent of the membership in May 2005, barely more so than in the lower chamber.

The House of Commons is overwhelmingly white. Of those elected up to and including the intake of 2001, all ethnic minority members belonged to the Labour Party. In 2005, of a record fifteen ethnic minority MPs, two Conservatives were returned. Four MPs in the current House are Muslims, an increase on the previous Parliament. Only two of the fifteen non-white members are female.

The Commons is also overwhelmingly middle class. Whereas Labour once saw it as its mission to bring 'workers' into Parliament, this is no longer the case. In 1918, 83 per cent of its MPs were working class; by 2005 the figure had dropped to 10 per cent. Many of its candidates are now drawn from the professions, a similar pattern to what has been happening with other social democratic and left-wing parties across much of Europe. The trend began in the 1960s, with an influx of Labour academics. Today, teachers in universities and schools are still strongly represented, as are other public-sector professionals, political staffers and lawyers. The legal profession tends to be well represented in most legislatures, there being an obvious connection between lawyers, who work in the law, and parliaments, which make it. Moreover, law provides a flexible work situation for candidates as they wage their campaign. They can also leave their job with relative ease and return to it, as they wish.

Other than the law, many Conservative MPs derive from business and City backgrounds, with a fair proportion of professionals who have worked in the media and public relations. Sixty per cent of them have been to public school, although far fewer have attended Eton than was the case a few decades ago. Many MPs of all parties have a degree (just over two-thirds), so that by occupation and education elected members are socially unrepresentative of those whom they serve.

MPs tend to be middle-aged, because most people attain the position having made their mark in some other employment. This can be said to provide them with experience of life, but it also means that the voice of young people is neglected, causing some to feel alienated from the political system. In Britain, following the 2005 election, eleven members were over seventy. The average age of Conservatives at Westminster is younger than their Labour counterparts (48, as opposed to 53), helped by the influx of some new members who were in their thirties. The Liberal Democrats have the youngest age profile, with the five youngest MPs – three under the age of thirty.

Most people would probably be relieved to know that MPs are experienced and have levels of educational attainment higher than among the population at large, for members deal with complex issues of public policy. It is essential that they are literate and fluent, qualities not possessed by all UK inhabitants. Similarly, it is no bad thing that the small minority of persons in the community suffering from emotional disorders and various forms of inadequacy are not represented at Westminster. In other words, it is undesirable that the House of Commons should be an exact microcosm or mirror-image of the whole population. Nor – in a chamber whose membership is elected – could that ever happen. Moreover, it is a fact that the people who come forward tend to be young to middle-aged, highly educated, white and male.

Women in the House of Commons

In 1919, Nancy Astor became the first woman to sit in the House of Commons. However, progress on women's representation was slow, and did not increase to beyond 5 per cent of the membership until 1987. In 1997, the number of women elected to the Commons exactly doubled to 120, a record improved upon eight years later when 128 were returned. This still leaves Britain with a lower proportion of female representation than many countries not traditionally known for their democratic credentials, from Rwanda (48.8 per cent) to Mozambique (34.8 per cent), from Cuba (36.0 per cent) to Argentina (33.7 per cent).

Other than in 1970 and 1983, the bulk of female MPs have been on the Labour side and today the party is well ahead of the others in moving towards gender equality. There is a long way to go, but women make up more than a quarter of the present Parliamentary Labour Party (98 MPs, 27.5 per cent).

Several factors contribute to the under-representation of women in Parliament:

- *Child-bearing and home-making responsibilities*, which have traditionally prevented many women from seeking a parliamentary career until the children have become teenagers, the more so given the long and still often unsociable hours that MPs work. Members of selection committees, particularly in the Conservative Party, tend to question women about their intentions and responsibilities with regard to their offspring.
- *The electoral system.* Whereas the use of proportional representation (see pp. 329–43) encourages the adoption of a gender-balanced list of candidates, the use of single-member constituencies makes their selection less likely.
- *The nature of parliamentary life*, which tends to be masculine and aggressive. Would-be female politicians may find themselves out of sympathy with the atmosphere of the House of Commons. The macho approach of some male members, obsessed as they are with

Table 3.2 The number of women MPs in selected elections since 1945

Election	Conservative	Labour	Liberal Democrat	Total number	% of members
1945	1	21	1	24	3.8
1964	11	17	0	28	4.4
1970	15	10	0	23	4.1
1983	13	10	0	23	3.5
1992	20	37	2	60	9.2
1997	13	102	3	120	18.2
2001	14	95	5	118	17.9
2005	17	98	10	128	19.8

NB Shortly after the 2005 election, the death of a Liberal Democrat reduced the party's figure to 9 and the total of women members to 127.

Box 3.5 Have women made a difference at Westminster? Varying viewpoints

The old days

'*Cor, we'd like to strip-search you too.*'
A comment shouted at Joan Ruddock (Labour) by one MP, as she raised the issue of police strip-searching of women, in the 1980s.

MPs used to barrack women; they got personal. I hated the throwaway comments we'd get after 10.30 when they've been in the bars. People assumed I couldn't be an MP just because I was a woman. I got stopped in the House of Lords corridors recently by a guard who said: 'Do you have your pass?' When I said, 'No', he said, 'And is your husband a member, madam?'
Anne Clwyd, Labour MP

On the immediate impact of the arrival of many new women MPs, in 1997

The changes are not just the obvious ones, such as installing more lavatories and providing a women's hairdresser. Nor is the importance merely that the male culture of men swapping banter at the Commons bar will be less noticeable, as women around the House will now be so much more in evidence. The arrival of 120 women means that the House is more likely to be dragged into the twentieth century.
D. Butler and D. Kavanagh, *The British General Election of 1997*, Macmillan, 1997

I have been warned that other members will assume I'm a secretary. It will take time to change that. But bringing in younger people, particularly women, brings in a different set of interests. It's important to get young people into politics – Labour has done this, and will get returns on it.
Clare Ward, Labour (at 24, the youngest female MP at the time)

Did it make a difference? Later impressions

The House is set up to be confrontational, with schoolboy behaviour of shouting and making disparaging [belittling] remarks the norm. Most of the women I talk to (and some of the men) regard it as counterproductive to what we're sent here for, and it's made more difficult for women because of their usually quieter, less strident voices.
Patsy Calton MP

Some women wanted to:

- change the image of the House of Commons from being less of an exclusive gentleman's club into a more 'user-friendly' body with good working conditions, more in tune with the needs of parents and children
- get rid of out-dated and complicated procedures
- have more discussion of 'bread and butter' issues, such as child-care, education, housing, environment and social services
- adopt a more consensual approach to solving issues (e.g. they wanted to try and find agreement rather than stress their differences, and wanted an end to applying the language of war to domestic politics)
- see an end to sexist banter. Clare Short has suggested that 'women, as the eternal outsiders, tend to work extra hard and be more sincere and much less inclined to indulge in the sleazy behaviour that so offends the public'.

Some of the changes above have been put into practice, including more family-friendly hours and an end to late-night sittings. But even here, there has been pressure from some male MPs to revert to the old hours. Patricia Hewitt, as Secretary of State for Trade, is keen to see the House retain the modernised hours. She fears a return to a form of late-night 'yah-boo', testosterone politics, will leave the public feeling even more removed from Parliament. On the others, the jury is still out and it remains to be seen whether the House will shed some of the worst aspects of its image. Many women members feel uneasy when Tony Blair and Michael Howard face each other at Question Time every Wednesday, and engage in their regular joust, with supporters on either side baying at their opponents. The macho attitudes of many men at Westminster make it a challenge to be a woman MP, even more so if you have children.

A survey of 83 current and recent women MPs conducted by Joni Lovenduski[16] and published in late 2004 contains startlingly frank testimony of Westminster's antediluvian attitude to women. It speaks of male MPs asking to 'roger' colleagues, juggling imaginary breasts and crying 'melons' as women try to speak in the chamber. Her conclusion is that women have undoubtedly made a difference to the House of Commons. But her fear is that if fewer women are returned in the future and with modifications to the family-friendly hours of work already in hand, the female influence could wane: 'I think it's too early to say . . . I prefer to be optimistic that the culture has changed for good, but I don't feel absolutely certain about it.'

point-scoring and abuse, is unwelcoming to them. They may not feel confident about coping in such a traditionally male preserve.

The campaigning organisation, Fawcett, claims that there is active discrimination against women, across the political parties, particularly in the candidate selection process. In addition, it suggests a neat summary of four other factors that can prevent women standing for Parliament – the four 'Cs' of culture, childcare, cash and confidence. Partly as a result of its persistent campaigning, the Sex Discrimination Act was amended in 2002 to allow parties to use positive measures such as all-women shortlists, to increase women's representation at all levels of politics.

In 2005, there were more female candidates than ever before (433), but only Labour took advantage of the legal change and insisted on the use of all-women shortlists in many targeted seats (particularly those in areas with less than 25 per cent women MPs in Labour-held constituencies, such as Wales). This would help its National Executive Committee achieve its long-term objective of 50:50 gender representation. The effect of the policy was evident after the election, for of the 40 new Labour MPs, 26 were women of whom 23 had been chosen via all-women shortlists.

Does the under-representation of women and ethnic minorities matter?

Several points can be made in support of the proposition that it does matter, among them:

- It is dangerous in a democracy if groups with less wealth and power are under-represented, not just women and members of ethnic minorities, but also young people and members of the poorest sections of the community. If they feel excluded, they may regard the legislature with some contempt and turn to other forms of political action to get their message across.
- Again, as long as certain groups are under-represented, there are likely to be fewer debates on issues affecting them, and the quality of debate may be poor as many members do not take the matters under discussion seriously. As a result, full scrutiny by the media of the impact of government policy on such groups may be largely absent from the political process.

- Legislatures need the services of the most able people available, but at present much talent goes unrecognised. This is the more unfortunate, because the more women and members of ethnic minorities that get elected, the more role models there are to encourage others of their own type to come forward and see politics as a realistic, attractive career option.
- All the mainstream parties talk of their aspiration to achieve a society in which people are able to progress on merit. They claim to dislike discrimination and to wish to encourage equal opportunities. It is therefore hypocritical for the legislature not to reflect these worthy principles in its composition.

Those who disagree, might argue that:

- In a representative democracy, we select MPs broadly to reflect the interests of their constituents. To achieve this, it is not necessary for Parliament to be a mirror-image of British society. The system is supposed to produce representation of people's political views. It is not essential or realistic to expect that membership will exactly be in proportion to the size of all the various groups within society.
- MPs should be able to represent the views of all their constituents, and it is not necessary to belong to a particular group or interest to put a case on their behalf. As long as they possess an ability to empathise with the needs of all sections of the population, they are capable of advancing its viewpoint. You don't have to inhabit a slum dwelling to appreciate that slums need to be cleared, even if your recognition of the full horrors might be more acute if you do so. Neither do you need to be a woman to understand that discrimination against women is hurtful, wrong and damaging to society.
- Women and other social groups are not homogeneous. They do not all possess the same needs and views. For instance, some women are pro-choice on abortion, some favour divorce and others are ardent feminists. Many take a contrary view. Class, employment, age, locality and lifestyle may be more important in determining political views than gender or race. For this reason, it is impossible to represent all women or minority communities as a group, even if one wanted to do this.
- Above all, what we need are competent and caring people to represent us. The personal ability and party allegiance of any candi-

date should be the main determinants of who gets elected. To draw attention to irrelevant factors such as gender in deciding on the selection of candidates may be unfair and result in reverse discrimination against the most suitable candidates for the job.

The pay and conditions of legislators

In terms of accommodation, equipment, staffing, library assistance and other amenities, American Congressmen are notably better placed than their British counterparts. Pay is markedly higher at $162,100 (January 2005), and perquisites are markedly more lavish. Perhaps the Commonwealth and Europe provide fairer comparisons, for countries are generally less affluent in these areas than in the USA. Australia, Canada and New Zealand all provide superior office accommodation with separate rooms for the members and the staff who serve them.

MPs earn £59,095 (2005–6), on which they are subject to normal PAYE rates of taxation. They get help with the maintenance of an office and staff costs, including:

- an annual staffing allowance designed to pay for between two and three full-time equivalent staff
- certain IT equipment for offices
- training of staff
- exceptional expenses (e.g. for MPs who have constituencies with special problems).

Some members still voice criticism of the lack of constituency help they receive, whilst others feel that they could do with more research assistance at Westminster. The paucity of information technology services is frequently condemned, although there have been significant improvements in recent years. The new Incidental Expenses Provision is intended to help with expenses in running an office, such as office rents.

In recent years, there has been a developing trend to increased professionalism in the House of Commons. It has proved increasingly difficult to combine membership of Parliament with any outside activity, in part because of the growing constituency and other demands made upon MPs but also because other professions increasingly require full-time commitment from those who work for them. In both main parties, the tendency is to adopt relatively young candidates whose outside career experience has been in politically related occupations. Some would argue that such **career politicians** lack the sense of broad perspective that derives from having done another job; they have not inhabited the 'real' world and may not always possess the judgement that comes from knowing what goes on beyond Westminster.

The case of Denmark

Parliaments tend to be more effective in countries where minority or coalition governments are common. Ministers tend to seek more cross-party agreement to get their bills through and often seek to gain a broad consensus of opinion behind them. The average life of Danish administrations is around two and a half years, half the figure for Britain and Sweden. In order to survive, they are very reliant on parliamentary acquiescence. They build coalitions among MPs according to the issue under discussion. As Budge et al.[17] put it:

> [Danish] governments depend upon Parliament rather than the other way round. But it is generally true that wherever coalitions are weak and quarrel internally, much more importance is attached to negotiations within Parliament, than where governments are confident of winning legislative votes. Generally coalitions are weaker the more parties they include.

A country of only 4.5m inhabitants, Denmark abolished its second chamber in 1953. Since then, special safeguards have been provided to prevent any legislation from being passed too hastily through the Folketing. For instance, one-third of the members of that chamber can demand a referendum on a bill which has yet to receive royal approval. Again, the legislative procedure of the Folketing was revised, so that more time is given between the readings and to committee stages.

The case of the European Parliament

The European Parliament, which meets in Strasbourg, has 732 members elected by peoples from across the European Union. Traditionally, it has been portrayed as little more than a 'talking shop', a role reflected in its original designation as an assembly rather than a Parliament. For several years, it served in this capacity, as a forum where members could come together and express their views. As they were appointed until 1979, it was not taken seriously and its powers were described in the Treaty of Rome as being only 'advisory and supervisory' (Article 137).

Their new-found democratic respectability after 1979 encouraged members to look for opportunities to expand their responsibilities. Their bid for a more meaningful position was recognised in the Single European Act of 1986, which allocated the Parliament greater powers. Additional powers were incorporated into the Maastricht Treaty (1991) and the Amsterdam Treaty (1997), and among other things these gave the Parliament powers of appointment and dismissal over the Commission. It also has budgetary responsibilities, having a joint say in fixing the annual budget.

Many MEPs still see the progress made as insufficient and feel thwarted in their aspiration to provide the Strasbourg body with a clearer identity and more meaningful tasks. It has never been a law-making legislature, though it has acquired a role of co-decision in certain areas of EU policy-making. Its voice is listened to with growing respect in this aspect of its work, and there is a developing convention that views expressed by members will be noted carefully – the more so if they are widely held. Yet as Holland observes[18]: 'The Parliament may react, influence and under certain circumstances even prohibit legislation, but it cannot direct the legislative agenda.'

It is easy to pinpoint the deficiencies in the workings and effectiveness of the European Parliament, but it is interesting to note that a growing number of politicians are interested in serving in it. They sense that the wind is blowing in the direction of a stronger assembly, for increasingly it is in Strasbourg that some of the more interesting political battles are taking place. The agenda for discussion is a highly relevant one, and for those who do not like the adversarial style of the House of Commons but rather seek a genuine consensus across party groupings, the European Parliament has more to offer than ever before.

The Strasbourg Parliament treats its members well. MEPs receive the same salary as do members of the national Parliament of the country they represent, but there are very generous allowances for members to defray expenses incurred in carrying out their parliamentary duties. Some MEPs have seen membership as a 'gravy train', and have exploited to the full the amounts they can claim for travel to places outside the EU.

The case of the USA

The Founding Fathers devised a constitution based on the idea of the separation of powers, in which each component element could act as a check upon the influence of the other two. They expected that Congress would be able to dominate the federal government, and significantly dealt with it in Article 1.

Congress is a bicameral legislature, comprising the Senate and the House of Representatives. Both are law-making chambers directly elected by the people. They have broadly equal powers, making the Senate the most powerful upper house in the world.

In the federal USA, the Senate acts as a check on behalf of the states upon the House of Representatives which is elected on the basis of population. The allotment of two senators to each state, irrespective of population, ensures that the voice of the states in all areas of the country is clearly expressed. Nevada with less than half a million inhabitants has as much representation as New York State with approaching 20m.

In the nineteenth century, Congress was normally dominant and only three presidents were able to alter the balance of power in their favour. Thomas Jefferson, Andrew Jackson and Abraham Lincoln all had a Congress comprising a majority of supporters from their own party, but this was – and is – no guarantee of presidential power; yet they were people of great charisma and had evident leadership quality.

Writing in the 1880s, Woodrow Wilson[19] (later himself to be a 'strong' president) observed that 'in the practical conduct of the federal government . . . unquestionably, the predominant and controlling force, the centre and source of all motive and of all regulative power, is Congress'. With only a very few other exceptions, greater power resided on Capitol Hill than in the White House right down to 1933. Since the days of Franklin Delano Roosevelt, Americans have become used to a more assertive presidency. His assumption of office led to a massive extension of federal power as he sought to implement his New Deal proposals to lift the USA out of economic depression.

By the 1960s, commentators were beginning to write about the imperial presidency. Some argued that presidents were acting too independently of Congress in both the domestic and foreign policy areas. It seemed that Congress could not act effectively in an age when federal activity had expanded so rapidly. In the early 1970s, it finally

Box 3.6 Are legislatures in decline across the world?

The constitutions of most countries describe the legislature, Parliament or congress as the key decision-making body in the realm, or else accord it equal status with the Executive. Yet in practice the reality is different, and over recent decades writers have often drawn attention to the alleged 'decline of legislatures'. In Britain, chapters have been written on the 'passing of Parliament', 'Parliament in decline' or 'the loss of Parliamentary control'.

As we have seen, there is a wide spectrum of experience concerning national parliaments. In a minority of countries, legislatures are an essential part of the decision-making process; in many more (including most Western liberal democracies) they have been dominated by the executive branch; in several cases they are manipulated by an authoritarian government; and in a very few they are actually abolished or suspended, perhaps as a result of some form of military coup.

In the nineteenth century, the number of legislatures grew and their political significance increased and parliamentarianism was a feature of the period. In Britain, there are references to the years between 1832 and 1867 as the 'golden age of the private member'. Yet this situation was not to last. Many observers claim that in the twentieth century, in Britain and elsewhere, there was a general decline in the power and status of legislatures, relative to the power of executives and bureaucracies.

Evidence of the weakness of contemporary legislatures

- Increasingly, legislatures react to policy initiatives from the Executive more than they create policy.
- Legislatures lack the support services (budgets, facilities and staffing) available to the Executive.
- The technical expertise and knowledge resources available to legislatures are far less than available to those within the Executive.
- Governments monopolise parliamentary time, often forcing bills through by procedural devices.
- Most legislation today emanates from the Executive, not the legislature. In the middle of the nineteenth century, most social improvements were brought about on the initiative of private members.

But is the picture of legislative decline universal?

Some argue that the thesis of legislative decline over-states the picture. Legislatures may have declined as policy-shaping bodies, but – in Blondel's[20] words – they have become more important as 'communicating mechanisms'. As television cameras have been allowed into many chambers, members can directly address the public, who – if only in snippets on the news – can see their legislators at work. This helps to raise the profile of MPs and emphasise the importance of the chamber as the central forum for national debate. Moreover, many assemblies have become more professional in recent years, improving the staffing and other resources available to members and adopting specialised committees to allow for more detailed scrutiny of the Executive.

Norton[21] points out that in the new democracies, legislatures have been created and in countries once under military rule such as Brazil and Greece they have been revived as soon as democracy was restored. In other words, the number of legislatures has greatly increased – 'they span the globe'. One reason for their adoption, he suggests, is that the public see them as important. Quoting Eurobarometer findings, he notes that 56 per cent of people in the UK saw Parliament as 'very important'. A majority of those surveyed in five countries examined similarly took this view.

Finally, in any case, the performance and power of legislatures varies. Not all assemblies are dying or impotent. Some are rather powerful structures, notably those of Denmark, Italy, Japan, Sweden and the United States – and the traditionally weak European Parliament has significantly developed since the introduction of direct elections for MEPs. In most other countries, legislatures can have significant impacts through their roles in enacting legislation, in representation and in oversight. At times, their power is shown to considerable effect, as in the case of the British Parliament today. Faced with a huge government majority, the two houses have been willing to challenge ministerial authority and on Iraq, foundation hospitals, tuition fees and casinos, members have shown that they are not mere ciphers.

As a result of the trend towards growing executive power, some parliaments are rather compliant. Even so, Hague and Harrop[22] warn against generalisation, and conclude that:

> To speak of the decline of assemblies in an era of big government is too simple. In several ways, assemblies are growing in importance; as arenas of activity, as intermediaries in the transition from one political order to another, as raisers of grievances and as agencies of oversight. The televising of proceedings in many countries is making assemblies more, not less central to political life . . . [Moreover] in the assemblies of Western Europe, backbench members are now more assertive; party leaders can no longer expect well-educated and well-researched backbenchers to be loyally deferential.

> In any case, any tendency towards decline is certainly less true of presidential systems. Congress is strong in the USA, as are assemblies in some Latin-American countries – though in the latter cases any display of assertiveness has sometimes provoked conflict with the administration and precipitated military coups. Even in the case of Congress, its main strength has usually depended more on blocking or delaying presidential initiatives, or scrutinising the performance and membership of the administration, than in actually in determining policy.

reasserted itself and streamlined its operations. Attempts were made to impose more control over the presidency (e.g. the **War Powers Act 1973**), and changes were made which were more to do with the internal organisation of Congress itself. As a result, Congress has been more willing and able to challenge presidential policy, and when – as now – the party in the White House lacks control of Capitol Hill, the opportunities for conflict soon become apparent. President Clinton found his authority undermined as his political opponents were more than willing to seize upon his sexual lapses as evidence of his unsuitability for the highest office – taking their opposition to the ultimate lengths of impeachment proceedings. He was only too aware that Congress was one national legislature which had become resurgent in recent decades. It remains the most influential legislature in the world.

··

 What you should have learnt from reading this chapter

- In recent decades, governments of many countries have often managed to muzzle legislatures. But they are not without influence. Indeed, in some cases their powers have been exercised more assertively in recent years, as our case studies illustrate. In more typical examples, they may have lost the power to initiate, lacking as they do the necessary technical competence. But they can play a part in starting up a great debate on policy issues which can be taken up elsewhere, particularly in the media. They can also exercise control over the Executive. In several legislatures, backbenchers have been active in seeking better resources to enable them to perform their role more effectively. Improved facilities, the use of specialist committees and the introduction of television cameras have all served to raise the profile of elected chambers.

- In Britain, the Executive dominates the legislature. The House of Commons is controlled by the government of the day, by means of its parliamentary majority. Such control is very evident when there is a landslide. The House has more influence when the majority is small. The unelected chamber has a relatively minor role, although it generally performs its tasks effectively. It is in the process of reform.

- Like many legislatures, Parliament is effectively a reactive chamber. It can sometimes significantly modify, but not initiate, legislation. Its effectiveness has been enhanced by the greater use of select committees, improved facilities for members and greater independence and assertiveness of the second chamber. But it finds it difficult to challenge dominant, strong administrations.

Glossary of key terms

Adjournment debate An opportunity for an MP to use a motion to adjourn the House of Commons to raise issues relating to his or her constituency or matters of public concern. There is a half-hour adjournment period at the end of the business of the day. Such debates are also held in Westminster Hall, in an attempt to give backbenchers more time to debate issues which cannot find space in the crowded schedule of the Chamber.

Bicameralism Refers to the existence of a two-chamber legislature.

Career politicians People committed to politics which they regard as their vocation. They know little else beyond the worlds of politics, policy-making and elections, perhaps having begun their career as a research assistant before working in the party organisation as a political staffer.

Impeachment The charging of a public official with an offence committed in office: the process by which the US Congress can remove officers of the national government, including the President, following charges laid by the House of Representatives and a trial in the Senate. The device was used in the United States to bring (unsuccessful) proceedings against President Clinton.

Standing committees Committees of the House of Commons which examine bills in detail, clause by clause, to tidy them up and make them more acceptable: composed of MPs in proportion to party membership in the House.

Unicameralism Refers to the existence of a one chamber legislature.

War Powers Act 1973 Measure passed in US Congress to impose a 60-day limit on the time for which a president can keep American troops abroad without congressional approval, treated with some disdain by subsequent presidents.

Likely examination questions

How might the House of Lords be made a more effective second chamber?

What is meant by parliamentary sovereignty? In what senses is Parliament no longer sovereign?

How and with what success does Parliament control the Executive in Britain?

How effective is the individual MP? What changes might make MPs more effective?

To what extent does the experience of the British Parliament support the theory of 'legislative decline'?

Helpful websites

www.Parliament.uk   Parliament site, with links to both chambers

www.fawcettsociety.org.uk   The Fawcett site, providing statistics and analysis of female representation in British politics at all levels.

www.europarl.eu.int   The European Parliament

Suggestions for further reading

Useful articles

S. Childs, 'Parliament, Women and Representation', *Talking Politics*, April 2002.

P. Cowley, 'The Marginalisation of Parliament', *Talking Politics*, Winter 2000.

P. Cowley and M. Stuart, 'Parliament: a Few Headaches and a Dose of modernisation', *Parliamentary Affairs*, 54:3, 2001.

P. Cowley and M. Stuart, 'New Labour's Backbenchers', *Talking Politics*, September 2002.

M. Grant, 'The Theory and Practice of Parliamentary Reform', *Talking Politics*, January 2004.

I. McAllister and D. Studlar, 'Electoral Systems and Women's Representation: a Long-term Perspective', *Representation*, 39:1, 2002.

P. Norton, 'Parliamentary Reform in Labour's Second Term', *Talking Politics*, September 2001.

P. Norton, 'Reforming the House of Lords: A View from the Parapets', *Representation*, 40:3, 2004.

C. Ridsill-Smith, 'Parliamentary Reform', *Talking Politics*, September 2001.

Useful books

A. Adonis, *Parliament Today,* Manchester University Press, 1993.

The Challenge for Parliament: Making Government Accountable, report by the Hansard Society Commission, 2001.

P. Norton, 'The UK: Parliament under pressure' in P Norton (ed.), *Parliaments and Pressure Groups in Western Europe, 1999.*

P. Norton, 'Parliament' in A. Seldon (ed.), *The Blair Effect*, Little, Brown, 2001.

CHAPTER 4

The Executive

Contents

Overview

The Executive includes not only the chief executive but also the entire
administrative system, for much of the actual work of policy implementation
is performed by the civil service. We can therefore distinguish between
politicians and civil servants. The **Political Executive** is the term used
when we are referring to the government of the day, and the **Official
Executive** is the term used when we are speaking of the bureaucracy
whose task it is to administer the policies that ministers have laid down.

In this chapter, we are primarily concerned with the work and growing
importance of the Political Executive, and the distribution of power within it.
We are more concerned with the chief executive than the head of state, in
cases where the two posts are separately held. At the end, we briefly
examine the relationships between ministers and the civil servants who
work in their departments.

Key issues to be covered in this chapter

- Relevant definitions and distinctions
- The work of political executives
- The distribution of power within political executives
- The structure, work and importance of the British Cabinet and committees
- The role and increased importance of the British Prime Minister
- The prime ministerial or cabinet government debate
- The description of modern prime ministers as 'presidential'
- The relationship of ministers and civil servants
- The ministerial responsibility of members of the Cabinet
- The cases of Brazil, Holland and the United States

Some matters of definition

The term 'executive' derives from the Latin *ex sequi*, meaning to 'follow out' or 'carry out'. The role of the executive branch of government is then to carry out the political system's policies, laws or directives. As long as there have been political systems, there have been individuals or small groups who assume the role of leadership. They have formulated and implemented public policy. At the apex of this executive structure, there is usually a single chief executive, be that person known as a president, prime minister, chief minister, supreme leader or monarch. On occasion, two offices may fulfil the executive role, as in France, where the presidency and prime ministership both have significant powers. On occasion, there may be a ruling junta exercising shared leadership.

Many writers use the phrase '**core executive**' to refer to the complex network of institutions and people at the centre that between them are charged with the day-to-day government of the country, the making of policies and the implementation of laws. The core comprises the first minister, the Cabinet and its committees, the offices that serve the first minister and Cabinet, and the departments headed as they are by senior ministers and including senior civil servants. These groups represent the pinnacle of the decision-making process.

Rather than focusing on the debate of whether we have **prime ministerial** or **cabinet government**, some British analysts prefer to think in terms of such a 'core' whose members circle around the Prime Minister and his or her colleagues. They point out that all of them are involved in a power network with other influential people and organisations in Whitehall and Westminster. Membership of the core is liable to change and it is not always clear who should be included at any given moment. During the invasion and occupation of Iraq, it will include the leaders among the military, but they would probably not normally be involved. Members of most – if not all – cabinet committees qualify for inclusion. In some listings, so also do the Chief Whip and even those who chair backbench parliamentary committees.

Parliamentary and presidential systems of government

In a situation of *parliamentary government*, the Executive is chosen from the legislature and is dependent for support upon it. Thus the British Cabinet is chosen from the House of Commons and is responsible to it – as opposed to the situation in a presidential system, in which the Executive is separately elected and in theory equal to the legislature.

Andrew Heywood puts it[1] well:

> A Parliamentary system of government is one in which the government governs in and through the assembly, thereby 'fusing' the legislative and executive branches. Although they are formally distinct, the assembly and the executive (usually seen as the government) are bound together in a way that violates the doctrine of the separation of powers, setting Parliamentary systems clearly apart from Presidential ones.

Most liberal democracies – ranging from Australia to Sweden, from India to New Zealand – have some kind of parliamentary government, often of a Westminster type. Historically, Britain had an era of legislative supremacy over the Executive. The situation evolved into one in which there was a relatively even balance between the two branches. The suggestion is that we have now moved towards executive supremacy. The Executive tends to dominate the legislature, because the party and electoral systems usually produce a strong majority government, what Lord Hailsham called 'an **elective dictatorship**'.

Parliamentary government appears to imply that government is checked by the power of Parliament which examines, criticises and checks its activities, via such activities as Question Time and the use of Select Committees. Ministers are individually and collectively responsible to Parliament, and should resign if the administration has been defeated on a vote of confidence (as happened with the Callaghan government in 1979).

The United States and several other countries have a system of *presidential government*. This does not refer to the fact that these countries have a president rather than a monarch as head of state. Both the Irish Republic and Germany have presidents in this role, yet both have parliamentary systems. As Heywood explains: 'A presidential

> **Box 4.1 Parliamentary and presidential government compared: a summary**
>
> In a parliamentary system, the governing parties are chosen from and remain members of the legislature. In a presidential system, after being popularly elected, the president directs the government and makes appointments to it. Neither he nor those appointed belong to the legislature. This is a key difference, one system being based on a fusion and the other on a separation of powers.
>
> In a parliamentary system, the first or prime minister and cabinet can be dismissed by a vote of no confidence in the legislature. In a presidential system, the president serves a fixed term and cannot be defeated in the legislature.
>
> In a parliamentary system, there is a plural executive. Government is collegial, with a first minister in various degrees dominant over his colleagues. In a presidential system, there is a single executive, power and responsibility residing in one person.

system is characterised by a constitutional and political separation of powers between the legislative and executive branches of government.' A presidential system is one in which the Executive is elected separately from the legislature, is outside of and in theory equal to it. The President is chosen by the people rather than from the legislative branch, and acts as head of the government as well as ceremonial head of state.

Presidential forms are common in African and Asian states, and have also been adopted in Latin America and the Philippines. They are regarded by supporters as capable of offering a blend of stability and security in government, in contrast to a parliamentary system in which changes of government may result if there are weak party systems and a lack of unity within parties.

In a parliamentary system, the key politicians include the ministers headed by a prime or chief minister. In Britain, the Political Executive comprises the Prime Minister, the Cabinet with which he or she works, and other members of the government, usually a total of around one hundred. Almost all of these people are elected, although some members may be chosen from the House of Lords.

Box 4.2 The leadership role: heads of state and chief executives

Two distinctive roles can be distinguished, although they may in practice be performed by the same person:

1. *The head of state* is an office of largely symbolic performance, being an office of formal authority. The incumbent embodies the authority and power of the state, acting as its leading representative on ceremonial occasions. The head of state is usually a president or monarch. Germany and Italy have non-executive presidencies of this type, whereas Britain, Belgium, Denmark, Holland, Norway, Sweden and Spain have constitutional monarchies in which the sovereign 'reigns but does not rule'. Heads of state may have some residual political influence, but for the most part their task is to award honours, assent to legislation and receive/visit dignitaries of other countries. They are – or should be – non-partisan figureheads, who shun political controversy and maintain a position aloof from party strife. Their existence implies that beyond the cut and thrust of daily political life, something more eternal and solid endures. As such, they can be a rallying point in times of trouble.

2. *The chief executive or head of the government* occupies a post carrying real political power and exercising a range of responsibilities connected with the performance of government.

On occasion, in the case of executive presidents, the two posts are performed by the same person. In France, Russia and the United States, the president wears 'two hats'. This may make the post demanding and time-consuming, but it also gives the holder a broad appeal as the focus for national unity and patriotism. The US president is in effect both in and beyond the political battleground.

The British Head of State: the monarchy

- The hereditary monarchy in Britain is the oldest of our national institutions. It is a constitutional monarchy, which means that it has lost its political role. In theory, it retains certain powers, but these are largely exercised by the Prime Minister. In a constitutional monarchy, the monarch fulfils essentially ceremonial duties.
- If the outcome of a general election were to be uncertain (with no party winning an outright majority), the monarch might be involved in calling the party leaders together to ensure that government could be carried on. But normally the monarch has no

influence over the choice of prime minister. The parties make provision to elect their leaders. In the event of a party winning the election or being in government already, the elected leader automatically enters 10 Downing Street.

- The monarch has no real political power during the lifetime of a government and has not had any for well over a century. On rare occasions advice may be given, for as the political commentator Walter Bagehot wrote in *The English Constitution* (1867) the monarch has 'the right to be consulted, the right to encourage, the right to warn' – in other words, the power of suggestion.

- The role of the monarchy is largely symbolic, that of a figurehead who receives visiting dignitaries, but the Queen and other leading members of her family also visit parts of the country to perform social functions (opening schools and civic centres), as well as touring abroad to represent Britain in the Commonwealth and elsewhere.

- Many people – especially the more elderly – find monarchy attractive, admiring the pomp, colour and splendour associated with royal occasions. For them, it seems to satisfy a popular need and evokes respect. It raises their morale and serves as a focus for their patriotic feeling.

- Others, members of younger generations often among them, are less enthusiastic. In their view, in our less deferential age, respect and loyalty have to be earned. Heredity is no guarantee of capacity. The monarchy seems outdated, an emblem of privilege and costly to maintain. It represents the past, not the future. It is time for the monarchy to be removed.

The role of political executives

Put simply, the task of a political executive – and particularly of the first minister – is to provide leadership. This involves taking the initiative in formulating, articulating and implementing goals. An effective chief executive becomes the spokesperson for the aspirations of the people, can galvanise their support for the identified goals and develop strategies for their accomplishment. The ability to mobilise people in the pursuit of an end vision is a crucial skill.

As part of this broad leadership role, we can identify several areas of responsibility:

- *Ceremonial tasks*, similar to those referred to under head of state; in effect, the person carrying out the duty is standing in for the state, embodying its authority and symbolising its unity. In this capacity, during the controversial state visit of George W. Bush (November 2003) the Queen welcomed the President to stay with her in Buckingham Palace, Tony Blair spent time with him on policy matters of mutual concern but also in social activities (such as the visit to the Prime Minister's constituency of Sedgefield) and other ministers met him and were involved in discussions.

- *Control of policy-making*, in effect directing and controlling the operations of government, developing as necessary coherent economic and social programmes, and conducting relations with other countries.
- *Political leadership*, ensuring that the public is aware of what the government is trying to achieve, mobilising support to ensure compliance and approval. The fate of the administration depends to a large extent on ensuring that there is public approval for what is being done.
- *Management of the bureaucracy*. The president or chief minister, and his cabinet secretaries, act as a top tier of management running the machine beneath them. Ministers head government departments and take political responsibility for particular areas of activity and the conduct of policy carried out by those who administer the programmes being implemented.
- *Crisis management*. When problems arise, be they international crises or a terrorist threat at home, it is the Political Executive that acts. Unlike legislatures, executives can respond quickly and the first minister and relevant members of his or her administration will, if necessary, declare a state of emergency as they struggle to cope with civil disorder and/or unrest.

The distribution of power within political executives: the trend towards first ministerial dominance

During the twentieth and twenty-first centuries, the power of political executives has been on the increase, for many of the reasons given for the decline of legislatures (see Chapter 3). Factors for this enhanced position include:

- The growth of party government, involving tight party discipline to ensure loyalty from elected representatives in the voting lobbies.

- The expansion of governmental responsibilities, in an age of interventionism in economic and social policy. This involves increased legislative tasks and has resulted in the growth of vast bureaucratic machinery to administer government programmes.
- International action and globalisation. In an age of speedy travel and communication, countries are today so closely bound up with each other, that first ministers and their cabinets are increasingly involved in issues of foreign policy, handling crises, responding to disasters and providing global leadership.

Today, the Political Executive (the government) dominates the process of policy-making. In many cases, it controls the agenda of the legislature and monopolises parliamentary time as it seeks to develop and implement its legislative programme. However, within the Political Executive, there has also been a shift in the balance of power. As Heywood[2] points out: 'By common consent, the main beneficiary of this process has been the chief executive.'

The widespread increase in the personal power of first ministers at the expense of their cabinet colleagues has been brought about by several factors: the centralisation of party machines; the growing importance of international diplomacy; and the development of the mass media (especially television), among them. Few political leaders are now merely *primus inter pares* (first among equals). We live in an age in which the focus of attention is on first ministers, to the extent that academics and commentators regularly refer to 'prime ministerial government'. However, the precise role and political importance of first ministers relative to their cabinets varies from system to system and also varies over time, according to the circumstances and personalities involved.

The increasing power of first ministers

Cabinets usually meet regularly and are chaired by the chief executive, in Britain the Prime Minister. Cabinets may share in the making of public policy, as well as offering advice to the political leader and helping in the broader coordination of government policy. They are part of a form of collective leadership, although in reality power has – in many democracies – become increasingly concentrated in the hands of the first minister.

First ministers operate under various labels. Germany has a chancellor, Ireland has a taoiseach and Britain has a prime minister. They are heads of government whose power derives from their leadership of the majority party – or coalition of parties – in the elected assembly.

There is a worldwide trend for them to exercise increased power. Germany has a chancellor who is appointed by and directly accountable to the Bundestag, or lower house. Article 65 of the German Constitution accords him a strong position, stating that 'the chancellor shall determine, and be responsible for, the general policy guidelines'. But in most cases, the support of a cabinet has traditionally been seen as crucial to his or her role. In Australia, Canada, India and New Zealand, first ministers operate through a system of collective cabinet government, but have found that there are increased opportunities for leadership in a television age, even if power varies according to the holder of the office and the prevailing circumstances. Commonwealth countries enjoy less freedom in matters of appointment than does the British incumbent. The power of British prime ministers to choose, reshuffle and dismiss ministers as they wish is formidable.

Not all cabinet systems are the same, an important distinction being that between single-party governments and those which are coalitions. Governments need the support of a majority in Parliament if they are to survive. In Britain and the Commonwealth, one-party government is the norm; only rarely do ministers find themselves struggling to gain the backing of a majority in Parliament. In most continental countries, three-or four-party coalitions are common.

In countries where coalition government is common, the trend to first-minister dominance is less apparent than where there is a single-party administration. In coalition situations, leaders of the largest party need to bargain with other party leaders over the allocation of ministerial offices and once the government has been established, they need to ensure that their partners agree on actions to be taken. There is less scope for personal dominance, the more so as the current first minister may find that around the cabinet table are seated others who have occupied his or her position. For instance, the Dutch Prime Minister is particularly constrained by a tradition of ministerial equality, as well as the existence of often closely worded coalition deals.

Box 4.3 Political leadership

We have seen that today there is a growing focus on 'leadership'. The term can refer to a pattern of behaviour, the influence exerted by an individual or group over other people to achieve selected goals. Or it can be seen as a personal attribute, as when we speak of the personal qualities that enable some people to influence others. In this second meaning, we are referring to attributes such as charisma and personal magnetism. As we have seen, television focuses on the importance of personalities and provides leaders with a powerful means of manipulating their public image. They (and those who advise them) are conscious of the importance of projecting their personalities as a means of mobilising electoral support.

'Strong' and 'weak' leaders

As we have noted, leadership styles vary. Leaders are not all alike and can exercise the quality of leadership in several different ways. Much depends on:

- their personality, vision and style
- their use of the means of mass communication
- events
- the institutional framework.

Some leaders want to 'be someone' and others want to 'achieve something'. Among the modern leaders who have wanted to transform their country and its prospects and reputation are Margaret Thatcher and Tony Blair. The former was noted for her style of 'conviction politics'. The latter, in the early years of his premiership, was criticised for being addicted to focus groups so that he could discern and follow public opinion. But as over Iraq, foundation hospitals and tuition fees, he showed that he had great strength of character (some would say stubbornness in the face of difficult obstacles) and was willing to lead. Although the gift of strong leadership may be seen as an asset, especially after a period of the weak and indecisive kind, it is not without its dangers. People can tire of it, the more so if it seems to drift into authoritarianism. Margaret Thatcher ultimately lost her personal ascendancy when she was overthrown in a leadership contest. As the Iraqi involvement has unfolded, Tony Blair has faced mounting rebellion on all sides from a party which admires his electoral skills but does not warm to his policy ideas.

> Strong leadership has its disadvantages as well as its advantages. It can certainly inspire and mobilise people, ensure people pull in the same direction and get things done. Yet it can also narrow the focus of debate, encourage top-down decision-making, discourage contributions from below and be associated with a serious lack of accountability.

The British Cabinet

The Cabinet typically comprises 23–24 leading ministers. It is the central committee which directs the work of government and coordinates the activities of individual departments. It has in the past been described as 'the core of the British constitutional system'.[3] Its members assume responsibility for all decisions on behalf of the government. It is common to describe the British political system in the early mid-part of the twentieth century as one of 'cabinet government'. Today, it is not uncommon to see references to 'the passing of cabinet government' or to 'prime ministerial dictatorship'.

Membership

Most cabinet members are drawn from the House of Commons, the dominant, elected chamber, although a small number sit in the House of Lords. Most cabinet members run a department such as Education and Employment, Health or the Home Office. Some are non-departmental ministers such as the Lord Privy Seal and Chancellor of the Duchy of Lancaster. Lacking departmental responsibilities, they have the opportunity to rove over the whole area of government and are available to take on particular tasks, as assigned by the Prime Minister.

There is a 'pecking order' within the Cabinet. In cabinet meetings, the attitudes and preferences of more senior ministers normally carry more weight than those of others present. The Prime Minister is at the helm, followed by the Chancellor of the Exchequer, the Foreign Secretary and then the Home Secretary. There may, as now, be a Deputy Prime Minister, whose ranking is usually below that of the Chancellor. The relationship of the Prime Minister and Chancellor is crucial. If they are united in their stance on a particular issue, other ministers will find it hard to achieve any contrary objectives.

Box 4.4 Some characterisations of the British Cabinet

'. . . the unique source of authority . . . the highest political prize in
the country.'
Patrick Gordon Walker, 1970[4]
'. . . the major instrument of government'.
A. Hanson and M. Walles, 1980[5]
'The Cabinet is the directing committee or board of management of
British government.'
P. Madgwick[6]
'. . . the Cabinet stands at the pinnacle of government.'
P. Norton, 1984[7]

The Chief Whip will normally attend cabinet meetings, although
the office does not really carry full membership of the Cabinet. The
Chief Whip is there to advise cabinet ministers of the feeling on the
backbenches of the party, in order to ensure that the leadership does
not lose touch with other MPs. This will help prevent damaging
revolts in the House of Commons.

The role of the Cabinet
The work of the Cabinet involves:

*   *Deciding on major policy to be followed at home and abroad.* Government
    policy has often been stated in the election manifesto and reflects
    prevailing party policy. But when in office, the priorities for action
    have to be decided and a legislative programme drawn up. Details
    of policy have to be filled in, in the light of prevailing circum-
    stances such as the financial state of the country and the advice
    received from key pressure groups.
*   *Dealing with unforeseen major problems.* New problems arise from time
    to time. There may be a crisis in the European Union, a sudden
    invasion of a friendly state, an outbreak of violence in an area of
    strategic interest, a fuel crisis at home, the discovery of a major
    human or animal disease (e.g. Aids, BSE or foot-and-mouth
    disease), a hospital bed shortage in a winter outbreak of a vicious
    variety of influenza or a tsunami (underground earthquake)

affecting many countries in the Far East. All of these issues require a response from government. They are liable to throw them 'off course', not least because they invariably require a substantial injection of funding.

- *Coordinating the policies of different departments.* If government is to function well and policy is to be successfully carried out, there needs to be coordination between government departments. In some cases, disputes may have to be resolved between departmental ministers or policies pulled together to ensure what Tony Blair sometimes refers to as 'joined-up government'. There is a natural tension between Treasury representatives and spending ministers who want more money for defence, education, health, transport and other issues.
- *Planning for the long term.* Ideally, this is a key area of policy-making, but governments are often preoccupied with the here-and-now. Moreover, ministers come and go, making it difficult to plan ahead with consistency of purpose. Yet some issues require long-term planning, such as those concerning the environment, defence and pension policy. Often this work is done in cabinet committees.

How the Cabinet operates

In the years after the Second World War, there were often two cabinet meetings a week. Nowadays, the Cabinet normally only meets on Thursday mornings. The session begins at 10 a.m. and traditionally lasts for two or three hours, although under Tony Blair some meetings have been much shorter and his attendance even more limited. The agenda is circulated by the Cabinet Office a day or two before the meeting. Many items are routine, such as the Foreign Secretary's report on the world scene and the discussion of forthcoming business; in the Blair government, considerable time is spent on the presentation of policy.

The number of topics discussed and the time spent on each of them is necessarily limited. The more time that is spent on individual items, the less opportunity there is to cover other matters. Those which have a low place on the agenda stand little chance of detailed attention. Prime ministers are able to manipulate the agenda, keeping off or giving low priority to those which may cause embarrassing disagreement.

Nigel Lawson[8], a chancellor under Margaret Thatcher, has written of the unsuitability of the Cabinet as a body for thrashing out problems and making long-term plans:

> A normal Cabinet meeting has no chance of becoming a grave forum of statesmanlike debate. Twenty two people attending a two-and-a-half hour meeting can speak for just over six and a half minutes each on average. If there are three items of business – and there are usually more – the ration of time just exceeds two minutes, if everyone is determined to have his say. Small wonder then that most ministers keep silent on most issues.

It is widely recognised that rather than providing a forum for detailed discussion of a wide range of policies, the main role of the Cabinet is to facilitate cohesion and coordination of governmental policies generally, and to provide or establish the parameters in which those policies are prepared and pursued. Many, if not most, government policies are developed in cabinet committees and then reported back to the full Cabinet for approval. In other words, the Cabinet tends to rubber-stamp decisions taken elsewhere.

Burch[9] has concluded his study of the Cabinet in operation with this analysis:

> In essence, Cabinet tends to resolve those issues that cannot be resolved elsewhere. It may also . . . lay out broad strategy and take a very general oversight role in relation to policy-making. It is, however, misleading to suggest that the Cabinet collectively and consistently controls policy-making . . . much decision-making on major items is spread outside the Cabinet. Many matters are decided amongst only a small group of Cabinet members or between ministers and civil servants or between a minister and the Prime Minister.

Beyond the Cabinet, decision-making takes place in:

- *Cabinet committees* (see Box 4.5).
- *Inner cabinets*. All prime ministers rely on some ministers more than others, some being personal friends as well as colleagues. At various times, Tony Blair has relied on David Blunkett, Gordon Brown, Peter Mandelson, and John Prescott, among others. On any major issues such as Iraq, he would want to be sure that his most senior ministers were in support.

- *Kitchen cabinets.* The term refers to the small coterie of advisers and confidants with which prime ministers like to surround themselves and talk over issues at the end of the day. It will usually include some members of the Cabinet, although in the present case more importance is attached to the views of key personnel such as Alistair Campbell and Peter Mandelson (both still in close contact, though detached from the day-to-day action), Philip Gould, Jonathan Powell and others.
- *Bilateral meetings* with individual ministers.

In assessing the importance of the cabinet as a whole, it is important not to exclude these other areas of policy-making. The role of the Cabinet meeting, particularly under Tony Blair, has been reduced. But if we use the term 'Cabinet' in an 'umbrella sense' to cover this network of decision-making arenas, its importance is very considerable. Power has been dispersed from the whole Cabinet, to some of its component elements.

Box 4.5 The work of Cabinet committees

Cabinet committees, small working groups of the whole Cabinet, have been used in many large democracies as key organs of decision-making. Usually, their use developed during wartime and thereafter it was convenient to formalise their use. They focus on specific areas of policy or on overall strategy. In recent years, they have been increasingly involved at the point of decision-making, their decisions being notified to and ratified by the whole Cabinet. In Australia, decisions cannot be reopened without the consent of the Prime Minister.

In Britain, committees existed in an unsystematic form in the nineteenth century, but it was the impact of two world wars and the rapid expansion of governmental activity in the post-1945 era which created the present committee structure. Up until the 1970s, their existence was officially denied, but within a decade academics and journalists had probed to find out more. Ministers are now willing to identify them.

There are two types of cabinet committee:

1. *Standing committees* are named, permanent committees responsible for a particular policy area such as Northern Ireland,

the European Union and local government. The most important is the Economic and Domestic Policy (EDP) Committee, chaired by the Prime Minister. It is, in effect, a kind of 'inner Cabinet' of senior government members.

2. *Ad hoc committees* vary in number according to the preferences and style of the Prime Minister. They are concerned with particular policy areas; it may be a sudden crisis (e.g. the Falklands invasion in 1982, the coal dispute in 1984-85) or an issue such as the abolition by the Thatcher government of the Greater London Council. A recent one dealt with the celebration of the millennium. Once the crisis has passed or the event ceases to be relevant, *ad hoc* committees are disbanded.

Important deliberative work is done in committees. They consider issues in more detail than does a cabinet meeting. Often, as was made clear in the *Crossman Diaries*[10], decisions are made in committees and not referred to the whole Cabinet, which only gets involved if there are major differences of opinion between ministers and departments. Decisions in committee are 'reported back' to the Cabinet, which can revise or veto committee proposals. But as the Prime Minister chairs several important committees, disagreement is not common.

Committees are today vitally important areas of governmental activity, with a major role in determining and resolving government policy. Crossman was worried about their constitutional impact. He saw them as one of the symptoms of the 'passing of Cabinet Government'. He observed the way in which the point of decision was being 'permanently transferred either downwards to the powerful Cabinet committees or upwards to the Prime Minister himself'. Certainly, the creation and composition of committees has been a key element in strengthening prime ministerial power.

See also recent prime ministers and their use of the Cabinet, pp. 126–8.

The work of the Cabinet Office and Secretariat

The Cabinet has a Secretariat of about forty senior civil servants whose job is to timetable meetings, prepare agendas and documents, and draft and circulate minutes. The Secretariat is so important that its head is the country's top civil servant, the Cabinet Secretary.

The Cabinet Secretary is in daily contact with the Prime Minister and cabinet members. He attends cabinet meetings, though not when party political items are being discussed, and some cabinet committees. The relationship between the premier and the Cabinet Secretary is a crucial one. Crossman revealed its importance, noting how the two men decided the cabinet agenda and the order of the items on it, and agreed the minutes afterwards. Over the **Westland Affair** (1986), these twin aspects were subsequently commented on by Michael Heseltine[11].

The Secretariat is assisted by a Cabinet Office of some 1,500 civil servants who prepare the work for committees and follow up their decisions. The term 'Cabinet Office' is now generally used to cover the whole machinery which services Number 10, the Cabinet and the departments, and the word 'Secretariat' rarely features. Apart from its traditional duties as outlined, there is within the Cabinet Office permanent machinery to cope with emergencies such as threats to fuel and water supplies, or terrorist activity. This is the Civil Contingencies Unit, which can, as the occasion demands, transform itself into a mixed committee of ministers, officials, the military, the policy and the security services, with the Home Secretary in the chair.

From an early stage as prime minister, Tony Blair and his team were keen to see a 'dynamic centre'. This involved more power for the Prime Minister's Office, which would work closely with the Cabinet Office. The Prime Minister[12] answered a parliamentary question on the future of the Cabinet Office back in 1998. He put it in this way:

> The role of the Cabinet Office has traditionally been to help the Prime Minister and the Government as a whole to reach collective decisions on Government policy. Since the election, the three principal parts of the centre – my own office, the Cabinet Office and the Treasury – have worked closely and effectively together, and with other Departments, to take forward the Government's comprehensive and ambitious policy agenda.

Since then, there has been a closer fusion than before between the Prime Minister's Office and the Cabinet Office.

Recent prime ministers and their use of the Cabinet

Prime ministers vary in the use they make of their cabinets. Clement Attlee, the post-war Labour premier, saw his role essentially as chairman of the Cabinet. He led an able team and although he could be assertive, it was meaningful to write of 'cabinet government' under his leadership.

Other prime ministers have had a different style, some tending to be forceful and dominant, others more content to delegate to those around them. At one extreme are the powerful (Thatcher, Blair), at the other those content to keep the shift afloat ('steady-as-she-goes' James Callaghan).

Margaret Thatcher used the Cabinet less than many of her predecessors, her annual average of meetings being 35 as against Harold Wilson's 59. She stated her own views at the beginning of cabinet meetings and was not a great listener. The longer she was in power, the more she surrounded herself with weak ministers whom she could easily control. Neither did she use cabinet standing committee meetings much, preferring to create *ad hoc* committees of her chosen membership as a means of bypassing full cabinet discussion. These often took important decisions on matters ranging from the American bombing of Libya to the introduction of the Community Charge.

John Major adopted a more collegial style. Taking over at a difficult time following the downfall of his predecessor, he saw the need to heal divisions and did so by including representatives of all shades of opinion in the party. Major's approach was more consensual, his cabinet meetings more friendly; he allowed the Cabinet to meet more regularly. He reduced the number of committees and did not use 'ad hocery' as a means of boosting his position and provided less leadership in Cabinet, preferring to hear the views of others and reach an agreed viewpoint. He did not insist too strongly on **collective responsibility** (see pp. 145–6). In his last years, his team was divided and his commentators portrayed his performance as weak and ineffectual.

Tony Blair uses his Cabinet much less than John Major and sometimes attends its meetings for only a short time. He tends to lay down his preferred policy, as on the Dome, and expect agreement. Generally, he has had cabinet backing because the party is relieved to be firmly established in power. There have been divisions, for he has some powerful figures around him. But his inclination seems to be to act decisively and strongly, though he has granted reasonable discretion to ministers to get on with their tasks as long as it is evident that they are in line with agreed policy. His position might in normal circumstances have been reinforced by a third election victory, but his publicly announced decision to stand down before the end of the new Parliament has meant that there is a tendency among commentators and some party colleagues to view him as a transient, 'lame-duck' figure.

Tony Blair has used *ad hoc* committees more than his predecessor, as on education and the millennium. Moreover, he was responsible for an innovation in his first term, inviting Paddy Ashdown and leading Liberal Democrats to serve on the Joint Cabinet Committee on Constitutional Reform.

The role of Prime Minister

The Prime Minister is head of the executive branch of government and chairman of the Cabinet. He has several responsibilities, ranging from oversight of the security services to liaising with the monarch in a weekly meeting, keeping her informed of what the government is doing and advising on matters such as the constitutional implications of a royal marriage or divorce. Among the chief tasks of the Prime Minister are the following:

• *Leader of his party in the country and in Parliament.* He owes his position to the party and in carrying out duties cannot afford to forget that connection. He will use his powers of leadership to keep the party united, working out compromise solutions as necessary. This role of managing the party is crucial to his prospects of survival. He cannot afford to grow out of touch with the people he leads. At times, the Blair premiership has been under threat, the lack of support among MPs for particular policies leading to major revolts in the voting lobbies.

• *Responsibility for the appointment and dismissal of members of the Cabinet (see Box 4.6), acting as it chairman; appointment of other members of the government.* In relation to the Cabinet, this also includes appointing members of cabinet committees, many of which he also chairs. Chairmanship of the Cabinet involves drawing up its agenda – in partnership with the Cabinet Secretary – and agreeing the minutes after the weekly meeting. His role in regards to the Cabinet enables him to steer the political agenda in his chosen way.

• *Leader of the government at home and abroad.* He answers questions in the House at Prime Minister's Question Time on Wednesday. He also acts as the country's voice on occasions such as the death of Princess Diana or some national disaster, and represents Britain in summit conferences in Europe, with the American President and at the UN. In this role of national leadership, he will sometimes appear on TV and address the nation directly.

- *Responsibility for a wide range of appointments, exercising a considerable power of patronage.* Appointments once made by the monarch are now mostly made on the advice of the Prime Minister. He appoints people from bishops to higher judges, from the chairman of the BBC to members of the Privy Council.
- *He determines the date of the next general election.*

Box 4.6 The Prime Minister and the Cabinet: the appointment and dismissal of ministers

Central to prime ministerial power is the ability to appoint members of the government and in particular the twenty or so members of the Cabinet. The power of hiring, reshuffling and if necessary dismissing colleagues illustrates the strengths and limitations of the Prime Minister's position.

On forming an administration, the premier has to decide how large the Cabinet will be and what offices of state are to be included within it. Government departments can be combined, created and abolished, so that post-war cabinets have varied in size from sixteen to twenty-four. Sometimes, a prime minister may create the post of Deputy Prime Minister. He or she may decide to have a combined Secretary of State for Health and Social Security, as opposed to separating the two roles as is currently the vogue. Transport may form a separate ministry or be part of the Department of the Environment.

Once the size and offices have been determined, prime ministers must then decide on the Cabinet's membership, who to include and who to leave out. They are constitutionally free to appoint whom they wish to the Cabinet, but in practice they are politically limited.

Their decision-making is likely to be influenced by several factors:

- *They will be members of the same party*, normally MPs. In the past, a very few non-political persons have been included, but they have normally been given a life peerage. The Prime Minister will need two or three cabinet members drawn from the House of Lords, in order to pilot government legislation through the chamber.
- *'Big figures' of party standing are usually included*. In every administration, there are some figures who almost pick themselves and who have a substantial say over which office they would like to

occupy. John Major would have found it difficult to omit Michael Heseltine, after the latter's strong challenge to the leadership of Margaret Thatcher at the time of her downfall in 1990. Tony Blair would have been ill advised to leave out Gordon Brown, Robin Cook and John Prescott after the 2001 election. They had been key members of his first administration and each had their own following and status in the party and country. Other than Cook, they were still senior figures in late 2005.

- *A balance of party opinion is ideal.* A prime minister normally wants to achieve a balance of left/right and pro-anti-European opinion in the party, so that all sections of the party feel that they have a voice representing their interests at the top. On occasion, a strong incumbent may feel able to shed members of a different viewpoint, but to do so is risky. It was President Johnson in the United States who concluded that it was safer to have 'his opponents on the inside of the tent pissing out than on the outside, pissing in'. By including persons not of the same persuasion, the danger to party unity is minimised. Senior figures who resent their omission or who leave a government under duress can be strong critics once they have the freedom of the backbenches.

- *The need to reward loyalty.* Prime ministers may wish to offer due recognition for those who have backed their battle for the party leadership or who have stood by them in cabinet discussions when the going was tough. Most prime ministers like to have some of their political – and sometimes personal – friends around them.

- *A blend of youth and experience is desirable.* There will come a time when figures of similar age to the Prime Minister – or perhaps older – have had their day. Wise prime ministers likely to recognise and encourage new talent, to ensure that there is another generation likely to take over the reins of leadership. When the Blair/Brown era has passed, the younger David Miliband/Ruth Kelly generation of MPs will be there to replace them.

- *The inclusion of members representing different groups in society.* Prime ministers normally ensure that women are represented near the top (as Tony Blair has done), and maybe – in the case of Labour – members of ethnic minority groups as well. Ideally, it is wise to choose a Scotsman as Secretary of State for Scotland, and similarly the same type of representation for Northern Ireland and Wales, as well.

- *Ability.* Hopefully, in having regard to the above factors, they will also bear in mind the need for personnel to have the relevant skills, experience and expertise. Prime ministers like to include some people 'with a safe pair of hands'. If they have good presentation skills and are persuasive on television, that is a bonus.

The debate about prime ministerial power

> For a Prime Minister to dominate the whole business of governing,
> he or she needs a formidable equipment and some good fortune.
> P. J. Madgwick, *An Introduction to British Politics*[13]

R. H. S. Crossman[14], a former Oxford don and then a Labour MP, was the first main exponent of the idea that Britain had acquired a system in which the Prime Minister had supreme power: 'The post-war epoch has seen the final transformation of Cabinet Government into Prime Ministerial Government', with the effect that 'the Cabinet now joins the dignified elements in the Constitution'. His observations were matched by those of another writer and politician, Professor John Mackintosh, who similarly discerned[15] the passing of cabinet government: 'The country is governed by a Prime Minister, his colleagues, junior ministers and civil servants, with the Cabinet acting as a clearing house and court of appeal.'

Similar claims have been oft-repeated since the early 1960s, observers suggesting that a prime minister presiding over a single-party government and equipped with the traditional prerogatives of the Crown is immensely powerful. But it was the premiership of Margaret Thatcher which provided the debate about whether Britain has 'government by prime minister' with a new impetus. She appeared to stretch the power of the office to its limits. So too Tony Blair has been accused of operating via a system of personal rule or 'too presidentially' (see Box 4.7).

Critics of this prime ministerial concentration of power have long pointed to its dangers. Former left-wing MP and ex-minister Tony Benn was specific in his challenge[18]:

> The wide range of powers . . . exercised by a British Prime Minister . . . are now so great as to encroach upon the legitimate rights of the electorate, undermine the essential role of Parliament, [and] usurp some of the functions of collective Cabinet decision-making . . . In short, the present centralisation of power into the hands of one person has gone too far and amounts to a system of personal rule in the very heart of our system of . . . parliamentary democracy.

Box 4.7 A presidential prime minister?

Academics, commentators and critics have often made the comparison between the power of the Prime Minister and that of the US President. Whilst some write of 'prime ministerial government', others use the phrase 'presidential [or quasi-presidential] rule'. It is possible to argue the case that the Prime Minister increasingly dominates the British political system, whilst quibbling about whether we live under presidential rule.

Those who detect presidential qualities in British prime ministers point to:

- the large apparatus in Downing Street with which modern premiers equip themselves. In particular, Tony Blair has developed the Prime Minister's Office which has become a *de facto* if not formalised Prime Minister's Department. Presidents – lacking the degree of backing a prime minister derives from the Cabinet – rely heavily upon an array of advisers and consultants, many of whom are located in the Executive Office.
- their pre-eminence in domestic and foreign policy, enabling them to assume much responsibility over substantial areas of governmental activity at any particular time, as the need or wish arises. After consultation with their political advisers, they decide what needs to be done and impose their inclinations upon cabinet colleagues.
- the priority attached to the presentation of policy and the way in which Tony Blair and some predecessors seek to manipulate the media, in order that they get their message across directly to the people. The Prime Minister has been criticised for making key policy announcements at staged and televised public events, rather than in the House of Commons – in which his record of attendance and voting have been criticised.
- elections have increasingly come to be seen as a duel between two leaders, in an age in which politics has become personalised. Television is a medium infatuated with personalities and has encouraged the emphasis upon personal characteristics.
- the quality of what Michael Foley[16] has called **'spatial leadership'**, a technique whereby prime ministers such as Margaret Thatcher and Tony Blair like to appear 'above the fray' of battle, sometimes talking about the government and what it must do, as though they were not the key force in shaping its direction and policies. This was a technique adopted by President Reagan, who seemed able to escape from any difficulties in which his administration was

mired. 'Teflon Tony' was a label applied to the Prime Minister, which drew attention to his ability to retain an aura of dignity and authority, unsullied by the events that happened to his ministers. The label has lost much of its relevance since his credibility and reputation were tarnished by the events surrounding the Iraq war.

The role of prime minister and president compared
There are several points that can be made in comparing the prime ministership and presidency:

- In Britain, we have separated 'pomp from power', having a chief executive and head of state. In the USA, the two roles are combined in one person, giving the incumbent enhanced prestige as he appears to be elevated above the daily political battleground.
- The President has greater security of tenure, having a fixed four-year term. Although prime ministers may serve five years if they choose to delay dissolving Parliament, they are liable to be defeated in the House (very infrequent) or to find difficulty in managing with a knife-edge majority (again, unusual). Arguably, the fact of being able to determine the date of the election and to engineer a situation in which the electorate 'feels good' (because of a thriving economy) tips the balance towards the Prime Minister.
- Britain has a plural executive, prime ministers and their cabinets being collectively responsible to the House of Commons. The US Cabinet meets less regularly, its members having less political standing in their own right. They are not rival contenders for the party leadership, as they may be in Britain.
- Prime ministers are accountable to the legislature, from which their governments are derived. They have to attend the House weekly at Question Time and sell/defend their policies in debates and before committees. Whereas Tony Blair felt it necessary to put the proposal to wage war against Iraq to a vote – which might have gone against him – the President did not have to struggle to achieve congressional approval. Prime ministers are always liable to defeat in the chamber, however, unlikely the scenario. Presidents are not answerable in the same way, their administrations not being formed from the legislature. They answer directly to the people in the next presidential election.
- Prime ministers derive much of their authority from their leadership of disciplined political parties. This enables them – especially if they have a sizeable majority – to pass the bulk of the programme outlined in the Queen's Speech. Presidents can find

it difficult to achieve their legislative programme, even when they have a majority in both chambers of Congress. Whereas Margaret Thatcher was able to reform the system of health service provision in the way that she and her ministers favoured, Bill Clinton was unable to do so a few years later. The strength which comes from party leadership gives the Prime Minister the edge in terms of domestic policy, in which presidents are more constrained. As Mayhew[17] points out: 'to suppose that an American party winning Congress and the presidency thereby wins the leeway of a British governing party is to be deluded by the election returns'.

- On foreign policy, the President has a clear advantage, not merely by virtue of America's pre-eminent global role. Post-war presidential power has depended heavily upon the incumbent's ability to act decisively at times of crisis. He can consult whom he wishes and then decide how to act. A prime minister may take key decisions in a Cabinet committee with a small group of ministers, but on a matter of major international policy would ultimately need to carry his Foreign Secretary and cabinet colleagues with him. Usually, prime ministers get their way, but they do not dominate the process of making and conducting foreign policy to the extent that the President is able to do.

Foley concludes that the Prime Minister has become presidential, but in a uniquely British way. He is not a head of state, nor does he derive power directly from the people. He cannot ignore the Cabinet, even if it is sometimes bypassed on individual policy matters. The constitutional position in the two countries does not make for real convergence. There is a fundamental difference between presidential and parliamentary government.

The central elements in prime ministerial power today are well known but difficult to measure. They include:

- the power of appointment and dismissal of cabinet and other ministerial offices
- power over the structure and membership of cabinet committees, any of which the Prime Minister may chair
- the central, overseeing non-departmental nature of the office
- leadership of the party
- single-party government

- the distribution of patronage
- (for some) wartime leadership
- a high degree of public visibility.

These features have operated for much of the century, but in recent decades some have assumed a growing significance. For instance, prime ministers are now much more visible than ever before, because of the growing trend towards international summitry and a high degree of television exposure. No occupant of Number 10 since the last world war has been anything less than very powerful. Any prime minister today has a formidable display of powers at his or her disposal.

Constraints on the British Prime Minister

Yet the thesis of prime ministerial government can be over-stated and suffers from the tendency to over-generalisation. Power can be seriously circumscribed and dependent on the circumstances of the time. It is not merely that some prime ministers are more powerful than others, but that any single incumbent will be more powerful at certain times than at others in the course of the premiership. Even the strongest among them are not always able to sustain the same degree of performance throughout their term.

Individuals have made a greater or lesser impact upon the office. All have been subject to some constraints, among them:

- *The Cabinet.* On major issues, even a strong prime minister will wish to keep his or her Cabinet united behind him. It normally comprises some figures of public and party standing, potential rivals if they are ignored or antagonised. In the build-up to the invasion of Iraq, it was essential for the Prime Minister that he could count upon the support of Gordon Brown, John Prescott and Jack Straw. The way in which prime ministers and their colleagues work together will depend upon the mix of personalities involved, the relationships being complex and fluid. Much depends on the issues and problems with which they are faced.
- *Party.* Strong premiers can be hard on party backbenchers, expecting loyalty in the voting lobbies even for policies they dislike. When ministers are going through a difficult period – and especially when party MPs fear for their seats in the next election – they may

Box 4.8 The Cabinet under Tony Blair: the verdict of Lord Butler

'The Cabinet is no longer a central organ of government. Cabinet Ministers still matter as heads of Departments, but Cabinet meetings no longer really count. The system is no longer collective. It is a centralised system directed by 10 Downing Street.' This was Peter Hennessy's[20] verdict on life under the Blair administrations, delivered in 2001.

The same commentator pointed to the weaknesses of the Blair approach in 2004, following the publication of the Butler Report[21] that had some scathing things to say about the way government has been conducted in recent years – an informal style with too many sofa chats, too many occasions when minutes have not been taken and a consequent lack of clarity about what has been decided. In restrained language, Lord Butler (an ex-Cabinet Secretary) barely concealed his disdain for 'the informality and circumscribed procedures' which marginalised the Cabinet's role in decision-taking over Iraq in the run-up to war against Iraq. He noted that the Cabinet discussed the subject on 24 occasions in the tense year before war broke out, but disapproved of the fact that the frequent reports of the foreign and defence secretaries and the Prime Minister were often unscripted: the defence and overseas committee did not meet at all. He concluded in this way: 'Without papers circulated in advance, it remains possible but is obviously much more difficult for the cabinet outside the small circle directly involved to bring their political judgement and experience to bear.'

find that support melts away. Prime ministers who lose backbench backing may find that they cannot rely on continued consent to their leadership, as Margaret Thatcher found out in 1990 and Tony Blair has found in late 2005.

- *Parliament.* Prime ministers need to retain support in Parliament to get their policies through the chamber. Even a prime minister who makes only limited other appearances in the House still has to appear every Wednesday to be grilled at Question Time, defend his policies to occasional select committee hearings and sell his policies on Iraq, tuition fees and other contentious issues. In March 2003, Tony Blair could not have gone ahead with his backing for President

Bush, if MPs had rejected his case for war. Primarily, getting parliamentary support means keeping government MPs happy, but over Iraq he wanted to ensure that there was sufficient agreement from the Opposition to his policy to help him defeat a Labour rebellion.

- *Events.* Harold Macmillan, the Conservative Prime Minister of the 1950s–60s saw 'events, dear boy, events' as his greatest danger. No prime minister knows what hazards are around the corner. Issues ranging from war to an outbreak of foot-and-mouth disease can derail or at least threaten an administration.
- *Hostility in the media.* Even a telegenic incumbent can have a tougher ride when the novelty and shine wears off. A poor performer on television will soon find that the medium is a two-edged weapon, useful to charismatic politicians but a problem for the less articulate or persuasive. Whereas Tony Blair had a remarkable degree of press support in 1997 and 2001, war and other issues inspired marked hostility from sections of the Tory press, in 2005.

Hennessy[19] quotes Tony Blair in a revealing conversation with the political commentator, Robert Harris, in which Blair admits that much

> is different from anything that you might have anticipated. The reality itself is more intense and more endless, even though in theory you would have anticipated that it would indeed be intense and relentless. And there are things that come and knock you about.
>
> But I have a very fixed view as to what I want to do for the country, and I haven't shifted in my belief that I can do it. But keeping a grip of that big picture and following it through is the toughest part of it.

There has certainly been a remarkable growth in the power of the executive branch of government in the last 100 years, but the distribution of power within the Executive is liable to change at any time. If there has been a gradual trend to prime ministerial dominance, it has been characterised by an ebb and flow of power, rather than a continuous increase. A much-quoted observation by Lord Oxford (formerly Liberal PM Asquith) reflects the varying nature of political power. He judged that: 'The office of Prime Minister is what its holder chooses and is able to make of it.' His emphasis on the ability, character and preference of the incumbent is generally accepted, as is the role of particular circumstances.

Prime ministers do not have unlimited power. If they did, they would be behaving as dictators. It is one thing to have dictatorial tendencies, another to be a dictator. Dictators cannot be removed, other than by a military coup or similar event. Prime ministers can always be evicted from Number 10 at the next election. The electorate is the ultimate limitation on even the most powerful premier. If leaders are seen as too powerful, remote, out of touch or untrustworthy, voters can react against them and bring their party down.

The extent to which Tony Blair surrendered his earlier popularity over Iraq and other issues is judged by an abortive all-party campaign to impeach him. Members argued that he was guilty of serious constitutional impropriety and invoked an antiquated – and, many commentators assumed, lapsed – procedure last used against Lord Palmerston nearly 150 years ago as a means of expressing their disapproval. Their complaints focused particularly on three main grounds – the claims that the Prime Minister made before the war about Iraqi weapons, his failure to tell MPs about new intelligence correcting those claims and the indications that he made an agreement with President Bush to go to war without the consent of the Cabinet, Parliament or the British people.

British ministers and their civil servants

As we have seen at the beginning of the chapter, the Executive in Britain comprises a political element (the elected politicians) and a non-political, administrative element (the unelected officials or civil servants). Theoretically, the position is that ministers make the policy decisions and civil servants administer them. Constitutionally, ministers are responsible to Parliament for the policies and administration of the departments they head.

The underlying rationale for this division of responsibilities is that politicians are elected on the basis of promises made at the last election. These priorities should determine their aims and approach to policy issues when in office. Civil servants, permanent appointees, are expected to be anonymous, neither receiving the credit nor blame for the success or otherwise of these policies. They provide advice to ministers to enable them to formulate and supervise the administration of policy decisions.

In practice, such a distinction is difficult to maintain. Not surprisingly, there have over many decades been suggestions that civil servants frustrate the will of ministers and governments. Some ministers of either party seem unable to impose their will on the departments they lead, whilst others have conflictual relationships with their higher civil servants.

Government ministers

By ministers, we are referring to around eighty to ninety senior government members, including cabinet ministers, ministers of state and parliamentary under-secretaries, who work in departments of state or ministries. These include the Treasury, the Department of Health, the Foreign Office and the Home Office (see Box 4.9).

Such is the volume of work in departments run by a cabinet minister, that other layers of ministers have been created. The thirty or so ministers of state and the same number of parliamentary under-secretaries are collectively known as 'junior ministers'. Below them, are the forty to fifty private parliamentary secretaries (PPS), who are the general assistants of ministers and really act as a kind of 'dogsbody'. They are unpaid for their work. Broadly, the more important the government department, the more ministers and junior ministers it will have. At the Treasury, there are two cabinet ministers and more than fifteen junior ministers.

Below these ministers there is a hierarchy of civil servants. The cabinet minister usually deals with them via his or her private secretary (normally a bright, up-and-coming civil servant charged with the responsibility for organising the minister's busy schedule) or through his Permanent Secretary.

Ministers are very reliant on the performance of the civil servants who work in their department. They are the people who organise the minister's day, arrange his or her appointments, write letters on his or her behalf, draft replies to parliamentary questions, arrange meetings and offer advice on how to deal with political issues as they arise. Yet ministers do not choose their civil servants. Ministers work with the people who are there when they come to office. For personal support in their dealings with officials, ministers rely on their junior ministers and their political advisers.

Box 4.9 The hierarchy of ministers at the Home Office

Home Secretary (Charles Clarke), cabinet member
Three Ministers of state for
    Crime reduction, policing and community safety
    Criminal justice, sentencing and law reform
    Citizenship and immigration
Three Under-secretaries of state for
    Community and custodial sentences
    Anti-drugs coordination and organised crime
    Europe, community and race equality
Four Parliamentary private secretaries

Ministers at work

Ministers have two main roles. They are MPs, elected politicians with duties in Cabinet and Parliament. They are also administrators of large Whitehall departments consisting of civil servants (officials).

As politicians, they have their normal constituency duties as a MPs, but as ministers this will involve them also in speaking in the House of Commons in debates, appearing before the relevant select committee, taking their turn at the Despatch Box in Question Time and piloting any legislation through the House concerning the department. Of course, also as politicians, they are in the Cabinet if they are senior party figures. Here, they will argue the case for their department in any issues that arise and take part in more general discussions of government policy.

As heads of a Whitehall department, their role is to supervise and take a keen interest in the work being done – managers who take responsibility and who take the key decisions. In theory, they listen to the advice put before them and uses their judgement – in practice, in a large department such as the Home Office, they perhaps decide only 10–15 per cent of the vast array of issues that come up. But they need to ensure that they run a smooth, well-oiled machine, have competent people on whom they can rely and be vigilant to see that they are getting the best advice.

Since the creation of new agencies under the **Next Steps programme** in the 1990s, the areas of policy-making and implementation in government departments have been separated in the cause of efficiency. This has reduced a minister's direct responsibility for what happens in whole areas of government work. Although ministers answer in the Commons on matters covered by an agency, the day-to-day management of such enterprises is left to chief executives, who take a share of responsibility for what happens.

Senior civil servants at work

The senior civil servants, often known as higher civil servants, comprise around 800 leading officials. Only this group will really be involved in working with ministers on policy, and the number likely to have much direct contact with them on a typical day will be considerably smaller than that figure.

At the head of the civil servants in each department is the *Permanent Secretary*, below whom will be the deputy and assistant secretaries (of course, some senior civil servants will now be working in agencies; these are said to be detached from the process of policy-making, although some senior officials are involved in offering guidance to the chief executive on advice which should be given to ministers).

The role of those core higher civil servants who work in Whitehall is concerned with:

- Preparing legislation, drawing up answers to parliamentary questions and briefing the minister.
- Administration – overseeing and carrying out the daily work of the department or some part of it. This may involve meeting up with representatives of pressure groups or dealing with difficult, non-routine casework.
- Helping to develop the department's attitudes and work, looking at alternative lines of policy, surveying the advantages and difficulties of these, foreseeing practical problems.

It is the Permanent Secretary whose role is crucial. He or she is a member of the highest grade of the civil service and is the leading official in the department. He or she is responsible to the minister for what goes on and given the minister's involvement in political work, the Permanent Secretary has to direct and supervise most of the department's normal work, perhaps 85–90 per cent of it.

What sort of people become higher civil servants?
Civil servants have been recruited on merit (by passing competitive examinations) since the middle of the nineteenth century. Often, those who were selected for entry were among the brightest and best graduates, with first-class degrees from older and more prestigious universities. However, by the 1960s, academics and commentators increasingly lamented their lack of relevant training and skills, and the narrow and unrepresentative social background from which they emerged. Their ability was not doubted, but the sort of degrees for which they studied (History, the Classics etc.) seemed to be of doubtful relevance to the work they would be doing in Whitehall. Moreover, they lacked experience of the outside world, having gone into the civil service on completion of their academic courses. The 1968 Fulton Report called for changes, so that there might be a movement away from this 'cult of the amateur' in favour of greater professionalism.

Over the last two decades or so, there has been greater effort to ensure that there are more temporary secondments between commerce, industry and Whitehall, and far more recruitment from the private sector. Under the Blair government, an attempt has been made so that there are more shorter and flexible secondments from the civil service into industry, especially civil servants at the junior level who operate outside London.

The persistent bias in favour of public-school students who become Oxbridge graduates has been more difficult to address, although since the early 1990s the issue has been taken more seriously. There has been a broadening of the basis of recruitment with:

- more recruitment of non-Oxbridge universities
- a movement away from arts subjects
- greater scope for women and members of ethnic minorities

It is increasingly considered important that those who advise ministers and influence policy-making should be more representative of the community, although there is still a long way to go before this is be achieved.

Some factors in the minister–civil servant relationship
- '*Ministers decide, civil servants advise.*' This is the classic statement of the relationship, the civil servants being 'on tap, but not on top'.

Box 4.10 The relationships between ministers and their senior civil servants

For many years, academics, journalists, politicians and top officials have engaged in discussion about where power lies in British government, with the politicians or with the bureaucrats who serve them. Much depends on the perspective of those who analyse the relationship.

For our purposes, three views of the relationship can be categorised:

1. *The traditional view*, namely that ministers decide issues in the light of the advice they are given by their civil servants. The officials loyally set out to serve their ministers' wishes, implementing the decisions made. The minister takes the praise or blame for what has been done, for good or ill.
2. *The radical perspective* adopted by critics on the left, which concentrates on the social background and attitudes of powerful civil servants who use their establishment connections and their wiles to frustrate left-wing ministers who want to change the direction of policy in a way that sharply challenges the status quo.
3. *The **New Right** approach* that stresses the way in which establishment civil servants with a vested interest in the expansion of public services are successful in pursuing their own interests and are immune from the market pressures that influence people in business and commerce.

Although they have a different vision and different objectives, non-consensus politicians of the left and right are liable to be frustrated by the way in which the civil service operates and may wish to see changes in Whitehall.

Officials are supposed to be non-partisan and impartial. They are there to serve any government, offering advice and suggestions but allowing the minister – who after all takes responsibility for what goes wrong – to make decisions. It is the minister who is the elected politician, responsible to the House of Commons; he or she has to be able to justify what has been done.

- Ministers are of course transient. They come and go, perhaps serving for a full administration or maybe being moved after a couple of years. By contrast, their officials may have been in the department for a long time and have developed considerable expertise. They become familiar with the realistic range of policy choices available and know the advantages or otherwise of various lines of policy. Their views will reflect a 'departmental view', but this may conflict with the government's or minister's priorities. In this situation there is scope for conflict between them.

Much has been written about 'mandarin power', mandarins being the very senior officials who have close and regular contact with ministers. It is suggested that often, because of their ability, experience and expertise, they exert a powerful influence over what happens in a department, especially over the policies that emerge. Radical commentators and MPs (and prime ministers such as Margaret Thatcher who wanted to 'get things done') are wary of mandarins, seeing them as a conservative force hostile to necessary innovation. At worst, they may frustrate the minister and be obstructive, concealing information. The suspicion is the greater because of their rather privileged public-school, Oxbridge background; some are to be seen in the best gentlemen's clubs in London.

Strong ministers will insist on their policy. It is often said that the first 48 hours will reveal whether ministers will be able to assert their individuality and strength, or whether they will be a pushover, excessively dependent on their officials. At best, there is a constructive relationship between both sides.

The conventions of ministerial responsibility

Ministerial accountability to Parliament has two aspects:

1. The collective responsibility of ministers for the work of the government
2. The individual responsibility for the work of the department they head

Both forms of responsibility are embodied in conventions which cannot be legally enforced. They developed in the nineteenth century and have been widely recognised as important elements of the Constitution ever since. However, in recent decades, they have been much modified in practice, leading some commentators to question whether or not they have the same significance once accorded to them.

Collective responsibility

The convention means that ministers are collectively responsible to the House of Commons for governmental policy. In public, they are required to stick to the agreed cabinet line and stay united. As a nineteenth-century prime minister, Lord Melbourne, once cynically remarked: 'It doesn't matter what we say, as long as we all tell the same story.'

There will be times when cabinet members feel uneasy about what is being proposed and there may be sharp controversy behind closed doors. They have the opportunity to voice their discontent. But when the policy is decided, they either resign because they cannot go along with it, or else they decide they can live with it and agree to stay silent about any reservations. The position was laid down clearly by Lord Salisbury, more than a hundred years ago: 'For all that passes in Cabinet, every member of it who does not resign if absolutely and irretrievably responsible, and has no right afterwards to say that he agreed in one case to a compromise, while in another he was persuaded by his colleagues.'

In recent decades, the policy has been extended downwards, well below cabinet level. All members of the government are bound to back official policy, even though only Cabinet members will have been present at the time of decision. Today, even the lowest rank in the administration, the unpaid Parliamentary Private Secretaries, are expected to 'toe the line'.

The doctrine still has its uses, for it:

- ensures that ministers 'sing from the same hymn sheet' and this helps to make policy clear and coherent
- avoids the confusion that can arise when different members of an administration say different things, as happens sometimes under US administrations.

Yet today, collective responsibility lacks the force it once had and is applied in a way that suits the government of the day. For instance:

- some ministers get round the obligation by leaking their views, perhaps in coded language
- others make speeches containing thinly veiled criticisms of government policy (Michael Portillo under John Major) or express personal views (Peter Mandelson on Europe, under Tony Blair)

- in 1975 Harold Wilson and in 1977 James Callaghan actually allowed ministers to agree to differ on divisive aspects of European policy, in the face of evident disunity.

The convention is liable to be waived when it suits the Prime Minister, which is why some commentators regard it as a 'constitutional myth'. The doctrine purports to make the government responsible to the House of Commons, the implication being that if a serious blunder is committed then the government as a whole is liable to be defeated. Yet governments have survived countless problems and crises from Westland to Iraq and no mass resignation of ministers has occurred. Party discipline ensures that MPs stay loyal in the voting lobbies, so that crises sometimes provide impressive demonstrations of unity (e.g. Westland, 1986).

Individual ministerial responsibility

Individual responsibility refers to the responsibility of each government minister for the work of his or her department. He or she is answerable to the House of Commons for all that happens within it. The positive aspect of this is that MPs know that there is someone to whom they can direct their questions and anxieties about policy, at Question Time, in committees, in debates and privately to MPs. The negative aspect is that thereby civil servants are kept out of the political arena and shielded from controversy, making it possible for any future administration to have confidence in civil service neutrality.

'Responsible' means on the one hand that ministers are required to inform Parliament about the work and conduct of their departments, explaining and if necessary making amends for their own and their officials' actions. They take the praise for what is well done and the blame for what goes wrong. In this sense, answerability and accountability still apply. But 'responsibility' goes further and implies liability to lose office, if the fault is sufficiently serious.

In this second sense, resignations for political or administrative misjudgements and mistakes have in recent decades become extremely unusual. In the nineteenth century, such resignations were not uncommon; few have occurred since the Second World War, notably Dugdale over the Crichel Down affair, Carrington over the outbreak of the Falklands War and Brittan over Westland. Many political blunders and misjudgements and departmental administrative failings are committed, but they go unpunished by the ultimate sanction. Today, whether or not a minister resigns under the convention will depend on his or her support from the party, Prime Minister and cabinet colleagues. If there is prolonged adverse publicity that may be damaging to the government, a resignation is more likely to occur.

In practice, the convention does then not normally apply. Its application has been watered down, for often MPs on the government side rally behind the beleaguered minister. Many commentators are sympathetic to ministers who find themselves in political trouble over an episode in which they had no direct involvement. In the Home Office, which deals with controversial issues that create much public anxiety, the volume of mail received every day is massive. It would be unreasonable to assume that ministers can read it all or know the details of every response sent out in their name. Finally, the creation of Next Step agencies has blurred responsibility. These agencies have a degree of autonomy, so that when a problem occurs – perhaps a mass prison break-out – there is an issue of who is to be held responsible, the head of the Prison Agency (responsible for administration) or the Home Secretary (responsible for the broad lines of policy). In the case of the Parkhurst gaol-break (1995), neither Home Secretary Michael Howard nor Sir Derek Lewis were willing to accept responsibility, each blaming each other.

The doctrine has its uses. First, it guarantees that someone is accountable, in that there is a minister to answer questions. In this way, it facilitates the work of MPs to investigate the grievances and press the claims of their constituents. Second, civil servants are not normally named when any error has occurred, but the knowledge that if they make a misjudgement then their minister will be answerable in the House helps to ensure that they act with care in handling departmental issues. Finally, it facilitates the work of opposition, in that someone has to justify what has been done to those who wish to expose departmental or policy failings.

Why do ministers resign?

Ministerial resignations have not been infrequent under the Major or Blair administrations. Some have been high-profile ones, such as those of Peter Mandelson and David Blunkett. Most of them have little to do with ministers taking responsibility for the work of their department, under the principle of ministerial responsibility. The clearest recent example of such a resignation would be that of Lord Carrington and his ministerial team who resigned after the invasion of the Falklands by Argentina, in 1982. His departure helped forestall probing questions and protect the Prime Minister from criticism. As an honourable man, he was willing to be a sacrificial lamb, a scapegoat who took the blame – even though at the time of the invasion, he was preoccupied with other events in world diplomacy.

Most other recent resignations fall into one of three categories (see Table 4.1):

1. *Personal misconduct.* Resignations have often occurred because of sexual or financial impropriety. Tim Yeo resigned after fathering a 'love-child' (1994) and Ron Davies did the same, having experienced a 'moment of madness' on Clapham Common involving the pursuit of homosexual experiences, which led to an assault (1998). Neil Hamilton left the Major government in disgrace, following financial misconduct (1994). An unusual resignation was that of Allan Stewart, who resigned from the Scottish Office, having waved a pick-axe at anti-road demonstrators (1995).

2. *Political misjudgements and mistakes.* Peter Mandelson resigned after failing to declare receipt of a large loan from a fellow minister to facilitate a house purchase. A potential conflict of interest was involved (1998). He resigned again three years later, after suggestions that he intervened to secure a fast-track passport application for the Hinduja brothers, financiers who contributed generously to the Labour Party. He gave an unclear initial explanation of what had happened, but the resignation probably owed more to his previous record and to the fact that he had many enemies in the party who wished to see his downfall. Estelle Morris quit as Education minister, following a series of departmental failures, although her resignation was ostensibly because of her feelings of inadequacy to shoulder the burdens with which she had to deal (2002). David Blunkett resigned as Home Secretary in December 2004, after an affair in which he had been involved had become a news item. More seriously, he had intervened to fast-track a visa application for his lover's nanny, thereby using his departmental influence to secure a personal favour. Given a 'second chance' of Cabinet office, he continued

Table 4.1 Departed cabinet ministers under the Blair leadership

Minister	Date of resignation	Reason for departure
Ron Davies	October 1998	Quit after 'moment of madness' on Clapham Common
Peter Mandelson, Geoffrey Robinson	December 1998	Loan revelations: Mandelson borrowed from Robinson and did not declare transaction
Peter Mandelson	January 2001	Resigned amid allegations that he was involved in a passport application: subsequently, seemed not to have done anything improper
Stephen Byers	May 2002	Following months of pressure, resigned after his reputation been seriously tarnished by a series of political misjudgements and amid suggestions of a seemingly misleading account of events
Estelle Morris	October 2002	Left saying she did not feel up to the job, bruised by adverse comments in media
Robin Cook	March 2003	Left in protest on the eve of the Iraq war
Clare Short	May 2003	After much hesitation, resigned over Iraq – when the war was over
Alan Milburn	July 2003	Resigned to spend more time at home

Table 4.1 (continued)		
Minister	**Date of resignation**	**Reason for departure**
David Blunkett	December 2004	Collapse of initial support from party and ministerial colleagues, as evidence of a clear paper trail over his lover's nanny's visa application damaged his political credibility
David Blunkett	November 2005	'Mistakes', 'misunderstandings' and unexplained share dealings; alleged conflicts of interest created media frenzy

to attract unwelcome headlines and resigned for a second time in November 2005, having been in breach of ministerial rules.

3. *Policy differences with the government.* On occasion, ministers can no longer support the policy of the Cabinet. Michael Heseltine could not support the pro-American stance of ministers over the sale of Westland helicopters (1986). Robin Cook resigned shortly before the invasion of Iraq (2003), because he felt the policy was dangerous and ill conceived.

The case of Brazil

Brazil has a history of military rule. It has been a practising democracy for just over twenty years, its present constitution dating back to 1988. Like the United States, it operates a presidential system of government. Both countries are large, heavily populated federations. Both are bicameral, with powerful second chambers. However, there is a significant difference between them in the power accorded to the president. As we see below, the powers of the US presidency are restricted and incumbents of the office frequently lament their inability to dominate the political machinery. By contrast, the Brazilian president has a much stronger position, particularly in relation to Congress. Most notably, he or she can:

- issue decrees (regulations having the force of law) for a sixty-day period without prior parliamentary approval and renew them once
- declare bills to be urgent, forcing legislators to act quickly upon them; in some areas of policy, only the president has the power to initiate bills
- propose a budget which is effective on a monthly basis, should Congress fail to pass a budget itself.

Yet in spite of such a range of formal powers, there are difficulties for any president. Congressmen can be surprisingly assertive. They represent a wide range of parties, so that the likelihood is that the president's supporters are in a minority in either chamber. Moreover, because party discipline is very weak (considerably more so than in the United States), members often transfer their loyalties. They cannot be relied upon to maintain their allegiance to the president, forcing him or her to look for informal coalitions of support from issue to issue. Given such difficulties, the Brazilian president, like his US counterpart, can find it difficult to deliver promises made during the heat of an election campaign.

The case of Holland

Holland employs a very proportional method of voting which results in the representation of several small parties. Not surprisingly, governments tend to be coalitions, so that the distribution of ministerial offices by the Prime Minister ('Minister-President') is limited by the often-lengthy bargaining which precedes the formation of a new administration. Once such an administration is formed, leaders are reluctant to conduct any reshuffle for fear of offending a partner in the government, a situation which, in the words of Hague and Harrop[22], makes for 'skilful conciliators, not dashing heroes'.

The style of Dutch government tends to be collegial rather than hierarchical. The fourteen or so members of the Cabinet are given considerable freedom to recruit their own departmental staff and group of personal advisers, rather than have to work with people imposed upon them. This further weakens the Prime Minister's power of appointment, so that he or she is not free to appoint, reshuffle or dismiss colleagues as he or she pleases, nor to take a hand in official appointments.

The result is that 'ministers serve *with* prime ministers, rather than *under* them'. In the age of television, in which 'media visibility grows apace', the Dutch Prime Minister is 'more than a chairperson, but remains far less than a chieftain'.

The case of the USA

Presidential power in the United States has waxed and waned, reflecting considerations of personality and style, circumstances and the limitations and opportunities presented by the office. Historically, Americans have swung back and forth in their views about the sort of president they favour. At times, they demand strong, assertive leadership and admire those incumbents who can provide it. Indeed, most of the highly rated presidents by academics and the rest of the population have been active presidents. Yet within a short period of being on the receiving end of such activism and vigour, there can be a reaction against it. In the words of one writer, Gary Wasserman[23], presidents have walked a thin line between too much and too little power in the White House.

Overall, the presidency has irregularly but vastly grown in power and significance from the limited role accorded it in the Constitution. The key roles that a president fulfils, covering as they do that of chief of state, chief diplomat, commander-in-chief, chief executive, chief legislator and party leader show how broad that power can be, particularly when exercised by a president who wishes to give a strong lead. By the 1960s, Americans seemed willing to accept a vigorous use of presidential power, as activists such as Kennedy and Johnson were willing to introduce a range of presidential initiatives at home and abroad.

Yet the experience of the 1970s illustrates the dilemma to which Wasserman has drawn attention. Following the resignation of Richard Nixon, there was a reaction against the **imperial presidency** of the past decade, as many Americans came to believe that the institution no longer seemed to be subject to adequate constitutional checks and balances. Since then, there has been more talk of the weakness rather than the strength of presidents, who are restrained by a variety of historical, legal and political limitations. Recent commentators have describe the office in such terms as the 'tethered' or the 'constrained' presidency. Back in the early 1960s,

Richard Neustadt[24] had noted that presidential power amounted to 'the power to persuade'. The ability of individual presidents to gain acceptance for their policies is dependent on their skill in selling these policies to other political players in Washington, their use of the media and their ability to control the bureaucracy. By 'going Washington' and 'going public', they have a chance of turning their programmes into political action.

There is an ambivalence about the presidency, to which President Kennedy drew attention: 'The President is rightly described as a man of extraordinary powers. Yet it is also true that he must wield those powers under extraordinary limitations.'

What you should have learnt from reading this chapter

- Executives have a key role in political life for it is members of the government who devise policies in the light of information and advice which they receive, and get them on the statute book. The official executive has the task of implementing the policies which the political executive has devised.

- Because of the expansion of governmental activity in the twentieth century, the powers of the Executive have grown; the chief executive is today far more powerful than one hundred years ago.

- Various circumstances, ranging from television to the new importance of international summitry and overseas visits, have provided political leaders with a new pre-eminence, and they are no longer national leaders alone but also world statesmen.

- Because of these trends, many writers have discerned a trend towards prime ministerial government in Britain and commented on the extent of 'presidential power'. The Prime Minister is indeed very powerful today, but the extent of that power and influence can vary according to the incumbent and the circumstances of the time.

Glossary of key terms

Cabinet government The theory that the Cabinet forms a collective political executive in which each member in theory has an equal influence. All power is vested in the Cabinet, which acts as a constraint upon the power of the Prime Minister. The principle of collective responsibility ensures that the Cabinet either makes or is consulted about all important political decisions. Some commentators claim that Britain has moved away from cabinet government towards a system of 'government by prime minister'.

Collective responsibility The convention or doctrine that requires all ministers to support governmental policy in public or else resign if they cannot do so.

Core executive The complex network of people and institutions which circle around the Prime Minister and Cabinet, including the Cabinet Office, the Prime Minister's Office and the leading civil servants in Whitehall.

Elective dictatorship The term coined by Lord Hailsham to describe the constitutional imbalance in which executive power has increased, only to be curtailed by the people's votes at the next election. In between, a government armed with a strong majority can drive its legislative programme through the House of Commons, helped by strong party discipline.

Imperial presidency A label for the increased authority and decreased accountability of the presidency, at its peak by the late 1960s.

New Right The term used to describe the outlook and policies of Margaret Thatcher in Britain and Ronald Reagan in the USA. They based many of their ideas on those advanced by neo-liberal political economists who urged a reduced role for the state and a market-oriented, laissez-faire approach to economics.

Next Steps programme Named after the short title of the Ibbs Report (1988), which saw the creation of executive agencies as a remedy for management failings and inefficiency within the civil service. The agencies have some managerial autonomy over the service for which they are responsible (e.g. Benefits Agency).

Prime ministerial government The theory that the office of prime minister has become so powerful that he or she now forms a political executive similar to a president. According to Crossman, one of the original advocates of the thesis, cabinet government had passed away, the Cabinet being relegated to becoming only a 'dignified part' of the Constitution. In contrast, the office of prime minister had become a powerhouse, 'the efficient secret of government'. Executive power is therefore concentrated in the hands of the Prime Minister.

Spatial leadership A reference to the way in which some recent US presidents and British prime ministers have tried to remain above the political fray and the problems in which ministers are mired, seeking to detach themselves from the fortunes of the government.

Westland Affair, 1986 A government crisis brought about by the failure of the Westland helicopter company. An American bid was lined up to take over Westland, but Michael Heseltine wanted the Thatcher government to show its support for European initiatives by backing a bid from a European consortium. He felt his views were sidelined, if not ignored. He dramatically walked out of the Cabinet over the failure of the Prime Minister to listen to his viewpoint, feeling that the Cabinet was not being fully consulted.

? **Likely examination questions**

How does do British prime ministers seek to control their Cabinet?

Discuss the view that 'cabinet government' in Britain has been replaced by 'government by prime minister'.

What are the main constraints upon the power of the British Prime Minister?

Discuss the view that modern prime ministers have too much power.

'The power to persuade.' Is this the only real power possessed by a chief executive in a liberal democracy?

Is the principle of the collective responsibility of the Cabinet worth preserving?

'The idea that the British Prime Minister has become a presidential figure like the American imcumbent ignores the substantial differences between the two roles.' Discuss.

 Helpful websites

www.number-10.gov.uk   The Downing Street site

www.cabinet-office.gov.uk/   The Cabinet Office site

 Suggestions for further reading

Useful articles

C. Brady and P. Catterall, 'Inside the Engine Room: Assessing Cabinet Committees', *Talking Politics*, April 2000.

M. Foley, 'Presidential Government in Britain', *Talking Politics* 6:3, 1994.

N. Jackson, 'The Blair Style: Presidential, Bilateral or Trilateral Government', *Talking Politics*, January 2003.

D. Kavanagh, 'Tony Blair as Prime Minister', *Politics Review* 11:1, 2001.

N. McNaughton, 'Prime Ministerial Power', *Talking Politics*, September 2002.

M. Rathbone, 'The British Cabinet Today', *Talking Politics*, September 2003.

M. Smith, 'The Core Executive', *Politics Review* 10:1, 2000.

Useful books

M. Foley, *The Rise of the British Presidency*, Manchester University Press, 1993.

H. Gardner, *Leading Minds*, HarperCollins, 1996. (An exploration of the nature of leadership.)

P. Hennessy, *The Prime Ministers: The Office and its Holders since 1945*, Allen Lane, 2000.

G. Thomas, *Prime Minister and Cabinet Today*, Manchester University Press, 1998.

CHAPTER 5

The Judiciary

Contents

Overview

The independence of the judiciary is regarded as an essential feature of democratic regimes. Because it is autonomous, it has often been regarded as having only peripheral interest for those who study politics. But in recent years, the dividing line between politics and the law has become blurred. Judges have become increasingly significant actors in the political system. Their greater willingness to concern themselves with issues affecting public policy has aroused disquiet among some elected politicians who see their policy-making role as being under threat.

In this chapter, we examine the political significance of the courts and the role of judges in commenting on and resolving political issues.

Key issues to be covered in this chapter

- The independence of the judiciary in theory and practice
- The notion of judicial neutrality
- The functions of the judiciary
- The impact of judicial review on the political process
- The effectiveness of judges in protecting civil liberties
- The increasingly political role of judges in politics
- Disquiet about the background and outlook of judges
- The cases of the European Court, the United States and dictatorships across the world

Judicial independence

The judiciary is the branch of government responsible for the adjudication of law and the arbitration between parties in any legal dispute. The term includes those individuals and bodies (primarily judges and the courts) which administer and interpret the meaning of laws.

In many states, the constitution provides for an independent judiciary. Its existence is a fundamental characteristic of **liberal democracies. Judicial independence** implies that there should be a strict separation between the judiciary and other branches of government. It is expected that the judicial system will be autonomous, able to function freely and without any interference from the government of the day. It is in regard to the independence of the judiciary that the key differences between authoritarian and liberal states become clear.

The degree of independence of judges from political interference varies from country to country, and even within a single country's history. In some parts of the non-Western world, there is a strong independent judiciary. India has generally retained the high standards of a judicial system put in place in the days of the colonial era. In Turkey, the constitutions of 1968 and 1982 'provided entrenched security of tenure for judges and prosecutors'. However, in several other states the judiciary is under constant pressure to deliver verdicts acceptable to the regime and those who exhibit a passion for justice can find themselves under considerable pressure.

Judicial independence in Britain

Lord Denning described the independence of the judiciary as 'the keystone of the **rule of law** in England' . . . It is the only respect in which we make any real separation of powers.' For politicians to interfere in issues before the courts would be seen as an affront to the idea of the rule of law. Yet in the way that judges have traditionally been appointed, there is room for doubt. According to John Griffiths[1], 'the most remarkable thing about the appointment of judges is that it is wholly in the hands of politicians'.

The independence of the British judiciary is supposed to be protected in three ways:

1. the way in which judges are selected
2. their security of tenure
3. their political neutrality.

In Britain, there is an additional protection. There is a tradition that the remarks and sentences of judges in court cases should not be subject to parliamentary debate or criticism. In the words of Lord Hailsham[2], parliamentary criticism was 'subversive of the independence of the judiciary'. Those involved in court proceedings – judges, juries, lawyers, witnesses and the accused – are all granted immunity from the laws of defamation for any comments made in court. Finally, judges receive fixed salaries that are not subject of parliamentary approval.

This tradition is on occasion breached. In the miners' strike (1984–5), a Labour MP was suspended from the House, on account of his reference to 'tame Tory judges'. Subsequently, some right-wing politicians, particularly in the Thatcher and Major eras, were much irked by the observations of certain judges and especially by the allegedly lenient sentences they imposed. They made their views known in the House of Commons.

The selection of judges

The recruitment of judges should not be influenced by political considerations or personal views. It should be done on the basis of merit or by popular choice. In practice, there are three main methods of selection: appointment, co-option by other judges and popular election (see Table 5.1).

The appointment of judges in Britain

At the beginning of the twentieth century, judges were appointed by the Lord Chancellor as a means of rewarding those who had provided political services. But since the days of Lord Haldane (Lord Chancellor), political allegiance has been relatively unimportant and merit (appropriate legal and professional qualities) has been paramount. Today, judges are still appointed by the government of the day. The most senior judges are appointed by the Prime Minister

Table 5.1 The recruitment of judges: a summary

Method	Examples	Merits or otherwise
Appointment	Practised in most countries, especially for senior judges (e.g. in Britain . . . and in appointments to the American Supreme Court).	Provides opportunity to choose people on basis of merit. Many of those selected have, at some time, had to pass examinations in order to demonstrate their abilities, before they can be considered for service. At best, it is possible to appoint judges from a wide variety of backgrounds. The dangers are that appointment becomes a means of rewarding relatives and friends (nepotism) and that people are chosen not according to their judicial merit but rather for their political leanings and known views on matters of public life such as the appropriate scope of state intervention in economic and social life (partisanship).
Co-option	Italy, Turkey	Good means of ensuring judicial independence, but may produce a judiciary out of touch with popular opinion – especially given the backgrounds and outlooks of many judges.

Table 5.1 (continued)		
Method	Examples	Merits or otherwise
Popular election	Some US states, such as Georgia	Judges are more responsive to the prevailing state of public opinion, and – in some cases – are liable to use of the **recall**. No guarantee that able, competent justices will be chosen. As Lord Taylor[3] observed some years ago: 'You wouldn't want the election of someone who was going to operate on your brain; you would want someone chosen because he knows what he's doing'. Moreover, those elected may feel unduly beholden to those who nominated them as candidates or to the majority of voters who favoured them. Minorities may not get a fair deal in states dominated by one party.

following consultation with the Lord Chancellor. High court judges, circuit judges and magistrates are appointed by the Lord Chancellor, mostly from the ranks of senior barristers, known as QCs (Queen's Council). He receives advice from the Judicial Appointments Commission, which scrutinises candidates for the judiciary and makes recommendations to the Lord Chancellor, but the final choice still rests with him. Since 1994, the Lord Chancellor's department has openly advertised for district and circuit judges, in the hope that this might broaden the range of candidates for consideration.

The appointment of judges is an important duty. If a prime minister has a long innings in office, it may be significant in determining the overall membership of the Bench. By the time of her departure, Margaret Thatcher had appointed all but one of the law lords and all of the lord justices of appeal. Appointments may be made on merit, but they can be contentious. There was press speculation that she had made Lord Donaldson Master of the Rolls, because of his political affiliations. In the Major years, some right-wing Conservatives were reported to be anxious about the appointments of Lord Bingham (Lord Chief Justice) and Lord Woolf (Master of the Rolls), because of their outspoken and often critical views on issues such as sentencing policy. Moreover, on occasion, there have been worries that judges chosen to hear politically sensitive cases have been selected for their known leanings.

Box 5.1 The hierarchy of judges in Britain

There are several categories of judges who preside over British courts. At the apex of the hierarchy is the Lord Chancellor. In his judicial capacity, he is effectively the 'top judge', responsible for the whole civil law and legal aid systems, and for many judicial appointments. As a member of the House of Lords (he is also its speaker), he may participate in the most important appeal cases that it handles. In this capacity, he is supported by up to eleven law lords. Each of these judges may deliver a separate judgement, the verdict being determined by a majority.

Below the Lord Chancellor are the Lord Chief Justice, who heads the Criminal Division of the Court of Appeal, and the Master of the Rolls (i.e. the roll of solicitors), who heads the Civil Division of the Court of Appeal.

The other group that is included within the ranks of the senior judges are those who sit in the High Court. All of the senior judges are chosen from barristers of at least ten years' experience.

Below them are circuit judges who sit in the crown courts, then the recorders (part-time judges) and at the bottom of the hierarchy are the magistrates (justices of the peace), lay people rather than trained lawyers.

However, new arrangements were announced by the Lord Chancellor in mid-2003 and became law in the **Constitutional Reform Act** passed two years later. A new Judicial Appointments Commission will look at the way in which judicial appointments are made. A key issue was whether or not it would have the power to make appointments or merely to advise on them (or perhaps to make more junior appointments and advise on more senior ones). At the time of writing (May 2005), the exact way in which the Commission will operate is unclear. It would seem that the Commission will put forward nominations, there being clear restrictions on the ability of the Lord Chancellor to reject them. For appointments to the new Supreme Court, the minister should receive only one name from the Commission. This solution owed much to Lord Falconer[4], the Secretary of State for the new Department of Constitutional Affairs. He was keen that the new judicial body should be accountable to the government of the day, which must have a stake in appointments 'so that it could defend them from the media'.

The security of tenure of judges

Once installed in office, judges should hold their office for a reasonable period, subject to their good conduct. Their promotion or otherwise may be determined by members of the government of the day, but they should be allowed to continue to serve even if they are unable to advance. They should not be liable to removal on the whim of particular governments or individuals. In some cases, they may serve a fixed term of office. They usually remain in position for many years. US supreme court judges normally serve for a very long period, although theoretically they may be removed by impeachment before Congress if they commit serious offences.

In Britain, the Act of Settlement (1701) established that judges be appointed for life. They are very hard to remove and serve until the time of their retirement. Today, those who function in superior courts are liable to dismissal on grounds of misbehaviour. This can be done only after a vote of both Houses of Parliament and has not actually happened in the twentieth and twenty-first centuries. Neither are lower judges normally dismissed. Dismissal only applies in cases of dishonesty, incompetence or misbehaviour. In 1983, one judge was dismissed for whisky smuggling!

Judicial neutrality (see also Box 5.3)

By convention, judges are above and beyond politics, apolitical beings who interpret but do not make the law. As such, their discretion is limited. But such a view is naive and a series of distinguished British judges from Denning to Devlin, from Radcliffe to Reid, have acknowledged that their role is much more creative than mere interpretation. This is because, apart from their work in relation to sentencing criminals, judges are involved in passing judgement in numerous cases relating to areas such as governmental secrecy, industrial relations, police powers, political protest, race relations and sexual behaviour. They are not simply administering the law in a passive way; there is much potential for them to make law as they interpret it.

In fulfilling their role, judges are expected to be impartial, and not vulnerable to political influence and pressure. They are expected to refrain from partisan activity and generally have refrained from commenting on matters of public policy. The 1955 **Kilmuir Guidelines** urged them to silence since 'every utterance which he [a judge] makes in public, except in the actual performance of his judicial duties, must necessarily bring him within the focus of criticism'. The Guidelines were later relaxed, but Lord Hailsham as Lord Chancellor in the early Thatcher years was keen to see their spirit observed. His Conservative successor, Lord Mackay, was sympathetic to a more relaxed approach, allowing judges to give interviews. More recently, in a greater spirit of openness, senior judges have been willing to express their views on public policy, although this is not to ally themselves with backing for one party.

The separation of judges from the political process is not quite as clear cut as the concept of an independent judiciary might suggest. Some holders of judicial office also have a political role, among them the Lord Chancellor, the Attorney General and the Solicitor General. Although they are supposed to act in a non-partisan manner in their judicial capacity, at times this can be difficult. The legal advice given to the Blair government by the Solicitor General over the legality of the decision to send troops into Iraq concerned a sensitive issue that has become more controversial in the light of subsequent revelations, with suggestions that he leaned over backwards to support the ministerial case for intervention.

In other ways too, judges may find themselves caught up in political controversy. They may be asked by the Prime Minister to chair important inquiries and make recommendations for future action. Lord Hutton was asked to inquire into the death of David Kelly, the former weapons inspector who committed suicide in 2003 after suggestions that the 'September dossier' arguing the case for military action against Iraq had been 'sexed up'. Sometimes, the findings of such inquiries are contentious and inspire criticism of the judge involved. Hutton was accused of producing a report that 'whitewashed' the Blair administration whilst heaping blame upon the journalist Andrew Gilligan and the BBC.

The reason why judges should remain politically neutral is clear. If they make a partisan utterance, it is felt that this would undermine public confidence in their impartiality. They need to be beyond party politics and committed to the pursuit of justice. Yet in practice there are real doubts as to whether judges can ever be completely neutral, for all members of the Bench have their own leanings and preferences. Because of such considerations, the issue of judicial neutrality has aroused much academic and political controversy.

By the nature of the role they perform, judges are expected to be somewhat detached from society. By virtue of their calling and training, they are likely to possess an innate caution and a preference for order. Not surprisingly, they are often seen as conservative and out-of-touch in their approach. There have been many examples when this has been the case, particularly in the United States in the 1930s. The nine supreme court justices disliked legislation that was intended to broaden the scope of governmental action. Key parts of the New Deal programme that had been enthusiastically endorsed by the electorate were struck down by the elderly judges who disliked measures that strengthened federal control.

Critics of the judiciary go further and allege that the social background of judges presents a subtle threat to the notion of judicial independence. In many liberal democracies the type of person appointed to judicial office tends to be middle class and affluent. As such, they are not representative of the society in which they operate. It is quite possible that their attitudes are unlikely to reflect those prevalent in society.

The background of judges in Britain

Many judges reached their eminence having practised at the Bar, the membership of which has long been held to be elitist and unrepresentative. As a result of the manner of selection (see pp. 158–62) and the choice available, judges were usually born into the professional middle classes, and often educated at public school and then Oxbridge. They tended to be wealthy, conservative in their thinking, middle-aged when first appointed (in their sixties before they attain a really powerful position in the House of Lords or Court of Appeal) and – like so many people in 'top' positions in British life – out of touch with the lives of people from different backgrounds. Observers sometimes complain that they are unable to understand the habits and terminology of everyday life, reflecting instead the social mores of thirty or forty years ago. They questioned the appropriateness of such persons to operate at a time of highly politicised argument on issues of human rights and civil liberties.

In an update of his original study, *Anatomy of Britain*, Anthony Sampson[5] has concluded that the social background of judges 'has changed less than that of senior civil servants or even diplomats'. Officially, there is no regard to gender, race, religion, sexual orientation or political affiliation in appointing judges, but the choice when making a senior judicial appointment is in practice extremely limited, often to a handful of candidates. His research illustrated the exclusiveness of the judiciary:

- 90 per cent of the judiciary were public school/Oxford or Cambridge educated
- their average age was 60
- 95 per cent were men
- 100 per cent were white.

With regard to the law lords at the time when Sampson was writing his revised version, all of them were male, educated at Oxford or Cambridge, half of them from three colleges that have a traditional reputation as 'nurseries for lawyers'. Only one of those educated in England had not attended a public school. Sampson acknowledged that they were persons of 'mostly original thinking, more liberal-minded and thoughtful than most earlier Law Lords, with a strong instinct for independence . . . But [they] could not claim to represent,

Box 5.2 The reputation of British judges

Back in 1936, Lord Chief Justice Hewart told a gathering at the Lord Mayor's Banquet that: 'Her Majesty's judges are satisfied with the almost universal admiration in which they are held.' The remark was criticised by one of his successors, Lord Taylor, in his 1992 *Dimbleby lecture* on 'The Judiciary in the Nineties': 'To our ears, such remarks sound breath-takingly arrogant and complacent'. Taylor recognised that the public perception of judges then fell far below that assumed by Hewart, the more so after a series of cases of miscarriage of justice had resulted in innocent persons being convicted and sentenced to several years in custody.

Some comments by judges on issues of gender and race caused controversy in the 1970s–80s, such as the suggestion by Lord Denning that blacks should not serve on British juries because of their 'alien' cultural backgrounds. But the most public controversy has been generated by cases involving rape or attempted rape. Comments by judges included the following examples:

Women who say no do not always mean no. If she does not want it, she only has to keep her legs shut and she would not get it without force and there would be marks of force being used.

It is probably that this girl would have been less severely injured if in fact she had submitted to rape by the mere threat of force rather than force being applied in the manner that it was.

There is some evidence to substantiate public concerns of judges being 'out of touch' with the mood and language of the day: during a murder trial, Lord Donaldson famously asked for an answer to his question, 'What is snogging?'.

Such comments were made a generation ago. More optimistic observers would suggest that judges' attitudes have to some extent changed in the light of the spirit of the age.

or know about, a wide section of the British population and most of them were candidates from a similar background to their predecessors of forty years ago.' The average age in mid-2003 was just over 68.

Since then, there has been a breakthrough in one respect. One of the last all-male bastions of the British establishment admitted a woman for the first time. The UK's first woman law lord, Lady Brenda

Hale, was previously a judge in the Court of Appeal. A former academic and specialist in divorce and the law on children, she argues that a more diverse and reflective judiciary will make a difference to how judging is carried out. She becomes one of the twelve members of the proposed new supreme court. Belatedly, Britain has followed the example of Australia, Canada, New Zealand and the United States, all of whom have had women judges in their highest courts. However, critics of the composition of the judiciary can continue point to the lack of female and ethnic-minority judges on the Appeal or High Court, and their serious under-representation on the Circuit Bench, as Table 5.2 highlights.

The Left in Britain has long been critical of judges and wary of the power they exercise. Throughout much of its history, many in the Labour movement have felt that their party has suffered from the decisions made by those on the Bench, particularly in the area of industrial relations. The most famous example of such treatment was the Taff Vale case at the turn of the twentieth century, in which the right of the unions to take strike action was seriously restricted. In the 1980s, a number of **sequestration** cases were heard, in which union funds were taken away as a result of judicial decisions. But the suspicion has not arisen solely as a result of the unfavourable verdicts that judges have often delivered to the Labour movement. It derives from a feeling that their judgements in court are influenced by their backgrounds, attitudes and methods of selection. In other words, they are biased.

This view was expressed in a Labour document entitled *Manifesto*[6] produced some twenty years ago: '[of judges] Their attitude to the political and social problems of our time is shaped and determined by their class, their upbringing and their professional life – their attitude is strongly conservative, respectful of property rights and highly authoritarian.' Other left-wing writers have suggested that in cases involving official secrecy, the performance of Labour councils and trade unions, the partiality of judges is evident. In their view, the nature of judicial backgrounds and the conservatism of their attitudes undermine the idea of judicial neutrality.

The most frequently quoted attack on the characteristics of judges was made by John Griffiths[7]. In his words, judges, 'by their education and training and the pursuit of their profession as barristers, acquire

Table 5.2 The representation of women and ethnic minorities on the Bench

Rank	Overall number	No. of women	% of women	No. of ethnic minority	% of ethnic minority
Lords of appeal in ordinary	12	1	8.33	0	0
Heads of division	5	1	1.20	0	0
Lord justices of appeal	37	2	5.40	0	0
High court judges	109	9	8.25	0	0
Circuit judges	632	65	10.28	9	1.42
Recorders	1,346	178	13.22	56	4.20
Recorders in training	49	14	28.60	49	12.24
District judges	434	92	21.20	14	3.20
Deputy district judges	797	186	23.34	20	2.50
District judges in magistrates court	126	33	22.30	4	3.17
Deputy district judges in magistrates court	148	25	19.80	11	7.40
Overall total	3,695	606	16.40	163	4.41

NB Figures adapted from those provided by the Department for Constitutional Affairs, as of 1 October 2004

a strikingly homogeneous collection of attitudes, beliefs and principles which to them represent the public interest'. He complains that
in exercising their discretion, judges rather assume that the public
interest favours law and order and the upholding of the interests of
the state, over any other considerations. His critique suggests that
judges are more willing to defend property rights than wider human
rights or personal liberties:

> They cannot be politically neutral because . . . their interpretation of
> what is in the public interest and therefore politically desirable is
> determined by the kind of people they are and the position they hold
> in our society: [and because] their position is part of established
> authority and so is necessarily conservative, not liberal.

According to this view, the backgrounds and attitudes of judges make
them unsympathetic to – indeed, biased against – minorities, especially strident ones, and hostile to ideas of social progress. Militant
demonstrators have often received harsh words and stiff punishments
from judges who dislike the causes and methods with which strikers
and others are associated.

The allegations of gender and social exclusivity, if not so much
those of political bias, made by Griffiths have been taken up by many
commentators and also by government ministers.

Is the attack on the background and character of British judges fair?

By virtue of their training, notions of restraint, caution, restriction,
respect for property and family, and obedience for law, come naturally
to judges. They have often revealed a leaning towards conventional
moral values, ones that are congenial to many members of the
Conservative Party – and probably to many Labour supporters as
well. In this sense, if the decision is not strictly determined by the
legal/factual material available to them, they decide cases on the basis
of values that are generally conservative, and their decisions may
have ideological overtones. There is no such thing as an absolutely
neutral decision.

The nature of their social backgrounds and professional training
are likely to incline them in a particular way. But it does not follow
that because people come from a certain type of social background

that they must all be biased in a particular direction. It is easy to make sweeping generalisations about judges and their behaviour. They are not a homogeneous group. There is a range of judges operating in different courts and at different levels, and if the Griffiths critique stresses their homogeneity so too the writings of Drewry[8] and Lee[9] have emphasised their diversity.

In any case, a generally privileged background does not necessarily render a judge biased in outlook or open to the allegation of possessing conservative opinions. Lee has suggested that an examination of the actual record of judges at work indicates that the attack on judicial neutrality is an unfair one. He makes the point that if historically judges have decided against trade unionists, it may not be because of their alleged conservatism but rather because, on the occasions concerned, the unions were behaving wrongly according to the law as laid down at the time.

Moreover, judges develop their outlook after their appointment. Whatever their background, their views are likely to evolve in the light of their experience. After some years of service, the tenor of their decisions cannot always be predicted on the basis of their class, education and training. Budge et al.[10] quote the example of a decision delivered by the late Lord Hailsham in the House of Lords in 1997. Here was an 'unambiguously political' judge who on occasion was more than willing to go against the grain. In giving a judgement in a case in which a woman was being prosecuted for breaking regulations governing over-crowding in boarding houses (though actually she was running a refuge for battered wives), he observed that:

> This appellant . . . is providing a service for people in urgent and tragic need. It is a service which in fact is provided by no other organ or our much vaunted system of public welfare . . . When people come to her door, not seldom accompanied by young children in desperate states and at all hours, because, being in danger, they cannot go home . . . the appellant does not turn them away . . . And what happens when she does? She finds herself the defendant in criminal proceedings . . . because she has allowed the inmates of her house to exceed the permitted maximum, and to that charge, I believe, she has no defence in law.

Hailsham then cast his vote against the side he undoubtedly favoured, because he felt constrained by precedent or duty. In this case, the law

Box 5.3 Judicial independence and judicial neutrality: being clear about the terms

Judicial independence and judicial neutrality are linked but distinct concepts. They combine to ensure justice, in the sense that disputes are settled in a fair and impartial manner. This implies, among other things, that the judiciary is able to uphold the rule of law and to protect individual rights and liberties, by avoiding becoming the creature of government or a legal defence for privileged and propertied groups.

Judicial independence has been described by Lord Denning[13] as 'the keystone of the rule of law in England . . . It is the only respect in which we make any real separation of powers.' It refers to the capacity of judges to resist political pressure from other branches of government. The judiciary is largely separate and distinct from them, in accordance with Montesquieu's theory, although the holder of the office of Lord Chancellor (now under review) is anomalous, as a party politician who sits in the Lords and is a member of the Cabinet.

Judicial independence is maintained by the fact that judges enjoy security of tenure and cannot easily be removed from office, even when their opinions become hostile to ministers. The conventions surrounding the parliamentary criticism of judges also help to protect them from undue political interference. The autonomy of the legal profession from political institutions and that the government does not train judges are also relevant.

However, the fact that judges are appointed by the Lord Chancellor (an office that is itself a political appointment in the hands of the Prime Minister) – admittedly after receiving advice – could be said to be an infringement of the idea of independence. Indeed, Griffiths[14] laments that 'the most remarkable thing about the appointment of judges is that it is wholly in the hands of politicians'. It is a defect currently being corrected.

Judicial neutrality is a necessary condition of judicial independence. It assumes equality before the law, that all persons can expect equal consideration of their case and be treated in the same way unless there are specific circumstances that mean they should be treated differently. Judges set aside any personal bias and issues of social background as they interpret the law. In this way, decisions can be taken objectively and disputes settled fairly and impartially, on solely legal grounds.

Judicial neutrality is guaranteed in several ways, notably that:

- judges are not expected to take any active, public role in party politics

- law lords are not expected to join the fray in debating contentious party political issues
- (in court) judges should follow points of law and confine themselves to the detail of the case
- if there are reasons to doubt the validity of judgements delivered, they can be challenged under the rules of appeal
- in some cases, there are other courts to which a person can go to seek redress (e.g. a decision in a case involving civil liberties may go to the Court of Appeal and then the House of Lords: it could ultimately end up in the Court of Human Rights in Strasbourg
- the watchful eye of the media: in the case of the extradition hearing of General Pinochet by the law lords, one of the five judges (Lord Hoffman) was revealed to be prominently involved with Amnesty International. The hearing had to be held again, with a replacement for him.

Are judges neutral?

On the whole, they do behave in as neutral manner as can reasonably be expected. Whatever the fears of the left about its treatment in some past cases and the views expressed by Griffiths and others, in the developing climate of judicial activism there is a greater willingness to take on government ministers. Indeed, it could even argued that the situation has changed from one in which judges were seen as anti-left to one in which they are seen as anti those in authority, challenging their decisions in several important areas. The issue of judicial review and the public statements made by senior law officers are important evidence of this trend.

was clear. Often it is not and here judges do have a wider variety of discretion. As we have seen, in a sense, the judiciary as an institution in every society, whatever the background of its members, is bound to be conservative, since its task is to maintain order and the stability of the state, This implies respect for precedents, history and the established way of doing things.

There has been in recent years a new breed of judges who are in no way anti-left, but much more willing to challenge government power. As we examine below (see judicial review), they are more willing to take on ministers and criticise their attitudes and approach. As Lord Taylor[11], the Lord Chief Justice who found himself in open disagreement with Conservative Home Secretary Michael Howard, has written: 'the suggestion that judges are biased towards the Establishment does not stand up to examination'. It is true that in the Blair era, Labour has again found itself under attack from the judges, but this has been precisely because it is judges who have been arguing the civil libertarian case on issues such as jury reform, official secrecy and sentencing policy, among other things. In 2002, Lord Woolf[12] argued that in the light of recent asylum cases, the judiciary had an important role in defending individual rights, given a tendency by government to override them.

There has been an attempt to widen the professional and social background of the judiciary in recent years. This process was carried further in October 2004 by the announcement from the Department for Constitutional Affairs that it was examining the issue of judicial diversity. It produced a consultation paper setting out proposals on how the judiciary of England and Wales can be made more reflective of society today, whilst ensuring that merit remained the basis of appointment. It is looking to identify the barriers that deter able candidates from wishing to become judges and to find ways of solving or minimising these problems in order to widen the pool of applicants for judicial appointment.

Functions of judiciaries

The judiciary is the branch of government that is responsible for the adjudication of law and therefore of arbitration between parties to a legal dispute. As the key figures in the judiciary, judges perform several functions:

- They peacefully resolve disputes between individuals, adjudicating in controversies within the limits of the prescribed law.
- They interpret the law, determining what its means and how it applies in changing circumstances.
- They uphold the will of the legislature, acting as guardians of the law, taking responsibility for applying its rules without fear or favour, as well as securing the liberties of the person and ensuring that governments and peoples comply with the 'spirit' of the constitution.

- They have responsibility for **judicial review** of particular laws and administrative actions particularly in states with a codified constitution.
- Senior judges may be asked to chair inquiries.
- If they are law lords, they sit in Parliament, contributing to its debates on public policy and sharing in the various tasks performed by the House of Lords.

The growing importance of judicial review

Judicial review is a key function of the courts. It refers to the power of the courts to interpret the constitution and to declare void actions of other branches of government if they are deemed to be in conflict with its requirements. Some countries have a very strong system of judicial review – Canada, Germany, India, Italy, Norway and Switzerland among them. The doctrine is common in Latin American states and is particularly important in federal systems. In the United States, it is the job of the Supreme Court to ensure that each layer of government keeps to its respective sphere and to settle any dispute that arises between them. It rules on constitutional matters in the same way that it has the final say on other legal issues.

Judicial review in Britain (see also pp. 50–1)
In Britain, there is no equivalent to the American Supreme Court, which can strike down legislation as unconstitutional. The task of judicial review has not until relatively recently been viewed as a feature of the courts. No court has declared unconstitutional any act lawfully passed by the British Parliament, the sovereign law-making body.

Yet, particularly since the 1980s, statistics indicate that there has been an increasing resort to the process of judicial review. The number of annual applications for permission to seek judicial review increased rapidly from the 1980s onwards, rising from around 500 in the early 1980s to nearly 4,000 by the late 1990s. (Many more applications for judicial review are initiated, but difficulties in obtaining legal aid and the High Court's refusal to grant leave for review, rule them out of consideration.) About a third of these cases refer to actions taken by local authorities, around a quarter by government departments. Lord Woolf[15] has noted that many of those involving a department fail, perhaps some ten for every one that is lost. What makes the news is because those that succeed are high-profile cases of political significance. They get the headlines.

The scale of increase has been made to appear more dramatic than it is, because of its concentration in two particular areas, immigration especially and homelessness. Beyond these two areas, the rate of growth has been much less apparent, which is in some ways surprising. Figures for cases involving the two contentious areas of the treatment of prisoners and entitlement to social welfare provision have remained low, perhaps because the victims of mistreatment have other means of remedy, such as tribunals, which they find successful, or more likely because they are unfamiliar with the processes of going to law, cannot afford to seek the advice of lawyers and lack the vigour to see a complex case through to a conclusion.

The Home Office is the department that has been most challenged in the British courts, attracting as it does some three-quarters of all challenges to government decisions. In the 1990s under the Major government, there were several cases involving the then Home Secretary, Michael Howard, who was found to have acted unlawfully in a number of cases. It was judged that he had wrongly delayed referring the cases of IRA prisoners to the parole boards and had failed to give a cult leader, the Rev. Sun Myung Moon, a chance to make representations before his exclusion from Britain. Under the Labour government there have been many more cases in which the verdict has gone against the minister. Often, they have involved issues of immigration and the rights of asylum seekers. Some Labour ministers have felt impelled to lament in public their concern about the activities of the courts in scrutinising government actions and striking them down with the regularity with which they do. Paul Boateng[16] pointed out that 'the judges' job is to judge, the government's job is to govern'. At various times, then Home Secretary David Blunkett accused judges of routinely rewriting the laws that Parliament had passed and bluntly made it clear that he did not agree with their findings.

Judicial review in Britain is a weaker doctrine than in the more usual continental and American experience. There is no written constitution against which the constitutionality of actions and decisions can be judged. Whereas elsewhere, the principle enables the judiciary to review and strike down decrees, laws and actions of government that are incompatible with the constitution, in Britain it means the right to determine whether the Executive has acted beyond its powers. It enables judges to assess the constitutionality of executive actions in the light of ordinary laws, using the doctrine of **ultra vires**. This is a much narrower and more limited version of judicial review, enabling the courts to declare the actions of ministers unlawful, but not allowing them to question the validity of the law itself.

The upsurge in cases involving this modest doctrine of judicial review has been striking. It reflects the growing human rights culture in Britain, with many lawyers willing to take up cases to challenge what they regard as the misuse of executive power. Attracting as it does much attention from the media, it has caused embarrassment to a succession of ministers and on occasion resulted in public confrontations between the courts and the politicians. It is an indication of the increasingly political role played by justices. Some politicians view this increase in **judicial activism** (see pp. 178–81 for further elaboration) with considerably anxiety.

The developing trend towards judicial activism

Judicial activism refers to the willingness of judges to venture beyond narrow legal decisions, in order to influence public policy. Its advocates take the view that the courts should be active partners in shaping government policy, especially in sensitive cases such as those affecting asylum, immigration and the rights of detainees in police custody. They argue that they are more interested in justice, in 'doing the right thing', than in observing the exact letter of the text and see a role for the courts in looking after the groups denied political influence, notably the poor and minorities.

Judicial activism has been a feature of recent decades in many parts of the Western world, as judges have become more willing to enter into the political arena. In some cases, judges have discovered hitherto undetected 'implied' rights in a careful reading of the constitution. In the Netherlands, Hague and Harrop[17] point out that although the constitution does not allow for judicial review, the Dutch Supreme Court has developed case law on issues on which Parliament has not legislated, especially in authorising euthanasia. The same writers have noted how the degree of judicial activism varies from country to country. On a least active to most active spectrum, there is a continuum ranging from the United Kingdom, Sweden and France at the least active end to Australia, Canada and the United States at the other.

In the United States, there has long been a conflict between those who subscribe to judicial activism and those whose preference is for the more conservative doctrine of **judicial restraint**. The latter believe that the task of judges is to apply the law and not to wander into wider, interpretative territory. They argue that the courts should limit themselves to adopt a passive approach and implement legislative and executive intentions rather than impose their views on other branches of government.

Judicial activism has been on the increase in many countries, because of:

- the increasing tendency of governments to regulate over new and broader territory, such as laying down new restrictive regulations on asylum seekers and deciding whether or not gay partners should have the same rights as married heterosexual couples. Such moves are contentious and open to challenge in a way that many of the decisions of government a half-century ago were not.
- the greater willingness of people on the political left to use the courts, a reflection of the decline of traditional socialist attitudes according to which judges were seen as defenders of the status quo, deserving of mistrust and suspicion.
- the post-war development of international agreements and conventions that have proclaimed more rights and encouraged the view that state decisions are open to challenge – the European Convention on Human Rights (1950) is an obvious example.
- the response of campaigning activists and media commentators to what they recognise as the growing confidence of judges in proclaiming on wider policy issues. The process is self-reinforcing. The more judges become involved in political decision-making, so too the more rights-conscious groups see scope for use of the courts as a means of redress.

The politicisation of British judges: growing judicial activism

The general political role of British courts has been increasing in recent years. Particularly from the 1980s onwards, judges have become involved in many areas from which they were previously excluded, most notably local–national government relations and industrial relations. In the former, the growth of centralisation under the Thatcher governments left many Labour-controlled local authorities seeking clarification and redress or defending their position in the courts, as their traditional rights were overridden. In the latter, the new corpus of law imposing restraints upon trade union action meant that judges were involved in making decisions on issues such as ballots prior to strike action, secondary picketing and sequestration of assets. If they did not act to extend their interpretative role, they nonetheless were regularly in the business of delivering judgements in accordance with the letter of the law. The print workers' union, SOGAT 82, found itself on the receiving end of financial penalties for a technical breach of the law, without in its view sufficient allowance being made for the special circumstances of the case. Other unions too felt displeased with the treatment they received in the courts.

Yet if the growing political involvement of judges in these cases worked in favour of the Conservative government, this was not to be the case in the following decade. We have seen that the increasing use of judicial review involved judges in conflict with ministers, as did the greater willingness of more European-minded judges to speak out in favour of the incorporation of the European Convention into British law and against ministerial policy on issues such as the sentencing of convicted criminals. The decisions of the Court of Human Rights in Strasbourg against the British government only added to ministerial misgivings during the Major administration, so that by the middle of the decade there was clear hostility between the politicians and the judges. Conservative spokespersons frequently denounced the trend towards increased judicial involvement in political controversies of the day.

Under the Labour government, it might have been anticipated that relations between the Blair administrations and the judges would have been better, given the promising start made by ministers by incorporating the European Convention into British law – in line with much judicial opinion. Yet the passage of the Human Rights Act itself offers the prospect of further politicisation of the judiciary, which could become more embroiled in the political arena, as judges seek to decide on the interpretation and/or validity of a particular piece of legislation. Furthermore, as we have seen, in several cases of judicial review decisions have gone against ministers, and judges at the highest level have been willing to confront publicly the policies pursued on issues such as freedom of information and trial by jury.

There are many politicians and some academics who regret the trend to politicisation of the judiciary. They feel uneasy about unelected judges stepping so boldly into the political arena. They stress that under the British constitutional arrangements, Parliament is the main protector of our liberties. It is a sovereign body and its members alone should make decisions. Because they are elected, politicians need to remain sensitive to the wishes of the voters, whereas judges lack accountability and are seen as a group remote from present-day reality. Ewing and Gearty[18] have asked whether it is

> legitimate or justifiable to have the final political decision, on say a woman's right to abortion, to be determined by a group of men appointed by the Prime Minister from a small and unrepresentative pool . . . Difficult ethical, social and political questions would be subject to judicial preference.

In other words, according to this view, the solution to inappropriate behaviour by the government of the day should be in the polling booth, rather in the courtroom. Politicians should not rely on judges to make difficult decisions and they are inappropriate persons to do so, given their narrow backgrounds and preference towards defending established interests in society.

On the other hand, the division of power between the three branches of government is a means of protecting people from arbitrary government, an antidote to potential tyranny. An independent judiciary is well suited to deciding difficult issues of the day, and if judges are not elected then at least – in the words of one American source – 'they read the returns too'. They are not immune from what goes on in society and can offer a view that commands respect, because of the broad esteem in which judges are held – a greater esteem than that currently enjoyed by politicians as a whole.

On issues relating to the liberties of the people in particular, judges have a role to play. Of necessity, it is a secondary one, in that the Executive has the initiative and introduces law, whereas judges react to them, reviewing them once they are in place. But it is an important role in any modern democracy and an independent judiciary is an appropriate body to exercise it.

Box 5.4 Judges as protectors of our liberties in Britain: some points to bear in mind

Judges protect our liberties well

- Judges always have had a role in interpreting common law and for centuries have been willing to defend the rights of 'freeborn Englishmen' to speak freely.
- Some judges have long shown an interest in the idea of a British Bill of Rights. For several years before the introduction of the Human Rights Act, more European-minded judges such as Lord Scarman were calling for its incorporation into British law. Judges in the Strasbourg Court (the European Court of Human Rights) issued several judgements from the 1970s onwards which enhanced the rights of British people, be they prisoners, victims of corporal punishment in schools or (for older citizens) public beatings on the Isle of Man, those caught up in immigration appeals or detained in the Maze prison.
- More recently, a limited concept of judicial review has been developed in which, if not the policy at least the lawfulness of governmental actions have been found wanting. See the example described on pp. 174–6.
- A number of judges have been willing to criticise aspects of government policy that seem detrimental to civil liberties – for instance, Labour ran into difficulties with its Freedom of Information Bill when it was going through the Lords, and in its attempts to make inroads into the principle of trial by jury. The law lords in the House of Lords ruled against the Home Secretary's right to set minimum tariffs for prisoners serving long-term sentences (November 2002).
- Above all, it is judges who are charged with interpreting the Human Rights Act, now that the European Convention has been

incorporated into British law. It is early days to say how they will exercise their powers, for numerous test cases are before them. But the Act offers a new weapon for aggrieved individuals and much will depend upon how judges react to cases brought under its terms.

Judges cannot be trusted to protect civil liberties

- Some groups in the community have always found judges intolerant on issues of civil liberties, because of their background and legal training, as well as their preference for the status quo. They tend to be intolerant of minorities, especially young protesters, minority activists and others prepared to question existing ideas and values.
- On the left, many would claim that over the last two centuries judges have used their discretion against trade unionists, individually or collectively. The right to strike has sometimes been put at risk by judicial decisions, as over the Tolpuddle Martyrs and Taff Vale.
- Other critics of the judges as protectors of civil liberties claim that they should not be so involved in the task anyway. It is Parliament's task to protect individuals, for MPs are elected to look after their constituents.
- Judges are not as socially representative as many would wish. There ought to be more members of ethnic minorities on the Bench, and more women and younger judges.

The judiciary has seemed increasingly concerned to uphold civil liberties in recent years, with the arrival on the scene of a new and perhaps more progressive body of senior judges in action. Although they have no home-grown British Bill of Rights upon which to base their decisions, the Human Rights Act has equipped them with a new weapon with which to defend the rights of individual citizens. However, it is still the case that a broadening of the recruitment and training of the judges would do much to improve people's faith in their suitability for the task.

The case of the European Court on Human Rights

The European Court in Strasbourg – not to be confused with the Court of Justice, which meets in Luxembourg and is part of the machinery of the European Union – comprises as many judges as there are member states of the **Council of Europe**, currently forty-five. A country can nominate a representative of a non-European state, as did Liechtenstein in 1990 when it selected a Canadian as its choice.

Before the Court considers a case, the country involved must have accepted its compulsory jurisdiction, as almost every signatory has. Written and oral evidence is heard at the hearing, and the judges decide whether a violation of the European Convention has occurred, on the basis of a majority vote. They can award 'just compensation'.

The British record in Strasbourg was for many years a poor one, especially prior to incorporation of the European Convention via the Human Rights Act. Among many other cases involving Britain, the Court criticised treatment of suspected terrorists interned in Northern Ireland, allowed prisoners to correspond with their lawyers and others, upheld the rights of workers not to join a trade union, declared immigration rules to be discriminatory against women and restricted the power of the Home Secretary to lock up under-age killers. Some of these judgements aroused the irritation – indeed anger – of sections of the Conservative right, some of whose members were prepared to contemplate British withdrawal from the Convention.

Although Britain has now incorporated the Convention into British law – and therefore most cases under its articles can be handled in the British courts – there is still the ultimate right of redress in Strasbourg, where many controversial cases are finally resolved. One of the more recent ones relating to the United Kingdom concerned the case of an eleven-year-old boy who had appeared before a Crown Court charged with attempted robbery. Although the trial of *S.C.* v. *the United Kingdom* was conducted in as informal a manner as possible, he was unable to understand fully and participate in the trial, given his low attention span. He had learning difficulties and impaired reasoning skills, and medical reports recommended that he be placed in long-term foster care rather than be given a custodial sentence. Yet he was given two and a half years' detention. The Court of Appeal refused leave to appeal against the verdict.

In this case, the Strasbourg Court found that in spite of the attempts to make the trial informal, the boy had not understood much of what was happening or grasped the fact that he faced a custodial sentence. It judged that he should have been tried in a specialist tribunal where more consideration of his handicaps could have been taken into account. The ruling was that he was unfit to plead and stand trial, to the extent required by Article 6 of the Convention, which lays down the right to a fair trial. By five votes to two, it was determined that a violation of the Convention had occurred and the Court made an award in respect of costs and expenses.

The case of the USA

In America, the highest judicial body, the Supreme Court, is clearly a political as well as a judicial institution. In applying the Constitution and laws to the cases that come before it, the nine justices are involved in making political choices on controversial aspects of national policy. The procedures are legal, and the decisions are phrased in language appropriate for legal experts. But to view the Court solely as a legal institution would be to ignore its key political role. As Chief Justice Hughes[19] once stated: 'We are under the Constitution, but the Constitution is what the judges say it is.'

In interpreting the Constitution, the justices must operate within the prevailing political climate. They are aware of popular feelings as expressed in elements of the media and in election results. They know that their judgements need to command consent, and that their influence ultimately rests on acceptance by people and politicians. This means that the opinions expressed on the Bench tend to be in line with the thinking of key players in the executive and legislative branches, over a period of time. Rulings in one age can be overturned by judgements delivered at another time. This was true of **segregation**. 'Separate but equal' was acceptable in 1896 in the *Plessey* v. *Ferguson* case, but by 1954 it was deemed 'inherently unequal'.

The question of how to use its judicial power has long exercised the Court, and different opinions have been held by those who preside over it. Some have urged an activist Court that enhances individual rights. They believe that the Court should be a key player in shaping policy, an active partner working alongside the other branches of government. Such a conception means that the justices move beyond acting as umpires in the political game, and become creative participants. Chief Justice Earl Warren was an exponent of the philosophy. His court was known for a series of liberal judgements on matters ranging from school desegregation to the rights of criminals. Decisions were made which boldly and broadly changed national policy.

The broadly progressive approach of the Supreme Court in the Warren and – to a lesser extent – Burger eras has come to an end under the leadership of Chief Justice William Rehnquist. More conservative in its membership and tone, his court has made inroads into past liberal decisions, notably on abortion and **affirmative action**. The nine judges have not viewed it as their task to act as the guardian of individual liberties and civil rights for minority groups. As Biskupic[20] puts it: 'Gone is the self-consciously loud voice the Court once spoke with, boldly stating its position and calling upon the people and other institutions of government to follow'. Yet for all the lip-service paid to greater judicial restraint, Yarborrough notes that 'most of the current justices appear entirely comfortable intervening in all manner of issues, challenging state as well as national power, and underscoring the Court's role as final arbiter of constitutional issues'[21].

The cases of dictatorships across the world: degrees of judicial independence

Power in authoritarian states tends to be concentrated in the Executive rather than being spread throughout the political system. The role of the courts is subordinate, although this subordination can be achieved in either of two ways. Ministers can declare a state of emergency in which the pronouncements are exempt from judicial scrutiny, or else make use of special, military courts. Usually, pressure is of a more subtle and indirect character. The notion of an independent judiciary is retained, but those who rule seek to influence the conduct of the judges.

In communist and former communist countries, there is often little direct intimidation of judges. Of course, this may be unnecessary, for in many cases people would not be appointed to their position if they possessed ideas known to be contrary to those of the prevailing regime. In their judgements, they are mindful of the need to help promote party interests and build socialism in a manner acceptable to the regime. In China, decisions hostile to the ruling party are often simply ignored.

Elsewhere, judges are left in no doubt as to what is expected of them. They might be wary of handing out judgements damaging to the regime. Pressure has sometimes been overt, as in Ghana, Nigeria and Indonesia.

Yet once appointed, judges have a habit of donning the clothing of judicial fairness. Even when there are insidious pressures, they can be singularly resistant and willing to offend the ruling administration. In several Latin American states, especially those functioning under civilian rule, judges are noted for taking a strongly liberal and independent line, displeasing to those who exercise political power. In Zimbabwe too, they have been willing to deliver judgements unpopular with the Mugabe regime.

Judicial independence varies widely. In many countries, judges are able to work independently and without fear of undue and improper interference. This is true of some authoritarian regimes, as well as of liberal democracies.

What you should have learnt from reading this chapter

- Courts of law are part of the political process, for governmental decisions and acts passed by the legislative body may require judicial decisions to be implemented. Courts need to be independent to be respected, but this is difficult to achieve in practice. There is never full independence as far as appointment is concerned. Moreover, as Blondel[22] warns, judges cannot be expected 'to go outside the norms of the society'.

- As a broad trend, the role of judges in the political system has increased in liberal democracies but also even in authoritarian societies. Some fear that this political involvement has gone too far and talk of a 'judicialisation' of political life.

- In Britain, senior judges have been more vocal in venting their views on issues of public policy. Recent pronouncements show that they are more than willing to challenge governmental decisions. Well before the passage of the Human Rights Act (a major development in enhancing judicial power), Lord Bingham[23] felt able to write: 'Slowly, the constitutional balance is tilting towards the judiciary. The courts have reacted to the increase in the powers claimed by government by being more active themselves.'

- Anxiety about the nature and politicisation of the judiciary has been voiced by several commentators and politicians. Lord Lloyd[24] is less concerned than many critics about the backgrounds from which judges are chosen, their competence or their capriciousness in adjudication. For him, Parliament – comprising the elected MPs – should decide on whether abortion or capital punishment is permissible, and what the age of consent should be: 'The fact of the matter . . . is that the law cannot be a substitute for politics. The political decisions must be taken by politicians. In a society like ours, that means by people who are removable.'

- Others emphasise their fear of judicial power. They are concerned that judges are unrepresentative and argue for a reformed judiciary.

Glossary of key terms

Affirmative action Policies and actions designed to compensate for the effects of past discrimination, by giving preferences to specified ethnic and gender groups.

Constitutional Reform Act A statute that signifies the most important shake-up in the relations between the judiciary and executive for many years. Passed after a stormy ride in Parliament, it provides for the creation of a new supreme court which takes over the judicial work of the House of Lords; for a new Judicial Appointments Commission to replace the Lord Chancellor's role in appointing judges; and for an amended position of Lord Chancellor under which he or she will give up the duties of Speaker of the House of Lords and perform a reduced role in relation to the judiciary. From now on, the Lord Chancellor can be from either the House of Commons or the House of Lords. The newly created Cabinet position of Secretary of State for Constitutional Affairs (originally created to wholly replace the Lord Chancellor's executive function) will continue, although the holder of that Cabinet post will likely also hold the ancient office of Lord Chancellor too.

Council of Europe An international body established in 1949 to achieve a greater unity between its members in order 'to safeguard and realise the ideals and principles that are their common heritage'. Open to any democratic European country, it was given a key task, namely to work for the 'maintenance and further realisation of human rights and fundamental freedoms'.

Judicial activism The idea that the courts should be active partners in shaping public policy. Supporters see the courts as having a role in looking after the groups denied political clout, such as the poor and ethnic minorities, and in protecting individual freedoms.

Judicial independence The constitutional principle that there should be a strict separation of powers, in which there is a clear distinction between the judiciary and other branches of government.

Judicial restraint The idea that the courts should not seek to impose their views on other branches of government. They want a passive role for the courts and feel that they should confine themselves to implementing legislative and executive intentions.

Judicial review The power of any court – strong in North America and Scandinavia – to refuse to enforce a law or official act based on law, because in the view of the judges it conflicts with the constitution. In much of Europe (including Britain), a weaker version applies, in which the courts cannot rule acts of Parliament as being unconstitutional but can review and squash ministerial actions based upon them that are deemed as being beyond their powers. The British rejection of a strong version is based on the idea that ultimate power rests with the democratically elected representatives of the people, not appointed judges.

Kilmuir Guidelines These guidelines were laid down in 1955 by the then Lord Chancellor to restrict the freedom of judges to pronounce on public policy, for example by speaking to journalists about judicial matters.

Liberal democracies Representative democracies in which there is limited government, respect for rights and a free media, among other characteristics.

Recall The US procedure whereby elected officials may be deprived of office by popular vote.

Rule of law The core liberal democratic principle that people should be subject to the law, rather than to the arbitrary rule of those who govern: no one is above the law, which should be the framework within which all conduct or behaviour takes place.

Segregation The practice or policy of creating separate facilities within the same society for the use of a particular group.

Sequestration The removal of (financial) assets from their owner, until the individual or owner complies with a court order.

Ultra vires Beyond the legal powers (of a person or organisation).

? Likely examination questions

Distinguish between judicial independence and judicial neutrality. To what extent and how effectively are they enforced in Britain?

Does it matter that the social composition of the judiciary is not a microcosm (mirror-image) of society at large?

Are judges biased?

'Judges make law.' Discuss.

Can judges stay out of politics?

How adequately do British judges protect civil liberties?

Why has the Labour Party been traditionally suspicious of the judiciary? Has it any reason to be suspicious today?

Helpful websites

www.dca.gov.uk   Office of Secretary of State for Constitutional Affairs. Information relating to judiciary in general and judicial appointments

www.europa.eu.int/cj   European Court of Justice (EU machinery)

www.echr.coe.int   European Court on Human Rights (Council of Europe machinery)

www.lawsociety.org.uk   The Law Society

www.justice.org.uk Justice.   A legal and human rights campaigning group

 ## Suggestions for further reading

Useful articles

G. Drewry, 'Judges and Politics in Britain', *Social Studies Review*, November 1986.

M. Garnett, 'Judges versus Politicians', *Politics Review*, September 2004.

L Jeffries, 'The Judiciary', *Talking Politics*, January 2003.

P. Norton, 'Judges in British Politics', *Talking Politics*, January 2004.

G. Peele, 'The Human Rights Act', *Talking Politics*, September 2001.

M. Ryan, 'A Supreme Court for the United Kingdom', *Talking Politics*, September 2004.

Useful books

L. Bridges, G. Meszaros and M. SunKin, *Judicial Review in Perspective*, Cavendish, 1995.

G. Drewry, 'Judicial Independence in Britain: Challenges Real and Threats Imagined' in P. Norton (ed.), *New Directions in British Politics?*, Elgar, 1991.

K. Ewing and C. Gearty, *Freedom under Thatcher*, Clarendon Press, 1990.

J. Griffiths, *The Politics of the Judiciary*, Fontana, six edns, latterly 1997.

R. Hodder-Williams, *Judges and Politics in the Contemporary Age*, Bowerdean, 1996.

A. Sampson, *Who Runs This Place? The Anatomy of Britain in the 21st Century*, Murray, 2004. (Chapter on 'The Law'.)

R. Stevens, *The Independence of the Judiciary*, Oxford University Press, 1993.

J. Waltman and K. Holland, *The Political Role of Law Courts in Modern Democracies*, St Martin's Press, 1988.

CHAPTER 6

Government beyond the Centre

Contents

Overview

In almost all countries, governments recognise the need to allow some scope for regional or local initiative. It would be impractical for them to involve themselves in the minutiae of detail and govern entirely from the centre.

In this chapter, we distinguish between unitary and federal states, noting the characteristics of the two types of governmental system and their benefits and disadvantages. We then examine the movement towards decentralisation in British politics and assess the 'areal distribution of power', the way in which functions and powers are allocated across the levels of government, in an era of devolution.

Key issues to be covered in this chapter

- The distinction between unitary, federal and confederal states
- The extent of federalism throughout the world and its merits and demerits
- Why power has historically tended to shift towards the centre in liberal democracies
- More recent moves towards decentralisation of power and decision-making
- British experience of devolution in Scotland and Wales
- British moves towards 'federal devolution'
- Developments in British local government
- Government beyond the centre in France, Spain and the United States

Unitary, federal and confederal states

Most political systems have found it necessary to create governmental structures below central administration, but the distribution and extent of power vary from country to country. However, broadly there are three types of governmental system, unitary states, federations and confederations.

Bullman[1] has classified European states into four categories. He distinguishes:

1. *Classic unitary*, in which there is no regional structure other than for centrally controlled administrative purposes, although there is likely to be a system of local government. Examples include Greece and Luxembourg.
2. *Devolving unitary*, in which there is some elected regional machinery with a (not necessarily uniform) degree of **autonomy**, with also a tier of local government. Examples include France and the United Kingdom.
3. *Regionalised*, where the directly elected regional governments are equipped with significant legislative powers (e.g. Italy and Spain).
4. *Federal*, where responsibilities and powers are shared between the centre and the regional or state units according to a written constitution and there is no possibility of central government abolishing the other tier. Subnational government enjoys constitutionally guaranteed autonomy. Examples include Australia, Germany and the United States.

In unitary states of either type, all legitimate power is concentrated at the centre. Central government has indivisible **sovereignty**. It may decide to delegate power or functional responsibilities to territorial units, known variously as departments, prefectures, regions or states. But such peripheral governments exist only at the behest of central government, which can revoke the functions and powers at its convenience. Most present European governments are of the unitary type. Examples of unitary states beyond Europe include China, Israel and Japan.

As we have seen, in unitary states, some devolution of power is possible, but this does nothing to breach the idea that control derives from the national legislature. Devolution involves the transfer of power to subordinate elected bodies, without there being any sharing of legal sovereignty. Devolved assemblies can be overridden by the parent authority. Devolution usually comes about as a result of dissatisfaction with centralised government when ministers appear to be unwilling to recognise local needs.

Unitary states have certain advantages. Because power is concentrated at the centre, there is little likelihood of tension between the centre and the periphery. Also, there is a clear focus of national loyalty. Citizens identify with the country as a whole, rather than with their state or region. On the other hand, government can become over-centralised, with too little scope for local initiative and there may be inadequate recognition of diversity, be it ethnic, geographical, linguistic or religious.

In federal states, there is a sharing of functions and powers between different tiers of government, a federal (central) government and regional governments, set out in a written constitution and – if necessary – arbitrated upon by a supreme court. The regions may have different names, being known as *Länder* in Germany and states in the USA. The different levels have guaranteed spheres of responsibility, the states enjoying autonomy within their sphere of responsibility and the central government conducting those functions of major importance, which require policy to be made for the whole country. The essence of federalism is coordination rather than hierarchy between the levels of government. Both tiers may act directly on the people, and each has some exclusive powers. Federalism thus diffuses political authority to prevent any undue concentration at one point.

Federal states vary significantly in character, there being clear differences between the German and American models. The Länder have considerable autonomy in Europe's most decentralised country, the federal government having only a limited capacity to implement its legislation and relying on the regional governments to do so. This requires a high degree of partnership between the centre and the *Länder*. Historically, the USA experienced a long-term centralising tendency, although in recent years there has been a greater emphasis upon the role of the states and a new spirit of cooperation.

Under federalism, it is still likely that there will also be a system of local government, although it can vary significantly in form. In the

USA, the federal government has little role in regulating the functioning of the local tier, which falls under the direction of the states.

Federalism is widely seen as desirable or necessary for a variety of reasons:

- In large countries, it is difficult to control the whole territory from the centre. Significantly, of the current federations, most operate in vast landmasses, such as Brazil, Canada, India, Mexico and the USA.
- In countries that have previously been governed by several loosely linked self-governing states, federations might be the answer as the need for greater national unity and central authority is recognised. When the American Constitution was being drawn up by the Founding Fathers at the Philadelphia Convention, they wanted a stronger central authority than that provided under the existing Articles of Confederation. But the states were unwilling to yield the bulk of their power to Washington.
- Federations can be a means of bonding diverse ethnic, linguistic or religious elements together. They accommodate sectional diversity, whilst providing the advantages of national unity. The Indian Constitution grants reserves specific powers to its twenty-five states, most of which are distinguished by a distinctive ethnic, linguistic or religious pattern.
- Federalism is a means of dispersing political power, preventing the degree of over-**centralisation** that is often a characteristic of unitary states by creating an additional set of checks and balances. In Germany after 1945, the experience of living under Nazi tyranny left many people keen to see that undue power should not be concentrated in the capital. Although the federal government exercises legislative power, the administration of the resulting national laws is carried out by the *Länder*.

Confederacies are a looser form of federalism, in which central control is modest and the component elements retain primary power. Confederations allow for structured cooperation between states as circumstances demand, but leave the initiative firmly in the hands of individual states. Switzerland is often described as a confederation. Its twenty-six cantons exercise substantial power and the Berne government exerts relatively little influence over key aspects of Swiss life. The Commonwealth of Independent States (CIS) formed out of the old Soviet Union in 1991 is a recently created example of the genre, which facilitates economic or military cooperation.

Devolved government in the United Kingdom

The United Kingdom is a unitary state. Other institutions exist, but their powers are subordinate to Westminster. The process of centralisation of power peaked in the Thatcher years, in which important elements of local government were abolished (e.g. the Greater London Council) and the remaining authorities were brought under tighter control from London.

Since coming to power in 1997, Labour has devolved power on a substantial scale and several new institutions have been created. The changes amount to a fundamental restructuring of the United Kingdom, leading some to view them as steps along the road to the creation of a federal state.

As to whether this devolution will satisfy the aspirations of those regions that have sought more control of their own affairs is an open question. There are various possibilities: the status quo could be maintained; there may be a clamour for greater power, with clear moves towards a more federal identity; the process could lead in the long term to the disintegration of the United Kingdom, with the eventual establishment of independent political units, each sovereign in their own right and becoming individual members of the European Union.

Devolution involves the ceding of power by Parliament to some new elected body. Bogdanor[2] defines it as 'the transfer to a subordinate elected body, on a geographical basis, of functions at present exercised by ministers and Parliament'. As such, it differs from federalism which

> would divide, not devolve, supreme power from Westminster and various regional or provincial parliaments. In a federal state, the authority of the central or federal government and the provincial governments is co-ordinated and shared, the respective scope of the federal and provincial governments being defined by an enacted

constitution . . . Devolution, by contrast, does not require the introduction of an enacted constitution.

The background to Labour's post-1997 devolution measures

The debate about devolution of power to Scotland and Wales did
not begin with the election of the Blair government. Against a background of rising nationalism in Scotland – and to a lesser extent in
Wales – the previous Labour government (1974–9) had spent a considerable amount of time on the issue. Arising out of the recommendations made by the Kilbrandon Commission – established by
an earlier Labour administration in 1969 – Labour ministers came
up with proposals for a directly elected assembly for Scotland with
a range of devolved powers. It also urged the creation of an elected
Welsh assembly, albeit one with more limited powers. Neither
proposal was implemented, both having failed to achieve the
required majorities in separate referendums in Scotland and Wales
in 1979.

In 1995, the Scottish Labour and Liberal Democrat parties, along
with other interested bodies, set out their proposals for a Parliament for
Scotland in the Scottish Constitutional Convention. In the same years,
the Welsh Labour Party put forward proposals for a Welsh assembly.
In both cases, the Conservatives – in office at the time – were hostile to
any devolution of power, arguing that the creation of devolved bodies
would lead to the break-up of the United Kingdom and in the process
weaken its component parts. By contrast, the Scottish National Party
was committed to national **independence** for Scotland within the
context of the European Union, rather than political devolution.
Devolution was portrayed as an inadequate halfway house, and a
recipe for tension between London and Edinburgh.

On coming to power in 1997, Labour quickly moved to announce
referendums in Scotland and Wales on the principle of establishing
new devolved machinery. In Scotland the outcome was an overwhelming 'yes' vote on two questions (see Box 6.1), but in Wales the
majority in favour was remarkably narrow. Via the Scotland Act and
the Wales Act 1998, ministers proceeded to establish devolved government in the two countries. The legislation laid down the composition, functions and powers of the new devolved machinery.

Box 6.1 The referendums in Scotland and Wales

Scotland

In 1979, as a result of a proposal from a Labour MP, a Scotsman who represented an English constituency, a clause in the devolution bill required that 40 per cent of the registered electorate in each country must support the proposals. The 'yes' vote amounted to only 32.9 per cent of the registered electorate.

In 1997, Scottish voters were asked two questions:

Do you support a Scottish Parliament?

Should a Scottish Parliament have tax-raising powers?

In the 1997 referendum, 74.3 per cent backed a Scottish Parliament and 63.5 per cent favoured one with tax-raising powers. The result was uniform across the country, with every one of the 32 voting regions opting for a Parliament and 30 of them also wanting the tax powers as well. The turnout of 60.1 per cent was higher than many pro-devolutionists had expected.

Support for devolution varied considerably, heavy in Glasgow (83.6 per cent and 75 per cent), markedly lower in Dumfries and Galloway (60.7 per cent and 48.8 per cent) and very low in the Orkneys (57.3 per cent and 47.4 per cent). As in 1979, the appeal of devolution was much greater in the parts of Scotland in closer proximity to Edinburgh where the Parliament would meet. More peripheral areas were less enthusiastic. To an inhabitant of the Orkneys, Edinburgh seems a very long way away, just as London always did to the majority of Scots.

The outcome shows the unreality of the earlier 40 per cent rule, for even though there was substantial support in Scotland for both propositions by those who voted, it remains the fact that barely 45 per cent of the registered electorate voted for the Parliament and only some 38 per cent for the tax-varying powers.

Wales

In Wales, the 'yes' campaigners won by the narrowest of margins, 0.6 per cent of the vote, on a fractionally higher than 50 per cent turnout. Almost three in four voters either did not bother to vote or said no.

Devolution for Scotland

Many Scots had long been dissatisfied with Westminster rule, feeling that London ministers did not attach priority to Scottish needs. They were too remote to understand the situation north of the border and this was an explanation often given for the higher than average levels of unemployment and the gravity of industrial decline in Scotland. More positively, Scots saw themselves as a nation. Scotland had always retained distinctive traditions and institutions, most notably its own coinage, educational and legal systems, and religion. There was in the late twentieth century a growing sense of **national consciousness** that exceeds the strength of regional feeling felt by Geordies in the north-east of England or Tykes in Yorkshire. It was nurtured by a Scottish culture and by Scottish sport and was expressed in surveys that showed that many Scots felt Scottish rather than British.

Scotland had experienced **administrative devolution** since 1885, the year of the establishment of the Scottish Office. In 1939 it moved from Whitehall to Edinburgh, its existence being an acknowledgement of the political need to bring Scottish government closer to the people for whom it made decisions. Prior to devolution, decisions were taken at Westminster and implemented in St Andrew's House. There was a Secretary of State for Scotland, who had an input into cabinet decisions and an overall responsibility for the activities of the Scottish Office. But the pro-devolutionists wanted to see decisions taken in Scotland by a Scottish Parliament, subject to democratic control. They wanted **legislative devolution**, with laws made and implemented by representatives of the Scottish people. Their resentment was all the greater in the 1980s and 1990s because although Scots were overwhelmingly clinging to their Labour allegiance at the ballot box, they were experiencing the Conservative government of Margaret Thatcher, for Labour was unable to win a majority at Westminster. This seemed particularly unfair, given the fact that Conservatism in Scotland was in decline: only ten Conservative MPs were elected in 1987 (out of seventy-two), eleven in 1992. In the 1997 election, Scotland became a Tory-free zone and Labour was elected to office with an overwhelming landslide. Devolution was back on the agenda.

Although nationalists in the SNP wanted more than they obtained, they campaigned for devolution in the run-up to the 1997 referendums. It was the best on offer and in the view of many SNP supporters it could provide a basis for future separation. Their backing meant that all parties in Scotland, other than the Conservatives, were in favour of the establishment of the Scottish Parliament.

Box 6.2 The Scotland Act 1998

Following the successful referendum, a Scotland Act was passed in 1998. Effectively, the first Parliament in 292 years was to assume the responsibilities previously exercised by the Scottish Office. This meant that it had primary legislative powers over:

Health

Education and training

Local government, social work and housing

Economic development and transport

Law and home affairs

Sport and the arts

Agriculture, fishing and forestry

The environment

Other matters

In all, there are 47 devolved issues grouped under these headings, so that the Parliament and the Executive chosen from it have a wide range of responsibilities. There are, however, a series of 'reserved matters' on which power resides in London, for it is considered that they can be more effectively handled on a United Kingdom basis. These include:

The Constitution

Defence and national security

Foreign affairs

Major economic policy and fiscal affairs

Employment

Social security

Transport safety and regulation

The machinery provided for in the legislation includes a Parliament of 129 members of the Scottish Parliament (MSPs), 73 of whom are elected by first-past-the-post (FPTP) as constituency representatives and 56 additional members chosen via a party list. An executive is selected from and accountable to the Assembly. The Executive is led by a First Minister, who is nominated by the majority party in the Parliament and appointed by the monarch. The First Minister chooses other members of the Executive, in the same way that the Prime Minister chooses the members of the Cabinet.

The merits and difficulties of Scottish devolution

As a result of the passage of the Scotland Act (see Box 6.2, above), a Scottish Parliament met in Edinburgh in May 1999 for the first time since the Act of Union was signed in 1707. A few yeas later it is possible to provide some initial assessment of the case for devolution and how it is working in practice.

Devolution is widely seen as democratic, in that it allows people to express their distinctive identity and have a say in the development of the life of their own particular regions. This is how Donald Dewar, then Secretary of State for Scotland and soon to become Scotland's First Minister, justified Labour's proposals when introducing the White Paper. The new system would 'strengthen democratic control' and 'make government more accountable'. In particular, the issues of control of decision-makers and their accountability to an elected body are key criteria in any democratic system. Moreover, many of those decisions are now taken in Scotland, as opposed to the time when they were made by ministers of 'British' institutions. In this case, control is ensured, in that decisions are taken by the Scottish Executive and Parliament, with ministers having to defend their decisions and policies before the elected representatives of the people, the MSPs, who were elected under a highly proportional and therefore 'fair' voting system. This means that the Executive can also claim 'legitimacy'. Indeed, in general elections, no post-war British government has based its support on more than 50 per cent of the popular vote, whereas in Scotland the 1999 Executive (a Labour–Lib Dem coalition) had 53 per cent backing from the electorate; in 2003, the figure was 50 per cent. This compares favourably with the 42 per cent and 35 per cent achieved by Labour at Westminster in the last two elections.

Another virtue deriving from the electoral system is that – able to vote in multi-member constituencies – the voters have been able to make a choice between candidates and vote in greater numbers for minority parties and groups such as women and ethnic minorities who otherwise might fare badly under FPTP. The social composition of the Scottish Parliament has an impressive gender balance, relative to that at Westminster. Of the 120 MSPs elected in 2003, 51 (39.5 per cent) were women. In Labour's case, the number constituted more than half (28/50) of its intake.

Devolution also has the merit of countering the dangers of an over-powerful, excessively centralised state. Indeed, in celebrating the referendum victory that preceded the passage of the Bill, Tony Blair observed that 'the era of big centralised government is over'.

Finally, devolution may be judged according to the results it has produced, in terms of distinctively Scottish policies. The Labour-dominated Executive, tempered by the need to placate its Liberal

Democrat partners, has introduced a range of measures that differ from those introduced by ministers at Westminster. Political leaders in London have been forced to accept that it is an inevitable consequence of devolution that policies in Edinburgh and London can diverge, even when the same party is in control in both capitals. Most notably:

- student tuition fees have been rejected in Scotland
- Clause 28 (on the teaching of homosexuality in schools) was abolished before the rest of the UK followed suit
- foundation hospitals have not been introduced
- elderly people have received entirely free care in nursing and residential homes
- fox-hunting has been abolished
- teachers' pay and conditions have been improved
- a cull in the number of unselected quangos has been gradually introduced undertaken.

Supporters would claim that the Parliament has made a difference and that when problems have arisen at least they have been debated in a genuinely Scottish forum. A poll in the *The Scotsman*[3] indicated that whatever reservations Scots had about their new Parliament, there was a rising sense of Scottish patriotism, and that 'a confident, modern and exciting' country was emerging. People were proud to call themselves Scots, 80 per cent of them seeing themselves as more Scottish than British and were optimistic about their country's future.

Yet devolution has in some respects had an inauspicious beginning. Two early difficulties are not of substantial long-term consequence but have been the cause of controversy. One reason for popular dissatisfaction has been the soaring cost of the new building. MSPs were temporarily housed in a building rented from the Church of Scotland, while the Holyrood site was eventually completed at almost ten times the original estimate. Moreover, leadership problems within the Labour Party have not helped. Donald Dewar's sudden death in October 2000 led to a leadership election, in which Henry McLeish defeated his rival Jack McConnell. Just over a year later, McLeish was discredited in the 'Officegate' scandal that cast doubt upon his integrity and judgement. McConnell took over, but not before his reputation was tarnished by allegations about impropriety in his private life.

More seriously, opponents see devolution as fraught with danger, often claiming that although in the United Kingdom the sources of unity are much greater than the sources of diversity, once parts of the whole are allowed to enjoy a measure of self-government then there is a danger of the whole edifice splintering apart, a kind of 'Balkanisation' of the UK. Such fears have been expressed by the Conservatives, who resisted the Blairite proposals in the 1997 election and referendum. They suggested that there was no real necessity for change, because unlike the situation in some other countries, the UK has not developed as a result of previously autonomous states coming together recently. They feared the ultimate disintegration of the UK if parts were able to go their separate ways, because the Scottish Nationalists would not be satisfied with devolution, a halfway house between unity and independence.

Indeed, the SNP does its best to expose the flaws in devolution as introduced, in the hope that this will fuel pressure for separation. It is a separatist party, its long-term goal being national independence for Scotland. It views with envy the experiences of the Baltic states that have in recent years gained their independence and argues that – given its resources – Scotland too has the potential to exist as a viable state. Leader Alex Salmond[4] rails against an executive 'which takes its policy and its motivation from London', noting the frequent use of **Sewel motions** as a means of preventing the making of Scottish decisions on Scottish issues, instead 'making unsuitable English policy apply in Scotland'.

One difficulty of devolution often cited by critics is the West Lothian Question (originally named after the now non-existent Scottish Constituency of West Lothian held by Tam Dalyell, and nowadays more usually called the English Question): 'Why should Scottish MPs at Westminster be allowed to have a say on purely English matters while English MPs will no longer have a say on Scottish matters?' Such a dilemma would not arise under a federal system, for under federalism the division of functions is clearcut. If ministers had opted for a system of elected regional councils for England, then each region (and Scotland and Wales) would have similar devolved powers, leaving the United Kingdom Parliament to deal with the residue of issues, those key ones affecting the four countries collectively. But as yet there is no public demand for legislative devolution across the UK (see pp. 207–9), and even if this were ever introduced it is doubtful whether the powers granted to regional bodies would ever be equal to those of the Scottish Parliament, so that statutory responsibility for English devolution would probably remain at Westminster.

The question was never a source of contention when, prior to Direct Rule, Northern Ireland had its own Parliament at Stormont while the province sent members to the House of Commons. (The situation arises again under the Good Friday Agreement that provides for an assembly and an executive body.) However, logic does not always apply in these matters, and there is a possibility that English people might feel disadvantaged. They may come to resent an issue primarily relevant to England being decided on the basis of Scottish votes in the House of Commons. Already, critics sometimes express doubts about the Scottish Labour contingent at Westminster who have helped ministers push through contentious policies on tuition fees and foundation hospitals.

Bogdanor[5] points out that the difficulties inherent in the West Lothian Question have been resolved – or at least accommodated – elsewhere without much difficulty. Devolution has proved perfectly feasible in countries such as France, Italy, Portugal and Spain. For instance, in Italy fifteen out of twenty regions have no exclusive legislative powers, but the other five have wide responsibilities in economic and social affairs; in Spain, seven out of seventeen have greater autonomy than the others. But there is no 'West Sardinian Question' nor any 'West Catalonian Question'.

Be that as it may, the West Lothian Question does raise the issue of whether in a unitary state it is possible to devolve substantial powers that are denied to other regions. Many commentators might argue that in Britain there was little choice. It would have been politically unrealistic to deny recognition to the Scots, whose wish for a change in their constitutional status had been so clearly stated in the elections of 1987–97. If the price of meeting their aspirations was the creation of an anomaly, then this was a price that had to be paid. However, Bogdanor does go on to observe that:

> devolution will alter the role of Westminster very radically, by introducing the spirit of federalism into its deliberations. Before devolution, every Member of Parliament was responsible for scrutinising both the domestic and the non-domestic affairs of every part of the

United Kingdom. After devolution, by contrast MPs will normally play no role at all in legislating for the domestic affairs of Northern Ireland or Scotland, nor in scrutinising secondary legislation for Wales . . . Westminster, from being a parliament for both the domestic and the non-domestic affairs of the whole of the United Kingdom, is transformed into a domestic parliament for England, part of a domestic parliament for Wales, and a federal parliament for Northern Ireland and Scotland. The West Lothian Question, then, draws attention to the fact that devolution will transform Westminster into the quasi-federal parliament of a quasi-federal state.

Devolution: the case of Wales

Wales has been a relatively neglected part of the constitutional reform argument. Politicians and commentators who have spent much time in consideration of the West Lothian Question and associated issues have rarely given much thought to the important features of the devolution debate distinctive to Wales.

It is not self-evident to many Welsh people why in 1997 they were offered a different form of devolution from Scotland. Welsh supporters of devolution pointed out that their country too has a distinctive identity and that even if their country lacked the unique institutions characteristic of the Scottish tradition, nonetheless they had something that Scotland lacked – a distinctive language. Ministers took a different view, arguing that Wales is less of a nation than Scotland, not least because of its smaller size and different history as a conquered territory. They were aware that nationalism in Wales was always more about preserving the Welsh culture and language than it was about self-government and pointed to the overwhelming rejection of devolution in 1979, as evidence that there was less demand for devolution in the province.

In the referendum, Wales was offered an assembly without legislative and revenue-raising powers of the kind given to Scotland. The modest nature of the proposals may in part have accounted for the lack of enthusiasm shown by the Welsh for devolution. They did not reject Labour's solution, but neither did they offer strong backing.

Under the terms of the Wales Act (1998) a National Assembly of sixty members was established, with members (AMs) to be elected in the same way as the MSAs (forty constituency and twenty additional members). The Assembly was not given the power to introduce primary legislation. It was responsible for secondary legislation, fleshing out bills already passed at Westminster and it could act as a pressure group on the London government for greater consideration of Welsh interests. From the Assembly, an executive was to be formed. Initially, a Labour minority administration assumed office, but this gave way to a Labour–Liberal Democrat coalition that survived up until the 2003 elections in Wales. Since then, Labour has governed on its own under the leadership of the First Minister, Rhodri Morgan. The office of Secretary of State for Wales (with a seat in the Cabinet) remains.

Critics dismiss the devolved machinery as a 'talking shop', pointing to its lack of effective power. It is true that the powers are limited, but this has not stopped Wales from embarking on some policy initiatives that distinguish Welsh arrangements from those in England. SATs tests for seven-year-olds and prescription charges for under 25-year-olds have been abolished and the first Children's Commissioner established in the UK. In addition, the quangocracy in Wales (much disliked by many Welsh people) has been tackled. Even before the new machinery was established, the Wales Act had provided for the removal of nine quangos and more were due to be abolished at a later date.

As in Scotland, the early history of Welsh devolution was not a triumphant success story. There was much dissension within the Welsh Labour Party over the way in which party managers in London so arranged the electoral process that a Blairite leader (Alun Michael) emerged as party leader and eventual First Minister. In 2000, he lost a 'no confidence' vote and the more popular Morgan took over. There were disputes within the Executive over controversial policies regarding EU funding, agriculture and teachers' pay, among other issues.

In the light of early experience, some Labour AMs, including the present First Minister, are keen to see more legislative power located in Cardiff. Plaid Cymru, as an officially nationalist party, believes in separation as a long-term goal, although in the short term it presses for greater recognition of Welsh identity and interests.

The former Secretary of State for Wales, Ron Davies, always claimed that devolution 'was a process, not an event'. This was true, and already a review of current arrangements has taken place against a background of increasing support for the idea of devolution. The present situation may well be changed in the not-too-distant future, with more effective legislative powers and budgetary discretion being the likely targets. The difference between the situation in Scotland and Wales is clear. In Scotland, there was a strong demand for some form of home rule long before it was eventually granted. In Wales, machinery had to be offered to, almost pressed upon, the Welsh people, before there were many indications that political devolution was wanted. Now that modest autonomy has been granted, there is a meaningful debate about the future direction that devolution should take. Welsh enthusiasts cast envious eyes upon the degree of self-government that the Scots have achieved.

Box 6.3 A note on devolution in Northern Ireland

Northern Ireland is the least integrated part of the United Kingdom. It is often viewed as 'a place apart', for the province has a distinctive history and political culture. Different political parties stand for election and the issues over which they contest are not based around those that influence the voters elsewhere. Religion is a significant force in voting behaviour, with Protestant and Catholic parties taking different views over the very existence of the six counties. Hatreds based on events that took place long ago still linger in people's memories and the emblems, flags, rituals and annual marches are always there to remind those who would forget the historical and religious-differences.

Northern Ireland poses a unique constitutional problem. The Protestant majority conclude that the province should be governed as part of the United Kingdom, whilst a large, predominantly Catholic minority would prefer to see the island united as one Irish republic. Protestant Loyalists are proud to be British, Catholic Republicans prefer to be considered Irish. Reaching any accommodation between two groups that adopt a very different outlook has been very difficult, despite the efforts in recent years of the British and Irish governments to bring about a peaceful solution. Whatever their religious allegiance, many inhabitants of the province would like to see a resolution of its problems, but much of the running in the discussion is made by hard-line politicians on either side who are reluctant to compromise in order to reach an agreement.

Under the terms of the Government of Northern Ireland Act 1920, the island was partitioned. This gave the Protestants of the six counties their own Parliament at Stormont, a chamber that was for years dominated by and organised in the interests of the majority Protestants. By the 1960s, many Catholics – who had been discriminated against in employment and housing, and were denied their full political rights – became dissatisfied and by the end of the decade were pressing for an end to their mistreatment. Rioting and the threat of a serious breakdown of order led the British government to send in troops, initially much to the relief of many Catholics who feared for their lives. However, the British army came to be viewed as an army of occupation by many Republicans. Their discontent made them an easy prey for the propaganda of the militant wing of the Irish Republican Army (IRA), which effectively exploited the genuine grievances of many people on the minority side. In this situation, the British government abandoned the Stormont Parliament in 1969, replacing it with **direct rule** from Westminster.

For years there was a cycle of violence. The greater the use of force by British troops, the more recruitment there was for the IRA and other extremist republican groups. Paramilitary action, random killings, bombings and explosions characterised the 1970s and 1980s, despite periodic attempts from London and Dublin to produce a settlement. The peace process that culminated in the present governing arrangements was initiated by the Major government in 1993. For the first time, Sinn Fein – the political wing of the republican movement – had the chance to become involved in the negotiations about the future of the province. After 1997, the Blair government gave the by then stalled peace process a new momentum culminating in the publication of the Good Friday Agreement in April 1998.

Under the terms of the Agreement, as ratified by the people on either side of the border, there was to be, among other terms:

- a devolved assembly with law-making powers in the province, elected on the basis of proportional representation
- an executive of ten ministers who would operate on the basis of power-sharing between the leaders of the two communities.

Ever since the conclusion of the Agreement, there has been a conflict over the decommissioning of IRA weapons, the reform of the police service, the continued presence of British troops and several other issues. The Assembly and Executive were established, although they have been suspended on four occasions, as they still are. Meanwhile, government continues via direct rule.

The Democratic Unionists and Sinn Fein are the more hard-line representatives of the two communities, and it may be the case that only if they can both be involved in an agreement, is there a chance of it being maintained. The announcement on 28 July by the IRA that it has 'formally ordered an end to the armed campaign' and decided to operate through 'exclusively peaceful means' could – if it truly means an end to Irish terrorism – be a statement of historic importance. It could ensure that the ballot can finally replace the bullet as the way of resolving issues in Northern Ireland. As yet, there remain unanswered questions, but meanwhile an uneasy peace prevails.

The degree of devolution granted to Northern Ireland is somewhere in between that granted to the Scots and the Welsh. Like the Scottish Parliament, the Northern Ireland Assembly has legislative powers, but unlike the former, the latter has no tax-varying powers. The members of the Assembly decide on many matters affecting the province, which continues to send seventeen MPs to Westminster. As in the case of Scottish MPs, they can vote on English issues, whereas English MPs cannot vote on issues affecting the six counties. But little is heard of the Belfast Question in British politics.

The form of future government in Northern Ireland is difficult to predict. As long as Protestants remain the largest element in the province, any major recasting is unlikely. British and Irish governments accept that change must have the backing of the majority of the population. However, demographic changes mean that within a couple of decades or so, there may be a narrow Catholic majority. If and when this happens, then alternative scenarios are possible, such as some scheme of joint sovereignty between London and Dublin or a united Ireland. Either way, the future of the United Kingdom could be markedly affected by developments in Northern Ireland.

Is Britain becoming a federal state?

As we have established, Britain is a unitary state. But there have been important changes in recent years to the pattern of government, and some of these seem to indicate a move in a more federal direction. Devolution has been the British route to decentralisation, so that power remains theoretically in Westminster's hands although it is politically hard to imagine any administration in London seeking to recover control over areas that have been delegated to Edinburgh or Cardiff.

Northern Ireland had a devolved assembly in the days before direct rule, so that the relationship between London and Belfast was essentially federal in character, with certain functions allocated to the national level of government and the rest to the provincial one. The new assembly formed as a result of the Good Friday Agreement (1998) was accorded similar legislative powers to the original Stormont body, minus limited opportunities to vary UK levels of taxation. However, the Executive and Assembly are currently suspended, so it is as yet uncertain how successfully this will operate and to what extent it can make Northern Irish divisions a thing of the past. If it can do so, then Northern Ireland, Scotland and Wales will all have devolved administrations, although the latter one has strictly limited powers.

Another development in Britain has been the introduction of an elected mayor and assembly for London. The adoption of elected mayors of the type to be found in American cities such as Washington and New York, and in European capitals such as Barcelona and Paris.

Box 6.4 The English regions

Ministers made it clear from the earliest days in office that at some point in the future regional development assemblies might be made accountable to elected regional assemblies rather than to an indirectly elected forum of local councillors. Much would depend on regional demand. In a White Paper produced in May 2002, referendums were promised in areas where there seemed to be 'sufficient public interest' to see whether an elected assembly was wanted. The first of these occurred in September 2004, in the north-east, where voters overwhelmingly rejected the proposal, by 77.9 per cent to 22.1 per cent. Support cannot again be tested in the region for seven years.

If the scheme had gone ahead, there was the possibility of a rolling programme of regional government, with some areas obtaining new machinery in advance of others. This now seems much less likely in the foreseeable future. The North-east was viewed as probably the area most likely to opt for an assembly. Such poor and more peripheral regions have a greater sense of identity than do the East or West Midlands.

It now seems likely that the idea of elected regional government will be indefinitely shelved. This dimension of the programme of constitutional reform is now effectively finished. It is likely that regional development agencies and unelected regional chambers will remain in place for the foreseeable future. Some suggestions have been made concerning an extension of 'new localism' or even a revival of the idea of elected mayors.

If these become the pattern of the future outside London, then we will perhaps experience what Coxall and Robins envisage[6]:

> [the development from] a unitary state to a mosaic of federal, devolved and joint authority relationships between core and periphery, with the English core becoming more decentralised as regional and urban identities find political expression.

When commentators speculate on moves towards a federal structure in Britain, they do not usually imply a uniform division of power between Westminster and provincial units formally set out in a written document. Rather, they envisage a situation in which the policy of devolution is gradually applied to all parts of the United Kingdom, just as it is now applied to Scotland and Wales. Such a pattern is more akin to the model proposed by some Liberals in the late nineteenth century, a pattern then labelled as 'Home Rule All Round'. Bogdanor seeks[7] to distinguish this from a strictly federal system, and refers to it instead as 'federal devolution'. (See Box 6.5 for a discussion of the feasability of federalism in the UK.)

The European dimension

Of course, another line of possible development is to imagine a more federal Britain in a federal Europe. The pioneers of post-war Europe who created the European Economic Community (now the European Union) always envisaged that their attempts at cooperation would take Europe towards some kind of 'United States of Europe'. British Conservatives have long feared the idea of a federal Europe, seeing this as a form of centralisation involving the creation of some giant Euro super-state. The formal creation of such a 'monster' may be as yet a long way off, but they see moves to integration (e.g. the single currency) as steps in that direction.

The British take a different view of federalism to most Europeans, who see it as decentralisation in practice. Whereas John Major was keen to insist on the notion of subsidiarity being written into the Maastricht agreement and sought to sell the Maastricht Treaty as a decentralising measure to halt the drift of power to Brussels, several other European leaders were bemused, for they could also endorse **subsidiarity**. They view it as the very essence

Box 6.5 Could federalism work in Britain?

The attraction of federalism is that it offers such a clearcut division of responsibility that could be neatly applied all round in the United Kingdom. There need be no jealousies between component parts, because all would have the same powers and be represented in the same way in the Westminster Parliament. A federal UK could be applied in two ways:

1. We could have parliaments or assemblies for England, Northern Ireland, Scotland and Wales, with these bodies looking after the main 'internal' policies such as education, welfare and transport. There would also be a UK Parliament still at Westminster. The trouble here is that England would predominate in the UK Parliament, for if representation was worked out on a population basis, England would need about 83 per cent of the seats. English representatives would be able to force any policy through, in spite of the opposition of Northern Ireland, Scotland or Wales. It would be unreal to expect England to accept that these three countries should be over-represented or have a blocking mechanism.

2. The alternative solution would be to recast England on the basis of 8–10 regions, similar to the ones used for the present regional chambers. Each region would have its own budget to provide its own educational, transport and other services, just as would the three countries that currently have devolved machinery. As we have seen opposite, this would mean that parts of England, especially those more remote from London (such as the North-east), would have their demands catered for. Given a blank sheet of paper, this might be a logical way of dividing up the United Kingdom. It is certainly a very decentralist approach. But in the present situation, is there enough regional consciousness to make regional government of this type worthwhile? Would it enthuse the voters? Having said it would permit indirectly elected chambers to opt to become elected should they wish to do so, ministers have since the 2004 referendum in the north-east lost much of their enthusiasm for the idea. Such a solution would have provided a clearer, neater division of responsibility between the centre and the nations and regions.

of federalism, for it involves the idea that decisions should be taken at the lowest level of government possible. As the Treaty puts it in Article 3b:

> In areas which do not fall within its exclusive competence, the Community shall take action, in accordance with the principle of subsidiarity, only if and in so far as the objectives for the proposed action cannot be sufficiently achieved by the Member states and can therefore, by reason of the scale or effects of the proposed action, be better achieved by the Community. Any action by the Community shall not go beyond what is necessary to achieve the objectives of this Treaty.

Box 6.6 A note on quangos

Quasi-autonomous non-governmental organisations (quangos) are so named because they are established by ministers and funded from the public purse, but yet have an independence of action usually denied to officials in the bureaucracy. This is because they are not controlled directly by national elected politicians. They fall into several categories, some having executive responsibilities (the Arts Council), some being Advisory (the Advisory Committee on Hazardous Substances), some judicial (the Employment Tribunal), some regulatory (the Audit Commission) and some tackling issues over a broad area (the Social Exclusion Unit). Examples include the BBC, one of the oldest quangos, and a variety of other authorities such as the Charity Commission, the Tourist Boards and the Welsh Development Agency.

The number of quangos has grown sharply over the last twenty-five years or so. Their increasing use in Wales caused particular upset in the principality. Although the Conservatives had committed themselves to curbing the growth of such non-elected bodies in 1979, their numbers increased according to several analyses. Charter 88 listed more than 5,000 organisations employing some 70,000 people, although ministers were much more modest in their estimate, suggesting that the number fell after 1979 from 2,000 to some 1,400 eighteen years later. If the range of quangos includes the executive agencies (created as part of the Next Steps programme in the early 1990s), health service trusts, opted-out schools and hospitals and Training and Enterprise Councils (TECs), then the opposition attacks based on 'the number's game' were justified. In any case, the reasons for criticism were wider than their alleged growth.

Critics targeted the twin issues of patronage and accountability. They disliked the way in which those appointed to serve on theses public bodies were usually men or women connected with or sympathetic to the Conservative Party, or – in some cases – wives of Conservative MPs. They saw them as being unaccountable to the general public. Moreover, ministerial accountability to Parliament is blurred when problems develop for which an agency is responsible. When there is a jail break, the Home Secretary can avoid taking responsibility by saying that this is an operational matter – the responsibility of the Director-General of the Prisons Agency – rather than an issue of policy for which the minister must accept the blame.

Since 1997, there has been no substantial attack on the quango-cracy, some older bodies being replaced by newer ones and most others being retained. Labour's distinctive contribution has been to create organisations with a broad remit, cross-cutting bodies such as the New Deal Taskforce. These are seen as 'filling in the gaps' between other agencies, to ensure the more effective delivery of policies.

In Wales, the new Welsh Assembly Government (WAG) has been tackling the issue of quangos. Some have been absorbed into the (e.g. the Welsh Language Board and the Welsh Development Agency), whilst others have had their remit curtailed (e.g. the Arts, Sports and Countryside Councils for Wales).

English local government

The need for a network of local councils

Given the size and population of Britain, it would be impossible to devise and operate all services from Westminster and Whitehall. Some intermediate system of administration is required to deliver services. Britain has traditionally operated several services on a regional basis, without there being any way in which the decision-making bodies are subject to democratic control. At the local level, the role of councils has gone far beyond merely administering services on behalf of the centre. Rather, it has played an important role in shaping and directing key aspects of public policy, although that role has been reduced in recent decades.

We have seen that the British political system is a unitary one, with constitutional authority emanating from the centre in Whitehall and Westminster. Local government is a creature of central government, working within a framework of parliamentary legislation. It can only act in those areas specifically laid down by Parliament. By contrast, French local government has a broad competence, which allows it to act except in areas specifically ruled out by national legislation.

The case for local government is based on two interrelated themes: democracy and policy effectiveness. Local government is based on the principle that public policy decisions should be taken as close to the people as is practicable. The rationale for this is that whereas centrally imposed solutions may prove inappropriate to many areas, councils can provide the most appropriate response to a particular situation based on their knowledge of the local. Councils are more accessible to people living in the community who can more easily seek redress for any problems they face. Such an approach has the additional benefits of diversity and flexibility, matching services to particular local needs. Individual councils can be used to experiment with new ideas and policy innovations.

In addition, because local government is closer to the people than central government, it is therefore more accountable. Elected local councils help to strengthen the democratic process, encouraging as they do the participation of citizens, by voting or standing for office. Moreover, the network of councils means that there are multiple centres of power, acting therefore as an important safeguard against an over-powerful central state.

Central–local relations: the growth of central control
Although the British system of local councils operates under a framework of controls from Westminster and Whitehall, it was for many years an active and vibrant one. Most obviously, in the period after 1945, it reached its heyday, in what now seems to have been in some respects a golden period for local government. The growth in local spending coincided with the creation and expansion of the Welfare state. Councils assumed additional responsibilities, particularly in areas such as social services, spending a growing share of the national income, employing more people and enjoying a considerable degree of freedom to determine local policy responses. Although the broad parameters of policy were laid down in London, local government was responsible for the direct delivery of the majority of public services that impacted upon people's lives, notably in education and housing.

Broadly speaking, in this expansionist phase, both local and central government directed their efforts to achieving the same goals, and relations were straightforward and lacking in tension. Central government was concerned to see that there was in place a pattern of local councils that were large and powerful enough to deliver a wide range of expanding services. In addition, it assumed the main role in policy-making but left detailed implementation to local government. As for the delivery of services, it had to be provided in a manner that complied with specified requirements and standards, but this left ample scope for authorities to adapt the specifics of public policy to local conditions, according to the mandate they received from their local electorate. Generally speaking, local councillors and officials were sympathetic to increasing local spending to provide a better range of services, an approach which in an age of growing affluence and welfare-state expansion sat comfortably with the framework established in London.

The situation began to alter in the mid–late 1970s, when the expansion of provision came to an end. But most noticeably, it was the impact of Thatcherism that began to change the political agenda as far as local councils were concerned. The relationship between central government and local authorities relates primarily to issues such as the arrangements for local government finance and the balance of national and local influence in policy-making. The arrangements in these areas became more sharply politicised after 1979, and profound changes affected the structure of local government and the way it was financed, and led to the more rapid creation of non-elected quangos.

Ministers wanted a greater role for the private sector in the delivery of local services, stressing the enabling rather than the direct service provision role of local government. In the field of public housing, in addition to the policy of selling council houses, active encouragement was given to the involvement of non-governmental agencies such as housing associations. In education too, previously an area of local autonomy, central control was increased in several ways, most obviously by the introduction of the national curriculum. The government placed the emphasis on consistency and efficiency, rather than diversity and choice.

Since the mid-1970s, the relationship has changed and fundamental disagreements have developed between the centre and local authorities concerning the appropriate direction of policy and the amount of money that could be raised to finance services. Labour introduced a number of changes to the way in which local authority expenditure was financed as part of a broader attempt to control the overall level of spending, primarily because of immediate economic pressures and in particular the perceived need to reduce levels of public spending. After 1979 Thatcherite ministers set out to curb local spending, but in their case the changes made stemmed from their ideological approach. If their outlook was hostile to high-spending Labour authorities, the situation was worsened because some local authorities fell into the hands of left-wing councillors who were intent upon challenging Conservative central government. This led to heightened controversy and conflict.

During the Conservative era, more than a hundred separate Acts of Parliament included provisions that made changes to local government in the UK. Broadly, they fell into three categories:

1. Those concerned with finance, particularly how local authorities raised or received their income and the rules and legislation concerned with how they spent their money.
2. Those concerning the activities in which local government was engaged.
3. Those related to the framework of local government, affecting its structure. These included the abolition of the six existing Metropolitan councils and the Greater London Council in 1986, as well as the creation of a number of entirely new authorities. The present structure of local government was laid down in the Major years. In addition to structural changes, there were other developments, most notably the development of the concept of local councils as enabling authorities which did not provide services directly (instead, they allocated contracts for service delivery to competing providers) and a raft of policy changes that tightened control just in the areas in which councils had previously had much discretion – namely education and housing.

As a result of the changes made, many commentators felt that after 1979 there was increased central control over local councils, involving a reduction in the degree of local autonomy. In 1997, the new Blair government was committed to giving councils a higher profile and restoring life and vigour into the way they function. The Prime Minister[8] was keen to revive this ailing area of British democracy. It would be 'modernised . . . re-invigorated . . . reborn and energised' under Labour rule. New Labour's plans for reviving local democracy included a proposal for an elected mayor in London and a new assembly.

For the most part, Labour has not been interested in major structural reform. It has preferred to concentrate on democratic renewal, internal management and service delivery. In particular, it gave councils throughout England the chance to consult the people in their vicinity about how they would wish to see their local authority operate in future. It wanted to see reform of the internal structure of councils, placing much emphasis on the nature and quality of local leadership. By 2003, the local consultations had taken place and of the options available, inhabitants in 316 areas chose a leader and cabinet, 10 an elected mayor and cabinet, 1 an elected mayor and council manager and 59 made alternative arrangements.

The impact of Europe upon local government
A further development over the past two decades has been the growing impact of Europe upon British local government. For a number of reasons, British local authorities began to develop direct relations with the institutions of the European Union (EU) and with partner local authorities on the continent. In the main, these circumvented British central government, indicating that a new dimension was emerging in central-local relations. The developing relationship between local authorities and the European Union took two principal forms:

1. The provision of EU funding through programmes such as the European regional and social funds. Some authorities such as Birmingham were notably effective in attracting European money to finance major construction projects.
2. Local authorities began to participate in European networks, working with councils in other countries in the search for common solutions and in a bid to influence the direction of Union policy.

This European dimension has assumed an ever-increasing significance in recent years, as councils have seen the EU as a potential means of protecting and fostering their autonomy. This is in line with the doctrine of subsidiarity laid down at Maastricht, notably that wherever possible governmental activities should be carried out at the most local level of provision. The doctrine was much praised by John Major, who was keen to see it 'beefed up' at the Edinburgh summit in 1992. He saw it as a means of ensuring that the European Union did not become too centralised and that Britain could retain decision-making over key areas in this country. He and other Conservative ministers were less willing to see power further devolved to British local authorities and regions.

The case of France

France has a history of centralisation, dating back to the time when its kings wished to increase their security by keeping the French nobility firmly in its place. The role and influence of the local aristocracy were carefully monitored, in order to lessen the likelihood of rebellion. Since those distant times, there has been little indication that French leaders have ever been willing to relinquish central control. Governments have preserved the idea that France is one unified nation. The Constitution of the Fifth Republic describes the country as a 'republic, indivisible' and even overseas territories are often portrayed as extensions of main-land France.

In 1982 changes were introduced that allowed for some regional-isation. Regional councils have increased their powers in recent years, but critics claim that they are still ineffectual and unable to exert really significant influence. Some groups continue to argue for an easing of the Parisian hold on rural French life. In particular the small Breton Democratic Union has long campaigned for some relaxation of central control and more rights for regions such as Brittany, which has a history marked by bouts of separatist feeling.

Corsican nationalists have long argued for greater recognition of the separate identity of their island. They accept the dependence of Corsica on central government for aid and support, but nonetheless want greater freedom from Parisian control. Following the murder of the prefect in 1999, the French government offered a package of mea-sures allowing for greater local control with the prospect of an eventual executive and assembly with limited powers. It failed to impress many Corsican nationalists and aroused antagonism from some politicians who feared that the concession could create a precedent for other regions seeking greater self-rule. The offer of a package tailor-made to meet the Corsican situation was withdrawn with the emergence of a new centre-right administration in France (2002), but the island has been promised that its interests and concerns will be recognised in any new scheme of modest decentralisation for the whole country.

The case of Spain

In Spain, seventeen autonomous regions – each with an elected assembly and government – were established under the 1978 Constitution. The extensive devolution of power to the regions was largely a way of enabling the new democracy to accommodate militant Basque and Catalan demands. The amount of devolution varies; 'ordinary' regions having less power, whereas the two regions above and areas such as Galicia and the Balearic Islands have more extensive competences. Issues other than defence and foreign affairs, social security and the direction of broad economic policy have been passed to the autonomous communities, but it is up to each one to decide how they exercise their new powers, the proviso being that they must do so in a way not in conflict with the Spanish constitution. Some regions have been unwilling or unable to assert their autonomy to any considerable degree.

The Spanish form of devolution has been labelled as one of 'differentiated' or 'asymmetrical federalism'.[9] Spain operates as a devolved unitary state over much of the country, yet there are parts of the country that function in a way akin to regions in a federal system. The central government in Madrid insists that Spain is an indissoluble state and would resist any attempt at secession. But if it is true that sovereignty legally remains at the centre, no government would contemplate any resumption of central control over the Basques and Catalans.

The experience of Catalonia was used by Scottish supporters of home rule in their campaign for effective devolution. They noted that devolution has not led to the break-up of Spain, but rather that it has weakened separatist demands. More extreme parties seeking national independence have lost much of their appeal, and the peaceful nationalist parties in Catalonia and the Basque country are now interested in making devolution work and getting the best possible deal for their region. However, there are in both regions many politicians who continue to work for some scheme of 'shared sovereignty' and a strong Basque terrorist opposition, ETA, which is not reconciled to the present constitutional arrangements.

The case of the USA

As president between 1981 and 1989, Ronald Reagan presided over a 'devolution revolution'. After his eight years in office, the states were funding more of their own programmes and the number run by the federal government in Washington was markedly curtailed. As a result of his initiatives and the approach of his successors, the last two decades or so have been categorised by Singh[10] as an era of 'devolutionary federalism'.

President Clinton (1993–2001) stressed the importance of cooperation between the federal and state/local governments. Whilst his belief in more active national government inclined him to be a centraliser in his approach, his background as governor of Arkansas made him sympathetic to states' rights. There was a modest increase in federal aid to the states and localities. There was also a shift in the balance of the federal–state relationship. Clinton offered support for state experimentation and was encouraged by the new-found vitality of state capitals.

Like his predecessors, an ex-state governor, George W. Bush portrays himself as 'a faithful friend of federalism'. Particularly in the early days in office, he leaned on the advice of leading state officials. But later developments have worked against such a pro-devolution policy, noticeably:

- the dislike of the **Religious Right** for some state laws, such as same-sex marriages in Massachusetts and euthanasia in Oregon
- the fears of the business community about excessive regulation by state governments
- the attack on the Twin Towers, which focused attention on Washington, as Americans looked to the White House for a lead in combating terrorism.

By British or French standards, the USA is a very decentralised country. Federalism has been beneficial in many ways, its advantages to Americans including the following:

- It recognises the distinctive history, traditions and size of each state, allowing for national unity but not uniformity. If the people of one state, such as Texas, want the death penalty, they can have it; other states, such as Wisconsin, which voted to abolish it, are not forced to follow suit.
- It provides opportunities for political involvement to many citizens at state and local level; state governments provide thousands of elective offices for which citizens can vote or run.
- States are still a powerful reference point in American culture, and many citizens identify strongly with their state as well as with their country.
- States provide opportunities for innovation, and act as a testing-ground for experiments which others can follow in areas such as clean air and health care.

What you should have learnt from reading this chapter

- In several democracies that have long exhibited a high degree of central control, there has been a move in recent years towards some decentralisation. In the Reagan and post-Reagan years, there has been a new mood of state renewal in the USA.

- Usually, the motivation has not derived from an ideological belief that excessive centralisation existed and that this should be reversed. It has sprung from recognition that the political aspirations of many peoples could not be met without some concession being made to their political aspirations. Elsewhere, greater decentralisation has been a response to the difficulties experienced by some countries in managing the process of decision-making. Blondel concludes[11]:

  one could argue that the regionalism that has been introduced in these countries constitutes an imitation of federalism – indeed, is federalism in all but name. Such a conclusion would not be valid for the French or Italian cases up to the mid-1990s, but where it was valid, as it might be in the Spanish case, it would mean that the difference between federal and unitary states is becoming smaller, not only in practice but formally as well.

- The devolution of greater and lesser power to Scotland and Wales respectively matches what has been happening in other EU states. In Spain, the people of some areas of the country have more control over their future than their fellow Spaniards elsewhere. It is as yet unclear whether, in the long term, the use of devolution as a means of defusing tensions and frustrations proves to be the antidote to separatism or a first step on the road to federalism.

- In the UK, the pattern is similarly confused, leading Ward[12] to conclude that: 'one's overall impression of Labour's constitutional design is how different the pattern of devolution in each country has been. Each of the assemblies has a different size and composition, a different system of government, and a very different set of powers.'

Glossary of key terms

Administrative devolution The transfer of administrative offices and responsibilities from central government (in Whitehall) to outlets around the country; decentralisation of the government machine.

Autonomy The right to a state of self-government: literally self-rule, a situation allowing people to be governed according to their own preferences and laws.

Centralisation The concentration of political power or governmental authority at the national level. Centralised governments are therefore those where all the major political decisions are made at the centre, in the case of the UK at Westminster and in Whitehall.

Direct rule The imposition in 1969 of rule from Whitehall/Westminster over the six provinces of Northern Ireland that had previously elected members to a devolved parliament at Stormont. Initially intended to be a temporary suspension of devolution while alternative arrangements were worked out, direct rule only came to an end when the Good Friday Agreement was implemented.

Independence The establishment of an independent state that has its own institutions and controls its own resources: national separation.

Legislative devolution The transfer of the power to legislate in certain areas from the national Parliament (at Westminster) to subordinate elected bodies (Scottish Parliament).

National consciousness The belief of members of a national community that they share common aspirations, culture and values: nationalism refers to the desire of such people to have their own separate, sovereign state.

Religious Right The label applied to a broad movement of conservatives who advance strict moral and social values in the USA. Most of its members are fundamentalist Christians who are unquestioning in accepting biblical doctrines. They wish to restore the godly principles that in their view made the nation great. They oppose the use of abortion and stem cell research.

Sewel motion A mechanism set out in the Scotland Act 1998 which allows the Executive to hand a decision or debate on a devolved matter over to Westminster, perhaps because it finds it too controversial or difficult to deal with, or when change might have UK-wide implications.

With Labour in power in Scotland, it is seen by critics as a means of stifling debate in Scotland and an indication that the Executive is too beholden to Labour at Westminster.

Sovereignty Supreme or unlimited power: in politics, the ultimate source of legal authority which – in the United Kingdom – is the Westminster Parliament.

Subsidiarity The notion that decisions should be taken at the lowest possible level, consistent with the demands of efficiency, as is written into the Maastricht Treaty: the idea is that each level of government has its most appropriate geographical area.

Likely examination questions

Explain the differences between devolution and federalism.

Examine the respective benefits and disadvantages of unitary and federal forms of government.

Why does the Scottish Parliament have greater devolved powers than the Welsh National Assembly?

Can devolution work in the United Kingdom?

Is devolution merely a staging-post en route to full independence?

Is the United Kingdom moving towards a quasi-federal system of government?

To what extent is the United Kingdom still a unitary state?

Helpful websites

Materials are produced and queries answered by staff associated with the Scottish and Welsh devolved bodies:

www.scottish.parliament.uk

www.wales.gov.uk

The Constitutional Centre produces regular updates on matters affecting the government of the United Kingdom, as does the Lord Chancellor's departmental site www.lcd.gov.uk

The Scottish National Party and Plaid Cymru sites offer a different insight into the governance of the two countries:

www.sup.gov.uk

www.plaidcymru.org

Two general local government sites are:

www.local.gov.uk and www.local.detr.gov.uk

Suggestions for further reading

Useful articles

D. Denver, 'The Devolution Project', *Politics Review*, September 2001.

P. Dorey, 'The West Lothian Question', *Talking Politics*, September 2002.

M. Rathbone, 'The National Assembly for Wales', *Talking Politics*, April 2003.

Useful books

Few books deal with the nature and development of nationalism in Scotland and Wales. It is still premature for much useful literature to have appeared on the character and workings of devolution in the United Kingdom. As soon as anything is written, it easily becomes dated by the pace of developments in Northern Ireland and at the regional level. Given these constraints, there is little to recommend at this time. However, the following are useful studies:

V. Bogdanor, *Devolution in the United Kingdom*, Oxford University Press, 1999.

R. Hazell, *Constitutional Futures: A History of the Next Ten Years*, Oxford University Press, 1999.

A. Trench (ed.), *Has Devolution Made a Difference? The State of the Nation*, The Constitutional Unit, 2004.

A. Ward, 'Devolution', in D. Oliver (ed.), *Constitutional Reform in the United Kingdom*, Oxford University Press, 2003.

Political Parties

Contents

Overview

Mass political parties were the key agency in mobilising the voters for much of the twentieth century. Unlike pressure groups, they sought to secure the levers of power and carry out programmes devised by people who shared a common identity and a broadly similar outlook. By the new millennium, there was some evidence that the Western European pattern was in decline.

Here, we examine the British party system and assess to what extent it retains its traditional characteristics. We ask whether the parties any longer offer radically different visions of society and retain their traditional supporters' allegiance.

Key issues to be covered in this chapter

- The role and importance of political parties
- The main types of party systems, including the British variety
- The two main British parties, Labour and Conservative
- The role and importance of third and minor parties
- Features of party finance, membership and organisation
- The alleged decline of parties: do they matter?
- Parties in France, Italy and the United States

Introduction

Modern democracy is unthinkable without competition between political parties. They are ubiquitous, existing in different forms under different political systems. They bring together a variety of different interests in any society, and by so doing 'overcome geographical distances, and provide coherence to sometimes divisive government structures'.[1] Via the electoral process, they determine the shape of governments. European, American and other democracies are party democracies.

The primary purpose of political parties is to win elections. This is the main feature that distinguishes them from pressure groups, which may try to influence elections but do not usually put up candidates for office. Parties are then organisations of broadly like-minded men and women who seek to win power in elections in order that they can then assume responsibility for controlling the apparatus of government.

Parties articulate the needs of those sectors of society which have created them and look to them to advance their interests. But they must go further, for to win an election they need wider support. If they wish to be in government – either in a single-party administration or some form of coalition – then they cannot afford to follow a narrow doctrinal programme, for this would alienate important groups in the community and make it difficult for other parties to contemplate cooperation with them. In the words of the old examination quotation: 'Pressure groups articulate and political parties aggregate the various interests in society.'

In the last two or three decades, there has been a noticeable decline in the fortunes of once-strong parties, several of which have lost members and voters in large numbers. They function in an era of **partisan de-alignment**, which has led to a far greater volatility in voting behaviour than ever before. Voting is no longer 'habitual and ingrained', as Punnett[2] described it back in the 1970s, and parties can no longer count on the degree of support they once could almost take for granted.

The functions of political parties

As we have seen, parties are defined by their central task of seeking office with a view to exercising political power. However, their impact on the political system is wider than this. They have several broad functions in most countries. They

- *serve as brokers for ideas and organise opinion.* They take on board the ideas of individuals and groups and aggregate and simplify these demands into a package of policies. In this way, they clarify the political process for the voter, who is confronted with a choice of alternative proposals, programmes and leaders. The voter is then able to choose the party that most resembles his or her own policy preferences. That choice can be made from a range of ideological parties deeply committed to particular goals (the German Greens) and pragmatic parties whose programme is flexible, moderate and incrementalist in approach (New Labour and the American Democrats).
- *are a source of political knowledge.* Even for voters who lack any strong party ties, their ideas and outlook are likely to be influenced by the information that parties offer and by their perception of what the parties support. In this way, parties socialise people into the political culture.
- *act as a link between the individual and the political system.* Most people rely on various political interests to represent their concerns and demands. Parties formulate, aggregate and communicate a package of such demands and if they win power attempt to implement them. In this way, parties facilitate the individual's integration into the political process. They act as bridge organisations, mediators between the conflicting interests of government and the electorate.
- *mobilise and recruit activists.* Parties offer a structure into which individuals can channel their interests. They provide contact with other individuals and groups and an opportunity to become political foot soldiers or local or national politicians. In many democracies, the recruitment, selection and training of parliamentary candidates is a key task. Parties offer candidates support during election campaigns and in many countries are responsible for the campaigning itself, both locally and nationally.

- *provide an organisational structure via which to coordinate the actions of government, encouraging those who belong to them to work towards shared objectives.* Leaders and their colleagues (including party whips) seek to persuade members of the legislature to vote for their policies and where necessary do coalition deals to secure a majority for particular programmes.
- *serve as a source of opposition.* The parties not in government provide explicit, organised opposition. In Britain there is a fully institutionalised party designated as Her Majesty's Loyal Opposition, with is own shadow ministerial team.

Types of party systems

The term 'party system' refers to the network of relationships between parties that determines how the political system functions. The most usual means of distinguishing between different types of party system is by reference to the number of parties involved. In a classic study, Duverger[3] referred to particular variations such as 'one party', 'two party' and 'multi party' systems. However, in addition to the number of parties is the issue of their electoral and legislative strength (e.g. whether or not parties have the prospect of winning or sharing political power). Some are 'major', others 'third', 'minor' or 'small' parties.

There are four categories of party systems:

1. *One-party systems.* There are several variants of this type, but they are mostly associated with authoritarian governments in which a single party enjoys a monopoly of power (e.g. in remaining communist regimes, there is no permitted effective opposition).
2. *Two-party systems.* In these systems, as in Britain, New Zealand and the United States, there are two major parties, each of which has a chance of obtaining a majority of seats in the legislature and capturing political power. There will be other parties – some sizeable – but they have not in the past meaningfully competed for office. They were never likely to win.
3. *Dominant party systems.* These exist in a country where there is free competition between parties, but only one party is likely to achieve an absolute majority of the votes cast and dominate governmental

office. There may on occasion be a sharing of power with another party, but the likelihood is that one party will enjoy a long period of continuous rule. Before majority rule, the Nationalist Party in South Africa was in this position. So too was the Liberal Democrat Party in Japan until the 1990s. In the 1980s, commentators noted that Britain had one-party dominance in a traditionally two-party system. Within a country, there may be a dominant party system operating at a regional level. In the rural Midwest of the USA, the electorate is overwhelmingly Republican.

4. *Multi-party systems.* These are common in European countries, such as Belgium, Italy and Switzerland. Government tends to be based on coalitions of more than one party, maybe three or four. Under this type of party system, there is not usually a clear distinction between government and opposition, for many of the broadly centrist parties tend to be members of the administration. Such systems are common where **proportional representation** is employed.

Box 7.1 Two-party systems in Britain and the USA: their causes, advantages and disadvantages

Conditions favourable to the development of two-party systems

- *The natural tendency for opinion on issues to divide into a 'for' and 'against' position*, which often follows the basic division between those who generally favour the status quo (Conservatives in the UK and Republicans in the USA) and those who wish to see innovation and a faster rate of change (Labour in the UK and Democrats in the USA).
- *The electoral system.* The simple majority system used in Britain and the USA means that the candidate with the most votes wins, whether or not he or she actually obtained a majority of all the votes cast. This discourages parties from splintering and restricts the growth of new parties. Duverger[4] noted that: 'The simple majority, single ballot system favours the two party system; the simple majority system with second ballot and proportional representation favours multi-partyism.'
- *The existence of broad broker parties that aim to win backing from all sections of the electorate.* The two main parties in Britain and

America accommodate their aims to the general feeling of the people, which keeps them moderate and middle-of-the-road. As such, there is little scope for a third party to establish itself on a popular basis.

- *The tendency of a two-party system to perpetuate itself.* Once established, the parties do all that they can to keep it that way and prevent a fractious section of the population from breaking away. If necessary, they modify their policies to cater for any new cause.
- *The absence (in Britain) of deep ethnic, linguistic, religious and sectional differences within the population.* In the USA, there is a much less homogeneous population, but many of the diverse elements within the population are accommodated within the melting pot of American life. The American Dream is widely shared, the belief that there is an opportunity for anyone to move from 'log cabin to White House'. There is a similarly common commitment to shared values of individualism and enterprise, which partly explains the failure of any left-wing socialist party from establishing itself.
- *The problems faced by third or other parties.* Lack of finance and other resources, the difficulty of establishing a distinct identity and the danger of being squeezed out by the two main rivals all make life hard for a new party trying to break through. In the USA, there are in addition several legal and other barriers to third-party advancement.

The advantages of two-party systems

- *They promote effective, stable and strong government.* The success of the British political system has often been attributed to the fact that there have been two strong parties, either of which is usually capable of forming a government on its own. Stability is promoted because a government can carry out its policies relieved of the possible fear that it will be suddenly overthrown by a coalition of the minority parties.
- *The system simplifies voter choice,* because only two parties are viable as governing bodies. Accordingly, the people can vote directly for or against an outgoing government, not merely for a party.
- *Government is clearly accountable to the electorate.* The voters know who to praise or blame for the policies in operation, whereas in a coalition situation responsibility is less clearcut. Governments can govern, but there is another one in waiting, should they fail.
- *Moderation is encouraged.* If an opposition party knows that its turn will come, this encourages it to be constructive and pose as

an alternative government, and not to lapse into extremism, which will probably alienate the large number of people in the political centre.

The disadvantages of two-party systems

- *Voter choice is restricted.* This matters less when the main parties are popular and command majority support, but is more serious when many voters feel alienated.
- *Two-party systems, far from promoting moderation, can be characterised by adversary politics*, with an emphasis on conflict and argument rather than consensus and compromise. Governments sometimes come in and undo the work of their predecessors.
- *There is a growing dissatisfaction with the performance of the main parties.* Especially in Britain in recent years, all has not been well with the adversarial two-party system. Governments have not always delivered the goods and neither has the main opposition party necessarily been appealing. Support for third parties (Liberal Democrats and Nationalists) has been growing, and in the USA a low turnout suggests that some people are unimpressed by the presidential challengers – in 1992, they showed a willingness to opt for a third candidate, Ross Perot.

The British two-party system (see also Box 7.1)

Historically, Britain has had a two-party system, Labour and the Conservatives being the dominant parties since the 1930s. In only one election since 1945, has one of the major parties failed to win an outright Commons' majority. The high peak of the two-party system was in 1951 when between them Labour and the Conservatives won 98.6 per cent of the votes and 96.8 per cent of the seats.

The two-party system has generally been resilient, although the rise in third-party support since the mid-1970s has made the picture become more confused. The two main parties have lost electoral support and their overwhelming dominance in parliamentary seats. Indeed, between 1979 and 1997 only one party (the Conservatives) secured victories at the polls, leading to suggestions that we had a dominant-party system, or a two-party system with one-party dominance.

The election of 2005 provided confusing evidence as to whether we still have a two-party system. The two main parties won barely over two-thirds of the popular vote, yet between them gained 554 seats at Westminster. Their joint share of the parliamentary seats was the lowest in any post-war election (85.6 per cent), with the third party (the Liberal Democrats) winning 62 seats, the strongest performance by a third party since 1923. No fewer than six parties (and two independents) won seats in Great Britain and another four did so in Northern Ireland. Moreover, in recent elections, there have been national and regional variations, that make the two-party system primarily an English phenomenon. Leaving aside Northern Ireland, which has a distinctive political system, Scotland and Wales both have a strong nationalist party, creating a situation in which there are four main parties competing for power. Labour is the largest of the four in both countries, so that in effect there is a one-party dominant, four-party system for Westminster elections.

A brief post-war history of the parties
The period 1951–79
In spite of fierce electoral competition and strong theoretical disagreements over the role of the state, private or public ownership of industry and the pursuit of greater social equality, there was between 1951 and 1979 a broad range of agreement between the parties over key economic and social policies, so that the period was often termed 'the era of **consensus** politics' (see Box 7.2). In those years, whatever was said by the party that was in opposition, once it assumed office it tended to follow broadly similar lines of policy to its predecessor. Governments of either party displayed broad support for:

- a **mixed economy**, which included retention of some nationalised public utilities
- the welfare state
- full employment
- the maintenance of strong national defences.

1979–present day
This period of so-called consensus came under threat in the mid to late 1970s, as the Conservatives under the leadership of Margaret Thatcher began to embark upon a radical overhaul of their post-war thinking and approach. Instead of following traditional evolutionary and conservative policies, her governments took a more radical,

Box 7.2 Consensus politics

Consensus implies a wide measure of agreement. In political life, it refers to a circumstance where a large proportion of the population and of the political community are broadly agreed upon certain values, even if there is some disagreement on matters of emphasis or detail.

The period 1951–79 is often described as an 'era of consensus politics', for there seemed to be general agreement about the policies to be pursued. Governments did seem to accept much of what their predecessors had done and found themselves adopting similar solutions to the problems that arose. Peace, prosperity and welfare were widely accepted goals. Some commentators portrayed elections as a contest to decide 'which team of politicians would administer the policies on which everyone was substantially agreed'.[5] Disputes were often more about the degree, the method and the timing of change, rather than representing fundamental conflicts. Even nationalisation, a hot potato of the late 1940s, had cased to be an area of major controversy. Hence Robert McKenzie[6] could portray a situation in which the two parties conducted 'furious arguments about the comparatively minor issues that separate them'.

Not all observers have seen the era of consensus politics in the same light. Reviewing the era, the late Ben Pimlott[7] saw the consensus as 'a mirage, an illusion that rapidly fades the closer one gets to it'. Other critics pointed out that there has always been a considerable level of agreement about fundamentals in British politics, such as support for key institutions and the commitment to peaceful change. Kavanagh and Morris[8] claim that 'the ideas and some of the practices of consensus existed before the Second World War', and state the extension of state ownership and intervention of the interwar years as evidence.

The 'era of consensus' was in no way an era of all-pervasive sweet reason and compromise and at times there were bitter party clashes. It was, after all, in the 1970s that Samuel Finer[9] first put forward the theory of '**adversary politics**'. (See Box 7.3 for a discussion of adversarial politics.)Pimlott noted that the word consensus was little used before the 1980s and that it was then used to distinguish **Thatcherism** from the period that preceded it. His point was that it was much easier to detect consensus in retrospect than it had been at the time.

NB On the continent, where proportional electoral systems are common, policies do tend to be more consensual. Many governments

> are coalitions in which representatives of the various parties involved
> do work together and hammer out policies acceptable to all of them.
> Commentators have often pointed to the example of West Germany,
> where stable coalition governments and economic prosperity were for
> many years seen as going hand in hand. Of course, the semi-circular
> shape of continental parliaments, in which deputies sit according to
> how far right or left they are, encourages cooperation among them,
> whereas the design of our House of Commons forces MPs to choose
> whether they are on the government side or on that of the Opposition.

neoliberal stance quite distinctive from that of previous post-war
Conservative administrations. Labour initially responded to its defeat
in 1979 by moving sharply to the left, so that in 1983 there was a
polarised contest between a right-wing Tory administration and a left-
wing Labour opposition. However, in response to successive further
defeats between 1983 and 1992, Labour moved back towards the
centre ground. By 1997, this process had gone so far that Labour had
become New Labour and jettisoned many of its traditional policies.
See pp. 243–8 for Blairite Labour attitudes and policies.

Under John Major and his successors (see pp. 238–40 for the attitudes and policies of recent years), the modern Conservative Party has
continued to espouse more right-wing policies than in the years of consensus. These have included support for privatisation and pro-market
economic policies; lower direct taxation; reduced governmental expenditure; a tough stance on immigration and asylum seeking: greater
emphasis on law and order; and a more hostile attitude to the European
Union and the issue of closer integration among its members.

The attitudes and beliefs of political parties

Parties are created around broad principles. Although most of their
members are not strict ideologues, these broad ideologies provide
recognition and mean something to many people. Budge et al.
describe[11] ideology as 'a theory about the world and about society,
and of the place of you and your group within it'. These ideologies
are important 'not only in telling leaders what to do but in telling their
supporters who they are and thus making them receptive to leaders'
diagnoses of the political situation'.

Box 7.3 Adversary politics

'Adversarial politics' are characterised by ideological antagonism and an ongoing electoral battle between the major parties. The term is used to refer to a period in which there is fundamental disagreement between the parties on the political issues of the day.

British politics are essentially adversarial in nature. In a two-party system, in which one main party is in office and the other is in opposition, the one defends its policies whilst the other attacks them. The opposite end of the spectrum would be the consensus model, by which policies are adopted only if there is widespread agreement as to their desirability.

Adversarial politics provide the public with a clear examination of the government's policies and of the alternatives posed by the opposition parties. Parliamentary business can sometimes be conducted in a very hostile manner, in which there is much point-scoring between either side and there can be opposition seemingly almost for the sake of it. The shape of the House of Commons encourages such conflict across the floor of the House, pitting as it does one side versus the other. Defenders of the adversarial approach would say that it serves democracy well, because ministers are forced to justify their performance and their policies in the face of a concerted onslaught.

The term 'adversary politics' was coined by Professor Finer[10], an American, to describe the British situation. He felt that the FPTP electoral system produced a regular swing of the pendulum, in which there was little continuity of policy. One party came in and undid what its predecessor had done, so that policies lurched from left to right. The electoral system was therefore based for polarising opinion. By contrast, the comparison was made with West Germany, where stable coalition governments and economic prosperity were seen as going hand in hand.

It was odd that Finer should have written his description in the early 1970s, at the time when Britain was experiencing what other writers would describe as an era of consensus politics. As we have seen, in the preceding couple of decades, ministers had often accepted what their predecessors had done and the differences between Labour and the Conservatives in office often seemed to be not very great.

Parties in many countries tend to employ similar names, so that across the continent words such as Christian, Conservative, Democrat, Green, Labour, Liberal and Socialist are in regular use. This suggests that they have assumptions and ideas that are similar. These common values and beliefs enable us to interpret events and policies more clearly.

Many voters still subscribe in some degree to causes such as **socialism**, in its various forms. However, even those parties within the socialist family can differ sharply over their vision of end goals and the tactics to be pursued in attaining them. Marxian socialism is probably the most developed and influential ideology, for many groups have been formed to argue for it, debate what it means or even react against it. Some socialists are fundamentalists who wish to stick to the ideas of Marx as they see them. Others are revisionists who wish to place them in the context of today's society, which has changed dramatically from the time in which he wrote. A small minority of adherents are willing to countenance violence and upheaval to achieve their aims, whereas the overwhelming majority pursue the democratic route to socialism. In practice, old-style social-ism has gone out of favour, the breakdown of Soviet control in Eastern Europe being widely hailed as a triumph for free-market soci-eties in which capitalism can flourish and individuals lead freer and fuller lives, as well as become more prosperous.

Parties can be classified according to their place on the political spectrum. The terms left and right were originally used to describe the attitudes adopted by different groups in the French Estates-General in 1789. They are still employed today. Broadly, those on the *left* support an increase in governmental activity to create a more just society in which economic and social problems can be addressed, whereas those on the *right* are more wary of state intervention and seek to limit the scope of government as much as possible.

Left and right in British politics

When people talk about party politics in Britain, they still often use the terms 'left', 'right' and 'centre'. Parties and their leading members are often described as left-wing or right-wing, although these labels can be misleading and confusing. People who seem left-wing on one issue may adopt a right-wing approach on another. More seriously, the division of left and right has become somewhat blurred, for supporters of New Labour increasingly employ terminology and adopt approaches traditionally associated with the British Conservative Party. Nonetheless, the terms remain a convenient shorthand by which to summarise different attitudes on important political, economic and social questions.

Very generally:

- *A left-wing person* challenges traditional attitudes and practices and wants to see reform. This involves a more active role for government in bringing about desirable change. He or she may also believe in higher levels of taxation to pay for improvements, some redistribution of wealth from the better-off to the least well-off and movement towards a more equal and less class-bound society. Some left-wingers are keen to see more state control over basic industries, believing that private ownership is unsuitable as a means of running the railways and other essential services.

  People on the left tend to believe in the ideas of 'liberty, equality and fraternity [brotherhood]' which was a popular cry in the French Revolution of the late eighteenth century. They also talk in terms of progress, reform and rights, and are more likely to be internationalists. (In other words, they see issues affecting Britain in world terms.)

- *A right-wing person* is more likely to support the status quo, keeping things as they are unless there is a very strong case for change. He or she is unlikely to favour too much government regulation, favours private enterprise over-state ownership and likes to think that people are left in freedom to run their own lives. Right-wingers will probably favour lower levels of taxation, good rewards for effort and enterprise, and freedom more than equality. An unequal society is accepted as inevitable, even desirable. Right-wingers tend to emphasise a belief in authority, duties, order and tradition, as well as seeing issues from a national rather than an international point of view.

In recent years, the broad left–right ideological divide of the past has become less clearcut. New Labour has shed its nominal socialism and positioned itself firmly in the political centre, seeking to maximise its appeal to moderates of the left and right. As the Liberal

Democrats inhabit similar territory, it means that the middle ground
is very crowded. People in the centre of the political spectrum tend to
support:

- a mixed economy
- acceptance of the marketplace as the best means of running the
  economy
- the duty of the government to take action to ensure that vulnerable members of society are not exploited
- tolerance towards ethnic and other minorities
- constitutional change, including a statement of personal rights.

Even if many members of the Labour and Conservative parties still
portray themselves as belonging to left or right, the leaderships are
aware of the need to attract and maintain support from a wide variety
of interests and from people with a wide range of political beliefs. To
some extent, as is common in most two-party systems, Labour and the
Conservatives are catch-all parties, in both cases having their own left
and right-wing, whose members advance a range of views on the
issues of the day. However, members and supporters of both main
parties share a number of distinctive ideas and philosophies, to which
we will now turn.

The British Conservative Party

British Conservatism has a long history. It embraces a broad spectrum
of ideas about the nature of humankind, society and political change.
It is a right-wing creed that emphasises preserving the best of the past
(including the traditions and institutions of the country) and allowing
society to develop gradually, adapting only where change is proved to
be necessary. At different times the party has placed more or less
emphasis on conserving the past and on reform.

The party was astonishingly successful in elections in the twentieth
century. In part, its success was brought about by a willingness to
adapt to changing circumstances. Unlike some continental right-wing
parties primarily representing the middle and upper classes, the
Conservatives never allowed themselves to be in the position of
opposing all progress just to preserve their self-interest. Under more
progressive leaders, the party reached out to working-class voters and

was of appeal to many of them. Without working-class support, it would never have won as many elections as it has in an age of mass franchise.

The party has always been concerned about electoral success. In the words of Glyn Parry[12], 'the primary and abiding aim of the [Conservative] Party is the achievement of power'. In the past, this mattered more than being too preoccupied with ideas. Indeed, an excess of ideological baggage was seen as a barrier to success. In matters of ideology, the wise Conservative 'travels light'.[13]

Key enduring themes for Conservatives are:

- a cautious approach to change
- distrust of the role of 'big government'
- an emphasis upon law and order
- an emphasis upon 'Britishness' (patriotism, defending institutions)
- a preference for freedom over equality, and private over-state enterprise.

In the post-war era, the Conservatives generally stuck to **one-nation** policies that were seen as pragmatic (practical, realistic). Most came to accept the welfare state and the need for more governmental intervention and regulation. In the 1980s, under Margaret Thatcher, the emphasis was rather different. She was committed to traditional party policies such as a firm stand on law and order, and promoting the idea of 'Great Britain'. But she scorned the timid 'wets' of the post-war era and wanted clearer, more distinctive Tory policies. Her New Right approach was markedly more ideological. Thatcherism was strongly in favour of free enterprise, market forces, lower taxes and more consumer choice, and hostile to trade-union power. She stressed individual effort, wanted people to solve their own problems and admired perseverance and self-reliance, which she wished to see rewarded. This more right-wing Conservatism endured after her retirement and the party continues to support less government and place emphasis on individual rather than collective values.

The battle to achieve free-market economic policies has been won. Conservatives of all shades (and New Labour too) are converts. In the last few years, there has been a different distinction among Conservatives between social liberals and more traditional Tories. Social liberals want to see the party become more inclusive, broaden its appeal and make itself more attractive to ethnic minorities, gays and others. Traditionalists are wary of social liberalism and feel more at home with traditional Tory attitudes, especially on such issues as support for authority, religion and family values.

Box 7.4 Recent Conservative leaders and their position on the party spectrum

The Conservative Party constitution describes the leader as 'the main fountain and interpreter of policy'. Leaders are therefore able to lead the party in accordance with their own ideas, values and preferences. Recent incumbents have been on the right of the party, although sometimes they have felt the need to stress their support for greater social tolerance in order to try and widen the party's basis of support. The tendency has been to revert to their more usual stance, as an election approaches.

John Major (1990–7)

John Major's policy outlook was not markedly different from that of his more famous predecessor. He fully embraced her free-market principles, so that some writers spoke of 'Thatcherism without Thatcher'. Indeed, his government embarked on some privatisations that even she had considered ambitious, notably the mines and the railways. He was also more able to make inroads into the social-security budget, by adopting a tough line on incapacity benefit. Yet others referred to Majorism as 'Thatcherism with a human face', for the Major rhetoric was milder, more consensual. His was a more emollient style, as was indicated by his preference for 'a nation at ease with itself', in which there were more opportunities for all, irrespective of background or colour. He was also by instinct more sympathetic to Britain's place being firmly planted 'at the heart of Europe', although events were to make this a position difficult to maintain.

What he lacked was Margaret Thatcher's resolve and firm approach to leadership. Although an electoral asset in 1992, his government became discredited. He was increasingly portrayed as weak and indecisive, as he attempted to hold together a diverse and not always loyal Cabinet.

William Hague (1997–2001)

William Hague was more right-wing than Major, especially more 'anti-European'. Yet he was also more libertarian than many

Conservatives. Following such a resounding defeat in 1997, the party had no clear policy position, it being difficult to take up new policies as members of the shadow cabinet were too closely associated with past unpopular ones, pursued when in office. At first, he saw the need to widen the party's appeal, by using inclusive language and making it clear that he wanted the Conservatives to embrace the cause of those who were unfortunate or disadvantaged. However, as the election drew near, there was an increasing tendency to populism on issues such as law and order, asylum seekers and the euro. In the 2001 campaign, he had little to say on the state of public services, the issue that mattered to many voters.

Iain Duncan Smith (2001–3)

After the 2001 debacle, Iain Duncan Smith (IDS) saw the need to emphasise issues of more direct concern to the public and in particular wished to emphasise the need to reform the public services, though by a more distinctively Conservative approach than New Labour. He found it difficult to resolve the conflict within his party between the social liberals and the traditional Conservatives. In particular, on gay issues he found himself leading a parliamentary party that was seriously divided. He had more success in uniting the party around European policy. Like William Hague and unlike John Major, he was happy to rule out membership of the Eurozone. His party was able to unite around his **Eurosceptic** position, which carried conviction as he had a past record as a **Maastricht** rebel and had at one time contemplated a British exit from the European Union.

Lacking charisma and an ineffective performer in the House, he found his leadership coming under sustained pressure as Conservatives noted the failure of the party to make headway in the polls. He resigned after defeat in a vote of confidence in his leadership (75 for, 95 against).

Michael Howard (2003–5)

A barrister by background, Michael Howard – a right-wing member of the Thatcher and Major cabinets – brought experience to the leadership. He also seemed a more heavyweight figure than his predecessors and was a more able performer in the House of Commons, with a lawyer's forensic ability to question and a natural and sometimes biting sarcasm. Conservatives hoped he could score points off Tony Blair, although few of them – other than in their dreams – seriously thought that he was likely to lead them to victory in 2005, for the task was a daunting one. He failed to increase the Conservative vote significantly, although the number of Conservative MPs increased to 198. He ceased to be leader in December 2005.

> On policy issues, Michael Howard was firmly planted on the right of the party, lukewarm on the European Union and keen to retrieve, where possible, powers lost to Brussels. He recognised the need for a broader Conservatism, so that although by instinct he was unenthusiastic to the notion of gay couples being allowed to adopt children he recognised the damage that might occur if he tried to enforce a traditionalist approach on his party.

Conservative problems and prospects

The Conservatives used to be the natural pattern of government. Their leaders managed to convey the idea that the party was uniquely capable of governing, whereas their opponents were derided as divided, ineffective, extreme or even un-British. By the end of the twentieth century, they had shed their reputation and advantages and were no longer seen as competent, united or well led. They were besmirched by scandals and sleaze.

In 2005, eight years after their heavy defeat in 1997, they still did not seem to be a credible alternative to New Labour. They had little distinctive to say on the main issues that concern the voters (in particular, the state of the public services); their leader was not popular in the country; and they were unable to develop any 'big idea' around which to campaign. Having marginally increased their share of the popular vote in 2001 (see below), they made further progress in 2005, benefiting from a 3.1 per cent swing in their favour and picking up 32 seats:

> 1997　31.5%　　　2001　32.7%　　　2005　33.2%

Electoral support is still not only low in percentage terms, but too heavily based on the elderly section of the population, some two out of three members being over 50 years old. There is an imbalance, because as members die, they are not being replaced by young recruits. At the local level, it is still hard to motivate volunteers to work for a party whose social profile is so heavily dominated by retired people.

The electoral challenge facing the Conservatives is formidable. The party has less MPs than did Labour in its dismal result of 1983. To win a bare parliamentary majority, it needs an additional 126 seats. The task is made worse by the in-built bias towards Labour in the electoral system, as it now operates. This is caused in part by the distribution of parliamentary seats, enabling Labour to win in many constituencies with small majorities (i.e. they are 'safe seats'). **Tactical voting** by voters in key constituencies has also in recent years exacerbated conservative electoral difficulties.

Apart from electoral hurdles, there are other difficulties. There is a lack of 'big hitters' on the party front bench. There are image problems associated with right-wing elements in the party membership, with some members still finding it difficult to accept the multi-ethnic society that Britain has become. The new leader takes over at a time when the party's fortunes remain at a low ebb. There is a need for fresh faces and a major rethink about the sort of party that the Conservatives wish to be. At present, they are widely viewed as too elderly, too out of touch and (surprisingly, in view of their historical record) too ideological.

Yet for all of their present difficulties, the record of the Conservatives suggests that their ability to transform themselves and update their organisation and policies to meet the challenges of the day stands them in good stead. The party has in the past pulled itself together under leaders able to modernise its image and platform, as the experience of Peel, Disraeli and the post-1945 Conservatives indicates. Other parties come and go, but it is likely that in some form the Conservative Party will always survive, for conservatism is an abiding element of the political scene.

The Labour Party

By its 1918 constitution, Labour committed itself to socialism. Socialism is not a precise term and different party thinkers and leaders have given it their own slant. However, many early socialists in the party saw the creed in terms of the original Clause Four of their constitution (see Box 7.5 on socialism, the old and new Clause Four, and Blairite thinking):

> To secure for the workers by hand or by brain the full fruits of their industry and the most equitable distribution thereof that may be possible upon the basis of the common ownership of the means of production, distribution and exchange.

Clause Four was for several years a 'sacred cow' of the Labour movement and the left of the party acted as its guardian. Traditionalists

Box 7.5 What is socialism?

Dictionary definition
'An economic theory or system in which the means of production, distribution and exchange are owned by the community collectively, usually through the state. It is characterised by production for use rather than profit, by equality of individual wealth, by the absence of competitive economic activity, and usually, by government determination of investment, prices and production levels.'

R.H. Tawney, *Equality*, 1931
'[Of socialism:] Its fundamental dogma is the dignity of man; its fundamental criticism of capitalism is, not merely that it impoverishes the mass of mankind – poverty is an ancient evil – but that it makes riches a god, and treats common men as less than men. Socialism accepts, therefore, the principles which are the cornerstones of democracy, that authority, to justify its title, must rest on consent; that power is tolerable only so far as it is accountable to the public; and that differences of character and capacity between human beings, however unimportant on their own plane, are of minor significance compared with the capital fact of their common humanity.'

Hugh Gaitskell, right-wing Labour leader of the 1950s to early 1960s
'[Of equality, "the central socialist ideal":] By this, I do not mean identical incomes or uniform habits and tastes. But I do mean a classless society – one in which the relations between all people are similar to those hitherto existing between one social class; one in which although there are differences between individuals, there are no feelings of superiority or inferiority between groups . . . one in which, although people develop differently, there is equal opportunity for all to develop.'

Anthony Crosland, *Socialism Now*, a revisionist work of the 1970s
'[Detected in socialism] a set of values, of aspirations, of principles, which socialists wish to see embodied in the organisation of society.'

Clause Four: key elements of the *revised* version, adopted in 1995
- The Labour Party is a democratic socialist party. It believes that by the strength of our common endeavour we achieve more than

we achieve alone so as to create for each of us the means to realise our true potential and for all of us a community in which power, wealth and opportunity are in the hands of the many not the few, where the rights we enjoy reflect the duties we owe, and where we live together freely, in a spirit of solidarity, tolerance and respect.

- To these ends we work for: a dynamic economy . . .
- a just society . . .
- an open democracy . . . a healthy environment . . . Labour is committed to the defence and security of the British people . . .
- Labour will work in pursuit of these aims with trade unions . . .
- On the basis of these principles, Labour seeks the trust of the people to govern.

Note two features of the new clause, both of which reflect the Blairite outlook:

1. The prominence given to enterprise, competition and the free market
2. The moral dimension, with references to personal responsibility, the family and our duty to care for each other.

These reflect two broad streams of influence on Blair's thinking. The first of these is Thatcherism – Tony Blair has been prepared to acknowledge that Margaret Thatcher got some things right, including the pursuit of economic realism, the need for Britain to compete in a global economy without the old protections afforded by state intervention. The second is a mixture of old and new, and is responsible for the moral side of the Prime Minister's thinking. On the one hand, there are the old traditions of ethical and Christian socialism; on the other, there are the more recent developments in political ideas, known as **communitarianism** (associated with the American thinker Amitei Etzioni) and the **stakeholder society** as elaborated by Will Hutton[15], two ideas that attempt to restate the relationship between the individual and society.

The Blair approach is a long way from traditional socialism. Some on the left of the party see it as little more than Thatcherism with a human face. Even some formerly on the right of the party such as Lord Hattersley lament that the previous importance attached to equality of outcome has now been downgraded to equality of opportunity. But others are attracted by what Tony Blair calls 'the third way', a mid-way position between pure capitalism and excessive state control. As he put it[16]:

[Labour] has a social conscience . . . [but] it recognises that we also need economic efficiency, trade unions given their place in our democracy but not confused with government . . . Labour believes in good business as well as a good society.

The third way
In Britain, the concept of the third way is most closely associated in academic circles with Anthony Giddens[17]. But the idea of a 'third way' is not entirely new. Harold Macmillan adopted a middle way for the Conservative Party in the 1930s. Essentially the third way is an attempt to find a middle route between left and right, between state socialist planning and free-market capitalism. It appeals to centre-left progressives and moderate social democrats. Giddens uses the term to refer to social democratic renewal. In his view, renewal was necessary in the late 1990s to adapt to the probably irreversible transformation of Britain by Thatcherism, the revival of free-market capitalism and the realities of globalisation.

The aim of the third way is basically to reject the old left and the new right and combine a market economy with a decent society, social justice with economic efficiency. Both markets and state should be disciplined by a public interest test. Legislation should provide redress for consumers and monitor the quality of state services (e.g. the Blair government's introduction of a minimum wage and measures against failing schools).

Equality is defined as 'inclusion' and inequality as 'exclusion'. Social inclusion refers in its broadest sense to citizenship, with its civil and political rights, its obligations and its opportunities for self-fulfilment and to make a contribution to society. It involves everyone having access to the requirements for a decent life, including education, health care, work and income. Measures need to be put in place to reduce the involuntary exclusion of the disadvantaged. The old social democracy was likely to provide rights unconditionally. Now the rights of citizens are accompanied by reciprocal duties and it is vital that there is mutual responsibility between individuals and institutions. For example, parents have the right to send their children to school but parents also are responsible for encouraging their children and supporting their school.

The third way is the theoretical basis of the Blair government's thinking and vision for the reshaping of British politics and society. It is also a strategy about creating a new left-of-centre progressive consensus in Britain and elsewhere. Its exponents share a commitment to practical social democracy. Shunning an excess of ideology, they proclaim that 'what matters is what works'.

wanted to preserve it intact and continued to see socialism in terms of public ownership of key industries, known as the policy of nation alisation.

After the Second World War, some leaders such as Hugh Gaitskell tried to get Clause Four rewritten. He and most moderate, right-of-centre Labour MPs saw socialism more in terms of the pursuit of greater equality, a more just and fair society. Socialism was about 'a set of values, of aspirations, of principles' (Anthony Crosland[14], one-time MP and minister). Like Gaitskell, he stressed that there should be equal opportunity for everyone to develop their potential. The welfare state, which the party did much to create, embraced many Labour ideas about the importance of society, humanity and care for one another.

Following a series of electoral defeats in 1979 and after, Tony Blair set out to reinvent the party as New Labour. He boldly tackled the party's constitution, rewriting Clause Four so that it now stresses community values such as equality of power, tolerance and respect, rights and duties, the emphasis being on society. He modernised the party, along similar lines to the way in which Bill Clinton had modernised the American Democrats. Its new values were tougher in some areas and on some groups who had traditionally looked to Labour to protect them (such as trade unions and the poor, whom he wished to give 'a hand-up rather than a hand-out').

Blairism in practice: 1997 onwards
While in opposition before the 1997 election and subsequently, Tony Blair has adopted some terminology more usually associated with the Conservatives. He has employed terms such as 'the market', 'achievement', 'opportunity' and 'aspirations', his whole approach representing an attempt to broaden Labour's appeal. In the process, his ideas and policies have upset many traditional Labour voters who claim that New Labour is too pro-business and that he is too concerned about pleasing Middle England.

A conscious aim of the Blair leadership has been to gather many of the moderates in British politics into 'Tony's big tent'. In the process, critics allege that he has transformed the Labour Party, shifting it not just from a socialist into a social democratic party, but abandoning even social democracy as well. They portray him as a modern-day New Liberal of the early twentieth century, the spiritual heir to Lloyd George and Asquith rather than a descendant of the previous post-war Labour prime ministers, Attlee, Wilson and Callaghan.

There is some truth in the analysis, but much of the language of Tony Blair still echoes traditional Labour vocabulary. He talks of community, cooperation, fairness, partnership, society and solidarity. Some of the actions of his government – constitutional reform, devolution, the introduction of a minimum wage, signature of the Social Chapter, the New Deal work programme and the injection of funding into education and the National Health Service – seem very much in the Labour tradition and are policies that Conservatives – even many moderate ones – opposed. In truth, Blair has been non-doctrinaire, borrowing from several traditions, socialist, social democratic, New Liberal, pragmatic One Nation Conservative and even Thatcherite, as the circumstances seem to make appropriate. There is no clear Blairite philosophy, rather Blairism represents a retreat from ideology.

Old and New Labour compared: some key features

Labour traditionally saw itself as a democratic socialist party, a term still used even in the new clause Four. The British road to socialism, as pursued by the Labour Party, was always based on a gradualist, evolutionary approach, not a revolutionary one. Marxism never made a great impact on many of the Labour Party's supporters.

Labour's boldest days were in the first post-war administration led by Clement Attlee, during which time the basis of the welfare state was established and many industries and utilities were taken into public ownership. Modern-day socialists look back upon the governments of 1945–51 with pride. By comparison, the Wilson and Callaghan administrations in the 1960s and 1970s were mildly reformist, often faced with a difficult economic situation.

Labour's manifesto in 1983 (dubbed 'the longest suicide note in history') was very Old Labour and leftish, advocating withdrawal from the European Community, the removal of American nuclear bases and the scrapping of the British nuclear deterrent, widespread nationalisation and abolition (without replacement) of the House of

Lords. Its heavy defeat led to an era of modernisation that began under Neil Kinnock, was continued by John Smith and taken much further with the creation of New Labour by Tony Blair. Now that New Labour has been tested in office, it is easier to see how far Labour has travelled over recent years. The party was and remains a coalition whose members possess differing shades of opinion, but there are discernible differences of old and new.

Characteristics of Old Labour
- Close to trade unions
- Willingness to raise taxes to finance high levels of public expenditure
- Committed to generous universal welfare benefits and full employment
- Belief in equality of outcome
- Nominal belief at least in old-style Clause Four, with its belief in nationalisation
- Working-class party with limited appeal to middle classes
- Lukewarm support/hostility for European Community
- Use of language of caring, compassion, social justice and equality
- Relatively little interest in presentation and spin/media manipulation
- Lack of prolonged majority government.

Characteristics of New Labour
- More detached from unions (Blair promise in 1997: 'no special favours')
- More harsh (some would say realistic) on welfare benefits
- Keen to keep public spending under control
- Keen to keep direct taxation down, or anyway not increase it (if necessary, willing to use 'stealth taxes' to raise funds)
- Belief in equality of opportunity
- Support for new Clause Four, with its emphasis on values
- Less appeal to traditional supporters, stronger bid for support of Middle England and 'big tent' approach
- Pro-Europeanism
- Interest in presentation and spin, concern with image
- Electoral success: three consecutive majority governments.

Is New Labour socialist?

- To some extent, it depends on the meaning of how you define socialism. Not in the traditional sense (Clause Four), nor even in the 'revisionist' sense of the 1950s and 1960s, implying a belief in a greater equality of outcome.
- Tony Blair hardly employs the word socialism, a term that has rather gone out of fashion following the end of Soviet control over Eastern Europe in the early 1990s.
- If it is socialist, it is socialism devoid of the traditional Marxian economic content. He is more in the tradition of ethical socialism, with its emphasis on values and a sense of community.
- The emphasis has been on appealing widely to aspirational voters who have wanted to better themselves. There is less emphasis on levelling down and more in creating opportunities for people to make the most of their talents. Blair talks of 'old ideas in a modern setting'.

Box 7.6 The two main parties compared: a summary of Labour and Conservative attitudes and policies

Some differences in their attitudes and ideas, past and present

- *The pace and extent of change*. Labour is in business to change society, to make it better, more just. The Conservatives are more interested in keeping things as they are, only changing as change proves necessary. They are wary of the idea that action by government can improve the tone of society.
- *The role of government*. Labour recognises an important role for government in changing society and is more willing to use the power of the state to improve conditions and stamp out injustice. Traditionally, it is a party of 'big government'. Conservatives want to see government play less of a role in the social and economic life of the nation, being more willing to allow individuals freely to live their own lives and businesses left unregulated.
- *Taxation*. Labour is traditionally more willing to tax the better-off in order to finance social reform. It is much less so now, although Chancellor Gordon Brown has resorted to 'stealth taxes' as a means of avoiding putting up levels of income tax. The Conservatives are traditionally a lower-tax party and although in

2005 their pledges were modest, they were keen to show that they wish to move towards lower direct tax. That is always a clear goal.

- *Government spending.* In his early years, the Chancellor constantly emphasised his message of 'prudence' and would not support high spending on social programmes, but in the last five years he has allowed much more spending on education and health. The Conservatives are keen to pare down spending, especially by cost-cutting initiatives and 'wars on waste'.

- *Public versus private provision.* Labour has always been committed to a publicly provided welfare state, and a NHS based on need on ability to pay. Under Tony Blair, it has been more willing to use the private sector to help offset pressure on the NHS and its solutions are more market-based than in the past. Some Conservatives dislike the idea of the welfare state and NHS and would prefer private provision. The party generally supports ideas to encourage private treatment in health care (e.g. tax concessions), and on welfare policy is keen to look at continental schemes financed by schemes of insurance.

- *Trade unions.* Labour was formed out of the trade-union movement and has historic and emotional links with the unions and TUC. Under Neil Kinnock and Tony Blair, it has distanced itself from the unions and Tony Blair has disappointed union leaders by often seeming more willing to listen to representatives of 'big business'. Yet the unions have benefited from some Blairite policies (e.g. the minimum wage) and find it easier to work with a Labour administration. In the Thatcher era, the Conservatives were tough on the unions and are still keen to portray Labour as unwilling to stand up to union power.

NB In the past there have been clear differences on two more issues, see below. It is less easy to detect them today, for the Blairite Labour Party has been tougher in its language and policies than past Labour governments used to be. Nonetheless, the Conservative attack on Labour for its alleged 'weakness' in tackling violent crime was again evident in 2005.

- *Law and order.* Labour used to be regularly accused by the Conservatives of failing to take action to maintain law and order. The Blair government has adopted a tough stand on the issue, 'tough on crime, tough on the causes of crime'. It currently targets hooligan behaviour, young offenders and those who cause disorder on the streets. It does also place emphasis on removing the causes of discontent in society, such as racial discrimination and racial tension. (Ironically, its action over Iraq has upset ethnic minorities, who in the past rallied to the party.) The Conservatives tend to be very tough on law and order, this being in the past one of their strongest policy issues. They have been less willing to emphasise the social causes of disorder, even in areas where there are clear problems being faced by ethnic minorities.

*   *Patriotism.* Labour was often accused in the past of not standing up firmly for British interests Over war in Iraq (2003), it showed that Labour can certainly take firm action when its leader sees this as being in the British national interest. Past Labour governments have tended to be more obviously supportive of the United Nations (UN). The Conservatives have always emphasised their patriotism and willingness to stand up for Britain, whatever the UN position might be. Officially, they were supportive of action over Iraq. The Conservatives also stress their support for traditional British institutions, such as the monarchy.

Third and minor parties in Britain and elsewhere

By a *third party*, we usually mean one that is capable of gathering a sizeable percentage of popular support and regularly gains seats in the legislature (e.g. the British Liberal Democrats). On occasion, it may win – or threaten to win – sufficient support to influence the outcome of an election.

By a *minor party*, we mean one that gains only a tiny percentage of popular support and almost never gains representation in the legislature (e.g. the British National Party).

The value of third and minor parties

*   *They take up particular causes neglected by the other parties,* such as Prohibition in America or abortion (Pro-Life Alliance in Britain). Similarly, the Greens in many countries give special emphasis to environmental policies.
*   *They ventilate certain grievances not being taken up by traditional parties* – as in the case of Plaid Cymru and the SNP, who long argued for more attention to be paid to their needs. The same could be said of far right policies such as the British National Party, which thrives on unease over immigration and race relations. Arguably, it is better that they should be allowed to articulate their cause via the normal political process, for otherwise they might be more tempted by anti-democratic methods.

- *They can act as a haven for protest voters.* The Liberals and their successors have often fulfilled this role in British politics, and so did Perot in America in 1992. Such protest can act as a spur to the traditional parties, saving them from apathy and indifference.
- *At times, they may affect the outcome of elections*, perhaps even exercise a balance of power. Ralph Nader's Green Party affected the Florida result in 2000 (and consequently determined who was to be president), just as Perot's intervention eight years earlier cost George Bush senior the contest versus Bill Clinton. In the British system, in which the government is dependent on majority support in the legislature, there may be times when a third party can maintain a government in power (e.g. the Liberals in the late 1970s).

On occasion, third and minor parties have made a major breakthrough. In twentieth-century Britain, Labour came to replace the Liberals as the second party in the interwar years. But more often, small parties are doomed to a peripheral role. It may be part of the definition of a party that it seeks political office in order to implement its programme. For most, the hope is illusory. In Britain and America there are many minor parties who are unlikely ever to gain more than one or two % of the votes in any election.

Box 7.7 British third and minor parties

The Liberal Democrats
The Liberal Democrats were formed as a result of a merger between the old British Liberal party and the Social Democrats, a break-away element from the Labour right. The new party soon established its own identity, but the past commitment to pro-Europeanism, racial justice and tolerance was preserved. Under Paddy Ashdown's leadership, the party moved nearer to the opposition Labour Party, abandoning its former equidistance. Labour and the Liberal Democrats cooperated on constitutional proposals before the 1997 election.

Under the leadership of Charles Kennedy, the Liberal Democrats distanced themselves from ministerial policies, especially as Labour ran into stormy waters. He and other Liberal Democrats criticised the timidity of the Prime Minister in not giving a clear lead in favour of Britain's early membership of the euro. They reserved their most profound criticism for the conduct of events leading to the Iraq war, deeply uneasy as they were about the decision to embark on hostilities.

In electoral terms, the party has fared well in recent elections. In 2005, it won nearly 6 million votes (22 per cent), its 62 MPs being a higher total than at any time since 1923. Yet there were reasons for disappointment. Having won seats from the Labour and Conservative parties, the Liberal Democrats also lost others back to the main opposition party. Many members of the party and outside analysts felt that they should have performed more strongly. In particular, their 'decapitation strategy', in which they targeted well-known Tory scalps, failed to deliver. They had hoped for substantial inroads into Conservative territory and this did not happen.

Other parties

Whereas the Liberal Democrats are a third force to be reckoned with, having substantial parliamentary representation, the other UK-wide parties have much less popular support and rarely gain any representation. Yet they do articulate the thinking of a section of the voters. The British National Party attracts much of its support from poor whites who see their position threatened by the post-war influx of Commonwealth immigrants and asylum seekers.

One of the fast-growing parties in Britain is the *UK Independence Party*, committed to outright withdrawal from the European Union. From 1994, it has put up a candidate in every parliamentary by-election and gained a strong result in the 2004 Euro-elections. It put up 496 candidates in 2005, but failed to get any elected. Robert Kilroy-Silk, an ex-chat show host, briefly led a breakaway party, *Veritas*, whose candidates in 2005 offered a similar right-wing Eurosceptic message to that of UKIP.

On the Left, the *Socialist Labour Party* comprises mainly ex-Labour members who find Blairism unpalatable. Members of *Respect*, a coalition of the Trotskyite Socialist Workers Party, some Muslim groups and remnants of Old Labour, echo such distaste for New Labour. The party strongly disapproves of Western military involvement in Iraq. The *Greens* also oppose this war. Primarily an ecological party, the Greens have tried to broaden their appeal by taking up other policy themes in recent years.

Of the other parties, the nationalists are by far the most important. The *Scottish Nationalist Party* (SNP) is a separatist party, wanting independence from Great Britain. It is now the second largest party in Scotland, after Labour. It does not emphasise the usual cultural nationalism of parties of the nationalist type. By contrast, *Plaid Cymru* has always been a more traditional nationalist party, speaking up for the culture and language of Wales. This has tended to limit its appeal to Welsh-speaking areas, although there are signs in the Welsh National Assembly elections that the party is now extending its support into the southern valleys.

Both the SNP and Plaid Cymru are pro-European and have contested European elections keenly. They have done relatively well in these and the devolved elections, helped by the use of proportional voting systems.

Table 7.1 Party membership in European democracies

1990–2000: membership as % of electorate

Austria	18
Finland	10
Norway	7
Italy	4
Germany	3
United Kingdom	2

(Adapted from P. Mair and I. Van Biezen, 'Party Membership in Europe, 1980–2000', in *Party Politics* (7), 2001)

Party membership in Britain, early–mid-2004

Labour	210,000
Conservatives	251,000
Lib Dems	74,000
SNP	11,000
Plaid Cymru	10,000

Figures provided by party headquarters

Party membership and finance

Party membership has been declining in Europe over the last few decades, as the figures in Table 7.1 indicate. There are exceptions to the trend such as Greece, Portugal and Spain, but as their peoples were living under or recovering from authoritarian regimes early in this period the comparison is made more complicated. Now living in more open societies, citizens of these countries have taken the opportunity to benefit from their newly won freedom and participate more actively.

Some writers see declining membership as an indication of a lessening of enthusiasm for and interest in political parties. They point to the loss of members by established parties and adversely compare it to the growth in pressure group activity. The low figures quoted may also reflect the fact that parties today spend less time on recruiting than in the past, for they once needed activists to engage in voluntary work and rally the local voters to turn out in support of their candidate. Nowadays, the 'nationalisation' of election campaigning has placed more emphasis on the whereabouts of party leaders and their senior colleagues. Finally, there may be too many other things that people can do with their time; for many, politics is a lower priority than once it was, perhaps because many of the 'big issues' of world peace and hunger have lost much of their impact on the European continent.

Of course, although changing electoral methods may provide an explanation, parties would be foolish to allow this to deter them from seeking to revive their membership. In Scandinavia the social democratic parties engaged in a drive for recruitment in the early 1990s. New Labour enthusiasts initially saw it as essential to create a mass membership, at a time when its trade-union links were being downplayed.

Finance

The role of money in political life is an issue of daily debate in old and new democracies alike. It is the driving force for modern competitive political systems, a point recognised some decades ago by a Californian politician, Jesse Unruh, who described it as 'the mother's milk of politics'. Party financing is a vital aspect of modern party politics. The ways in which parties get access to money can influence the outcome of elections, determine the relationship between party leaders and members, affect the number of women elected and condition the level of public trust as a whole. Parties everywhere are finding difficultly in raising sufficient income to meet increased costs.

The widespread fall in figures for party membership has implications for party finances. In many European countries, the decline in income from membership has been compensated for by the establishment of some form of state funding of party activity. Such aid is normally unconditional, being dependent upon the support achieved in the previous election. German parties receive generous subsidies that often constitute well over a quarter of their income.

In Anglo-Saxon countries, Australia, Canada and the United States have seen state funding as a necessity to bridge the gap between the expenditure that is necessary for political purposes and the funds raised from voluntary donations to parties and candidates. America has a scheme of federal funding for candidates willing to accept strict limits upon raising and spending corporate money. It is conditional aid, the amount being triggered by the decisions of private individuals. Political finance is almost completely candidate-oriented, whereas in Canada and the UK in particular, campaigns are run predominantly by parties.

Parties receive funding from three main sources, other than by public subsidy:

1. Subscriptions from individual party members
2. Donations, either from companies or from individuals (sometimes these are one-off sums from generous benefactors or take the form of bequests)
3. Contributions from associated bodies, such as affiliated trade unions.

Many people feel uneasy about huge contributions from wealthy businessmen, particularly those who reside outside the country concerned. However, it is the income from business organisations and trade unions that generates the greatest anxiety. There is a common perception that 'he who pays the piper calls the tune'; money may be given not just because an organisation shares the broad outlook of the party it is backing, but in the hope and anticipation that decisions taken by ministers will be favourable to it.

The finance of British parties

Operating a political party is an expensive enterprise. British parties need funding for four main categories of expenditure:

Table 7.2 Party incomes, (%): a summary (year ending December 2003)

Source	Conservatives	Labour
Donations and fundraising	56.1	36.8
Membership fees and subscriptions	5.8	12.8
Affiliation fees (trade unions)		25.1
Commercial enterprises		11.6
Grants	30.4	
Other, including investment income, notional interest, legacies etc.	7.7	13.7
Total	100 (£13,619,000)	100 (£26,940,000)
Surplus/deficit	−£2,415,000	+£2,637,000

NB This was a non-election year and neither was an election looming. The Conservatives received heavy pre-election donations in the run-up to the 2005 election but were nonetheless unable to match the Labour party's spending on the campaign: Labour £17,939,617 Conservatives £17,852,240 Liberal Democrats £4,324,574.

1. *Maintaining headquarters* – day-to-day running costs and an administrative machine to deal with relations with branches who need back-up support. In particular, as far as the public is concerned, the educational work of the parties is important. They conduct research and produce pamphlets, contributing to broader political understanding.
2. *Reserve funds* – to deal with any emergency that may arise, such as repairs to central headquarters.
3. *Campaign costs* – fighting general and other elections requires heavy spending on propaganda, speaking tours and the services of sophisticated agencies and political consultants, to help get the message across. With the advent of European, devolved and

mayoral elections, the campaigning costs have significantly increased in recent years.

4. *Local constituencies* – these have their own expenses, again maintaining headquarters, printing leaflets and meeting costs incurred in-fighting the constituency election campaign.

The finance of British parties has been more tightly regulated in recent years, following the publication of a special report (1998) of the Neill Committee on Standards in Public Life. Labour broadly accepted its recommendations and embodied many of them in its

---

Box 7.8 State funding in Britain: for and against

In favour
- The nub of the case for political funding is concerned with the importance of party activity to the democratic process. Political parties and their competition for political power are essential for sustainable democracy and good governance. Visible party competition requires well-entrenched political parties that need to be encouraged to develop and strengthen. Adequate resources are required for necessary activities. With state aid, they would be less preoccupied with ensuring their survival and more with genuine political activity. The present trend for parties to reduce expenditure in an attempt to balance the books results in less agents and less staff at headquarters to deal in research or answer queries from the public. This can be said to be detrimental to the political process. By investing in political parties, we invest in democracy as well.
- That it would reduce the excessive dependence of the two main parties on their large institutional backers, companies in the case of the Conservative Party and companies and trade unions in the case of Labour. State funding avoids the perception that wealthy backers are able to buy influence over the operations of a political party. Too much reliance on funding from either the private or the public sector of society is unwise. Democracy involves pluralism in all things, including sources of finance.
- Parties of the centre-left tend to be at a disadvantage with those of the right, for they do not have the means to compete. Labour still derives much of its strength from the inner cities, where voters tend to be relatively poor. By contrast, many Conservative

voters are more affluent and can afford to be more generous in their political giving. They are also more likely to join a political party. Working people do not tend to be 'joiners' of organisations to the same extent. Political parties that do not have such backing are placed at an unfair disadvantage, being unable to spend so heavily on expensive poster campaigns. For smaller parties, the situation may seem particularly unfair. Such difficulties are compounded when several elections arise together as in 1979 and 1997, making the annual costs of electioneering high.

The principle of some state assistance to British political parties has already been conceded. Help is given to opposition parties (the so-called **'Short' money**) to assist them in the performance of their parliamentary work, and at election time facilities are made available to them at no cost. The amount of money involved in terms of government spending on such assistance is small. By ensuring that payment is dependent on a certain level of success in the last election, the difficulty of the state financing small and extreme parties such as the British National Party is removed.

Against
Critics of state funding tend to emphasise these arguments:

- Politics is essentially a voluntary activity. If parties are currently short of funds, then they must either curtail their costs or seek funds in other ways such as more local fundraising by volunteer workers. With state funding available, there would be little incentive for parties to go out and recruit a mass membership.
- The decline in membership and waning popularity of the two main parties suggests that they are not as popular as they once were. The answer is that they need to pursue policies which are more in tune with the needs and wishes of the voters. When they are perceived as being 'in touch', they will be more attractive to voters who are potential recruits.
- Taxpayers who are not interested in politics might resent being asked to finance party activity. Cynicism and disillusion with politicians are widely prevalent. They would be increased if the public was expected to spend money on their activities. Sceptics might suspect that any extra money be spent on needless extravagances, such as glossy brochures and advertising material.
- Popular support for state funding has often increased when corruption seems to be all-pervasive, but there is little evidence that state funding ends corruption, and some people even argue that it can increase rather than diminish it. In Italy, assistance was initially introduced in 1974 to reduce the bribery and scandals so

endemic in political life; by 1993, as details of illegal payments and the abuse of power were exposed, it was dropped because of its misuse. Other countries which have state aid have also experienced financial improprieties – France, Germany and Spain among them. Much depends on the traditions of public life in the country concerned.
- 'The time is not ripe.' For many voters it never will be. Subsidising parties seems a low priority in good or bad times.

Political Parties, Elections and Referendums Act 2000. Among other things, this Act imposed a ceiling on general election expenditure, currently fixed at almost £20 million (see p. 317).

The three main parties all have financial problems and are prone to heavy indebtedness. Today, Labour finds itself heavily reliant on gifts from corporations and wealthy individuals. The Conservatives have a small number of donors who substantially fund their election campaigns. They all need money from sources that do not undermine the integrity of the political process. Many academics and commentators have pointed to state funding in other developed countries as the way forward for Britain (see Box 7.8 above). The concept is supported by Labour and the Liberal Democrats, the parties who have most to gain from such an experiment.

In Britain, surveys suggest that the vast majority of the public is currently against the funding of political parties by taxpayer's money. A MORI poll for the Electoral Commission published in September 2003 found that:

- Few people feel informed about how political parties are funded at the moment: 72 per cent admitted they knew little or nothing at all about the issue
- 76 per cent think parties should be financed by their own fundraising
- 56 per cent do not think that parties would necessarily become more honest if they were funded through taxes.

The belief that parties should stand on their own financial feet is underlined further by the third of voters who feel it would not harm the democratic process if political parties were allowed to go bankrupt. On the other hand, there is also strong support for the principle that people should have the right to make donations to parties they support (79 per cent), although this is tempered by a majority view (70 per cent) that there should be a limit on how much people can donate. Interestingly, in spite of their reservations about state funding, 70 per cent of respondents believe the voluntary system is unfair and at risk of abuse, as it presents a risk that wealthy donors might buy influence.

Party organisation: general trends

The last few decades have also seen developments in party organisation. Originally spurred on by the creation of a mass electorate in the days when universal franchise was granted, parties saw the need to create national and local organisations to ensure that they were in a position to maximise their support. They needed to raise funds, organise canvassing and provide opportunities for the new voters to become involved, among other things. Usually the organisation operated on a top–down basis, under which national organisations were created and they were given the task of supervising the activities of local branches established throughout the country. Decisions were taken at the centre, and policy statements and lists of likely candidates were handed down to the local associations where much of the everyday voluntary work of mobilising the voters was carried out.

This pattern has not been as true in recent years. Older parties have had to adapt to changing conditions, and the arrival of television, has as we have seen, made local organisation less essential; indeed, some party clubs have lapsed to such an extent that they have effectively disappeared, only to be briefly resurrected at election time. In Britain, Labour has been concerned to modernise its image and organisation, and since its defeat in 1997 the Conservative Party has engaged in an overhaul of its traditional approach, streamlining the party and making it more open in its operations. In both cases there has been a new emphasis on making the party more democratic in the sense that members should have a greater say in how the party functions, whilst also seeking to ensure that the leadership retains key powers to act to keep out dissidents who might bring discredit on the organisation.

In Europe and in America too, parties have seen the importance of employing new techniques to galvanise the electorate via mass mailings and other devices. The US Republican Party has been effective in using modern technology in campaigning and in mastering the complicated laws that affect how money is raised and spent. Since the 1980s, they have employed a substantial professional staff to conduct such activities. The Democrats, with a smaller staffing, have nonetheless followed suit, although they contract out much of their work, such as direct-mail fundraising, to campaign consultants. In both cases, the national party has been strengthened.

Newer parties are wary of formal party organisation, seeing it as a means of stifling dissent or ignoring the views of party supporters. They have been more democratic in their workings from the beginning. Green parties in most countries have tended to shun the central control associated with established parties, and often operate more casually via a network of informal local organisations. In as much as they need leadership, they have sometimes been willing to experiment with new forms, such as having joint leaders or a troika of decision-makers. The emphasis has been on democratic consultation with the membership, rather than on strong leadership that manipulates the rules to keep decision-making effectively in its own hands.

The German Greens have allowed members to have a key role in initiating policy. However, as they became more potent in their electoral challenge, there were pressures on them to adapt their behaviour and adopt procedures more familiar in the older parties. In an age of television, the voters expect to see a familiar face as leader, and find twin leadership or other forms confusing. When the Alliance parties (Liberals and the Social Democrats) fought the 1983 election with joint leaders (Jenkins and Steel), this served to confuse some voters who wondered who would lead the party and become prime minister in the event of a major breakthrough.

The experience of the new democracies of Central and Eastern Europe has been of interest to those studying political parties. Once the old systems of state control disappeared, the formation of parties was an early priority, a point to bear in mind when considering whether parties are generally losing their importance. In several cases, the pro-democracy movement soon split once freedom was achieved, and several strands of party opinion appeared. They dominated the early elections, but within a few years the discredited communists reappeared and re-grouped. They benefited from the fact that they had a long history, during which they had a network of branches, members and lists of former members. By contrast, the new 'freedom' parties lacked such organisational assets, and having only a central organisation they failed to mobilise all of their potential support.

The organisation of British political parties

In studying party organisation, the key issue is where power resides. The two parties are organised very differently, reflecting their different origins. The Conservatives developed as a party at Westminster back in the early nineteenth century, before the extension of the vote to working people. Once the franchise was extended, they needed to ensure that their MPs were supported by a network of local associations to organise support within the constituencies. They developed a Central Office to act as the professional headquarters of the party.

Central Office controls the activities of the provincial areas and the constituency agents. But such organisation, local, regional and national, was there to serve the parliamentary party and the leadership. The leader's influence over the machine has always been a strong one, it was his or her personal machine to help the occupant pursue the desired goals and prepare the party for election success.

Labour originated outside Parliament, and developed out of the wish of trade unions, early socialist societies and others to get working people elected into Parliament. Its 1918 constitution made provision for the control of the party by the extra-parliamentary elements. In other words, the party in Parliament was made responsible to the party outside. Labour was therefore keen to avoid a focus on the figure of the party leader. The affiliated organisations, the Constituency Labour parties and the Parliamentary Party are all important elements in what is a federal structure.

Both parties have several tiers in which people can be active, local, regional and national. They may join the local party organisation as fee-paying members and participate in its political and social activities within the constituency, ranging from fundraising to canvassing and distributing party literature. Labour associations have affiliated organisations, including trade unions, socialist societies and young socialists. Party members have a voice in the selection of the constituency candidate, when a vacancy occurs. Periodically, they will also have a chance to take part in a leadership election, when there is a contest for the top position. This is the grass-roots level of party organisation, the party in the country.

One of the pleasures for grass-roots members is the opportunity to attend the annual party conference.

Party conferences in Britain

The party conference is the most important annual gathering of the Conservatives and provides the main forum for the expression of opinion by all sections of the party. It serves as a rally of the faithful, who enjoy the opportunity to vent their feelings and urge the party forward. Representatives of the constituency associations have complete freedom to speak and vote as they choose. They are not delegates committed to act in a certain way.

The agenda is carefully controlled and only rarely are formal votes taken at the conclusion of a debate. Revolts can occur over sensitive issues such as Europe, immigration and law and order, on all of which forthright views are held. However, many debates are anodyne and in any case they are only advisory, having no binding effect on the people at the top. However, the conference sets a mood and a wise leadership will take its view into account. Today, there are more revolts than in the past, along with stronger expression of feeling, but this is combined with a strong sense of deference to the leader.

By contrast with the Conservatives, the Labour conference was given the supreme function of directing and controlling the affairs of the party. The 1918 constitution established that party policy is the responsibility of conference and that decisions taken by a two-thirds majority are supposed to be regarded as sacrosanct and included in the next manifesto. However, although opposition leaders pay greater respect to the sanctity of such decisions, Labour prime ministers have often treated them in a more cavalier manner,

The role and significance of the Labour conference has long been a matter of controversy and academic debate. Strong leaders, even in opposition, can override its decisions if they have the backing of the National Executive Committee, the administrative authority of the party which acts as the guardian of conference decisions. As the unions have lost much of their former status in the party and the left has been effectively sidelined in recent years, so conference has lost much of its former status. It has a diminished role, for the modernisation of the last decade or more has seen the development of alternative sources of power and influence. In particular, the centralisation of the party structure around the leader, his or her office and entourage, has concentrated media attention on the person at the helm. Prior to the 1997 election, when there was a scent of victory in the area, delegates were reluctant to rock the party votes in front of the television cameras. From time to time, reassertions of conference's authority may occur, but more generally the tendency is to listen to and applaud appearances by the party luminaries.

In both parties, conferences are now heavily stage-managed. The leaderships are conscious of the television coverage they receive and speeches are seen as a chance to communicate directly with the public as well as a chance to address an audience at Blackpool or Bournemouth.

Party leaders: how they are chosen by the main British parties

There have been changes to the way in which both main parties choose their leader in recent years. Labour reformed its selection process in 1981 and the Conservatives did the same twenty years later. In both cases, the membership now has a say in the choice and there is provision to rid the party of an unwanted incumbent. At election time, the contest enables the party to resolve issues of personality, as well as party policy and direction.

The two main parties have different approaches to the way in which they choose their leaders. Labour was the first to involve party members in the choice, back in the early 1980s, but its arrangements are more complex because it has affiliated bodies such as trade unions to consider. Under William Hague, the Conservatives – after much pressure from within the party to adopt a more democratic method – devised a new procedure. In both parties, the candidates are already sitting MPs. The present arrangements are set out below.

The Conservatives
The sitting leader can be challenged if 15 per cent of the parliamentary party express no confidence in the leader (at least twenty-five MPs,

Table 7.3 The Conservative system in operation: the choice in 2005

Round one: votes of MPs		Round two: votes of MPs	
Cameron	56	Cameron	90
Clarke	38	Davis	57
Davis	62	Fox	51
Fox	42		

Round three: votes of party members, November–December 2005

Cameron	67.6%
Davis	32.4%

at present). They would need to sign an open letter to the chairman of the backbench 1922 Committee. The sitting leader needs to win 50 per cent + one in a secret ballot on a motion of confidence in his leadership. Should he or she fail, then he or she is excluded from the contest. At this stage, other candidates step forward. The parliamentary party holds as many rounds as it takes to choose two candidates, with the worst-performing MP eliminated from each ballot. Then, the party members vote and the candidate with the greater number of votes wins.

If a vacancy occurs because of the resignation or death of the incumbent, then the parliamentary party moves straight into a series of ballots of MPs.

In 2001, five candidates stood for the leadership. The bottom two (Michael Ancram and David Davis) tied on the first round and stayed on into the second, in which they were eliminated. In a third ballot, the bottom candidate (Michael Portillo) was eliminated. Party members then chose Iain Duncan Smith rather than Kenneth Clarke. In 2003, when Duncan Smith failed to secure enough votes in a vote of confidence on his leadership, there was no contest. Michael Howard was the undisputed candidate for the job.

Following a further defeat in 2005, some leading Conservatives were keen to return to their previous system, election by MPs. The involvement of party members was widely blamed among party professionals for the choice of Duncan Smith, whose leadership was generally regarded as ineffective. However, there was grassroots resistance to any change. Accordingly, the election of David Cameron was conducted under the same method as was used in 2001. Party members voted for him by a decisive margin of 134,446 to 64,398 votes.

Labour

Labour uses an Electoral College to choose its leader. It includes a 33% share for each of the Parliamentary Labour Party, the party members and the trade unions who form an integral part of the party structure.

Those MPs who wish to become leader need 12.5 per cent of Labour MPs to back them if there is a vacancy or 20 per cent if there is a challenge to a sitting leader. To be elected, a candidate needs to receive an absolute majority of the votes cast. If no one achieves this, then further ballots are held on an elimination basis. To avoid repeated balloting, voters are asked to express second and third preferences.

In 1994, the procedure worked relatively smoothly to elect Tony Blair, who won a majority in each of the three elements of the party vote. He received 57 per cent of the vote overall, out of 952,109 votes cast. The election was widely seen as the biggest democratic exercise in European party politics, giving the winner what his admirers called 'a million vote mandate'. Nonetheless, some people within the party would like to see the College abandoned and instead a more straightforward system of 'one person, one vote', in which each vote counted equally.

The Liberal Democrats

The Liberals were the first party to involve party members in the choice. Under the constitution of the Liberal Democrats, the candidate for the leadership must be nominated and proposed by two other MPs and supported by at least 200 members in no less than twenty local parties. The leader is elected by a simple 'one person, one vote' method of all members, including, of course, MPs. The system was used to elect Paddy Ashdown and Charles Kennedy, and worked well on both occasions.

In January 2006, Kennedy was forced to stand down following widely expressed anxieties among MPs about his personal situation and more general dissatisfaction with the energy and commitment of his leadership. Four candidates obtained the necessary support within the parliamentary party, three of whose names were listed on the ballot form which went to the party membership in January 2006.

The systems compared

The Conservatives traditionally took the view that MPs alone were best able to judge the merits of the candidates. They feared that giving a say to the party outside Parliament could lead to MPs having a person imposed on them in whom they did not have confidence and whose views did not accord with their own. Accordingly, until recently, the membership of the party played no formal part in the process, though it could put pressure on their sitting MP to use his or her vote in a particular way when a contest arose.

The present Conservative system has several advantages. There is still provision for MPs to have a say, enabling them to demonstrate who they feel they can work with and support. But more positively, 'one person, one vote' provides the opportunity for party members to exercise their choice. It is a transparent and democratic method.

Labour's procedure has for a long time recognised the need for a wider involvement than that of MPs alone. In its present form, the scheme has some sound democratic credentials, but there are anomalies. 'One person, one vote' is applied to each of the three individual elements within the party, so that each union levy-payer is entitled to vote within the contest staged by the union. But some Labour supporters may belong to more than one union or to a socialist society, as well as a local association in the constituency where they reside and the one they represent. Hence, Neil Kinnock was able to cast seven votes in 1994.

This is probably not the definitive Labour scheme. That would be for all members of the Labour Party, either those who pay the levy-plus through their union or who join the party directly, to have a vote on the choice of leader. There would be no Electoral College, but a large mass party with an increased membership. That would be a genuine 'one person one vote' approach.

The powers and security of party leaders

Any leader of a main political party in a two-party system is either an actual or potential prime minister. As such, he or she is bound to have great authority, for either now or in the future, there will be a chance to distribute ministerial offices and make or break the careers of rivals.

The opposition leader is a key figure. Traditionally, he or she has been more powerful in the Conservative Party, although the experience of recent years points the other way: Neil Kinnock and Tony Blair operated a highly centralised system of control and leaders from Hague to Howard have had difficulties in establishing their undisputed authority. If leading the country as prime minister he or she becomes so powerful, writers describe Britain as having 'government by prime minister'.

The Conservatives

At face value the Conservative leader has enormous power. Many years ago, Robert McKenzie[18] described the incumbent as possessing greater authority and being subject to less restraint than his or her counterpart in any other democratic country. The leadership was once described by the American writer Austin Ranney[19] as 'one of autocracy tempered by advice and information'.

In particular, the leader has exclusive responsibility for writing the election manifesto and formulating party policy, does not have to attend meetings of the 1922 Committee of Conservative backbench MPs, has enormous control over the activities of Central Office and the party machine, appoints (and dismisses) the party chairman, vice chairman and treasurer and chooses the Cabinet or shadow cabinet. This is an important package of powers, a recognition of the fact that the party embraces the idea of strong leadership. It developed as a party within the House of Commons, its MPs wanting to see a powerful leader who could espouse the party cause and dominate the chamber.

Yet the position is one of leadership by consent and there is ample precedent for power melting away and that consent being withdrawn. This is particularly the case when the party is in opposition, although the experiences of Margaret Thatcher (challenged in 1989 and 1990 and forced out of office) and John Major (challenged in 1995) suggest that even a prime minister is not as secure as a formal reading of the leader's powers would suggest.

When the party has been defeated in an election or appears to be making little electoral headway, it can act harshly against its leaders and make them scapegoats for failure. It likes and has in the past been used to electoral success. Several leaders have lost the support of MPs and been under pressure to go, including William Hague, following the 2001 defeat, and Iain Duncan Smith, who never even had the opportunity to lead his party into an election. After the latest defeat, Michael Howard soon announced that he would be standing down (on grounds of age) once the party had rethought the process for choosing a new leader.

Labour

Labour originally had a chairman of the Labour MPs in the House of Commons, but no leader. It only appointed a leader when it had become a party large enough to mount a significant electoral challenge to the Conservatives and Liberals. The way the party developed and a bad experience of excessive leadership power in 1931 combined to make party members reluctant to recognise the supremacy of the leader over the Labour movement. They have always wanted to ensure that he or she is accountable.

Accordingly, the 1918 constitution imposed restrictions on the power of the leader, in order to ensure his subservience to the party in Parliament and to the mass organisation outside. Leaders have to attend backbench meetings of the Parliamentary Labour Party; (in opposition) work with a shadow cabinet, the membership of which has been elected by MPs; implement policies in line with conference decisions; attend conference and give an annual report of their stewardship. They also lack the control over the affairs of the party organisation that Conservative leaders possess.

Yet in recent years, Labour leaders have become markedly more dominant than this portrayal suggests and the leadership has accumulated ever-greater power. The process gathered pace under Neil Kinnock, who did much to weaken internal opposition. In the Blair era, the leadership has maintained an iron grip, so that dissident voices have been weeded out, the union ties loosened and power concentrated in the leader's hands. Starved of victory for many years, many Labour members have been willing to give Blair a remarkably free hand, although as he has become more out of touch with grass-roots opinion there are many members who might lament this centralisation of power. He has strained the bounds of party loyalty by many of the policies that he has adopted.

The Labour Party has been less severe on its leaders than the Conservatives, many of them enjoying a lengthy period of service. It shows less brutality to those who lead it, so that although there were often muttering about the performances of Neil Kinnock in the House and real doubts about whether he was an electoral asset, talk of a replacement was infrequent. He easily survived a challenge to his position in 1988.

Since 1945, whereas the Conservative party has had eleven leaders, Labour has had only eight. Recent experience suggests that the Conservatives have found it difficult to find a strong figure who can unite the party, impart vigour to its performance and achieve electoral success. Generally speaking, parties accept strong leaders when they are delivering the goods (electoral success or the prospect of it). If that strength shows signs of becoming too over-bearing, particularly at a time when electoral success is proving elusive, a reaction sets in. The leaders then need to watch their backs.

The decline of political parties: do they still matter?

Some writers point to a crisis in party politics, noting the decline in party membership, increasing partisan de-alignment and the rise of extremist parties. Parties such as those of the far right in many parts of Europe are sometimes labelled 'anti-party parties', in that they aim to subvert traditional party politics, rejecting parliamentary compromise and emphasising popular mobilisation.

Established parties in several countries are finding their task more difficult. They have been the victims of public disillusion, as voters compare the promise and performance of parties in government. They have also lost support because many young people especially feel that they do not speak about issues that matter to them. Their ideas seem less relevant to a post-materialist society. On topics such as animal rights, gender, nuclear power and the environment, pressure groups articulate popular feeling more successfully than parties.

Why have traditional parties lost some of their support?

- *Single-issue protest politics seem more relevant and exciting,* particularly to the young. They seem to prefer more loosely organised, less authoritarian and centralised parties, compared with the oligarchical established parties whose membership is often inactive or engaged in dull, routine tasks.
- *Traditional parties having served in office – and the politicians who represent them – have been tainted by power and lost their freshness and appeal.* They are seen as sleazy, jaded failures, sometimes prone to lapses of financial probity. They have often been unable to make their performances match up to the promises once made and have lost respect.
- *Perhaps countries are today more difficult to govern.* People have high expectations which politicians find hard to match, because often their capacity to influence events in an age of globalisation is strictly limited.

Blondel[20] finds that the prospects for parties are less bleak in the Scandinavian countries than elsewhere. For the rest of continental Europe, he believes that the loss of support is clearly perceptible, and that 'the representation of interests and views is increasingly provided by groups which are closer to the people than parties'. He distinguishes between the situation in continental Europe and that in the USA, and divides the Western scene into three distinct scenarios:

1. In Europe he finds that the traditional parties have lost ground to newer parties which seem to be more attuned to the people's interests. This has resulted in the development of a growing number of significant parties, this fragmentation making it more difficult for any one party to emerge with 'a true grip on political life'.
2. Britain and the older Commonwealth countries have largely avoided the above trend, because of their attachment to the First-Past-the-Post electoral system, which has enabled them to think still in terms of the old adversarial conflict of government and opposition.
3. In America, he detects a different scenario. Parties have a more symbolic role. 'They do not propose programmes; they do not even select candidates, since these are in effect chosen by primaries which are outside the control of party leaders. On this basis, they

survive . . . [but] remain in existence because people apparently feel that there have to be parties in a democracy.'

It is possible to exaggerate the extent of party decline. Party systems have always undergone change, with new ones emerging to replace those that have lost their original justification. In emerging democracies, new parties have been created, and the removal of dictatorships in Greece, Portugal and Spain inspired a growth of new organisations, as did the breakdown of communist rule in Eastern Europe. There have, it is true, been shifts of support in an increasingly volatile age, and inevitably more recently established parties in long-standing democracies have had to pick up their support from existing ones.

Party fortunes are generally in a state of flux. Budge et al.[21] make the valid point that electorates in Europe have been broadly stable in the left–right allegiance, and that there has been no sign of a dramatic shift from one end of the spectrum to the other side. Rather, it has been a case of 'significantly shifting support' between left and right parties as blocks. On the right, for example, there has been an erosion of support for traditional parties balanced by a growth of right-wing, nationalistic ones. Such splintering has been apparent in several internal elections but also in the European elections of 1994, 1999 and 2004.

The case of France

In the first half of the twentieth century, France had a multi-party system, as opposed to the two-party systems to be found in Britain, the Commonwealth and the United States. In part, this reflected the use of proportional electoral systems that encouraged a multiplicity of parties. So too it reflected the various historical and social divisions in French society, such as the cleavage between monarchists and republicans, clericalists and anti-clericalists, workers and the bourgeoisie. Compromises were difficult to achieve in such a polarised situation and so rather than sheltering under a large umbrella, a number of small parties concentrated on the issues that mattered to them and competed for power.

At that time, parties were internally weak, often loose networks of local leaders. They made little attempt to mobilise mass support and develop a national programme. French socialists such as François Mitterrand, later to become a president under the Fifth Republic, were elected on the basis of their personal appeal and programme. On election, they might join up with like-minded individuals, but there was little party discipline within any parliamentary groupings.

Party fortunes have fluctuated throughout the years of the more stable Fifth Republic, created by and for General de Gaulle in 1958. In the first decade, the Gaullists dominated political debate and a coalition of groups supporting de Gaulle evolved. By the 1970s, the various socialist groups were developing a more united front that was to enable them to capture the presidency in 1981. Thereafter, the influence of the traditional parties was challenged by the growing prominence of new political forces, including the extreme right National Front and the ecologists. Although the old social and ideological cleavages still shape the political scene, there have been substantial shifts in voting preferences which have forced older parties to reconsider their approaches, strategies and tactics.

As in most democracies, electoral success in France continues to depend on organised political parties which bring together people who share similar beliefs about how society should develop and the policy approaches that are necessary to achieve this common vision. However, individuals often play an important part in French politics and parties are sometimes formed and maintained around backing for a particular personality, such as Jean-Marie Le Pen of the National Front. Stevens[22] notes that the Union pour un Mouvement Populaire (UMP) was formed in some haste out of a confederation of other groupings in 2002, to assert support for Jacques Chirac who had just won the presidential election, and his chosen prime minister. It lacked a developed set of ideas and policies. In her view, 'some parties seem at times to be little more than convenient vehicles for personal political ambitions'.

The French party system remains weak and fragmented, all the more confusing because of the multiplicity of groups which contest elections, some of which are transient, some more durable. It is in their interests to stand, for under French electoral law registered parties that put up at least fifty candidates are entitled to a state subsidy. In this way, small parties and leaders use elections as a means of attracting extra resources.

The case of Italy

For several decades after 1945, Italy was regarded as a byword for governmental instability. Between 1947 and 1992, there were forty-seven governments, an average of one per year. This was the period when the centre-right Roman Catholic Christian Democrats dominated the political landscape, serving in every administration. Appealing widely to all anti-communists (the communists were the second largest party), the party was able to put together a series of coalitions, keeping itself in power by its generous use of patronage. It rewarded its backers with contracts and jobs, enabling it to secure support in both the more affluent north and the poorer south.

There were so many parties that coalitions were inevitable. As in France, parties were created to represent many political traditions and personalities. They benefited from the proportional electoral system that encouraged small party representation in the Chamber of Deputies. In the absence of a few strong parties, coalitions often involved four or five parties working together. When disagreements emerged, they tended to break up. New coalitions were then formed, after negotiations between the dominant Christian Democrats and the other parties. The members of one government tended to reappear in a later one, and prime ministers often experienced at least two periods of national leadership.

Italy has experienced a massive change in its party system in recent years. Of the traditional adversaries, the Christian Democrats have vanished and the communists reformed as the Democratic Party of the Left (PDS). In their place, loose 'umbrella' groupings have been formed under the influence of high-profile personalities such as Silvio Berlusconi, who has twice served as prime minister.

The new pattern of party activity has much in common with that prevailing in the 'new democracies' of Central and Eastern Europe. Parties lack ideological cohesion and a mass membership, and, as Hague and Harrop point out, take the form of 'shells for ambitious politicians . . . the parties are more like campaigning institutions before elections than permanent institutions propagating ideology. In that respect, post-communist parties follow the American rather than the Western European model'.[23]

The case of the USA

From a historical and international perspective, American political parties have always seemed weak. They have never had the solid class-based electoral support common in other developed countries. Given the weakness of party discipline in the United States, they have never been sure that they could turn any detailed policy commitments into legislative effect. Maidment and McGrew[24] regard them as 'vast and disparate coalitions with no coherent sets of beliefs'. Other comment-ators have written about public disillusion with the two parties and the politicians who belong to them, suggesting that they are all as bad as each other.

Various factors explain the historical weakness of American parties, notably:

* *the federal system of government*, which means that the attitudes adopted in each party vary from state to state
* *the operation of the idea of the separation of powers*, which encourages members of all parties in Congress to act as a watchdog in the Constitution, checking the actions of a president with whom they are in nominal political agreement
* *the notion of consensus in American politics*; both Democrats and Republicans subscribe to the ideals of the 'American Creed', liberty, equality, individualism, democracy and the rule of law
* *the ethos of individualism in American society*, which stresses the role of the individual citizen in shaping his or her own destiny.

In the twentieth century, the parties became even weaker than they were, a process helped by:

* *the growing use of primary elections*, which took power away from the party bosses
* *the development of the mass media*, which placed more emphasis on candidate-centred electioneering
* *the arrival of new issues on the agenda* in the 1960s and 1970s which cut across the party divide (feminism, environmentalism, civil rights and Vietnam)
* *the increasing importance of pressure groups and political action committees*, which meant that there were more causes in which Americans could participate and alternative bodies for fundraising for candidates

- *the breakdown of traditional allegiances among sections of the electorate and a growth of volatility in voting behaviour.*

If for much of the twentieth century, there were signs that political parties had fallen on hard times, in the closing two decades there were indications of renewal. In particular, party organisation became more effective, as first the Republicans and shortly afterwards the Democrats saw the potential of high-tech fundraising. Hence Herrnson's observation[25] that: 'The parties' national, congressional and senatorial campaign committees are now wealthier, more stable, better organised and better staffed than ever before.'

Parties have shown a greater ability in recent years to raise money by new techniques of fundraising and have become more organised at the federal level. Moreover, some of the 'new issues' have lost much of their earlier impact. For all of their alleged weaknesses, parties have not been displaced. They:

- still serve as a reference point for the voters, the bulk of whom still think in terms of Republicans and Democrats
- remain a reference point for presidential candidates and congressmen, almost every one of whom belongs to one of the major parties.

· ·

✔ What you should have learnt from reading this chapter

- Most political parties have not been stable over a long period. Stability is associated more with the Atlantic and Commonwealth countries than the rest of the world. The disappearance of Soviet control in Eastern Europe has shown that even strong single-party systems are not endurable.

- Yet for all of the signs of weakness and fragmentation in party systems, parties are unlikely to become extinct. Even if the bonds are somewhat tenuous, they remain the only mechanism which links the voters and those who rule them, and they continue to perform useful tasks, notably recruiting representatives for national legislatures; educating the electorate by developing, elaborating and 'selling' policies; and offering an opportunity for popular participation in the political process.

- In Britain, there has been a regular alternation of Conservative and Labour rule, but third parties have gained ground. The use of the FPTP electoral system for Westminster elections tends to reinforce the dominance of the two main rivals.

🔎 Glossary of key terms

Adversary politics A style of politics in which there is a fundamental ideological disagreement between the main parties. Finer's suggestion was that this meant that a change of government resulted in a sharp change of direction in key areas of policy.

Communitarianism The set of beliefs associated with Etzioni, arguing that both liberal individualism and massive state interventionism have failed and that the best way forward is through individuals recognising the importance of community. As citizens, they have rights but must also be aware of the duties and responsibilities to society.

Consensus Consensus implies general agreement. Consensus politics means that there is substantial agreement between the politics of all parties and the public over fundamental values and policies, even if there are differences of emphasis and degree. 'Consensus politics' refers to a style of politics based on compromise and conciliation. In Britain, the era of consensus (usually described as being 1951–79) was associated with widespread acceptance of the need for full employment, a mixed economy and a welfare state.

Euroscepticism The term that became fashionable in the 1990s to describe the attitude of someone who is opposed to European integration and is sceptical of the EU, its aims, policies and practices. Usually, Eurosceptics wish to try and reverse the tide of integration and often they talk of 'repatriating' powers to the UK.

Maastricht Treaty The treaty signed in 1992 that turned the old European Economic Community into the present European Union. Among other things, it created two new 'pillars' to deal with justice and home affairs, and the common foreign and security policy. It also laid down 'convergence criteria' for monetary union and made us all citizens of the EU.

Mixed economy An economy in which there is a significant role for both private and public ownership, as existed in Britain between the late 1940s and the 1980s – before Margaret Thatcher embarked upon her programme of privatisation.

One-nation Conservatism One-nation Conservatism originally derives from the era of Disraelian supremacy, in the 1870s. It stresses the need for the Conservative Party to seek to maintain a broad appeal to all groups and in all areas of the country. Adherents emphasise the desirability of flexibility over matters of doctrine, enabling conservatism to adapt to changing circumstances.

Partisan de-alignment The theory explaining how the public increasingly dissociates itself from both main parties; the erosion of party identification, as reflected in an increase in voter volatility.

Proportional representation The collective term for electoral systems that award seats in the legislature in proportion to the number of votes cast for each party.

'Short' money A grant payable to opposite parties to assist them in their discharge of parliamentary duties; named after the leader of the House of Commons who originally introduced it.

Socialism Socialists believe that unrestrained capitalism is responsible for a variety of social evils, including the exploitation of working people, the widespread existence of poverty and unemployment, gross inequality of wealth and the pursuit of greed and selfishness. They are in favour of a social system based on cooperative values; emphasise the values of community rather than of individualism; believe in the need for a more equal and just society, based on a sense of social solidarity; and in the case of Marxian socialists have a clear preference for common ownership (nationalisation) of the commanding heights of the economy. Marxian socialism has a strong economic as well as ethical dimension. It also emphasises the importance of a class analysis to society's problems.

Stakeholder society Originally deriving from Japanese business experience, it suggests a society in which people possess rights and opportunities, but also responsibilities and obligations; everyone has a stake and nobody is excluded. New Labour rhetoric has often stressed the need for 'social inclusion'.

Tactical voting The willingness of some voters to vote for a candidate other than their first preference in order to ensure that their less preferred candidate is unsuccessful. In 1997 and subsequently, Labour and Liberal Democrat voters in some seats have been willing to use their vote in such a way as to 'keep the Conservatives out'.

Thatcherism The creed associated with Margaret Thatcher, involving a market-based economic system, emphasising competition, free enterprise, lower taxes and curbs on trade-union power.

❓ Likely examination questions

Why are parties essential to a democracy?

Why is the United Kingdom usually described as having a two-party system?

Do the terms left and right any longer have relevance in describing the British political scene?

In what respects is New Labour different from Old Labour?

To what extent can the Conservative Party still be described as Thatcherite?

Discuss the manner of choosing, the power and the security of tenure of British party leaders.

'Political parties do not matter any more.' Are parties in long-term decline?

Helpful websites

www.keele.ac.uk/depts/por/ptbase.htm   Keele Guide to Political Thought and Ideology

www.conservative-party.org.uk

www.labour.org.uk

www.libdems.org.uk

 Suggestions for further reading

Useful articles

N. Jackson, 'Two, Two and a Half and Three Party Politics', *Talking Politics*, January 2004.

R. Kelly, 'The Third Way', *Politics Review*, September 1999.

R. Leach, 'From Old Labour to the Third Way', *Talking Politics*, January 2002.

N. McNaughton, 'The Changing Nature of UK Political Parties', *Talking Politics*, April 2003.

R. Tillson, 'Is the Party Over for the Conservatives?', *Talking Politics*, April 2005.

Useful books

R. Garner and R. Kelly, *British Political Parties Today*, Manchester University Press, 2000.

R. Hefferman, 'Political Parties and the Party System', in P. Dunleavy, A. Gamble, R. Hefferman et al. (eds), *Developments in British Politics* 7, Palgrave, 2003.

P. Norton, 'The Conservative Party: Is There Anyone Out There?', in A. King (ed.), *Britain at the Polls*, 2001, Chatham House, 2002.

Pressure Groups

Contents

Overview

Pressure groups are organised associations that aim to influence the policies and actions of those who hold government office. They operate in the space between government and society, consulting with ministers and providing continuous opportunities for citizens to become involved in political life.

In this chapter we survey the range of pressure groups that exist and the nature and extent of group activity, before exploring how organised interests play a part in the government of the country.

Key issues to be covered in this chapter

- The distinction between pressure groups and movements
- The differences between pressure groups and political parties
- The different ways of classifying groups
- The nature and scale of group activity
- How groups operate
- Changes in pressure group activity since 1979
- Factors influencing group success
- The contribution of groups to the workings of democracy
- The characteristics of groups and their impact in France, Scotland and the United States

Group activity in modern societies: pressure groups and movements

Pressure groups are voluntary organisations that seek to influence public policy by defending their common interest or protecting a cause. Their nature and degree of influence vary from country to country. Generally speaking, business is close to government, for what government does affects business just as the decisions of the business community in areas such as job creation and investment have important repercussions for ministers. However, many other interests in society are also affected by ministerial decisions and wish to make their views known in the appropriate quarters. Employees are organised via the trade-union movement, and various other groups represent farmers, churches and a host of civic, environmental and social causes.

There are myriads of British groups, covering the whole spectrum of policy issues. Some 34,000 organisations are recognised by the Directory of British Associations, but there are many more that

---

Box 8.1 Pressure groups: a note on terminology

There is no agreed terminology to cater for pressure group activity across the world. The Americans talk mainly of interest groups and lobbying, whereas in Britain the tendency is to use the term 'pressure groups' and then to classify them into different categories. The word 'pressure' is unfair to the many groups that operate without resorting to any degree of coercion. In this case, pressure usually amounts to influence and persuasion, rather than use or threat of intimidation. It is because of the negative connotation of the term pressure groups that campaigning voluntary groups such as Cafod and Oxfam tend to now describe themselves as non-governmental organisations (NGOs).

The term 'interest groups' is unsuitable as a description of the myriad of promotional or single-issue groups that seek to propagandise on behalf of a cause and have no self-interest in the matter in the issue with which they are involved. For our purposes, 'pressure group' is a convenient general label to cover the range of organisations under discussion.

operate at the local level. Groups are as diverse as they are numerous, ranging from the high-profile National Farmers Union to the rather more obscure group that campaigns for the provision of better public lavatories.

In particular, there has in recent years been a surge of interest in single-issue campaigning, on subjects from gay rights to the export of live animals to the continent, from gun control to the siting of a motorway or other public amenity. Over the last two or three decades, the number of these and other pressure groups has soared, and there are additional outlets at which they can target their propaganda. New techniques of putting across ideas and information have emerged, in particular the growth of professional lobbying.

The behaviour of activists in the campaigning field has raised important questions about the role of pressure groups in modern democracies. Many of the issues are relevant to European and American experience as well as to life in the United Kingdom. In all countries, the increasing trends towards the development of privatised industry and market economies, and the inevitability of globalisation have had clear repercussions for the way in which groups function and the influence they can wield.

Pressure groups exist in all societies. Free societies are **pluralist**, in that a variety of organisations are allowed to exist and compete for influence over government. In some pluralist societies, there are strongly antagonistic ethnic, linguistic or religious groups; others may be based more on social class. In Western liberal democracies, thousands of bodies seek to influence the conduct of power and make their views known. In a free country, groups seek to exert influence via many avenues, mostly peaceful, but on occasion they may resort to more violent forms of protest. No single group can exert a monopoly of power and manipulate the system for its own advantage.

Pressure groups differ considerably in their internal operation, some being democratically structured, others led by a powerful elite that dominates proceedings on a regular basis. Some are large, others are small; some operate at a national level, others do so regionally or locally; some are particularly effective and have popular appeal, others cater for minority interests and needs. Some are durable and make a great impact, others are short-lived and make little impression.

Box 8.2 Pressure group activity under authoritarian regimes

Rulers of authoritarian countries view group activity as a threat to their survival. In as much as such groups can exist under such authoritarian regimes, they usually live in peril, liable at any time to be closed down or have their offices raided. In some cases, groups may be allowed to function, but under the watchful supervision of government. Any leaders who seek to foment discontent will be quickly removed. Elsewhere, they may be suppressed completely. If they try to continue their work, they have to operate in an underground manner.

In the communist states of the Soviet era, at some periods interest groups were not usually allowed to exist at all. When they were tolerated, they were carefully managed and subject to the whims of the Communist Party. Trade unions, professional associations and youth groups were in effect agencies of the party, there only in as much as they were of use to those in power. Yet by the 1980s, in Hungary, Poland and Yugoslavia in particular, there were more signs of sectional activity that was tolerated as long as there were clear limits to the expression of any serious discontent. In China today, the All-China Federation of Trade Unions is controlled by party officials.

Movements and the politics of protest

Since the 1960s there has been what Heywood[1] has referred to as an 'explosion in pressure and protest politics'. In his view, this burst of activity 'may be part of a broader process that has seen the decline of parties and a growing emphasis on organised groups and social movements emerging as agents of mobilisation and representation'. The **new social movements** that have emerged since the 1970s are less structured and cohesive than pressure groups. They tend to have a core group that provides general direction and a network of widespread supporters who are only loosely organised. Often, their activities arise at grass-roots level, before later evolving into national crusades. They are broadly united around a central idea, issue or concern whose goal is to change attitudes or institutions, as well as policies. Characteristic concerns include equality for women and ethnic minorities, the environment and animal rights, globalisation and international peace.

Those who involve themselves in social movements often provide a radical critique of mainstream societies and institutions, and are interested in finding different ways of organising political activity. They want fundamental change to the status quo and the dominant values in society. Members of pressure groups may want to see substantial changes in public policy, but broadly they are more likely to support the existing political and social framework in society, and the dominant values that underpin it.

Pressure groups and political parties: their differences and similarities

Pressure groups differ from political parties, for they do not seek to win elections to gain political office. Indeed, they do not usually contest elections and if they do so, it is mainly to draw attention to some matter of national concern. Their goals are narrower, in that they do not attempt to advance ideas covering the whole range of public policy. Indeed, some of their aspirations are non-political.

Yet there is some overlap between parties and pressure groups. Both types of organisation are vehicles through which opinions can be expressed and outlets for popular participation. Both have a role in the workings of government, in the case of parties by forming or opposing an administration, in the case of groups by providing information and assisting in governmental inquiries. There is also some duplication between their activities. For example:

- There may be a close relationship between pressure groups and political parties. Many trade unions are actually affiliated to the Labour Party and form part of the wider Labour movement in the country. Some staff are active in 'social' pressure groups and in the ranks of the Labour or Liberal Democrat parties.
- Within the parties there are groups that seek to influence party thinking, such as the Tory Reform Club and the Bruges Group in the Conservative Party and the Tribune Group in the Labour Party. These tendencies or factions are effectively pressure groups within a party.
- Some **think tanks** act alongside the political parties. Members share the broad outlook of the party, but act independently and

seek to have an impact on the general thrust of public policy. Examples are Demos and the Institute for Public Policy Research on the moderate left and the Adam Smith Institute and the Centre for Policy Studies on the right.

• Some groups actually put up candidates in an election, as have Friends of the Earth in the occasional by-election and the Pro-Life Alliance in recent general elections. In these cases, the point is not any desire to attain office, but rather to achieve publicity for a particular cause. In the case of the Pro-Life Alliance, in 1997 it fielded enough candidates (53) to qualify for a party election broadcast, thus providing a good opportunity to air members' thinking on issue such as abortion, fertilisation and embryology.

Classifying pressure groups

In an early study of pressure groups, Samuel Finer[2] distinguished between groups involved in different areas of activity, such as the 'labour lobby', 'civic' groups, and 'educational, recreational and cultural' ones. There are two more usual ways of classifying them. The first describes them according to what and whom they represent, the second in terms of their relationship with government and the way in which they operate.

Protective and promotional groups (see Table 8.1)
The distinction originally made by Stewart[3] and subsequently employed by many others, divided groups into a. those which seek to defend the interests of persons or categories of persons in society (protective, interest or defensive groups), and b. those which seek to advance particular causes and ideas not of immediate benefit to themselves (promotional, propaganda, cause or ideas groups).

Protective groups
These are primarily self-interested bodies that seek selective benefits for and offer services to their members. Business interests are among the most powerful players in pluralist societies such as Britain, France, Italy and the United States. They are of strategic importance in the economy and governmental interests and their own often tend to coincide. Many of them are represented in peak

286 British Government and Politics

organisations, which bring together within one organisation a whole range of other bodies and coordinate their activities and speak on their behalf. Such umbrella groups may represent the broad interests of capital (the Confederation of British Industry and the Institute of Directors) or the firms belonging to specific industries (Motor Manufacturers' Association). They are usually well organised and financed.

Trade unions are probably the best-known protective or interest groups. They exist to represent the interests of organised working people, by defending and improving their wages and working conditions. They have a closed membership, for only those who work in an industry or possess a particular skill are eligible to join them. In many countries that membership is vast, covering millions of workers. Individual unions often belong to an umbrella organisation, in Britain 69 being affiliated to the Trades Union Congress (TUC) and in the United States 96 belonging to the American Federation of Labour and the Congress of Industrial Organisations (AFL/CIO). In recent decades, trade unions have lost much of their bargaining power in Britain, Europe and America. The decline of manufacturing industry and high levels of unemployment in the 1980s, the trends to globalisation of national economies and the increase in new and less unionised employment have seriously affected their membership and have generally taken a toll of union influence.

Farmers constitute a third important group in many countries, although they are losing some of their former political strength, for in many parts of Europe farming has become less dominant in national economies. Farmers have one advantage over the other two groups, in that whereas employers and workers each have to combat their antagonists on the other side of the industrial fence, farmers do not face a powerful and articulate voice to argue against their influence. Usually, there is little organised opposition to agrarian interests, many people actually being sympathetic to farmers, who are seen as maintaining the countryside and upholding the values associated with the rural way of life. The National Farmers' Union has long been considered to be one of the most effective protective groups, representing as it does a clear majority of British farmers. Its views are listened to with respect in Whitehall.

Other highly significant protective groups cover the interests of those engaged in the professions, doctors, lawyers and teachers among them. Because they represent clear occupational interests, protective associations are often well established, well connected and well resourced.

Promotional groups

In contrast to protective groups, *promotional groups* seek to advance ideas and causes which are not of benefit to their membership, other than in a most general sense. They are selfless rather than self-interested in their concerns. They are also open to people from all sections of the community who share the same values, whereas members of interest groups have a shared experience. Again, unlike the many interest groups that have been in existence for several decades, many promotional ones have a short span of life, disappearing once their cause has been appropriately tackled.

Promotional groups are defined by the cause or idea they represent. The Electoral Reform Society advocates a change in the electoral

Table 8.1 Examples of British protective (interest) and promotional (cause) groups

Protective	Promotional
Confederation of British Industry	British Association for the Advancement of Science
Institute of Directors	Catholic Truth Society
Trades Union Congress	Electoral Reform Society
National Farmers' Union	Shelter
Buddhist Society	League Against Cruel Sports
Association of British Adoption Agencies	World Wide Fund for Nature
English Collective of Prostitutes	United Nations Association

system, Help the Aged tackles the needs of the elderly, Greenpeace urges greater environmental awareness, Anti-Slavery International takes up issues of human rights and Amnesty International campaigns on behalf of political prisoners. Many cause groups are today **single-issue** ones. In Britain, Snowdrop had a brief existence. It lobbied effectively for a ban on handguns and when the goal was attained, its raison d'être was removed. Single-issue groups were first identified in the United States, many being on the left of the political spectrum.

Protective associations are traditionally stronger than promotional ones, better organised and resourced. Many promotional groups operate with limited funds and few, if any, full-time staff. They have a tendency to split into rival factions. They also tend to have less access to government.

Hybrid groups

Hybrid groups have some characteristics associated with protective and promotional groups. The Roads Campaign Council works for road improvement, but was established and is financed by interest

Table 8.2 British groups: their characteristics summarised

Characteristics	Protective groups	Promotional groups
Aims	Defend interests of membership	Advance an idea or cause
Focus of their attention	Executive (Whitehall) and legislature (House of Commons), and EU institutions	Legislators, public opinion and international bodies such as EU
Membership	Restricted to those in trade or profession	Open to all
Status	Usually insider groups, with a consultative role	Often, but not always, outsider groups; not usually consulted by government

groups, including the Society of Motor Manufacturers. In addition, several protective groups combine the two elements of interest and cause. The Royal Association for Disability and Rehabilitation (Radar) defends the interests of its members who are disabled, but works for the general betterment of the lot of disabled people. The British Medical Association (BMA) engages in campaigning on general health issues such as diet and smoking, although it primarily exists to defend the interest of professionals involved in health care.

Insider and outsider groups

Groups may also be classified by an alternative typology developed by Wyn Grant[4]. He finds the protective versus promotional distinction unsatisfactory because along with it there tends to be the assumption that protective groups are more influential than cause groups, because they represent powerful interests. Also, it is easy to assume that promotional groups are of greater benefit to society than protective ones, because they are more concerned with the general good rather than personal advantage.

Grant's preferred approach is based on the relationship of groups with the central decision-makers in government. For him, the key issues are whether any particular group wants to gain acceptance by government and – if it does – whether or not it achieves that status. In his words:

> The principle on which such a typology is based is that in order to understand pressure groups, one needs to look not just at the behaviour of the groups but also at the behaviour of government.

Grant divides groups according to whether they are insider or outsider ones. *Insider groups* are regularly consulted by government, having good access to the corridors of power. *Outsider groups* either do not want such access or are unable to attain recognition. Many but not all protective groups are insider ones, and have consultative status. Similarly, in most cases promotional groups are outsider ones, but there are several exceptions, such as the Council for the Protection of Rural England, the Howard League for Penal Reform and the Royal Society for the Protection of Birds (RSPB), all of which are in frequent touch with representatives of government. The status of others fluctuates over a period.

The Grant typology has itself come under some criticism. It has been pointed out that:

- Some groups pursue insider and outsider strategies at the same time, so that the distinction is not clearcut. Tactics such as peaceful public demonstrations and letter-writing campaigns are compatible with insider status, but more violent direct action is not. In Greenpeace, tensions exist over tactics. Over the years, it has shifted towards more dialogue with government and business, whilst maintaining direct-action activities that attract money and popular support.
- More groups have insider status than Grant originally suggested. It is not hard to be consulted – some 200 are on the list for consultation on issues relating to motor cycles, but their influence may be marginal. In other words, consultation is not a special privilege.
- If the insider versus outsider distinction was valid several years ago, it is less valid now because new forms of politics have arisen in the 1990s and subsequently. Pressure group politics has changed, with more middle-class involvement in animal welfare and anti-roads protests. Also, there are more arenas than before, most obviously the European Union. Some groups concentrate much of the time on Brussels, and this gives a new dimension to talk of access to the corridors of power in Whitehall.

The methods employed by pressure groups

In any free society there are **access points**, formal parts of the governmental structure that are accessible to group influence. Where the emphasis is placed will vary from democracy to democracy. In Britain, the most obvious ones are:

The Executive (ministers and civil servants)
The legislature (MPs individually and as members of the party)
Public opinion.

In Britain, the approach adopted depends on the type of group involved. Large, powerful protective groups have close contacts in Whitehall, for in a highly centralised country decision-making is concentrated: key decisions are made in government departments. They may also have contacts in Westminster, and in the case of the unions have close links with several MPs. By contrast, many promotional groups will have very infrequent contact and little influence in Whitehall, unless they are an insider group such as the RSPB. They may have some spasmodic support at Westminster but will try to persuade public opinion in their favour in the hope that the press and MPs will then take up the cause if it proves to be one of much concern. The Campaign for Nuclear Disarmament (CND) has little contact and even less influence in Whitehall, has a number of sympathetic MPs (and in the early to mid-1980s, the Labour Party) to speak in the House, but mainly seeks to create a public mood in favour of unilateralism.

Pressure groups and government

In almost all countries, interest groups target the executive branch of government. Sometimes, they deal with ministers directly, but elected politicians mainly set out what Hague and Harrop[5] refer to as the 'broad contours' of policy. More often, lobbyists – who are interested in the small print of policy – have contact with senior figures in the various departments of state. Groups require access to the seat of power, and it is in the departments that decisions are made and the details of legislation finalised. Matthews[6] explains why this is so:

> the bureaucracy's significance is reinforced by its policy-making and policy-implementing roles. Many routine, technical and 'less important' decisions, which are nonetheless of vital concern to interest groups, are actually made by public servants.

Most British interest groups have close contacts in Whitehall. It is the higher civil service which offers advice to the Secretary of State, the political head of a government department, and so it is very worthwhile to contact senior civil servants. Civil servants and ministers find the Lobby (the network of groups with whom they are in dialogue) very useful. They can get technical information and advice, and maybe help in carrying out a policy. In return, the groups learn the department's current thinking and hope to influence its decisions and get bills drawn up in line with their recommendations.

The concentration of power in the British Executive makes it an obvious focus for group activity, contact being arranged via formal and informal links – government-established committees, the circulation of government documents and widespread consultation conducted in other ways. The National Farmers' Union (NFU) and those employed at the lower end of senior policy grades in the Department of Farming and Rural Affairs (DEFRA) are in frequent contact. The NFU values its consultative status in Whitehall and likes to operate in a quiet, behind-the-scenes way which avoids too much publicity. Only when a row breaks out will it turn to open public methods.

Pressure groups and the legislature

Groups often voice their views via parliaments and assemblies, although whether they place much emphasis at this level depends in part on how much influence the representative body can wield. As we shall see on p. 309, the US Congress is a major channel through which groups can communicate, as is the French National Assembly (see p. 306) and the Italian Chamber of Deputies, which is able to modify and even create policy. This is less true of the British and Canadian parliaments. In both countries, there is a strong system of party discipline, so that MPs are likely to be less responsive to group persuasion. Powerful British groups prefer contact with the Executive, but MPs are much lobbied by them, as well as by promotional groups. Both types have shown increasing interest in lobbying the European Parliament, its MEPs and committees, the more so as its powers have increased.

British groups lobby Parliament because it can influence public policy. In one study[7], 75 per cent of them claimed to be in regular or frequent contact with MPs and more than half also maintained contact with the House of Lords. They might rank its influence below that of the executive branch, but the trend since the 1980s has been towards more lobbying of the legislature. This has been in part because of the growth of the select committee system as another target for influence, but also because the Thatcher and Major governments were less receptive to group campaigners, professional lobbying of MPs has increased. In addition, the existence of governments with large majorities means that it is sometimes more productive for groups to work on backbenchers in the hope of persuading them to oppose what ministers are trying to steamroller through the House.

Elected representatives have often worked as businessmen and women, lawyers, teachers or trade unionists in their earlier life, so that there are likely to be members more than willing to speak up for the interests of various groups in the community. They may be willing to champion individual causes or even put forward a private member's bill. MPs who draw a high position in the annual ballot to introduce such a bill soon find themselves contacted by campaigners who hope to persuade them to introduce a measure relating to their cause. They may have a draft bill ready or else provide assistance in devising one; for example, pro-life groups are keen to find someone willing to introduce legislation restrictive of the circumstances under which abortions can be carried out.

Influence at the parliamentary level can be elected representatives, committees or even a particular party. Prominent British pressure groups often claim to be non-political, though some have clear party leanings. CBI attitudes on 'free enterprise' broadly coincide with Conservative ones, and the unions have historic links with the Labour Party and some are affiliated to it. The TUC is not formally linked and plays no part in the Labour organisation, though there is regular contact between the two bodies and they share a common desire to change society for the benefit of working people.

In lobbying Parliament, groups hope to:

- amend or sponsor legislation in a direction favourable to them
- influence the climate of discussion on relevant issues of public interest
- gain parliamentary backing for causes they may have first raised outside the chamber.

The appeal to the public
Groups try to influence the public who, after all, are the voters in the next election. American groups have long gone in for this style of pressure, especially *background* campaigns, which over a period seek to create a favourable impression for a cause. In Britain, Aims for Freedom and Enterprise, a long-time crusading organisation against nationalisation, keeps up a steady flow of information, and becomes more prominent at election time. A dramatic **fire-brigade campaign** may quickly rally support and get MPs and government ministers to take notice. The Snowdrop campaign in 1996–7 used this blitz approach.

Whereas the public level seemed to be the least influential a few years back, in the last couple of decades it has become more common. The coming of television has provided opportunities for publicity and some organisations now campaign via this medium. By persuading voters to take an issue on board, they hope to generate public interest and raise awareness. Environmental groups have grown rapidly in the last decade, and such bodies have consciously sought to mobilise support through the use of television images and discussions.

For those groups which employ direct action, television can provide valuable publicity. The prolonged Greenham Common anti-Cruise missile protest of the early 1980s attracted some attention, and the campaigns against the M3 extension at Twyford Down and against the Newbury by-pass a decade or so later gained extensive coverage. More recently, so have the campaigning activities of Fathers 4 Justice.

Other outlets

The courts are another focus for the attention of lobbyists. In the USA, litigation is a powerful weapon of campaigners who may bring a class action on behalf of others who share their concern. As yet, British groups have made less use of the legal route, although bodies such as the Equal Opportunities Commission and Greenpeace have won considerable victories in the courts. The Countryside Alliance used the judicial route in an attempt to delay the implementation of the ban on fox-hunting, claiming that it was a denial of members' rights under the European Convention.

Other than by direct approaches to the three tiers of government and the public, groups can be effective in other ways, by working with political parties, lobbying other pressure groups and companies, and using the mass media to create a favourable climate of opinion for their action. There also other layers of government which provide access, at the local, devolved and European levels.

The European dimension to pressure group activity

From the time the United Kingdom joined the European Community in 1973, some groups saw the need to lobby its institutions. The larger manufacturing interests and organisations such as the National

Farmers' Union were first off the mark. Since then, many others – including bodies such as Friends of the Earth and Greenpeace in the environmental field, and the British Veterinary Association and the Royal Society for the Prevention of Cruelty to Animals operating in the topical area of animal welfare – have seen the need to embrace the European dimension. Indeed, in Baggott's[8] survey (1992) of some 100 groups, more than 60 per cent reported an increase in contact with EC institutions over the previous decade.

The European Commission is a relatively open bureaucracy and the views of various 'interests' are carefully considered in the early stages of draft legislation. MEPs and their party groupings, and committees of the Strasbourg Parliament are also the focus of attention. MEPs are a useful avenue through which more attention can be paid to the Commission. The Commission estimates that around 10,000 people are engaged in lobbying at the European level. The increase is not merely one of volume but also of quality, for there is today a growing professionalism and sophistication in much group activity.

With the passage of the Single European Act and the opening up of the single market, more and more decisions are being taken in Brussels. European institutions are an obvious target for British lobbyists. Three avenues are open to groups that wish to lobby the European machinery:

1. *Placing pressure on the national government.* Many groups try to influence the stance adopted by their governments in EU discussions and to influence the implementation of EU decisions. They can do this by entering into discussions with ministers and senior civil servants in the relevant Whitehall ministry. Some groups prefer to operate via the British government rather than make a direct approach to the Union.

2. *Operating through Euro-groups.* Many groups feel that in addition to utilising their contact with their own governments, they wish to exert pressure via a European-level federation of national groups. Back in 1992, Baggott found that 75 per cent of the groups he surveyed were members of such an organisation. The TUC is a member of ETUC, a Eurogroup that currently represents 77 national organizations from 35 countries.

3. *Direct lobbying.* Direct contacts with Union institutions are becoming increasingly important for many groups. A few large ones have established offices in Brussels, as a means of closely monitoring European legislation and issues of interest to British trade unions and also as an outlet that can offer protection for members working in the EU. More usually, contact takes other forms, such as working via MEPs, approaching formally or informally a commissioner or writing letters to or phoning Union institutions.

Box 8.3 Lobbying the European Union: the case of the RSPCA

Since the 1970s, much of the legislation on animal protection in the UK has been enacted by the European Community/Union. Examples cover regulations concerning the transport of wild, farm and laboratory animals. This is a trading activity carried out in several countries and across borders. It involves other industries such as farming, slaughter, scientific research and the sale of animals as pets or public zoo exhibits. As a result of successive EU treaties, the Union's capacity to deal with issues such as these has been increased. Nearly all of the legislation on farm animals derives from the Union. So too, the Union has tackled issues of the protection of native wild animals and their habitats.

Not surprisingly, the EU is an extremely important part of RSPCA campaigning. It lobbies at several levels:

- The Council of Ministers
- The Commission
- The Committee of Permanent Representatives (COREPER)
- The Parliament.

The RSPCA now has an office in Brussels, run by the umbrella Eurogroup for Animal Welfare, a federation of national pressure groups in the field of animal welfare. Via its office and by working with the Eurogroup, the pressure group has been particularly active since May 2004, in seeking to improve, apply and enforce animal welfare standards in the newly enlarged European Union of 25 countries, aware as it was that standards of care have varied considerably across the more recently admitted member states.

Pressure groups in the Thatcher to Blair years

In the 1980s, Tory governments had large majorities and could override most backbench rebellions, with the notable exception of the attempt to change the law on Sunday Trading in 1986, which ran into serious opposition from the trade unions and religious lobby. The Government was not well disposed to group activity, and in that same year the then Home Secretary, Douglas Hurd, issued a sharp rebuke to groups. He attacked then as 'strangling serpents' which created unnecessary work for ministers and made it difficult for them to reach decisions in the public interest. He argued that they distorted the proper constitutional relationship between the Executive, Parliament and the electorate.

Along with some other senior Tories, he seemed to be casting doubt on the right of groups to have their say in the formulation of policy. This was particularly the case in relation to the unions, for ministers were wary of **corporatist** arrangements through which unions and big business could develop a close relationship with government. Margaret Thatcher was especially hostile to the idea of negotiating with such groups, which she viewed as essentially self-interested.

The then Government's reaction differed according to the type of group in question. If unions and many welfare groups aroused suspicion, others which were more sympathetic to Conservative policy received a different response. Some had views which were music to the ears of ministers, such as the Adam Smith Institute with its espousal of free-market economics, and the Freedom Association, which stressed the rights of individual workers rather than organised labour and was opposed to excessive governmental intervention in our daily lives.

By contrast with the Conservatives, the Labour Party is in the business of seeking to change society, and often there is an overlap between pressure group activists and Lib–Lab supporters. Some of its MPs and ministers were once group activists. Patricia Hewitt once worked for the National Council for Civil Liberties (now Liberty) before becoming an MP and then achieving cabinet status. Even if Labour governments often disappoint them, groups in the social field will often find that their staffs, supporters and objectives sit more easily with a Labour administration, which at least shares some of their values and priorities, than with a Conservative one.

Yet since May 1997, many pressure groups have been disappointed with the success achieved. The unions desperately wanted a Labour government and have achieved some of the goals which mattered to them – action on a minimum wage and youth unemployment, the signing of the Social Chapter and the recognition of unions at GCHQ. But in other respects the Blairite party has been a disappointment to them. From the beginning, key spokespersons for New Labour made it clear that they would do 'no special favours' for the unions, and that they would listen to and consult with any body whose views they wished to hear. In that spirit, ministers have met business as well as union leaders frequently. Businessmen and women have played a prominent role in government, with some actually serving in office at a high level.

For social groups their enthusiasm for the Government was weakened by the adherence of the Chancellor to the strict spending limits on expenditure in the early years. Subsequently, the 'tough' policies adopted on welfare policy (towards lone parents and the disabled) left many quickly disillusioned.

Generally, the environmental lobby has fared well in the last two decades, a reflection of the increase in public interest and media attention since the late 1980s. Margaret Thatcher had an interest in aspects of the environmentalist agenda, and some members of Friends of the Earth and other organisations found a receptive ear for some of their ideas. Their efforts have led to modest 'greening' of the policies of the three main parties.

Some trends in group activity

There has been a dramatic increase in nation-wide popular movements. More single-issue groups have emerged, and via television have achieved enormous publicity, and demonstrated the extent of popular feeling in favour of their campaign. So too have certain causes such as the countryside and environment gained popular backing. On the one hand, there is the success of the Countryside Alliance, whose march on London in 1997 showed ministers the scale of unrest in country areas about trends in governmental policy in recent years. More typical of the situation in most European countries are the new social movements about which we have written. As we have seen, new left politics are characterised by the involvement of younger and better-educated people within society, who take up issues such as minority rights, anti-nuclear protest, international peace, anti-globalisation, poverty in developing countries and the environment in general. Using tactics ranging from boycotts to passive resistance, and engaging in activities such as protests or more violent demonstrations, these unconventional forms are no longer new, having become an accepted feature of group activity in Western societies.

The increasing use of professional lobbyists

In recent years, pressure groups have developed a more sophisticated approach to the ways by which they seek to influence 'pressure points' in the political process. Some have turned to the use of the new commercial 'lobbying industry', an American-style import. Professional lobbyists were defined in a House of Commons report as those who are 'professionally employed to lobby on behalf of clients or who advise clients on how to lobby on their own behalf'.

These agencies trade their political knowledge and expertise to clients in return for considerable financial reward. They are hired for their inside knowledge of the workings of government and their contacts. There are around sixty of them, and they have represented groups as diverse as British Airways and Tottenham Hotspur FC. Some are small specialist bodies, such as Political Planning Services. Others have a much larger client base. Most major pressure groups either have a specialist lobbying department or employ the services of one of the professionals.

Concern has been raised over the activities of these professional groups, especially over their close relationship with certain MPs. Most MPs do not provide very much in return for payment as consultants, mainly reporting back to the group monthly on relevant political developments of interest to the company, and acting as 'eyes and ears'. From the lobbyists' point of view, they are pleased to be able to use the MP's name on the top of their notepaper. It creates the impression that the group has access to and influence in the 'right places'. The fear is that in some cases that connection might be misused, and that companies are buying influence over legislation, influence which is denied to smaller, less well-funded groups within the community.

Some MPs have been less than open in disclosing their connections. In particular, several cases arose in the early to mid-1990s which cast down on the honour of the House of Commons and its members. There was widespread anxiety about the way in which MPs were willing to accept money from outside sources. This led to the establishment of the Nolan Committee, which in 1995 made recommendations regarding payment from outside sources. MPs went further than the committee suggested, and prohibited the practice of any paid advocacy by MPs. They can no longer advocate a Particular cause in Parliament in return for payment, and have to disclose money from outside bodies that is paid to them by virtue of their status as MPs. For instance, income from a company for advice on how to present a case to government now has to be declared.

The increasing use of direct action

In the last two or three decades, there has been an upsurge in the growth of forms of **direct action** by individuals and groups. These range from demonstrations and 'sit-in' protests, to squatting and striking, from interrupting televised events and non-payment of taxation to the invasion of institutions in which the activities conducted cause offence. Groups committed to opposing abortion in the United States and hunting or other forms of alleged mistreatment of animals in the United Kingdom have often been willing to resort to forms of direct action to voice their protest. On a global scale, the 1990s saw the emergence of a widespread movement of opposition to **globalisation**, in which a wide variety of groups – environmentalists, campaigners for debt relief, human rights activists and so on – took part in a series of demonstrations, such as those in 1999 (in London on May Day and in Seattle at the World Trade Organisation conference) and in 2001 at Genoa at the time of the G8 summit, where 100,000 demonstrators gathered in protest.

Many local action and promotional groups have used direct action as an additional tool. There are many examples of the 'not in my back garden' (NIMBY) types of groups which have used this approach in their bid to block moves to build a housing estate on green-belt land, or stop the felling of some ancient tree in the name of progress. NIMBY groups have mushroomed, often using media-oriented tactics in their campaigning. Mothers and Children Against Toxic Waste (MACATV) is a Welsh example of the genre. It sought to prevent the burning of toxic waste by a chemical processing plant.

Box 8.4 Direct action, 2004-style: Fathers 4 Justice

On 19 May 2004, two members of Fathers 4 Justice caused a security alarm at Westminster when they hurled purple powder at Tony Blair. There were immediate fears that it might be a chemical or biological toxin, but later it was proved to be harmless flour. The two protesters had managed to evade the newly installed glass screen, for they were seated in the front three rows of the gallery outside the security fitting.

Fathers 4 Justice is a direct-action fathers' rights group, formed to campaign on behalf of fathers who claim to have suffered injustices in the quagmire of divorce proceedings and feel that the legal system is stacked against them.

Often, groups have used direct action when they have campaigned against the use of fur for clothing, hunting foxes or laboratory experimentation on live creatures. Animal rights activists and anti-motorway protesters have been in the forefront of such campaigning, and have often been adept in arranging for the media to be present at their demonstrations. A reading of the local papers on any day will probably reveal the activities of groups who seek to gain publicity by some dramatic gesture. The object of many demonstrations is to generate publicity. It can be effective, for several polls have indicated that opposition to fox-hunting has increased because of widespread coverage of anti-hunt activities.

Factors influencing the success of different groups

Different pressure groups experience varying degrees of success. For these purposes, success may be interpreted as meaning:

- gaining access to a centre of decision-making, and
- exerting influence over the development of policy.

Baggott[9] has distinguished three general considerations that determine the effectiveness of groups:

1. Their resources
2. Their political contacts
3. The political environment in which the pressure group operates.

Traditionally, protective groups are thought to have possessed more power in Whitehall than promotional ones, but their success may vary according to these specific factors:

- *The degree of government support for the aims and ideas of the group*: e.g., (particularly in the past) the unions may benefit more from a Labour administration, business from a Conservative one.
- *The government's need for cooperation and support*: The NFU and BMA – among other organisations – are in a position to provide valuable information and assistance to ministers.
- *The bargaining power of a group within the economy*: some groups have the capacity to withhold their support and thereby cause hardship and inconvenience. The BMA has much power, for ultimately its members could (and have) threatened to withdraw from the operation of the National Health Service. The National Federation of Old Age Pensioners (NFOAP) can cause relatively little disruption, although the growth in the number of old people means that the electoral potential of senior citizens is an ultimate weapon which the NFOAP is beginning to exploit.
- *Timing is all important*: If there is general public feeling in their favour, it can work to the advantage of pressure groups. In 1972–4 the miners had widespread public sympathy at a time when their produce was much needed because of the quadrupling of oil prices in the Middle East. Coal was seen as vital to the economy in the1970s, and expendable or replaceable by other sources of energy in the 1990s; the time for coal had passed, in the eyes of Conservative ministers.
- *The representativeness of the leadership*: any union or organisation which speaks for the vast majority of people in its sector and is perceived as being representative of opinion (as is the NFU) is in a better position to advance its claim. In the early Thatcher years, it was easier to ignore the views of union leaders, who were criticised as being unelected or elected for life, and not accountable to those who put them in their position.

Generally, promotional groups are viewed as less powerful than groups which consult with Whitehall, though as we have seen, some such organisations are influential insiders. Lacking such access, most operate more directly with the public. Factors of relevance here include:

- *The attitude of the government.* CND is unlikely to make any significant impact on a Conservative government, Aims for Freedom and Enterprise on a Labour one.
- *Proximity to an election.* Ministers might be more susceptible to influence when an election looms.
- *Parliamentary support from all parties.* Wide backing may smooth the passage of a bill being promoted in the House, and may suggest to the government that there is a wide consensus on the issue.
- *A good case*, well informed and well argued, and not too partisan.
- *The climate of opinion.* Attitudes may change over a generation, and whereas the Lord's Day Observance Society could wield considerable influence post-war, its position is undermined by the waning of religious devotion today.
- *Media attention.* Television exposure offers cheap publicity, and can demonstrate that a group's interest corresponds with public concern; it is then more difficult for ministers to ignore the case presented.

The benefits and disadvantages of pressure groups

In recent years, the tendency of many politicians has been to criticise pressure group activity as damaging to the democratic process. Groups are seen as essentially self-interested and lacking in concern for the needs of the wider public. Yet this is only part of the picture, for they also raise issues of popular concern and provide a useful channel through which preferences may be expressed. Democracy would be unable to function without them, for they are at the heart of the policy-making process. Given such a position, the need is to monitor their activities and ensure that they are efficient, open and representative, rather than to imagine that their contribution can be either ignored or removed.

Among the specific arguments advanced in favour of and against their contribution to democracy are the following.

In favour

- In a pluralist society, in which power is dispersed in many different locations, pressure groups are seen as being at the heart of the democratic process. In particular, they perform a valuable function within the political system, for they allow participation in decision-making by ordinary individuals. Many people otherwise only participate in political life at election time, but they can indirectly do so by joining groups that can influence the decisions of public bodies.
- They provide valuable information to government departments based upon their specialist knowledge of their field. In some cases, this is backed by cooperation in administering a particular policy and monitoring its effectiveness. They are indispensable to governmental decision-making because they are available for regular consultation. Indeed, this may be on a very frequent basis, there being continuing dialogue between a government department and a key interest group such as the CBI or the BMA. The government knows that a group of this type represents the bulk of people in that particular sector. Most farmers are in the NFU, and therefore its voice is representative.
- They act as a defence for minority interests, especially those connected with parties not in government.
- They counter the monopoly of the political process by political parties, and sometimes they raise items for discussion which fall outside the realm of party ideas and policy, and which do not tend to get in the manifestos. They made the running in the 'green' arena, before the parties took up ecological issues.
- In a democracy such as ours, they are an inevitable feature. The chance to freely voice a viewpoint is basic to a democratic system. The group system has mushroomed in recent years and this growth is unlikely to be reversed.

Baggott[10] has summarised their value effectively:

> The views which pressure groups convey are legitimate interests . . . Modern democracy would not exist without pressure groups. As a channel of representation, they are as legitimate as the ballot box . . . They can mediate between the government and the governed.

Against

- A frequent criticism is that not all sections of the community are equally capable of exerting influence, though virtually everyone is free to join a group. There is not a level-playing field for influence. Some, especially ideas groups, are much less likely to be acknowledged. Campaigners can point to the failure of the Child Poverty Action Group and other welfare groups to prevent Labour from cutting benefits to one-parent families and the disabled. Of the interest groups, the voice less frequently heard is that of consumers, who are difficult to organise, other than via the ballot box. By contrast, the producer groups, the unions and, particularly in the Tory years, the industrialists, have easier access to Whitehall.
- The leadership of some groups is unrepresentative. This was the case with a number of unions before a change in the law forced them to hold elections for the post of general secretary. It is important that any government knows that people it talks to do genuinely reflect their members' wishes, and that deals made with leaders will stick because they have the backing of group supporters.
- Some people worry about the secrecy under which bargains between interest groups and Whitehall departments are made – hence Finer's[11] plea for 'Light, More Light'. Also, they fear that too many MPs are beholden to outside groups and business commitments.
- A pressure group by definition represents a number of broadly like-minded citizens in society. In other words it is a 'sectional' interest, in the way that the NFU represents farmers and the NUM miners. Governments have to govern in the 'national interest', and consider the views and needs of all sections of the community, not the voice of only the powerful. The TUC still represents a substantial proportion of working people, but by no means all workers; the miners' voice on pay may be strong, but consumers may have to finance their pay by spending more for their coal/electricity.

The case of France

At the beginning of the Fifth French Republic (1958), President de Gaulle expressed the view that the state was more than 'a mere

juxtaposition of particular interests, capable only of feeble compromises . . . [it was] an instrument of decision, action, ambition,
expressing and serving only the national interest'. His first prime minister, Michel Debré, was more directly hostile to powerful pressure
groups. His comments echoed the view that they are 'strangling serpents', for he saw them as vested interests which 'divide the state and
leech upon it with scarcely a thought for the nation or the citizens'.

Such comments were a reflection of the experiences of some
French politicians of life under the previous two republics, the Fourth
of which was commonly known as the 'régime des intérêts'. Then,
with a weak executive branch of government and a powerful
chamber, groups were able to exert considerable leverage – the more
so as party discipline was particularly weak.

French pressure groups operate in a similar way to those in the
United States and elsewhere. But they have some distinguishing
features:

- French interest groups tend to be more ideologically fragmented
  than in some other countries, this being especially true of the trade
  unions. The largest and oldest body is the Confédération Générale
  du Travail (CGT), a federation of constituent unions which has
  a history of supporting direct working-class action; it has a traditional affinity to the French Communist Party. The Force Ouvrière
  (FO) is staunchly anti-communist, but stresses the need for unions
  to distance themselves from involvement with political parties. Big
  business is more unified.
- Agrarian organisations have traditionally been particularly influential, although in recent years there has been a decline in the
  number of farms and farmers. Governments find it hard to ignore
  farming interests, for the agricultural way of life is closely linked to
  the survival and future of particular regions that would suffer from
  rural depopulation if the industry foundered. Accordingly, the
  French Farmers' Federation (FFF) has influential insider status, its
  representatives sitting on state commissions and advisory councils.
  Its ex-leaders sometimes move on to assume ministerial responsibilities. Access to the focus of power does not prevent French
  farmers from engaging in radical action to draw attention to their
  grievances. The FFF is on occasion willing to countenance such

tactics, illustrating how powerful insider groups sometimes accompany their consultative dialogue with more theatrical forms of protest.

- Non-occupational groups have not traditionally had the same impact that they have in some other countries. There are relatively fewer of the large national voluntary public interest associations common in many other democracies. Stevens[12] notes that there is no equivalent to the British RSPB or the US National Rifle Association, and that French consumerism was slow to take off. But the French have a tradition of membership of clubs and associations, many of which are small and local, but may still have an indirect impact on policy-making. They operate in areas ranging from women's issues to the environment.

- There is a tradition of protest politics. Many associations, voluntary groups and individual citizens take part when there is what Waters[13] calls 'a spontaneous movement of public defiance', seeking major policy change. These gatherings fall into the 'social movement' category, large and loose groupings that derive their impetus from people who often do not belong to the classic political organisations. They lack a regular membership, programme or constitution, but arise from the circumstances of the day. Examples include the movements for students, gay rights, Corsican autonomy, ecology, women's rights and anti-racism.

The case of Scotland

Following the introduction of devolved government in 1999, many UK pressure groups have shifted their focus in response to the new arrangements. This is particularly true north of the border, for the Scottish bodies have greater powers and responsibilities than those created in Wales. Before the creation of the Scottish Parliament, there were exclusively Scottish interest groups. However, since 1999 their range and number have significantly increased and they now concentrate much of their attention on the Scottish Parliament and Executive. Moreover, several UK groups have developed separate Scottish branches in order to lobby more effectively. Those groups that regularly come into contact with the Edinburgh machinery generally appear to have a positive view of the process.

From the beginning, the Executive has encouraged groups and individuals to become involved in the process of consultation. The presence of Labour and the Liberal Democrats in office may facilitate a close relationship, for there is some movement of personnel between social group activists and the two broadly progressive parties. So too, MSPs have encouraged campaigners to petition Parliament and liaise with its committees. Committees engage in consultations, in a bid to discover public opinion on a wide range of issues prior to proposed legislation.

The resulting growth in activity has inspired the media to report on group demands, so that some issues have been extensively covered by journalists. The **Souter referendum** and the subsequent repeal of **Section 28** were high-profile events that generated much journalistic activity and discussion.

Overall, those groups recently contacted by the author[14] generally had a positive attitude towards devolution. They felt that their input was being taken into consideration as decisions were made. In addition, they find it convenient to be able to lobby in Edinburgh, rather than in London, the access point in the days before devolution. They feel that they are in close proximity to the key political players and of course also benefit from savings in time and travelling costs. These are early days in which to come to anything other than a tentative judgement about the efficacy of groups in the consultative process. But there is no doubt that an important new dimension to group activity has been created by the passage of the Scotland Act.

The case of the USA

American groups vary considerably in size, influence and resources. Among the protective groups are large institutional bodies such the US Chamber of Commerce (representing businesses across the nation) and the American Medical Association. Among the promotional groups, some are based on support or a single issue such as the National Abortion and Reproductive Rights Action League, whereas others are concerned to promote a wider range of causes within a given area, such as Friends of the Earth.

Groups operate at all levels of government, federal, state and local, benefiting from the number of access points available in a federal system of government. Congress is a particular focus for lobbyists. Both chambers, the Senate and the House of Representatives, are powerful bodies with a key legislative role. Many legislators are financed by substantial contributions from political action committees, the political and financial arm of American groups. Elected every two years, representatives are also aware of the need to keep their constituents 'back home' contented. Many of them come from areas where a substantial proportion of the population is engaged in a key interest, such as farming in the Midwest.

Activity at the Congressional level is more overt than that aimed at the Executive, much of which often takes part behind closed doors. Congress is a key part of the policy process, especially its committee system; moreover, party discipline is much weaker than at Westminster. As with the French Chamber of Deputies, group activists have a real opportunity to influence votes by their campaigning. Weak party discipline and strong pressure group activity at the legislative level tends to coincide, whereas by contrast – as the experience of Britain and Canada indicates – tighter discipline makes lobbying of elected representatives less worthwhile.

America has the most developed system of group activity of any democracy. Groups benefit from:

- a constitution that provides protection in the First Amendment of the Bill of Rights for freedom of speech and expression
- the participatory tradition of the American people
- an open form of government, with powerful freedom of information laws
- a fragmented party system
- issue-based rather than party-based election campaigns.

American groups differ from British groups in several respects:

- There are more of them, reflecting the participatory tendency of Americans and the greater number of access points for them to lobby.
- They exist in an atmosphere conducive to their operations, with constitutional protection and an executive and legislative framework much influenced by federalism and the separation of powers.

- They employ a range of different methods, including fundraising via political action committees, paid political advertising and the use of technology.
- They make more use of the courts, both federal and state.
- They are less likely to target the Executive, for whereas in Britain this is the location of key decision-making, in America the role of the legislature (i.e. Congress) is very influential in policy-making.

....

 What you should have learnt from reading this chapter

- The influence and effectiveness of pressure groups varies according to the country and its internal circumstances, as well as to the time and the nature of the cause.

- There is greater scope for group action in more advanced nations than in more backward ones. Groups flourish in liberal democracies, which have a range of access points to which they can apply pressure.

- Overall, there has been a change rather than a decline in pressure group power in Britain in recent years, a situation reflected also in other countries. Traditional groups have in many cases lost some of their former influence, but local action organisations and enthusiasts for new causes publicise their case strongly. Often, they employ different methods than those characteristic of more familiar organisations.

Glossary of key terms

Access (or pressure) points Those parts of the governmental structure which are accessible to pressure group influence.

Corporatism Corporatism refers to the tendency of governments to incorporate leading peak organisations (such as the CBI) into the process of policy-making, thereby institutionalising group consultation. Tripartitism refers to the three sides involved in such consultations: government, business and the unions.

Direct action Any action beyond the usual constitutional and legal framework, such as obstructing access to a building or the building of a motorway. Terrorism is an extreme form. Essentially, it is an attempt to coerce those in authority into doing something they would not otherwise do.

Fire-brigade campaign A dramatic type of group campaign designed to rally support quickly.

Globalisation Globalisation refers to the increasing interdependence of people, organisations and states in the modern world and the growing influence of global cultural and economic forces or trends. For many critics, it is the process whereby life is increasingly shaped by decisions or events taken at a distance from them. Anti-globalisation protesters worry especially about the influence of American capitalist values, seeing the United States as the cause of many of the world's difficulties, such as a degraded environment and world poverty and indebtedness.

Hybrid groups Groups that do not neatly fit into the protective versus promotional typology. They exist to protect the interests of their members, but also do a substantial amount of promotional work. In some cases, they are established by interest groups but exist to propagate a cause or an idea.

New social movements Organisations that have emerged since the 1960s in order to influence public policy on issues such as the environment, nuclear energy, peace and women's rights. They have wider interests and are more loosely organised than most pressure groups, tend to have supporters rather than members and do not operate through detailed involvement with government. They are concerned to bring about fundamental change in society.

Pluralist Pluralism refers to the belief that power in modern societies is widely distributed between a multiplicity of competing interests. From time to time, new groups emerge, ensuring that there is further competition in the political marketplace. Pluralist societies are ones in which group activity can flourish, the various organised groups each having the opportunity to articulate their various demands.

Section 28 Introduced by the Thatcher government in its 1988 Local Government Act, the clause prohibited the 'promotion of homosexuality in schools'. It was offensive to many sections of the community. Labour has acted on its pledge to remove it both in England and Wales, and in Scotland.

Single-issue groups Groups that concentrate their attention on the achievement of one specific objective.

Souter Referendum A privately funded ballot of all Scottish people on repeal of the contentious Section 28. On a 34 per cent turnout, 87 per cent wished to retain the section, 13 per cent to remove it.

Think tanks Groups formed to research and develop policy proposals, and campaign for their acceptance among opinion formers and policy-makers. They are often ideologically based, their ideas sometimes being influential with the parties with which they share a broad affinity (e.g. the Institute of Policy Research and the Labour Party).

❓ Likely examination questions

Why is the distinction between pressure groups and political parties often unclear?

Examine the main differences in the methods by which protective and promotional groups operate.

Why do many leading British interest groups concentrate their attention on Westminster rather than on Whitehall?

Account for the growing impact of the European dimension to British pressure group activity.

Compare the activities and tactics of environmental groups with those of other types of pressure groups.

Discuss the view that the activities of pressure groups constitute a threat to the operations of liberal democratic systems of government.

 ## Helpful websites

For basic information on pressure groups, their characteristics and influence, and on pluralism, consult:

www.historylearningsite.co.uk/pressure-groups.htm

Most individual pressure groups have their own sites, covering such aspects as the history, objectives and organisation of organisations. Some are listed below.

www.demos.co.uk   Demos

www.cbi.org.uk   Confederation of British Industry

www.etuc.org   European Trade Union Confederation

www.countryside-alliance.org   Countryside Alliance

www.greenpeace.org.uk   Greenpeace

 ## Suggestions for further reading

Useful articles

N. Jackson, 'Pressure Group Politics', *Politics Review*, September 2004.

D. Watts, 'Lobbying Europe: An Update', *Talking Politics*, September 2004.

D. Watts, 'Pressure Group Activity in Post-Devolution Scotland', *Talking Politics*, January 2006.

Useful books

R. Baggott, *Pressure Groups Today*, Manchester University Press, 1995.

B. Coxall, *Pressure Groups in British Politics*, Pearson, 2001.

W. Grant, *Pressure Groups and British Politics*, Palgrave, 2000.

J. Greenwood, *Representing Interests in the European Union*, Macmillan, 1997.

CHAPTER 9

Voting and Elections

Contents

Overview

All Western countries hold regular elections. They are central to any definition of a representative democracy. The right to vote is the primary symbol of citizenship in a democratic society, allowing citizens to decide who shall govern them. By an election, we mean a competition for office based on a formal expression of preferences by a designated body of people at the ballot box. Such a contest holds those in office to account and if necessary provides a means for their replacement. In this chapter, we are concerned with the conduct of elections; the choice of electoral system; the nature of campaigning; influences upon people when they cast their vote; reasons for non-voting; and the growing popularity of direct democracy across the world.

Key issues to be covered in this chapter

- General characteristics of elections
- Various types of electoral system and their impact
- Electoral systems currently in use in the United Kingdom
- Trends in election campaigning, particularly the influence of television
- Role and importance of money in modern elections
- Trends in voting behaviour
- Turnout in recent elections in Britain and elsewhere
- Growing interest in forms of direct democracy
- The experiences of France, Germany and the United States

General considerations

Elections in established democracies are generally free and fair. In a report for the Commonwealth Parliamentary Association, two Canadian writers, Gould and Jackson[1], see the key determinant of 'free and fair' as being whether 'the will of the majority of voters is expressed, freely, clearly and knowledgeably, and in secret'. Today, more countries hold elections that meet these criteria than ever before. In the last quarter of the twentieth century, millions of people acquired the right to vote for the first time. In 1994, South Africa held its first free election in which the previously disenfranchised millions were entitled to vote. On the African continent, elections providing a choice of candidates and multi-partyism are now the norm. In the newly emergent Eastern European countries there is free and open competition. Even countries such as communist North Korea allow for a narrow range of candidates.

Elections can range from being a meaningless exercise in which there is no genuine voter choice to a downright fraud, because of the tampering with votes or the lack of freedom under which polling is carried out. Yet even in countries with dubious democratic credentials, elections are still recognised by the ruling authorities as being useful. They create the illusion of popular participation. Hence they are not only a means of filling public offices, but confer legitimacy on the government. In Britain, we may only get a vote in a general election every few years, but at least there is a genuine opportunity to express an opinion on those who have presided over our fortunes and to indicate whether it is, in our view, 'time for a change'.

In most countries, the voting age has been lowered, 18 being the most common age for qualification. Of course, entitlement to vote is not the same as the ability to vote, and in a democracy it is important to ensure that there is an effective procedure by which people can be registered. In several countries there are permanent registers, amended at periodic intervals, as in Britain and most of Europe. Elsewhere, registers have to be created from scratch, so that in most American states it is necessary for the would-be voter to register his or her vote before polling day; this reflects the American emphasis on the mobilising effect of elections. Such an approach tends to be less efficient in ensuring eligibility and is likely to result in low turnouts.

Whatever the system, it is likely that some voters – perhaps 5–10 per cent or more – will not be registered. Of those who are registered, others will be unable to cast their vote because of illness, absence or other pressing circumstances. Some people are just unwilling to make the effort, especially if obtaining a postal vote is a complex process. Hence the remedy introduced in several countries, compulsory voting. Australia, Austria, Belgium and some Latin American states are among those which have resorted to this method, but in most cases its effectiveness is limited by the low level of fines and the difficulties in collecting those which are due.

Election campaigning

Campaigns and campaigning are an integral part of the democratic process. The task of those who run campaigns is to make sure that the electorate is well informed about the personalities and issues involved. In particular, campaign managers wish to reinforce wavering voters, recruit those who are undecided and convert those whose initial preference is for another party. Above all, they need to see that there is a maximum turnout of their own sympathisers on polling day.

British election campaigns are much shorter than American ones. Even though there is much speculation and a pre-election atmosphere in the third or fourth year of the lifetime of a Parliament, the campaign proper lasts only three to four weeks. Campaigns for all elective offices in America are longer, especially for the presidency.

Election campaigns have never been the same since the televising of politics began in the late 1950s. New styles of campaigning have developed, so that in recent years there have been innovative polling techniques, the wider use of focus groups, the introduction of professional advisers and an emphasis on the training of candidates. This greater professionalism of campaigns has been fairly general in all political systems, as has the increasing attention given to the qualities of the candidate rather than the party. In this world of more **candidate-centred campaigning**, professional **consultants** have acquired a new importance. For years major parties have brought in outside agencies to advise them, but now they maintain a core of their own **spin doctors** and image and marketing specialists who are either employed permanently at headquarters or are easily available.

Skilful use of the media has become something of an art-form in modern elections, and campaigns are often based around opportunities for media coverage, particularly on television. Like the cinema, television is a medium of entertainment, so parties, politicians and their advisers have seen the need to attune performances to its demands. The focus in political campaigning is now increasingly on broad themes rather than policies, emotion rather than rational debate. **Sound-bites** have often been a substitute for genuine discussion.

Media consultants are always on the look-out for opportunities to maximise free television coverage. Election advertising is expensive, whether the money is spent on American-style paid advertisements or on poster hoardings. So rallies and speeches addressed to large meetings are often scheduleds that they gain as much exposure as possible on news bulletins.

In presidential countries such as the USA, the marketing of politics has been particularly well developed. Electioneering has always been more candidate-centred, parties having been less entrenched in the political system. The new techniques of electioneering have crossed the Atlantic, leading to accusations about the 'Americanisation of elections'. Britain has in many ways learnt from the American experience, for there has been an increasing emphasis on walkabouts, photo-opportunities and pseudo-events created for the media. As in other countries, parties have adjusted to the changes to the changed environment in which they now operate.

In some states such as the Netherlands and the USA, party access to television time is unlimited, but in most countries governments have regulated the situation to ensure that justice is done to all parties. In Ireland, New Zealand and the United Kingdom, time is allocated according to the proportion of support obtained in the last election, whereas in Denmark and France, among other examples, there is equal access to all parties irrespective of their size.

Box 9.1 A note on the importance of money in campaigning

The issue of funding election campaigns has become highly controversial in recent years. The necessity for heavy party spending has been increased by the trends in modern campaigning, with their emphasis on image and marketing. Best-financed parties have a clear advantage, being able to commit greater resources to advertising on hoardings or (in the USA) on television. Between a quarter and a third of the total campaign expenses in American congressional elections goes for radio and TV advertising. In all countries, much of the money that does not go on direct advertising is still focused on the media. The work of campaign consultants in developing and testing themes and strategies, targeting audiences, surveying focus groups and conducting polls is done in preparation for taking the party's or candidate's message to the media for transmission to the voters.

In Britain, the Conservatives have traditionally been able to outspend Labour and the Liberal Democrats, although their advantage has been markedly curtailed since 1997. Then and four years later, Labour was almost able to match their expenditure. The possibility of one party being in a stronger position was much reduced by the passage of the Elections and Referendums Act (2000), which – among other things – imposed a limit on how much any party can spend (currently the ceiling on campaign spending is £30,000 per seat contested, which adds up to £19,380,000 if a party fights every constituency).

British election campaigns and campaigning

In a sense, parties engage in continuous campaigning, but as legally defined the campaign in British elections must last at least for the three weeks prior to polling day. Campaigns follow a fairly regular form. At the constituency level, candidates and volunteer helpers continue to canvass, address meetings and deliver election addresses to electors' homes, although the amount of energy devoted to arranging meetings for the candidates and doorstepping has markedly declined.

Constituency campaigning has been transformed in recent years into something much more sophisticated than it was until the 1980s. Party headquarters now plays a significant role in planning and managing local campaigns. Resources are increasingly targeted on marginal constituencies, often referred to as 'target seats', and in particular on categories of voters within them such as 'school gate mums'. The use of computers and telephone banks has enabled party campaigners to develop a profile of individual voters and send them an appropriate message.

Party leaders now engage in frantic tours around those constituencies that may change hands. Their itineraries are planned in great detail, as they are whisked from one end of the country to another in a carefully controlled schedule of meetings and events. They address gatherings in the large towns and cities, sometimes attend and make statements at the daily morning press conferences, and prepare for their television broadcasts, interviews with established interrogators and appearances before studio audiences.

During the campaign, the amount of political activity intensifies dramatically, and great political expertise and professionalism are employed to get the message across. *But does all of the massive and expensive effort actually make any difference to the outcome of the election?*

The traditional academic view of election campaigns was that they had little impact on the voters. In an age when voting behaviour was more habitual and predictable, then the campaign was less likely to influence the firmly held loyalties of the voters. In this context, party managers saw the purpose of the campaign as being to stimulate interest and maximise their potential turnout on polling day. Particular attention was concentrated on the marginal constituencies where the extra effort might affect the outcome. The floating voters – especially those in marginal constituencies – were the key target of the party managers: a small shift in opinion or an increase in their turnout could prove decisive.

In recent decades, the combination of **class** and partisan **de-alignment** and the development of television as the main form of mass communications have led to a questioning of these earlier assumptions. It is commonly agreed that the electorate is more volatile, and notions of class and party identification are less deepseated. In this situation, there are likely to be more people who are undecided before the campaign proper gets underway. According to Heath et al.,[2] the number of voters who only made up their minds during the campaign doubled to 24 per cent between 1970 and 1992.

If voters are more open to persuasion, then it is reasonable to assume that campaigns ought be more significant. Nonetheless, it remains difficult to prove that the impact of the campaign is very extensive. In 2001 and 2005, the ratings of the two main parties did not significantly shift in the weeks before polling day. As often happens, the third party benefited from the increased publicity that an election generates.

British electioneering, past and present: marketing the party image

An interest in publicity and marketing is not a novel concern for parties and politicians. Early in the twentieth century, the Conservatives were keen to exploit the opportunities offered by the new forms of media, be they radio or film. Strategists of what was referred to as the 'psychology of the electorate' were keen to promote 'party image' as far back as 1908, when Graham Wallas[3] first coined the term. A few years ago Fletcher[4] could write that:

> So far from political advertisers copying baked beans and detergents, as the oft-repeated cliché has it, baked beans and detergents have been copying political advertisers, for ages. This should not be surprising. Persuasive communication is the essence of politics, and it has been since the dawn of time. The marketing of branded consumer goods is a relative newcomer to the scene.

However, it is from 1979 onwards that there developed a new professionalism in the arrangements for handling matters of image, propaganda and marketing. In the Thatcher era, it was inspired by the partnership between the Conservative communications director, Gordon Reece, Saatchi executive Tim Bell and the leader herself. Since then, packaging and presentation have been central to the campaign, leading some to observe than the essence of modern politics is style rather than substance.

Much of this concern for party image is reflected in the skilful use of television, the main medium of communication today. Bowler and Farrell[5] refer to the 'increasing importance of television as a tool in election campaigning'. Two writers[6] in their survey of marketing and strategies note how today electoral contests are 'media-driven', and suggest that 'free elections in a modern democracy would easily collapse if the **mass media** . . . were to ignore election campaigning'.

British electioneering in the television age

Television first played a significant part in British electioneering in 1959. Ever since the election of that year, it has dominated our political life, not just at polling time but throughout the duration of every parliamentary session.

Election campaigns today are made for television. Television dictates the form and style of electioneering, and in addition it has a significant influence over the agenda for discussion. **Agenda-setting** has an important effect on what people learn about the politicians and their beliefs. Television producers have the power to draw attention to issues which they believe to be interesting and/or contentious, and so they help to determine the content of election discussion. By stressing some areas and ignoring others, they can assist in shaping the impression the public acquires of particular parties, leaders and policies.

Television producers like a good story (particularly one with pictures), and party media advisers seek to ensure that they are given a plentiful supply of both. In other words, skilful politicians and their consultants themselves help to determine the agenda, by maintaining a regular flow of material 'ready-made for television'. Most leaders have been willing to take advantage of **photo-opportunities**, carefully stage-managed episodes in which the leading figure is set against a particular background perhaps to demonstrate concern for the area or its industry. The advisers to Margaret Thatcher were aware of the humanising potential of the photo-opportunity. One of their most famous contributions was the image of the leader cuddling a newborn calf on a Norfolk farm in 1979. Another was the incident in 1987, of which Rawnsley[7] has written:

> She inaugurated a new softer image with a charge down a Cornish beach with a borrowed King Charles spaniel: 'I would love a dog', breathed the Prime Minister, 'but my job won't allow it'.

In the campaign, leaders visit local party committee rooms, take part in staged events, visiting places where they can be photographed by television cameramen and doing campaign walkabouts. Just occasionally, for all of the careful pre-planning, something happens to disturb the arrangements. In 2001, an angry Sharron Storer waylaid the Prime Minister as he entered a Birmingham hospital, protesting at delays in the treatment for her partner, a victim of cancer. The scene was much relayed on screen. So too was the famous or infamous Prescott punch when Deputy Prime Minister John Prescott landed a punch on an egg-throwing farmer in Rhyl.

It is quite possible for a party to run an impressively organised and professional campaign and still lose the election. In 1987, Labour was widely credited with winning the campaign but it still contrived to lose the election by a substantial margin and added only 3.0 per cent to its total vote from its record low of 1983. In 1992, it added only another 3.6 per cent, again in spite of running what was judged to be a broadly superior campaign. In 2005, its campaigning efforts were widely seen as inferior to those of the Conservatives, but nevertheless the party achieved a third successive victory. As Kavanagh[8] observes: 'Packaging and presentation can only do so much.'

Box 9.2 The lack of television debates in British elections

Several countries hold television debates, the USA since 1960, Germany since 1969 and Australia since 1984, among them. In these and other democracies, they are now an established part of the political process and attract large audiences. In November 2004, the American presidential debates were of a high standard and many enthusiasts for political discussion found them enthralling. They were good television and made for good political debate. Most of the major issues received an airing and clear differences of character, style and policy between Senator Kerry and George W. Bush emerged.

In Britain, it is usually opposition parties that argue for debates, seeing them as providing a useful opportunity to attack the Prime Minister. Managers on the government side are wary of allowing their leader to be subjected to them. In 1997 negotiations became embroiled in the detail of whether the Liberal Democrats should take part, and under what terms. As a result, it was only too easy for those who were never convinced that it was a good idea to ensure that the obstacles proved overwhelming and no agreement could be reached.

Those who favour them argue that a leader's debate, in whatever form, would engage voters and increase public awareness, an important consideration given the low turnouts of recent years.

Carefully moderated contests of some 90 minutes or thereabouts would force the politicians to discuss policy, rather than indulge in highly confrontational and personalised 'yah-boo' politics and easy sloganising. Such debates might take the form of one between the three main party leaders, a second between the Chancellor and the two shadow chancellors and a third between, say, the Home Secretary and those who shadow him.

There are difficulties with such contests, not least that:

- British voters are not asked to choose directly between two or three party leaders. Instead, they vote for a party or – more precisely – for a local party candidate, making a debate between the leaders in a sense irrelevant.
- Whereas American voters choose between two presidential candidates, three at most, British voters might be in practice choosing from among candidates from the main parties, with possibly those of Respect, UKIP and the Greens and others, as well. This makes it harder to determine who should be involved in a debate.
- Perhaps more seriously, such a televised debate would tend to encourage presidential-style politics at a time when many people lament the decline of Parliament. Debates would help to personalise further the political process and therefore reduce the role of the House of Commons as the main political arena.
- Finally, it can be argued that there is less need for such a televised clash in Britain than in the USA. American presidents are not members of Congress and do not have to attend to account for their actions. Every week, prime ministers face a grilling in the House, not least from their main opponents. On issues such as Iraq, Tony Blair has had to justify his policy and persuade the House to back him in major debates. George W. Bush was under no such pressure from members of the legislature. We actually fund a leader of the Opposition to oppose, attack and present an alternative choice to the incumbent of Number 10 and he or she has many opportunities to question the Prime Minister of the day.

The campaigns in 2001 and 2005

In 2001, the campaign was poorly received. There was much public apathy about the election. Even the broadsheet newspapers did not always lead with an election story or feature election news on the front page and the tabloids and middle-market papers reduced their coverage. On television, the audiences for interviews with party leaders were smaller than in 1997 and news programmes cut back on their coverage. The campaign aroused little passion or interest, perhaps because the outcome seemed to be a foregone conclusion. There were no significant shifts in opinion on either issues or the parties' ratings on them.

In 2005, the national opinion poll ratings (see Box 9.3) of the main parties followed a similar pattern, but again the figures for the Liberal Democrats revealed a steady advance – particularly in the final week. Although the Labour Party maintained a consistent lead throughout the campaign, the outcome was unclear, not least because of doubts about the willingness of its reluctant supporters to turn out and vote. Overall, MORI found more than 30 per cent who claimed to be undecided two days before the election.

Box 9.3 Opinion polls and their value

Opinion polls are a familiar feature of modern election campaigns. Polling has been carried out in Britain since 1938, but it has been since the 1950s that it has been done on a regular basis. Two main methods have been tried: random and quota sampling. Random sampling, based on the Electoral Register, has been used in conducting the majority of surveys in the last three elections, with only MORI continuing with face-to-face interviewing. As random polling has been refined with the use of more phone contact, it is increasingly favoured by polling companies, because:

- It has a lower probability of error.
- It is now possible to get higher response rates.

The recent record of the pollsters
In the early years of regular polling, in the 1950s and 1960s, the record of the polling companies was very good. They were remarkably successful in pinpointing the actual outcome of elections, often within a small percentage of the result achieved by each party. In 1970, 20 out of 21 got things badly wrong, only one poll getting the winner right. Thereafter, fortunes were mixed. In an age of greater voter volatility, as class voting began to break down, it was less easy to gauge the true intentions of the electorate and to be sure that those who inclined to one party would actually turn out and vote for it. The performance in 1992 was particularly poor. Most polls predicted a 'hung Parliament', in which Labour would be the largest

party. The error in the predictions of the likely gap between the two parties was greater than it had ever been.

Ever since the failings in 1992, there have been serious doubts about the performance of the opinion polls. In 1997, they were accurate in predicting the winning party, although bearing in mind the scale of the Labour victory this success was unsurprising. Again, in 2001 it was no great achievement to pinpoint the leading party. However, yet again, there was a vast variation in the Labour lead, which ranged from 11 per cent (Rasmussen) to 17 per cent (MORI) in the final polls taken.

Between 1992 and 2001, there was a consistent pro-Labour bias in almost all of the surveys. They over-stated Labour support and understated the Tory vote. Each polling company took steps to correct such biases, but their solutions depended on what they saw as the causes of past error. Three explanations were available:

1. *Defective sampling methods*: the polls tracked down too many Labour supporters and too few Conservatives.
2. *The spiral of silence*: some shy Tories claimed to be undecided, being unwilling to admit their allegiance to a stranger asking questions. This may be because they think that they might be perceived as acting selfishly, if they back a party with a tax-cutting thrust.
3. *Turnout*: in assessing their data, pollsters made insufficient allowance for differential turnout of Labour and Tory supporters. Labour supporters are more likely to stay at home, especially in safe Labour seats.

2005
Throughout the campaign, the polls generally agreed that Labour seemed destined to win, but with a reduced majority. They differed on how much the majority might fall. Of the final polls, that taken by NOP was the most accurate although none of the major polling companies was far out. Collectively, their surveys were the most accurate predictions ever made of the outcome of any British general election. As can be seen from Table 9.1 no estimate was, on average, more than 1.5 per cent adrift from the final outcome, and every individual estimate was within 2 per cent of the result for each party.

Do polls have any influence and importance?
In the early days of polling, the successes of many pollsters led many commentators to accept their findings without question. Problems in some elections since 1970 have led to greater caution in the use of poll findings. However, whatever the reservations, poll results are still

Final opinion poll results during 2005 campaign

	ICM %	MORI %	NOP %	Populus %	YouGov %	Result %
Labour	38	38	36	38	37	36
Conservatives	32	33	33	32	32	33
Liberal Democrats	22	23	23	21	24	23
Other Parties	8	6	9	9	7	8
Average Error	1%	1%	0.25%	1.5%	1%	

Information based on data provided on the MORI website and covering surveys conducted wholly or partly after Monday, 2 May 2005. The accuracy of each estimate is shown by the use of average error, being the average of the percentage differences between the estimates and the final result.

viewed with much interest by politicians, the media and many members of the public – especially when an election is looming.

Parties do their own private polling to find out about which voters they should target. Polls are useful to party leaders to help them assess their party's standing with the electorate. They may also assist them in devising their policies and strategies, for when there is evidence that a party is failing to appeal to a key group among the voters or that its policies in one area are out of touch, then it may be wise to make an adjustment.

Prime ministers may find polls helpful in determining when to call an election. Some have been skilful at 'playing the polls', in other words timing the election date to coincide with a period when the polls are showing that their party is 'riding high' in public esteem. However, today, in an age of greater electoral volatility, it is less easy to count on people voting as they say they will. They are more likely to change their minds at the last minute.

Certain academics and journalists have claimed that polls may affect voting behaviour. Some of them have suggested that there is a bandwagon effect in favour of the party in the lead, whilst others have mentioned a contradictory boomerang effect in favour of the party in second place. There is no consistent evidence one way or the other.

According to supporters of the bandwagon effect, the polls encourage voters to climb on the winning party's bandwagon, so they end up backing the victorious side. If such an effect operates, then this should lead to an increase in the lead of the winning party throughout the campaign and between the publication of the final pre-election polls and the election itself. The results of several elections disprove this. In 1992, following several poll leads, Labour lost in the only poll that really mattered, the one on election day. In 1997, the margin of victory in percentage terms was smaller than what polls were suggesting.

Similarly, if there is a boomerang effect in which electors are encouraged to change sides and support the losing party, there ought to be a consistent set of results showing that the margin of the leading party should be cut between the final polls and polling day, whereas the performance of the second party should improve. This is not easy to demonstrate. Results in post-war elections do not uniformly show that the trailing second party improved its rating on election day.

Some countries ban publication of polls in the build-up to polling day, lest there is any influence on voting. To many commentators, such a measure seems illiberal in a free country, for companies have a right to publicise what people think, just as have the voters the right to know their findings. In any case, if we do not know for sure what effect polls might have, the case for banning seems unproven. Furthermore, if findings are not published, the results can still leak out; it would be hard to stop poll findings from being published abroad.

Electoral systems

Electoral systems and the issue of electoral reform have been on the political agenda in many parts of Europe and beyond in recent decades. In the 1970s, those Mediterranean countries (Greece, Portugal and Spain) that moved away from dictatorship to become fledgling democracies had to decide upon the most desirable method of election. In the early 1990s, the creation of 'new democracies' in Central and Eastern Europe meant that several more countries faced a similar decision. Apart from this interest in electoral systems in countries where the system of government had changed, there has been developing interest in the subject in long-established democracies, ranging from Italy to Japan, from New Zealand to the United

Kingdom. In established democracies, change does not come about easily in peacetime, because the political parties in power have a vested interest in the system that elected them.

The choice of electoral system is important. To a considerable degree, it shapes how the body politic operates. As Farrell points out[9]: '[Elections] are the cogs which keep the wheels of democracy properly functioning.' They are relevant to any discussion of representation, parties and party systems, the formation of governments and the politics of coalition. Indeed, the interim report of Labour's Plant Committee[10] on the subject observed that: 'There can be nothing more fundamental in a democracy than proposals to change an electoral system.'

The choice of system raises issues about the nature of representative government and the purpose of elections. Representative government is based on the idea that the legislature represents the will of

---

Box 9.4 The criteria for any electoral system: the Jenkins Inquiry[11]

There are different views of the criteria necessary for a good electoral system. The then Home Secretary, Jack Straw, set out four for the Jenkins Inquiry into the most appropriate way of electing our MPs. Its brief was to

observe the requirement for broad proportionality, the need for stable government, an extension of voter choice and the maintenance of a link between honourable members and geographical constituencies.

These were not absolute conditions, and indeed in some respects the four 'guidelines' were not entirely compatible. On proportionality, there was little difficulty, for a concept may be deemed as 'broad' without too many problems of definition; to have asked for 'strict' proportionality would have tied the hands of those involved. 'Stable government' was another general phrase, capable of differing interpretations. Again, similar flexibility was displayed in the words 'a link', for 'the link' might have seemed to imply that the existing bonds had to be maintained in their present form. As for 'voter choice', this too sounded important, but was capable of divergent explanations.

the people. For some, it is crucial that the elected chamber should mathematically reflect the voters' wishes and be sensitive to every shade of opinion, thereby catering for minority views. Out of the resulting chamber, a government will be formed. For others, it is less important to have a system that mathematically reflects the way electors vote. In their view, an election very broadly represents the swing in the public mood, so that in Britain in 1997 few would doubt that the country wanted a change of government, even if the scale of the Labour victory was exaggerated. According to this view, it is more important to find a system that produces strong government, based upon an effective parliamentary majority. This enables those in power to develop coherent and consistent policies, without facing the risk of regular defeats in the legislature.

Types of electoral system

Controversy over electoral systems centres primarily on how votes are converted into seats. Broadly speaking, there are two categories of electoral system, those which are proportional and those which are not. Within both groups there are many potential variations, each of which has its merits and disadvantages (see Table 9.1). Moreover, it is possible to combine elements of the two categories.

Non-proportional systems are the simplest to explain and to operate. The key point about them is that voters are not rewarded strictly according to the share of votes they obtain. In proportional systems, the opposite is true. Their guiding principle is straightforward, namely that parties are awarded seats directly according to the number of votes they win. In its most perfect form, this means that a party winning 45 per cent of the votes cast will receive 45 per cent of the seats available. In practice, although the mechanics are designed with that goal in mind, most systems are not exactly proportional and tend to offer some modest bonus to the largest party – although far less than applies in non-proportional system.

Non-proportional systems: plurality and majoritarian methods of voting

The most straightforward non-proportional system is the British *First-Past-The-Post (FPTP)* method, under which the successful candidate is the one who receives the most votes in the single-member constituency. In any contest, a simple plurality of votes is necessary for victory, not a majority. Nationally, FPTP normally leaves one party with a parliamentary majority. The largest party – and sometimes the second party – gains a substantial bonus in seats. Because of this, one party will usually win an outright majority in the legislature.

Other non-proportional methods are majoritarian ones, in which the candidate needs a majority of the votes cast to win the election. This requires a run-off election between the top candidates in a second ballot. The case for such a system is that it ensures that no candidate represents only a minority of the voters. In this category, the French *Double Ballot*, the *Supplementary Vote (SV)* used to elect the London Mayor and the Australian *Alternative Vote (AV)*. The **Jenkins Inquiry** recommended the AV for the geographical aspect of its proposal for a mixed-member system known as *AV-plus*.

Proportional systems

There are many different forms of proportional representation (PR), all of which are designed to ensure that the number of seats allocated in the legislature is broadly in line with the number of votes won by each party in the election. Unlike the plurality and majoritarian systems above, they operate in multi-member constituencies. Two main subdivisions are:

1. *The list method*, the most widely used form in which the elector votes for a list of party candidates rather just for a single person. The number of votes won by a party determines how many of its candidates are elected from the party list. Lists may be closed or open. Under the closed lists used in countries ranging from Portugal to South Africa, voters have no choice over candidates and simply cast a party vote. At the other extreme are open lists of the sort that enable Swiss voters to vote for individual candidates. Most list systems allow for some element of voter choice.
2. *The Single Transferable Vote (STV)* is used for local and European elections in Northern Ireland. It is the option favoured by the Electoral Reform Society. Voters list candidates in order of preference, and can, if they so wish, choose contenders from more than one party. To get elected, a candidate needs to obtain a quota

determined by a mathematical formula. The candidates with the least votes are eliminated and have their votes transferred to the remaining candidates on the basis of the second preferences, a process that continues until all seats are filled.

There are also *hybrid systems* such as the *Additional Member System (AMS)*. These have developed in the post-war era, in a bid to obtain something of the best of both worlds. They have become popular in the new democracies of Central and Eastern Europe. They combine the geographical representation of the plurality method with the party representation of the proportional schemes and do so in a way that also delivers a broadly proportional outcome. Again, schemes vary significantly in detail, but in Germany half of the seats in the Bundestag are filled by plurality voting in single-member seats (thus ensuring a geographical link of an elected member and his or her constituency), whilst the other half are allocated to parties with the aim of achieving a proportional result overall. The victorious candidates under the proportional element are taken from the party's lists.

Variants of proportional representation might well produce a more representative parliament whose composition fairly reflects all or most shades of popular opinion. They are less likely to yield a 'strong' government.

The 2005 election in the United Kingdom

The anomalies that can arise under the British FPTP system were again in evidence in 2005 (see Tables 9.2 and 9.3 for the results). Among the foremost of them:

- There was a clear discrepancy between the proportion of total votes gained by the parties and the seats they won. The winning party benefited from the system. Labour again won a highly exaggerated victory, based on the support of just over 35 per cent of those who voted, a mere 22 per cent of the 44 million electorate. Its lead over the Conservatives was barely 3 per cent, yet it obtained 159 more seats. Third parties suffered, although the Liberal Democrats improved their overall position. Other small parties fared badly, the Greens, UKIP and BNP failing to win any seats in spite of securing 3.4 per cent, 2.8 per cent and 4.3 per cent

Table 9.1 International voting systems

	Where Used	How it Works	Merits	Demerits
FPTP	UK, USA, Canada, India	Leading candidate elected in first and only ballot	Simple Easy to operate. Normally produces clear outcome, makes one party government likely. Retains MP–constituency link.	Produces distorted results, greatly favouring governing party. Some areas of country are dominated by MPs of one party (e.g. Wales). Leads to election of 'minority' MPs. Harsh on third and small parties, poor for election of women and minority candidates limits voter choice.
AV	Australia (Lower House)	Voters rank candidates in order of preference 1, 2, 3, 4 etc. Candidates eliminated from	Fairly simple to graft on to present system. Keeps MP–constituent link, ensures	Can produce very distorted results, as it would have in 1997, 2001 because of

Table 9.1 (continued)

Where	How it Used	Merits Works	Demerits	
		bottom up, votes allocated to others until someone gets 50%.	winning candidates have majority support at local level. More fair to smaller parties, but single-party government possible.	tactical voting. In some parts of country, one main party can gain few or no MPs. Not fully just to third and small parties. Poor for election of women and minority candidates.
SV	London mayoralty	Variation of AV. Votes rank only 1, 2. All but top two candidates eliminated, their votes allocated to those remaining.	Fairly simple to graft on to present system. Keeps MP-constituency link, ensures winning candidates have majority support at local level. More fair to smaller parties, but	Can produce very distorted results, as it would have in 1997 and 2001 because of tactical voting. In some parts of country, one main party can gain few or no MPs. Not fully just to third

			single-party government possible.	and small parties. Poor for election of women and minority candidates.
AV-Plus	Urged by Jenkins	Mixed system in which up to half seats are elected by AV, the rest distributed to candidates on a party list.	Limited, no radical change. Depending on exact division of constituency and top-up seats can produce a fairly proportional result, yet still make single-party government possible. A compromise between stability and fairness.	Can be unfair on third and small parties, much depending on division of seats. Role of 'top-up' MPs unclear – who do they represent? Might they be seen as second-class members? Could lead to coalitions, which have some disadvantages.
List PR	Israel, most of Europe, Latin America	Electors vote for a party's list of candidates. Parties win seats according to votes they obtain.	Usually a strong connection between votes won and seats obtained. Fairer to small parties,	Closed lists place power in the hands of the party managers who can position trouble-some

	Where Used	How it Works	Merits	Demerits
		Successful candidates taken from list.	good where there are minorities in population. Open lists allow for voter choice. Likely to produce coalitions, which have their advantages. Good at securing election of more women and other minorities in legislature.	candidates near the bottom. They deny voter choice. PR makes coalitions more likely, with all their alleged dis-advantages. No link of MP and con-stituency.
STV PR	Irish Republic, Malta	Voters list candidates in order of preference. Candidates need to obtain quota to get elected. Their surplus votes are redistributed according to second preference shown on their	Good connection of votes and seats. Fairer to small parties, good where there are minorities in population. Also allows voter to choose between candidates of same party.	A more complex system than the others, although the difficulty is for the Returning Officers rather than the voters, meaning slower results etc.

Table 9.1 (continued)

		ballot papers Then, step-by-step elimination of candidates from bottom, until all seats are filled.	Likely to produce coalitions, which have their advantages. Good at securing election of more women and other minorities in legislature	Makes coalitions more likely, with all their alleged dis-advantages. No link of MP and con-stituency.
AMS	Germany, Hungary, Japan, UK devolved elections	Some seats allocated on a plurality basis (FPTP), others on a party basis using PR. The latter acts as a 'top-up' to secure an overall proportional outcome.	Produces effective proportional results. Fairer to small parties. Keeps MP-constituency link. Makes coalitions – with their possible advantages Good at securing election of more women and other minorities in legislature.	Doubts re status of 'top-up' MPs, as to who they represent and whether they are seen as second class. Makes–more likely. coalitions more likely, with all their alleged dis advantages.

of the vote, respectively, in the seats where they stood. Overall, it took only 26,872 votes to elect a Labour MP, 44,531 to elect a Conservative and 96,485 to elect a Liberal Democrat.

- As in 1997 and 2001, the second party, the Conservatives, did not benefit from the workings of the FPTP system. The bias in the electoral system, brought about by a combination of Labour having many sparsely populated inner-city seats plus the fact that

Table 9.2 The operation of FPTP in the British general election of 2005

The result

Party	% votes obtained	No. of seats obtained	% of seats obtained
Labour	35.22	356	55.10
Conservatives	32.33	197	30.49
Liberal Democrats	22.05	62	9.59
Others	10.42	30	4.64

Table 9.3 The outcome in Scotland

Party	% of votes	No. of seats	% of seats	Votes per MP
Labour	39.5	42	71.2	21,962
Lib Dem	22.6	11	18.6	48,007
SNP	17.7	6	10.2	68,711
Conservative	15.8	1	1.7	369,388
SSP*	1.9	0	0.0	n/a

NB SSP* = Scottish Socialist Party

Labour's overwhelming domination in Scotland rests on the backing of less than 40 per cent of the popular vote. The Conservatives were more harshly treated by the electoral system in Scotland than in England. For almost a sixth of the vote, they secured only one MP. With a similar share of the vote in the 2003 elections for the Scottish Parliament, they gained 18 out of 129 seats. In Scotland, 39 out of 59 MPs are currrently 'minority' ones.

English constituencies are historically larger than those in Scotland and Wales (where Labour does better) and the effects of anti-Conservative tactical voting, again operated against them. As a result, although they gained 50,000 more votes than Labour in England, they won 92 fewer victories.

- The 'electoral deserts' recognised by the Jenkins Inquiry were once more in evidence. Conservative voters were effectively disfranchised in much of Scotland (see Table 9.4) and northern England. Labour supporters across whole swathes of the south were left unrepresented. Although more than 235,000 (45.1 per cent) votes were cast for the Liberal Democrats and Labour in Surrey, the Conservatives control all eleven constituencies in the county.
- More MPs than ever before (some 66 per cent) were minority ones, in that they did not receive the support of 50 per cent of their local electorate. Notably, George Galloway, who won Bethnal Green & Bow standing for Respect (an anti-war coalition party) against Labour's Oona King, was not the preferred choice of 64.09 per cent of the voters in that constituency; he won under 20 per cent of the backing of the whole electorate.
- Women and members of ethnic minorities were under-represented. Only 19.8 per cent of the successful candidates were female and only 2.3 per cent belonged to ethnic minority groups.

As a result of such anomalies and distortions, there were demands from politicians of all parties that the issue of electoral reform should

Table 9.4 UK electoral systems currently in use: a summary

General and local elections	First-Past-The-Post
European elections	Closed List PR
Scottish and Welsh devolved elections	AMS
London Mayoralty	Supplementary vote
London Assembly	AMS
NI local/assembly/European elections	STV PR

be reconsidered. They suggested that in a three-party situation, FPTP is a particularly blunt instrument whose bizarre outcomes are a travesty of democracy. On the flimsy basis of just over one-third support of those who voted, Labour dominates the House of Commons, fuelling charges that a government formed in this way is in effect an 'elected dictatorship'.

Labour's claim to a mandate has to be set in context. 9,556,183 people voted Labour, fewer than in any other post-war election since 1983, an election that has gone down in history as a never-again disaster. A combination of a 61 per cent turnout; the growth of multi-party politics; and the unfairness of the electoral system combine to mean that no administration since 1929 has been elected by as few voters as the one elected in 2005.

Some arguments surrounding the debate over FPTP versus PR

For FPTP and against PR

Farrell[12] has neatly summarised the three main themes in any defence of the British system, as 'simplicity, stability and constituency representation'. These points are worthy of further consideration:

- *The FPTP system is easy to understand,* especially for the voter who marks an 'X' on the ballot paper. It has the alleged merits of simplicity and familiarity, and, as such, is widely accepted.

Table 9.5 Party majorities in recent elections

1987	101	(Conservative)
1992	21	(Conservative)
1997	178	(Labour)
2001	146	(Labour)
2005	66	(Labour)

- *It usually leads to the formation of strong, stable, single-party governments* with an overall majority (see Table 9.5); coalition government other than in times of emergency is virtually unknown. Single-party governments pinpoint political responsibility. The voters know whom to praise or blame, when things go right or wrong. Such administrations are also said to be capable of providing effective leadership for the nation. This is viewed as more important than achieving a proportional result. In Britain, we know who is to form the government immediately after the election is over. There is no need for private deals to be done by politicians who bargain in smoke-filled rooms, away from the public gaze; it is the voters directly who choose which party is in office.

- Because we have single-member constituencies *there is a close relationship between the MP and his or her constituency.* The one member alone has responsibility for that area which he or she can get to know well. Once elected, the MP represents all who live in the area, not just those who voted for one particular party; all citizens know whom to approach if they have a problem or grievance needing resolution. This is very different from what happens under some more proportional systems, in which several elected members represent a broad, geographical area.

In his inquiry, Lord Jenkins[13] himself recognised that FPTP is not without benefits, referring to the 'by no means negligible' merits of the present system. In addition to the points above, the commissioners made the point that it enables the electorate sharply and cleanly to rid itself of an unwanted government; in other words, it is easy to punish those directly responsible for their errors.

Apart from the positive case for FPTP, there are disadvantages associated with proportional representation. Among specific criticisms often made, it is suggested that:

- PR encourages minor parties to stand for election and makes it more difficult for any one party to emerge victorious. Duverger's[14] observation is often quoted, namely that: 'The simple-majority, single-ballot system favours the two party system; the simple-majority system with second ballot and proportional representation favour multi-partyism.'

- The primary anxiety of those opposed to an abandonment of

FPTP is that it would greatly increase the likelihood of perpetual coalition government. As neither has ever secured a majority of the votes cast in any election post-war, it is unlikely that single-party government would result.

For Proportional Representation

The case for the use of a proportional scheme of voting in Britain has much to do with the allegedly adverse effects of FPTP. Among its anticipated benefits, a proportional electoral system:

- *would not exaggerate movements of opinion within the electorate* and produce landslide majorities that are often based on an ever-diminishing proportion of the national vote.
- *would not allow a government to exercise power on the basis of minority popular support*; e.g., Labour obtained power in October 1974 with the support of only 39 per cent of those who voted, and with under 30 per cent of the backing of the whole electorate.
- *would provide greater justice to small parties.* Traditionally, it has been the Liberals in their various guises who have suffered from FPTP, although in 1997 the Conservatives lost all representation in Scotland in spite of gaining 17 per cent of the vote.
- *would yield governments which have the backing of the majority of the electorate*, and therefore could claim legitimacy; they may be coalition governments, but the parties which voted for them would in toto have a broader appeal than is the case at present.
- *would avoid the geographical divisions brought about by FPTP.* In 1997 the Conservatives were wiped out in Scotland, Wales and the large English provincial cities, just as Labour had suffered badly in the southern half of England back in the 1980s.
- *would overcome a problem much emphasised in the Jenkins Inquiry, namely that there are 'electoral deserts' under FPTP*, areas more or less permanently committed to one party, in which the opposition can make little impact and get even less reward. Many seats in the House of Commons rarely change hands, so that supporters of the minority parties (e.g. Conservatives in Glasgow) have little likelihood of ever securing the election of a representative who supports his or her views. Significant sections of the population are condemned to almost permanent minority status.

- *would, unlike FPTP, be better at producing parliamentary representation for women and ethnic minorities.* For instance, since the introduction of a more proportional system in New Zealand, there has been a marked increase in the percentage of women elected.

In addition, of course, there is a positive case for proportional representation and coalitions. Proportional representation is:

- *fair* because it produces a close relationship between votes and seats
- *gives minority parties more representation* and encourages voters to back them in the knowledge that they will not be wasting their vote
- *makes coalitions more likely.* Coalitions can provide government that is stable because it rests on broad backing, legitimate because it has wide popular support and encourages the politics of consensus, cooperation and moderation.

Some general points about coalitions to bear in mind
The primary anxiety of those who oppose any abandonment of FPTP for Westminster elections is that it would greatly increase the likelihood of perpetual coalition government. In that a 'third force' (probably the Liberal Democrats) would gain a greater share of influence, this would be at the expense of the two main parties. Because of its implications, the pros and cons of coalition government are highly relevant in any discussion of electoral systems.

Inevitably, on either side of the argument, examples are used selectively and the case tends to be over-stated or oversimplified. Coalitions can be strong or weak, successful and unsuccessful. Much depends on the nature of the country involved and its political system. Some points are, however, worth stressing, notably that:

- In Europe, where proportional electoral systems are used, coalition governments are common.
- In many of these countries, there is no tradition of a two-party system where voters know that the party they vote for will be able to put its programme into effect. At best, their party will be part of a governing coalition, able only to carry out the parts of its policy that its partners agree upon. By contrast, in Britain, the voter knows that the winning party (yes, because of a distorted

electoral system!) will be largely able to carry out its programme, and thus an election is a choice of a party and set of policies to govern. The idea of coalition arrangements (with bargains and deals over policy after the election) is alien to our tradition. This may not matter but has to be appreciated.

- Coalitions and PR may be associated with greater instability of government but not all countries experience this. Under the Weimar Republic, before Hitler's take-over in 1933, Germany did use PR and experience instability, but the country was then facing acute problems; post-Nazi Germany has had coalitions and stable government. Much depends on the social and political system, on whether or not there is a tradition of stable politics and whether there are many parties, reflecting the existence of many groups within society or acute regional differences. Modern Germany is often cited as producing strong, effective coalitions which have ruled well. Is it this which has produced the economic policies that have given the country prosperity, or is it because of these economic successes that governments have been long-lasting? Of course, we have the experience of Scotland's devolved government to draw upon. The Executive has been governed by a Labour–Liberal Democrat coalition since its creation in 1999. The arrangement has proved a stable one, with ministers capable of implementing an agreed programme.

- Where coalitions have not lasted nearly as well, as in France's Fourth Republic to 1958, one can over-state the instability involved. Coalitions including socialists, radicals, Mouvement Républicain Populaire and independents frequently broke up because of disagreements on colonial and foreign issues, and stalemate could result. Italy still has such disagreements, but though – as in the Fourth Republic – ministries often collapse and a game of 'musical chairs' is played over government positions, there has often been much continuity of policy and considerable economic achievement in both countries.

- Sometimes these coalitions have taken a few days to form, often longer. Back in pre-1958 France, one took a month; similarly, Israel in late 1988 experienced very prolonged bargaining. Yet if, when formed, these are stable administrations which can last a few years, then the wait may seem worthwhile. At least, the changes made by such a government will be agreed ones, backed by a group of parties who have more electoral support than a British government normally has.

- Germany has been quoted as having stable and generally effective governments. Stability implies continuity, a lack of conflict, and for Germany the system seems to have worked well. To be effective, government doesn't always have to be so stable and governments which are stable don't always produce effective policies.

No best electoral system

A judgement about electoral systems is ultimately a judgement about the primary function of an election, as to which goal is the more important – choosing a representative legislature or choosing a government. Generally, on the continent the emphasis is upon choosing a representative assembly. From its midst, a government can be constructed that commands sufficient support – usually, a coalition. In Britain, the emphasis is upon choosing a government that is likely to be stable and strong, allowing ministers to get on with the job.

Of course, governments can still be effective if they are coalitions, and the virtues of strong administrations can be overplayed. Different writers reach different conclusions about what constitutes strength. Norton[15], as a defender of the First-Past-The-Post method used in British elections, sees strong government as a situation in which one party dominates the House of Commons. In contrast, Bogdanor[16] argues that a government cannot be strong unless it represents the majority of the voters. By this definition, no post-war British government would have passed the test.

There is no perfect system that is necessarily best in all circumstances, ideal for all countries at every period of time. In countries with acute social or political divisions (Israel, Northern Ireland and South Africa, among them), a proportional method is appropriate in that it ensures some representation for minority groups and reduces the danger of tyrannical majority rule. In stable countries in which government changes hands at fairly regular intervals, there is arguably not the same need to show concern for opposing and minority viewpoints.

Indeed, it is quite possible to have different types of election within a particular country, as Britain currently experiences. All of them have their merits and demerits.

Voting behaviour and turnout

Social changes have occurred in all developed countries, and these mean that old nostrums have had to be reconsidered in the light of experience. This applies to Britain and the USA, as well as on the continent.

The trend in most countries is now for voters to be less committed to their long-term allegiances. Stability rather than change was once the established pattern in voting behaviour, and many voters were reluctant or unwilling to deviate from their regular habits. In recent years, partisan de-alignment has occurred, and this means that there has been a weakening of the old loyalties, and a new volatility among the electorate.

Social class was once a key determinant of voting, with the working classes tending to vote for the more progressive party and the better-off inclining to the political right. It was still important in the 1980s and 1990s. For instance, Ball[17] shows how in the French presidential contest of 1988 more than two-thirds of the business, agrarian and professional classes voted for the conservative candidate, Chirac, whereas an even higher percentage voted for the socialist, Mitterrand. In the same way, Labour in its bleak years in the 1980s

Table 9.6 The relative importance of class voting: some examples

Importance	Examples
Low	USA, 'new' democracies (e.g. Hungary, Poland)
Relatively low, little evidence of decline	Ireland, Netherlands, Spain
More significant, but in decline	Austria, Belgium, Germany
Relatively high, but in decline	Denmark, Sweden, UK

Based on data provided in T. Bale, *European Politics: A Comparative Introduction*, Palgrave, 2005.

continued to find its core support from the least well-off in the inner cities, and in regions such as Scotland and Wales.

Class voting varies considerably between countries, relatively significant in some, much less so in others, as Table 9.6 indicates. However, the hold of class is not what it was. Whilst there were always many voters in Britain and the rest of Western Europe who deviated from class voting, that number substantially increased in the 1980s as right-wing administrations managed to increase their appeal among the more skilled working people who had aspirations to upgrade their lifestyles and prospects. Old class structures have broken down as many sections of the population have become better off and the manual working class has diminished in size.

The personality of the candidate has assumed greater importance, the more so as party leanings have become less firm and voters are able to learn and see so much more about those who would lead them via the mass media. Furthermore, political issues and election campaigns have also become more significant, with the increase in votes 'up for grabs'.

Determinants of voting behaviour

Long-term influences include:

- *Party identification and loyalty.* Electors identify with a particular party and loyalties are forced, so that there exists a strong long-term alignment (partisanship). Family influences are often reinforced by the membership of particular groups and later social experiences.
- *Social class.* Whereas in the United States, the deep-seated association with a party was often stressed, in the United Kingdom and on the continent more attention was paid to membership of some social grouping. As Hague and Harrop[18] put it: 'Their social identity anchored their party choice.'
- *Other factors relating to the social structure, such as age, gender, occupation, race and religion.*

Short-term influences include:

- *The economy.* This covers indicators of inflation, unemployment and disposable income) and in particular how voters view their future prospects (whether or not they 'feel good'). Governments like to 'go to the country' at a time when people will feel good about their material circumstances and their future prospects.

- *The personal qualities and appeal of the party leaders.* These are more important today given the media's infatuation with personalities.
- *The style and effectiveness of party campaigning.* This has already been explored in some depth on pp. 315–23.
- *The impact of the mass media.* As we have seen in the above, the media now play an important part. They may or may not have a direct influence on how voters vote (see pp. 352–4), but they help to determine what the election is about and the issues that are impor-tant. They provide information and – in the case of the press – dramatic headlines which can damage the standing of leaders (e.g. the damaging portrayal of Neil Kinnock in 1987 and 1992, in the *Sun*).
- *The events leading up to the election.* The 'Winter of Discontent' wrecked Labour's chances in 1979, in the same way that the humil-iating circumstances of British withdrawal from the ERM (1992) and the connection in the public mind with the Major government with sleaze seriously undermined faith in the Conservatives in 1997. More recently, the handling of the war with Iraq seriously damaged the reputation of the Labour administration, and in par-ticular made many votes question the integrity of Tony Blair. In contrast, the successful outcome of the Falklands War boosted the prospects of Margaret Thatcher in 1983.

Box 9.5 The impact of the mass media on voting: conflicting theories

Extensive research has been done into the effects of the mass media – in particular, television – on public attitudes and voting behaviour. None of it has been conclusive. Nor can it be so, not least because the influence of television is difficult to distinguish from the impact of other long- and short-term factors.

Between the wars, in an era when dictators were aware of the power of propaganda, it was common to believe that the organs of communication must have a significant impact in moulding people's outlooks. Studies often used the hypodermic model, by which a passive and gullible public was seen as highly vulnerable to a syringe injection of indoctrinated material. It was assumed that the electorate would be unable to withstand the malign influences of those who sought to manipulate them.

This 'manipulative theory' was soon challenged, for American researchers were unable to find any evidence to substantiate it in a democratic country. They developed a *minimum effects model* that suggested that voters used the media to reinforce their own outlook. They know what they need from the media and take that and that alone. In other words, as free agents rather than mindless victims, they filter information which substantiates their own pre-determined beliefs. Hence the name sometimes employed for this theory, *the uses and gratifications model*, a term used by Blumler and McQuail[24] in their 1967 study.

The reinforcement theory held sway for many years, but as television became more pervasive and played such a key part in people's daily lives, its adequacy was called into question. It gave way in the 1970s to the theories advanced by the Glasgow University Media Group. Its members emphasised the importance of *agenda setting*, stressing that by deciding on the issues that are granted coverage, television and papers help to determine what the public is thinking about, if not actually what they think. As Walter Lippman[25] put it in 1938, in speaking about press influence: 'It is like a beam of a searchlight that moves restlessly about, bringing one episode and then another out of the darkness and into vision.'

In an election campaign, the media directs our attention to the candidates and the issues, determining what will be discussed on a particular day. If the manner in which stories is presented tends to reinforce consensual values and portray 'extremists' in an unflattering light, then this might be an important influence.

The most recent studies often refer to the *independent effects model*. This recognises that the impact of media messages will vary according to the person or group that receives the message. Indeed, media messages may have different effects on different people, and at different times, but that it is common sense to assume that as today's voters spend so much time viewing TV programmes they are likely to be influenced by them in some degree – the more so in an age when traditional allegiances have substantially been eroded.

The suspicion nowadays is that the media have a greater importance than that accorded to them in reinforcement theory. At the very least they provide plenty of information, so that people should know more than did those who lived in previous generations. Particularly on areas of policy on which they are ignorant or lacking much knowledge, it is reasonable to assume a greater degree of influence, borne out by the admission that voters get most of their information from television.

The difficulty is to measure the extent of any media influence on voters. It is hard enough to do this over a short period, but to do so over the long term is almost impossible. The cost of establishing research over many years and the complexity of the task of interviewing the same people are enormous barriers to investigation, so that analysts are bound to rely on reasonable speculation in this area. However, we do have some research from studies of cultural effects of television and the printed word.

Gill and Adams[26] quote the example of a survey of reactions to the TV programme *Nationwide* in 1980, which noted that 'media effects depend on both the images projected and the cultural background of the audience'. The writers elaborated in this way:

Groups of bank managers accepted the content of the programme, but didn't like the style, while groups of shop stewards liked the style but criticised the assumptions behind what was being said. Young blacks found the programme boring, because it seemed to be about a foreign world of middle-class shoppers and businessmen.

The same writers also referred to Glover's[27] findings in 1984, which suggested that women's magazines 'mould and reinforce women's views of themselves and their place in society', and noted that men's magazines do the same for their male readership. Such findings suggest that the influence of television in particular may be greater than had previously been recognised.

Controversy continues to surround the issue of media influence. Cultural attitudes, social values and political opinions are all liable to media influence, but the extent and nature of that influence is difficult to ascertain and continues to be a matter of academic contention.

Generally, the long-term factors have declined in their importance in British politics and the short-term ones have assumed an increased significance. The breakdown of these traditional associations has been of considerable importance for the parties, which can no longer count on the support they once took for granted.

Table 9.7 Average share of the vote for each party in post-war elections (%)			
	Conservative	**Labour**	**Liberal/Liberal Democrat**
1945–70	45.3	46.0	7.1
1974–2005	37.9	36.3	19.4

The case of the United Kingdom

Voting behaviour in Britain: post-war patterns
The features most noted in the post-war years up to 1970 were:

- the stability of voting patterns, as people stayed loyal to the party they had always supported. As Punnett[19] put it in 1971: 'For most people, voting behaviour is habitual and ingrained.'
- that elections were determined by a body of floating voters in key marginal constituencies, whose votes needed to be targeted by the parties if they were to have a chance of success
- the uniform nature of the swing across the United Kingdom, which showed that voters in one area tended to behave in much the same way as those elsewhere
- the domination of the two main parties, which between them could count on the support of the majority of the electorate. This reached a high point in 1951 when the Conservatives and Labour between them gained 96.8 per cent of the vote, but in 1966 they still obtained 89.8 per cent.

In the past thirty years many of those assumptions have proved to be no longer valid. The parties can no longer anticipate the degree of support they once enjoyed. Since the 1970s, the rise of third parties has made inroads into the share of the vote the two parties can command, as the figures in Table 9.7 indicate.

Voting behaviour in recent years
In 1994, Madgwick[20] concluded that: 'Voting is still related to social class, but the relationship is complex, and there is less confidence

about the significance of the term.' His conclusion was heavily influenced by the work of Ivor Crewe, whose researches in the 1970s and subsequently showed that not only was class identification weakening,

Box 9.6 Social class as a determinant of voting behaviour in Britain: some key points

- As the manual working class has numerically declined, Labour has had to extend its appeal to 'middle England'. This has been a successful strategy, but one achieved at the cost of disillusioning some of its traditional supporters who are now less likely to turn out on polling day (see p. 356).
- Service industries have becoming increasingly important, as old industries have shrunk. In 'post-industrial society', other distinctions such as ethnicity and gender have become significant in shaping allegiance.
- The availability of education and more information via the media has created a society in which people are more willing to think for themselves and make a calculated choice based on their appreciation of the issues, lessening the tendency to vote by habit.
- With more people now enjoying a decent standard of living, their preoccupations have in some cases moved away from their perceived economic interests to enable them to concentrate on values or issues that seem important today: for example, elements of the professional middle class may be tempted by socially liberal or green parties, working people by parties of the far right.
- With the decline of party identification and the connection between class and voting, voting is increasingly about issues (primarily economic ones – perceptions of how well people have done and might expect to do), values and party leaders. It is about making a judgement on a range of factors whose importance may vary from election to election.
- For all of the above considerations, and the greater volatility in voting behaviour that they have helped to bring about, class remains an important factor in influencing voting choices. It relates to region, with people in the peripheries of Great Britain (the north, Scotland and Wales) being more likely to vote Labour than those in the central south-east. These strong regional differences in party support are in part related to the class structure, for the more socially deprived and solidly working-class areas are those furthest from the centre.

but so was party identification generally. (See also Box 9.6 for further analysis of class and voting behaviour.)

Sarlvik and Crewe's publication of *Decade of Dealignment*[21] was a psephological milestone. Using data from Essex University's *British Election Study*, Bo Sarlvik and Crewe analysed elections in the 1970s, culminating in the Conservative victory in 1979. They showed the extent to which the two parties had steadily lost their once reliable supporters, people who voted for the same party in successive elections. In particular, the writers discovered that demographic changes were taking their toll on Labour, for the old working-class communities were being destroyed by redevelopment schemes and inner cities were emptying. Workers moving to new towns and expanding small towns around London were less likely to vote Labour. Areas of population decline – like the north and south Wales – were traditionally Labour, while growth areas – mainly in the south-east – were strongly Conservative, a point emphasised by constituency boundary changes. Labour's electoral base was being eroded, a point which led Kellner[22] to write that the 'sense of class solidarity which propelled Labour to power in 1945 has all but evaporated'.

Table 9.8 Social class: categorisation in common use by polling companies		
Category	**Current % of population**	**Groups included**
A/B	28	Higher/lower managerial, professional and administrative
C1	29	White collar, skilled, supervisory or lower non-manual
C2	19	Skilled manual
D/E	23	Semi-skilled and unskilled manual/residual, casual workers, long-term unemployed and very poor

The Crewe study was particularly famed for its distinction between the old and the new working class. He wrote of: 'the traditional working class of the council estates, the public sector, industrial Scotland and the North, and the old industrial unions . . . the affluent and expanding working class of the new estates and new service economy of the South [the new working class]'. By the 1980s, it seemed that **embourgeoisement** was a significant factor favouring the Conservatives, for in 1979 members of the skilled 'new' working class were seduced by Thatcherite support for tax cuts, and shared certain Conservative attitudes on race, unions, nationalisation and crime.

Labour's claim to be the party of the working class took a strong blow in the 1980s. It may be true that the Labour vote remained largely working class, but the working class was no longer largely Labour. To be successful again, Labour had to succeed in attracting more skilled workers back into the fold. Under the Blair leadership, the position dramatically improved. In 1997 and 2001, New Labour did well in all social categories (as listed in Table 9.8), and only among the AB voters did the Conservatives retain a lead. In 2005, Labour suffered a sharp decline in the number and percentage of votes it polled (see Table 9.10). There was a marked regional variation across Great Britain.

What influences British voters today?

We have noted the broad trend in all democracies away from group or party voting. This is not to say that there has been a complete de-alignment, but rather a weakening of existing patterns and attachments. But the consequences of this de-alignment have been profoundly important in voting behaviour. In particular, there is now a more volatile and sceptical electorate who are liable to be influenced by a range of factors. These include the short-term factors to which we have already referred:

- Political issues
- The economy
- Party leaders
- Party image
- The effectiveness of party campaigning.

In more pragmatic times, voters come to a general assessment of the parties, based on what they have done and what they propose to do.

Table 9.9 Voting behaviour in the 2005 election

Category	Labour	Conservative	Lib Dem	Other
Social class				
AB	28	37	29	6
C1	32	37	23	8
C2	40	33	19	8
DE	48	25	18	9
Gender				
Men	34	34	22	10
Women	38	32	23	7

Based on figures provided by *The Observer*, 8 May 2005.

They look for competence and the skill of consultants and other marketing advisers is to generate an impression of confidence and trust in the abilities of ministers and would-be ministers. They are much influenced by prevailing economic conditions, particularly their disposable income, and levels of inflation and unemployment, rewarding success and punishing poor performance. In 1997, the perception that the Conservatives were no longer competent in economic management was a devastating blow to party prospects.

Voting is now much influenced by the opinions and judgements of the voters, what Denver[23] calls 'judgemental voting'. As he concludes:

> People will disagree over what exactly the judgements are about – issues, ideologies, images, personal economic prospects, party leaders – and this may vary from election to election; but it is the transition from an aligned and socialised electorate to a dealigned and judgemental electorate that has underpinned electoral developments in Britain over the past half-century.

Turnout in elections

Voting is the most usual form of political participation. Voter turnout refers to the percentage of the voting-age population that actually turns out on election day. A good turnout of voters is often considered to be a healthy sign in any democracy, as this appears to indicate vitality and interest.

Many advanced countries have turnouts consistently above 75 per cent, some over 90 per cent, but those with exceptionally high figures (Australia, Belgium and Italy) have compulsory voting laws. Among European countries that do not compel people to vote, Austria, Denmark, Germany, Norway and Sweden have had impressive turnouts in recent elections. All of them have arrangements that facilitate easy registration. Britain has usually fared less well than the established European democracies over the last few decades, its 59.4 per cent figure in 2001 being dramatically down on its more usual 70–75 per cent turnout. Turnout in elections for local councils, devolved assemblies and the European Parliament have usually been abysmally low.

Turnout is lower in the United States than almost any other advanced industrial democracy in the world. Many analysts would say that the way in which American states organise and administer voter registration explains its lower voter turnout to a significant degree. Piven and Cloward[28] have shown that of the Americans who do register, more than 85 per cent turn out on election day. This places them much further up the turnout league for the world's democracies than the percentage who actually voted in the 2004 election (itself the best figure since 1960) would suggest.

Most democracies have found that the figures for turnout have declined in the last few elections and this has led to alarm about the degree of apathy about or even alienation from the political system that many voters now experience. Many voters across Europe and America seem increasingly disillusioned with the performance of parties in office and with the politicians who represent them. Promise has not always been matched by outcome and, in the eyes of many voters, the parties and politicians all seem as bad as each other. Moreover, party differences have narrowed as some of the big issues of capitalism versus communism, and peace and warfare in the Cold

War, have ceased to be so relevant. The distinctions between party programmes are not often fundamental ones.

It may be the case that the descendants of the committed voters of yesteryear are perhaps today's pressure group campaigners who see involvement in environmental and community issues as more worthwhile. Perhaps in a post-materialist age in which the majority of people live a much better life than their predecessors, what matters more are quality of life issues such as ecology and minority rights issue. Pressure groups arguably represent these causes more effectively than do the parties that contest elections.

Some writers would suggest that rather than lower turnouts being a sign of apathy and resentment, they may be healthy, reflecting broad contentment. There is less tribalism and partisanship has decreased, compared to a few decades ago. Non-voting may amount to general satisfaction with the conduct of affairs, so that voters do not feel stirred to express their feelings at the ballot box. Of course, the motives of voters may vary among different groups, some feeling that they don't need to go out and vote because all seems to be going along satisfactorily, whilst others – often the young, the poor and members of ethnic minorities among them – may feel that there is nothing in the choice of party or candidate relevant for them.

Box 9.7 Some international comparisons

Turnout in the post-war era appears to be higher in the established democracies of Western Europe, and less so in countries which have gained their freedom more recently. In South Africa, the excitement produced by the first democratic elections inspired many people to queue up to vote. In the USA, where elections are so often held, there is no such enthusiasm.

The figures for turnout in the most recently held election to the end of 2004 in an assortment of countries were as follows (in %):

Austria	80.5	Denmark	89.3
Finland	80.1	Italy	81.4
Japan	59.9	New Zealand	75.4
Rwanda*	96.5	South Africa	89.3
Spain	77.2	Sweden	80.1
Switzerland	45.6	USA	59.4

* First democratically held election

Table 9.10 Post-war turnout in the United Kingdom (%)

General elections		European elections	
1945	72.7%		
1950	84.0%		
1951	82.5%		
1955	76.8%		
1959	78.7%		
1964	77.1%		
1966	75.8%		
1970	72.0%		
1974 Feb.	78.1%		
1974 Oct.	72.8%		
1979	76.0%	1979	31.6
1983	72.7%	1984	32.6
1987	75.3%	1989	36.2
1992	77.7%	1994	36.5
1997	71.4%	1999	23.6
2001	59.4%	2004	38.8
2005	61.3%		

Turnout in the United Kingdom: the 2005 election

Turnout in general elections has varied considerably in the post-war era. The variation from constituency to constituency is also very large, often ranging from well in excess of 80 per cent to just over 50 per cent. The trend in national turnout has been broadly downward, interrupted by occasional better results.

The turnout in 2001 and 2005

The average turnout in post-war British elections up to and including 2001 was 75.2 per cent, but in the election of that year there was a sharp decline in participation, the worst in living memory. Many voters may have felt alienated from the political world, including young people who saw the party battle as increasingly irrelevant, sterile and out of date. Older people who did not turn out may have failed to do so either because:

- (as Labour supporters), they felt disappointed or disillusioned with a government that had let them down
- in the absence of any credible alternative, they were content to let Labour to get on with he job that it had undertaken of improving the public services; it seemed to be on the right lines, but there was much to be done.

In 2005, there was a modest increase in turnout on the very low base of four years earlier. Indeed, 26.2 million voted, but voter interest varied substantially from the high of Hampshire East (90.5 per cent) to the low of Liverpool Riverside (41.5 per cent). The difference in turnout between Conservative-held and Labour-held seats was marked, 65 per cent as against 58 per cent.

Many voters clearly remained unimpressed by the choice on offer and did not feel inclined to vote. They feel disengaged from the political process and feel that party politics has a limited relevance to their lives. Traditional Labour supporters had been alienated by policies towards Iraq, foundation hospitals and student tuition fees and were unwilling to turn out and support the Blair government. Others did so, in spite of their serious misgivings.

Yet the turnout was slightly better than in 2001, perhaps the reason being that there was the prospect of a closer contest. Although the Conservatives lacked popular appeal, there was the opportunity to give a verdict on the Prime Minister and give him a 'bloody nose'. There was greater reason for interest than in the previous election in which the result seemed to be a foregone conclusion. Significantly, in

Table 9.11 Comparison of turnout in marginal and safe seats, 2001 and 2005 (%)

Type of seat	2001 turnout	2005 turnout	Change
10 most marginal seats in England and Wales	66.0	68.8	+2.8
10 safest seats in England and Wales	50.0	51.4	+1.4

those constituencies where there was a genuine prospect of political change, turnout was higher, as the figures indicate in table 9.11.

One explanation often given for recent lower turnouts is the decline in the intensity of party identification and an increase in the number of voters who see no obvious ideological or policy difference between the two main parties. New Labour's drift to the centre ground may have been a strategically wise move as a means of winning elections (for that is where many voters are positioned), but its core vote is not enthused by the prospect of Labour ministers pursuing allegedly Conservative policy solutions. It may be that if a greater policy divide opens up between the parties and there is the prospect of a real likelihood of a change of party control at Westminster, then the higher turnouts of the past could be restored.

Direct democracy: initiatives and referendums

Elections are a feature of representative democracies. They give the people a chance to choose who will decide issues on their behalf. By contrast, referendums and similar devices, such as the initiative and the recall, are a means of direct democracy, in which the voters give their own verdict on the issues under consideration. They ensure that those in power are aware of and act in accordance with the express wishes of the electorate.

Whereas a general election provides an opportunity for the electorate to offer a general judgement on the overall performance of the government of the day and of the suitability of the opposition parties

Box 9.8 Direct democracy: some definitions

The referendum Magleby[29] defines the referendum as a 'vote of the people on a proposed law, policy or public expenditure'. In other words, it is a vote on a single issue of public policy, such as a constitutional amendment (e.g. the British devolution referendums, 1979 and 1997, see pp. 194–5 and 202).

The initiative is a procedure through which an individual or group may propose legislation by securing the signatures of a required number of qualified voters. In several countries and American states that have referendums, there is also provision for the right of popular initiative as well (e.g. in November 2004, voters in six US states were asked to vote on propositions outlawing same-sex marriages).

The recall is a much less frequently used device that enables a certain number of voters to demand a vote on whether an elected official should be removed from office (e.g. the Californian recall (2003), that enabled state voters to reject Gray Davis as Governor; as a result, Arnold Schwarzenegger was elected to the office).

as an alternative, a referendum and associated devices are votes on a single issue. Such a vote gives the electorate a chance to answer a simple 'yes' or 'no' to whatever question is asked of it.

The increasing popularity of direct democracy worldwide
Direct democracy was employed in the early years of the twentieth century in some American states. In most cases, they opted for the initiative and referendum. However, for several years it went out of fashion in the United States. Nor was it widely popular elsewhere, although in the Nazi and other dictatorships of the interwar era it was not unusual for the leadership to seek popular approval from the people directly. This is why referendums (or plebiscites as they were often called in a non-democratic context) incurred odium in free countries. The British Prime Minister Clement Attlee (1945–51) described them as 'devices alien to our traditions' and saw them as instruments of 'demagogues and dictators'. He pointed to their often suspiciously high turnouts.

More recently, referendums were used by the notorious Chilean dictator General Pinochet. His use of them showed how the wording of the question could be so framed as to get the answer required. He gained 75 per cent acquiescence for the proposition: 'In the face of international aggression unleashed against the government of the fatherland, I support President Pinochet in his defence of the dignity of Chile.' Sometimes, referendums have been used in democratic countries with authoritarian overtones such as the Fifth French Republic of Charles de Gaulle (1958–69). Again, there was suspicion that the wording was designed to secure the desired response. There was also strong pressure on the media to publicise the ruler's case.

It is the memory of such past experience that troubles some democrats who fear the purpose and management of such means of consultation with the public. However, the undemocratic overtones have largely disappeared from the debate about the merits of direct democracy. Initiatives and referendums are now used with increasing regularity in countries and states with impeccable democratic credentials.

Referendums and initiatives have been used more widely in recent decades. Since the 1970s, a growing number of American states have used them to decide on contentious moral issues, from the use of cannabis for treatment of the sick to the right to 'death with dignity' via euthanasia, on social issues such as the rights of minorities to health reform and on constitutional issues such as term limits for those who serve in positions of political power. Some member states of the European Union have used them to confirm their membership or to ratify some important constitutional development. In Switzerland, the heaviest user of referendums among European countries, they are built into the regular machinery of government, and are held on a three-monthly basis. The new democracies of Central and Eastern Europe, particularly the fifteen republics of the former USSR, have used them to decide a range of issues relating to the form of their new governments. Among highly significant ones in the last decade were those that enabled white South Africans to reject the prevailing system of apartheid (separate development of the races) and East Timorians to vote for their independence from Indonesia.

Of 728 national referendums held across the world between 1900 and 1993, two-thirds were held in the last thirty-three years[30]. The issues broadly covered three main areas:

1. *Constitutional matters* – for example, the ratification of treaties and change to the electoral system in Italy and New Zealand.

2. *Territorial matters* – for example, the decision of a country as to whether it should join a larger unit such as the European Union and issues relating to devolving power to regions or provinces.
3. *Moral/social matters* – for example, whether to allow abortion, gambling or the legalisation of soft drugs.

We have mentioned above how questions can be worded to achieve the desired outcome. In other ways, it is possible to limit the impact of what the voters decide. There are also controversies relating to the timing and status of referendums. Even in democratic countries, they are normally held at the most propitious moment for the government. In 1997 Labour was careful to hold its vote on devolution in Wales after the similar one on Scotland. The Welsh were known to be

---

Box 9.9 Why has direct democracy become more important in recent decades?

Direct democracy caters for the need of many people to feel that they are involved in the decision-taking that affects their lives. Whereas they can only participate in a general election infrequently, initiatives and referendums provide an opportunity for popular involvement at intervals in between. Moreover (especially where they are used to resolve social issues), they enable voters to decide issues that are of importance to them.

Direct democracy is popular with pressure group activists, who – in the USA – see initiatives as a means of moving issues up the political agenda. As part of their growing professionalism, they have brought in a growing army of consultants who help them handle initiative campaigns. Organising direct democracy has become a growth industry. It has been encouraged by the media, who like to provide coverage of causes and those who support them.

In Britain, two factors have contributed to the use of referendums. First, governments of both parties have found them helpful in resolving controversial issues which cut across the party divide, such as devolution and Europe. Second, Labour has been converted to their value, and during the lifetime of Labour governments has been willing to use them to decide thorny constitutional issues and local issues such as the fate of grammar schools. It has been able to portray such consultation as an extension of democracy and voter empowerment.

lukewarm over the proposals, whereas the Scots were enthusiastic about gaining greater autonomy.

Referendums may be binding or advisory. In Britain, with its commitment to the idea of parliamentary sovereignty, only Parliament can cast a decisive vote on any issue, but it is unlikely that a majority of legislators would make a habit of casting their parliamentary vote in defiance of the popular will as expressed in a referendum. In 1975 Prime Minister Wilson accepted that a majority of even a single vote against so doing would be enough to take Britain out of the European Community. Both ministers and MPs accept that they should treat the popular verdict as mandatory, in the sense that it was morally and politically binding. The Swedish government had no such qualms in 1955, when the people voted to continue to drive on the left and it chose to ignore their decision. Swedish minister showed a similar reluctance when in 1980 the voters opted for the decommissioning of nuclear power stations; it took almost twenty years before the first reactor was taken out of action. Most governments have accepted that to consult and then to ignore the people's verdict is worse than never to have sought their opinion.

The merits and demerits of direct democracy

In favour of votes on single issues
Perhaps the strongest argument is that they give people a chance to take decisions which affect their lives, whereas in a general election they can only offer a general verdict. If democracy is supposed to be based upon the people's will, surely a referendum is the most direct and accurate way of getting their verdict. Such an exercise in direct democracy has an intrinsic appeal, for the idea of 'letting the people have their say' appears to gel with the usual understanding of what democratic government involves. A *Guardian* editorial[31] recognised the strength of this case, when it discussed the idea of a vote on electoral reform. It noted that Britain suffered from 'an enormous and increasing democratic deficit' and saw a need to encourage politicians to go out and persuade people of the merits of their standpoint: 'imaginative means have to be sought to redress the imbalance . . . [a referendum] would generate an urgent civic discussion which will never take place with such purpose in any other way'.

Otherwise, it can be pointed out that:

- They stimulate interest and involvement in public policy.
- They may exert pressure on the legislature to act responsibly and in the public interest, and in the case of initiatives raise issues that might otherwise remain undiscussed.
- They help counter the special interests to which legislators can be beholden.
- They help overcome the obstructionism of out-of-touch legislators and therefore make reform more likely.
- They allow governments to put difficult issues to the people that they would rather not take themselves, perhaps because they are internally divided or because the issue is a major and controversial one that has to be decided but on which support and opposition cut across the party divide. A 'yes' vote can strengthen the ministerial hand, as they seek to resolve an impasse. As Hague and Harrop[32] vividly put it: 'Like a plumber's drainrods, referendums resolve blockages.'
- Referendums resolve questions in such a way that there is a final solution to an issue which will not go away. The 1979 referendum resolved the devolution issue for several years, as did the European vote in 1975, even if that particular matter has returned to haunt some politicians. Critics of a particular policy are more likely to accept the result if they know that it is the public view, which is why Labour held its referendums on devolution in 1997 before the House of Commons began the legislative process, rather than after. Tony Benn, a leading opponent of British membership of the European Economic Community, explicitly made this point after the 1975 poll: 'I read the message loud and clear. When the British people speak, everyone – including ourselves – should tremble before their decisions.'

Against votes on single issues

The key point is that they fit uneasily into representative democracies. These are based upon the idea that people do not have to decide specific issues for themselves, but rather elect MPs or deputies to act on their behalf. Being close to the centre of the argument, these representatives are able to inform themselves fully on an issue, then vote accordingly. If we do not like how they exercise that choice, we can deny them our vote at the next election. If government and Parliament pass the question back to voters for their determination, then they shirk the responsibility which representative government clearly places upon them. Other arguments are that:

- Campaigns can be expensive and therefore to the advantage of well-funded groups. Money is too dominant in the process. Business interests have far more scope to influence the outcome to their own economic interests.
- Many issues are too complex for voters to handle. Their resolution requires a degree of knowledge and understanding that make it difficult for the average voter, who can provide a worthwhile general verdict on a government's performance in a general election but not easily deliver a specific judgement about the case for using the euro as a single currency.
- The result of a referendum can get muddled up with other issues. In 1979 opinion polls suggested that the majority of Scots favoured devolution, but there was a background of governmental unpopularity. It is significant that the Conservatives campaigned for a 'no' vote and argued that this was a vote against the Labour government's plans and not against the principle of devolution; indeed, they promised to bring forward proposals of their own!
- Initiatives and allied devices undermine political parties and therefore weaken the democratic process.
- They encourage single-issue politics, rather than debate based on a conflict of broad principles.
- They can work to the disadvantage of minorities, who can be persecuted by the majority (e.g. blacks and homosexuals).
- The referendum only tells what the public are thinking at a particular time, on a particular day. Logically, further votes are necessary to ensure that ministers are acting in line with the public mood. On Europe, in particular, another vote is necessary to give people a chance to express their viewpoint, bearing in mind how much the Community has changed over the last three decades as it was transformed into a Union.
- Votes on constitutional issues may be a good idea, but there are dangers in allowing popular opinion to determine issues such as

abortion, capital punishment and homosexual sex. The fear is that these contentious topics generate much passion and that voters may be swayed by emotion rather than reason, particularly after seeing images of unborn foetuses or in the aftermath of a brutal killing.

The use of referendums in the United Kingdom

Britain has until recently had very little experience of voting on a single issue, even though the case has often been canvassed in the twentieth century. A Conservative leader and former prime minister, Arthur Balfour, told the House of Commons back in 1911 that 'so far from corrupting the sources of democratic life [referendums] would only be a great education for political people'.

There is no procedure for the use of initiatives in Britain. The only UK-wide referendum was when in 1975 voters were asked whether or not they wished the country to remain in the European Economic Community. Before 1997, there were also local votes on the future status of schools and the ownership of council estates, and in Wales the issue of 'local option' on the Sunday opening of pubs was decided in this way.

Since May 1997 referendums have already been used to resolve the issue of devolution, and the future shape of London's government. Also, in concurrent votes, popular approval of the Good Friday Agreement was given by electors on both sides of the border in Ireland. When New Labour took office, it was committed to a vote on electoral reform at some time in the future, but this has not taken place. In the unlikely event that there should be a decision for Britain to join the single currency, then this too will be submitted to the people for popular backing. A referendum was promised on the draft EU Constitution, but the rejection of the document by French voters in 2005 has effectively sounded its death-knell, so that no vote is likely to be held.

New Labour has been more willing to allow the public a key role in the decision-making process on constitutional matters than the Conservatives, although it had to be placed under sustained pressure to concede one on the European Constitution. Ministers knew that Europe was an unpopular issue with the British public and were

Table 9.12 UK experience of national referendums

Year	Topic	Turnout (%)	Outcome
1973	Border poll in Northern Ireland: electorate asked if it wished to remain a part of the UK or join the Republic of Ireland.	61%	Massive majority to remain in UK
1975	UK's membership of EEC: electorate asked if it wished to stay in the Community or withdraw from it.	64%	2/3 majority to stay in (43% of whole electorate)
1979	Devolution to Scotland and Wales: each electorate was asked if it wanted a devolved assembly.	62.8% / 58.3%	Scotland: narrow majority in favour / Wales: majority against
1997	Devolution to Scotland and Wales: each electorate was asked if it wanted a devolved assembly.	60.1% / 50.1%	Scotland: strong majority for / Wales: very narrow majority for
1998	Good Friday Agreement on Northern Ireland: voters north (and south) of border asked to endorse the package.	81.0%	Overwhelming majority in favour

unenthusiastic about asking for what they considered to be unnecessary public endorsement. Maastricht and other European treaties had never been placed before the British electorate for its consideration by Conservative ministers in office, but in opposition they knew that in campaigning for a vote on the Constitution they had a strong possibility of public approval for their stance. Parties and politicians tend to view referendums according to the chances of victory or defeat.

In their approach to referendums, Labour has mainly taken the view that:

* the device is a democratic one in that it gives people a direct say in decision-making, so that any decision taken has legitimacy
* it is particularly appropriate for deciding constitutional issues that bind future as well as the present generations.

Cynics would suggest that Labour's willingness to resort to a popular vote has much to do both with governmental prospects and a reluctance to take difficult and divisive decisions. Ministers were happy enough to allow a referendum which they thought they could win, such as the vote on devolution in Scotland. In that case, the people's wishes were not in doubt. Prior to the Euro-elections (2004), they agreed to permit a future vote on the highly contentious issue of the European Constitution, in order to take the sting out of any Conservative attack on the failure to consult the people. Should the verdict not be the one favoured by ministers when it is eventually held, they are unlikely to feel under any pressure to resign from office.

The case of France: the use of referendums

France has used referendums more than most European countries, other than Switzerland. The 1958 Constitution made provision for such direct consultation with the voters. Nine had been held by the year 2000, all on constitutional issues. However, a constitutional amendment passed in 1995 allows for the use of direct democracy on economic and social policy, and the services that implement these.

Constitutional topics tackled include self-determination and later independence for Algeria (1961–2), enlargement of the European Community (1972), ratification of the Maastricht Treaty (1992) and the introduction of a five-year presidency (2000), all of which issues were approved. Only twice has the ministerial recommendation been defeated, the first time was in 1969, when the failure to achieve support for reform of the Senate and the creation of regions led to the downfall of Charles de Gaulle. He had tended to regard referendums as 'plebiscitary confirmation of his own standing.'[33]

Of the votes held since 1960, that on the Maastricht Treaty attracted a turnout of around 60 per cent. Most recently, the vote on the quinquennat, the five-yearly presidential election, failed to inspire public enthusiasm and resulted in the lowest turnout yet recorded in a French referendum. In 2005, President Chirac was unenthusiastic about putting the proposed EU Constitution up for popular approval, perhaps recognising that it might be a difficult cause on which to campaign. He reluctantly agreed to do so, but the plan backfired. In May 2005, on a 70 per cent turnout, voters rejected the document by 54.9 per cent to 45.1 per cent. Those registering a 'no' vote came from across the political spectrum, including communists, dissident socialists and supporters of far-right groups. The outcome was widely seen as being not just a verdict on the people's view the future of European integration. Other issues played a part, including the voters' disapproval of the governmental economic record.

The case of Germany: voting behaviour

Voting behaviour in Germany has undergone several of the changes that have characterised the situation in other democracies in recent years. Social class and religion continue to have an important influence, but they lack the hold they once held over many voters. Today, only 38 per cent of Germans work in manual occupations, so that as in Britain there is a shrinking working class from which the left-wing party can draw support. The Social Democratic Party has needed to widen its appeal, as it successfully did in the late 1990s under Gerhard Schröder's leadership. Similarly, the old middle class of farmers, shopkeepers, doctors and lawyers now forms a much smaller part of the electorate, so that for Christian and Free Democrats it has been necessary to adapt and broaden their support. In religion too, there has been a profound change. Religion has lost its hold over many Germans, and the number of weekly church attenders has dropped from over 40 per cent to just over 20 per cent in the period since the 1950s. According to Colomer[34]: 'Church-going Catholics were about as likely to vote for the CDU/CSU in 1990 as they were in the 1950s, [but] their numbers and hence the aggregate impact of religion on the vote have declined.'

At election time, the decline in traditional allegiances and the greater volatility of voting behaviour mean that personality counts for more than in the past. So do too the policies and images of the parties, for voters are more willing to make their decisions on the merits of the case. Many young voters are tempted by the 'new politics' represented by the Green movement. They find their idealism been better represented by Die Grünen than by Gerhard Schröder's pragmatic Social Democrats. They are inspired by a platform emphasising environmental matters, peace and disarmament, opposition to nuclear power and women's rights.

The case of the USA: election campaigning

American elections are far more focused on candidates and their personal qualities and/or failings than on their party label or particular issues. With the backing of **political action committees**, candidates run much of their own campaigning, parties assisting them in a supportive capacity. Candidates seek to put together a winning coalition of support. They do this by making sure that there are sufficient funds to allow them to get their message across as widely as possible, so that everyone knows who they are and what they stand for.

Campaigning has always demanded certain qualities from the person chosen: a pleasing voice, a gift for public speaking, the ability to sell one's personality and to persuade people of the merits of a particular case. A half-century ago, such assets were deployed 'on the stump', as speakers addressed a gathering in the local marketplace or school hall. John F. Kennedy conducted very active speech-making tours and sometimes spoke from the rear of a railway carriage, as he campaigned across the country. However, nowadays any deficiencies are a serious liability exposed before the whole nation, whereas previously many voters did not know of them. Personal failings are also highlighted in the blaze of publicity surrounding a modern election campaign.

Whether the election is for Congress, for the presidency or for some other position, the trend has been towards far greater professionalism than ever before. Some argue that elections today are increasingly about presentation and style rather than substance, in that television simplifies and trivialises issues, and the political message is sold like soap-powder or cosmetics. Too often, the point has to be conveyed in visual terms, and rather than analysis and depth of discussion, the trend is increasingly for candidates and their backers to buy 15 or 30 second slots of prime advertising time, which are then often then devoted to creating a negative impression of one's opponent.

· ·

 ## What you should have learnt from reading this chapter

- Elections and election campaigns are the process by which democracies choose the path they will take in the future. Everyone has a chance to affect that crucial decision, but many voters fail to take the opportunity to do so.

- Those who do vote do so in the light of many influences, party identification and social class being declining factors. In highly visible campaigns in which information is readily available, candidate attributes and policy positions are more important than in the past and can lead voters to abandon their long-term allegiances.

- Campaigns are increasingly candidate-centred, media-driven and negative. These features may have contributed to the decline in turnout.

- Voters in the United Kingdom now have a range of elections in which they can vote, such as European, devolved and mayoral contests. A variety of different voting systems are employed. The outcomes illustrate that proportional systems encourage the success of smaller parties and make coalition administrations more likely.

Glossary of key terms

Agenda-setting The media's function of directing people's attention to particular issues for their consideration: giving some issues special – some would say, disproportionate – coverage; the way in which the media influence not only what we think, but what we think about.

Candidate-centred campaigning A campaign in which the emphasis is on the role and activity of the individual candidate, rather than on the party he or she represents. Consultants and volunteers coordinate campaign activities, develop strategies and raise funds, although parties are likely to be involved.

Class de-alignment Class de-alignment refers to the weakening of the traditional links between voting and the social class to which a person belongs – for example, the majority of working-class people are now less solidly supportive of Labour than they once were.

Consultants Used increasingly in recent decades, most of them specialise in some aspect of campaigning, such as fundraising, personal image and presentation, polling, speech-writing, spin-doctoring and staging media-covered events. First coming to notice in the United States and then spreading to other democracies, all are in the business of 'selling' politicians. They tend to associate themselves with the party with whom they have some affinity.

Embourgeoisement The theory that as working-class people became more affluent and acquired more material possessions, they increasingly behaved more like middle-class people in their voting habits.

Jenkins Inquiry The Jenkins Commission was established by Tony Blair to recommend a new system for electing MPs. It reported in October 1998, members recommending the use of AV Plus, a scheme under which the bulk of seats would be fought on a single-member constituency basis using the Alternative Vote, while a top-up of additional members would provide for a greater measure of proportionality.

Mass media Those means of communication that permit messages to be conveyed to the public, such as broadcasting by radio and television, the press, books, cinema and, more recently, videos and computers. They reach a large and potentially unlimited number of people at the same time.

Photo-opportunities Carefully stage-managed events in which the leading figure is set against a particular background, perhaps to demonstrate concern for the location. Such occasions have a humanising effect, suggesting that the candidate is a so-called 'regular guy'.

Political action committees Organisations formed by individuals, companies and other pressure groups to fund the election campaigns of candidates who sympathise with their aims.

Spin doctors 'Spin' refers to the attempt to change the way the public perceives what is happening, by putting a gloss on events and information to make them appear in a better light. The term derives from the spin given to a ball in flight, in various sports (originally in baseball). It is a new name for an old practice, public relations management. Spin doctors are those in the media team whose skill is to 'spin' stories, to make them more flattering to the candidate or party. The term has become pejorative of late, Labour's skilful use of it being said to encourage disbelief about ministers' true convictions.

❓ Likely examination questions

'Theoretically admirable, but in practice unworkable'. Discuss this verdict on the differing varieties of proportional representation.

Does the use of First-Past-The-Post for Westminster elections mean that Britain will always have a two-party system?

'UK experience of PR has so far failed to establish a convincing case for its use in Westminster elections.' Discuss.

'Turnout in British elections has long been unimpressive by European standards and appears to be in long-term decline.' Does it matter?

'Modern elections are more about personalities than issues.' Discuss.

How important are election campaigns in determining the outcome of elections?

Discuss the view that the media tend to reinforce the existing views of the votes rather than fundamentally alter them.

Do the links between social class and voting matter any more?

Helpful websites

www.keele.ac.uk/depts/po/ptbase.htm   Keele Guide to Political Thought and Ideology, containing information about many aspects of elections and voting

www.charter88.org   Charter 88 Information on use of different electoral systems

www.electoral-reform.org.uk   Electoral Reform Society. Useful source of ideas and statistics concerned with alternative voting systems, particularly its favoured STV

Suggestions for further reading

Useful articles

A. Batchelor, 'Direct Democracy', *Talking Politics*, January 2002.

J. Curtice and M. Steed, 'And Now for the Commons? Lessons from Britain's First Experience with Proportional Representation', *Politics Review*, 2000.

I. Davenport, 'Electoral Reform', *Talking Politics*, September 2004.

D. Denver, 'Whatever happened to Electoral Reform?' *Politics Review*, September 2003.

P. Donleavy, 'How Proportional are the British AMS Systems?', *Representation* 40:4, 2004.

R Gibson S. Ward and W. Lusoli, 'The Internet and Political Campaigning: The New Media Comes of Age', *Representation* 39:3, 2003.

R. Johnston and C. Pattie, 'The Growing Problem of Electoral Turnout in Britain', *Representation* 40:1, 2003.

P. Norris, 'Does Proportional Representation Promote Political Extremism?', *Representation* 40:3, 2004.

M. Rathbone, 'Referendums in Britain', *Talking Politics*, September 1999.

D. Watts, 'The Growing Attractions of Direct Democracy', *Talking Politics*, September 1997.

E. Wild, 'Modern Myths of Electoral Apathy', *Talking Politics*, 2003.

Useful book

D. Denver, *Elections and Voters in Britain*, Palgrave, 2003.

CHAPTER 10

Democracy in Theory and Practice

Contents

Overview

Democracy is the most stable and enduring governing idea in modern politics. It arouses widespread approval, even in states that may seem undemocratic. In this chapter, we trace the development of ideas about democracy, from the time of the Greeks to the present day. We then examine the characteristics of modern liberal, representative democracies, before assessing how democratic the British system is in practice and noting possible areas where action is required.

Key issues to be covered in this chapter

- How and why the term 'democracy' has been extensively used
- Direct democracy in ancient Greece
- The development of modern ideas on democracy
- Indirect and liberal democracy
- The various other models of democracy that have been suggested
- British democracy, its virtues and blemishes

Democracy in vogue

According to Abraham Lincoln, democracy is:

a system where no man is good enough to govern another man without that other's consent.

On another occasion, he described it as:

government of the people, by the people and for the people.

Today, almost all of us describe ourselves as democrats and more people than ever across the world live under conditions of democratic rule. This is not to be complacent about the nature of some regimes and the brutalities and breaches of human rights that they practise. Rather, it is a statement of the fact that tolerable levels of democracy prevail more widely and over more people than ever in the past.

Doctrines such as capitalism and socialism are called into question, but democracy is an abiding principle to which most of us feel attached. Hardly any group would disown the label, even though they might think very differently about what it entails. Communists and conservatives, liberals and socialists, anarchists and fascists often try to hijack the word, as though they have a particular understanding of its meaning. In fact, very few groups would like to be described as undemocratic and the same is true of countries as well. North Korea calls itself the Democratic People's Republic. Sri Lanka sees itself as a Democratic Socialist Republic. The nature of the world's 'democracies' varies spectacularly. In many cases, they are far removed from those that operate in Western Europe and the United States, with their emphasis on representative and limited government. Perhaps unsurprisingly, Bernard Crick[1] felt impelled to refer to democracy as 'the most promiscuous word in the world of public affairs . . . she is everybody's mistress and yet somehow retains her magic even when a lover sees her favours being illicitly shared by another'.

Whatever the definition of democracy employed, democracy is in practice a model form of government to which it is easy to aspire but difficult to achieve. Even those states commonly regarded as among the most democratic often have blemishes upon their record in particular areas.

The development of democracy

The city-states of ancient Athens provide the first great experiment in democracy. Essentially it was a form of government based on mass meetings, with major decisions being made by the Assembly, to which every citizen belonged. Pericles described the experience as a system in which government was the concern of the many rather than the few. From our point of view, however, there were obvious flaws in the Athenian model, in that the right to vote was limited to free citizens, men of Athenian ancestry. Foreigners, slaves and women were denied the chance to participate in decision-making.

From the collapse of the Roman republic in the second century BC until the eighteenth century, **autocracy** was the usual form of government, although in Britain from the seventeenth century a concept of parliamentary control over the arbitrary actions of the monarch began to emerge. The American Declaration of Independence, chiefly written by Thomas Jefferson and based on the ideas of the English philosopher John Locke, marked an important development. Its basic theme was that King George III had violated the contract between people and their leader. It contained many references that today sound profoundly democratic. It spoke of 'inalienable rights' and proclaimed that 'all men are created equal' and that 'governments derive their just powers from the consent of the governed'.

In the *Federalist Papers* which followed the drafting of the American Constitution, the protagonists wrestled with key issues of government, such as how to make it strong enough to keep order and protect liberties and basic rights, yet ensure that it was not so strong that it limited their freedoms. The answer was indirect, representative democracy, with certain checks and balances to guarantee the protection of minority rights.

There was considerable interest in France at the American experiment and ideas were exchanged between leaders of the American Revolution and the early leaders of the French Revolution of 1789. The National Assembly drew up a Declaration of the Rights of Man, modelled on the American experience. It spoke of men as being 'free and equal in rights', of the principle of 'popular sovereignty' and the importance of 'equality before the law', among other important policies. For many years, the Declaration was the watchword of all European reformers, who were stirred by its battle-cry of 'liberty, equality, **fraternity**'.

Democracy: its main forms

The word 'democracy' derives from two Greek terms, *demos*, meaning people and *kratia*, signifying rule of or by. Many people therefore see democracy as meaning 'people power', with government resting on the consent of the governed. There are two main types of democracy:

1. *Direct or classical democracy*, the situation in which it is possible for all the citizens to come together in one place to make decisions as to how the state should be run.
2. *Indirect or representative democracy*, the form of democracy which emerged to replace the direct form, in which the voters choose representatives who will govern on their behalf and according to the wishes of the majority.

In modern states, the growth in population and the size of the area to be governed meant that the old Athenian form of direct democracy was no longer viable, other than in very small communities. It went out of fashion. In the nineteenth century, representative democracy developed in Britain, with the extension of the right to vote and the evolution of a constitutional monarchy.

The characteristics of representative democracies

Key elements of a modern representative democracy include:

- *Popular control of policy-makers*. Government must be subject to control exercised through elected representatives, popularly chosen.
- *The existence of opposition*. Without a right to oppose, there can be no democracy.
- *Political equality*. Every adult must have the right to vote, each having only one vote.
- *Political freedoms*. There must be a free choice of candidates and a range of basic liberties and rights – free speech, assembly and organisation among them.

- *Majority rule.* The right of the majority to have their way may seem just, but it needs to be accompanied by toleration of and respect for any minority.

From this listing of criteria, we can piece together the following definition: a democratic political system is one in which public policies are made, on a majority basis, by representatives subject to effective popular control at periodic elections which are conducted on the principle of political equality and under conditions of political freedom.

Other forms of democracy

Liberal democracies

Democracy involves more than people having voting rights. It is essential that there are opportunities for citizens and the media to exercise freedom of speech, assembly and political opposition. There are checks on the power of government to protect citizens from arbitrary or unfair action, so that a liberal democratic regime is characterised by:

- *pluralism* – the existence of diverse centres of economic and political power
- *limited government* – constraints on the power of government
- *open government* – non-secretive government which can be seen to be fair and accountable
- *independent judiciary* – a just, impartial legal system.

In liberal democracies, the power of government is limited by the recognition of free play between autonomous voluntary associations within society. There are several checks and balances. Important foci of power include trade unions, professional associations and private companies. The task of government is to reconcile and coordinate these various interests, only imposing coercion when other methods of harmonisation fail to operate effectively.

Liberal democracies are characterised by a spirit of tolerance towards competing groups and particularly towards the views of minorities. There is due recognition of everybody's interests, but it is understood that government should be concerned with the good of the whole community.

Participatory democracies

Despite the general acceptance in the West of representative and liberal democracy, some writers see this view of democracy as incomplete and say it concentrates on the government of the many by the few and involves the idea of the mass of the citizenry only in a very minimal way. Writers from Jean-Jacques Rousseau to Peter Hain have argued that individual and group participation should be a distinguishing feature of a democracy. They stress the educational and integrative effects of political involvement. The goal of participationists is not merely active participation in government, but a participatory society in which democracy is no longer seen as a means of good government but as an end in itself.

Semi- or façade democracies

The versions of democracy outlined above are based primarily on the experience of Western Europe and North America. In other parts of the world, newer forms of democracy have been developed which cannot be included within the orbit of liberal democracy. Hague and Harrop[2] refer to them as semi-democracies, blending features of a Western-style representative democracy with more authoritarian impulses. They have been developed in countries whose conditions are very different to our own and are an attempt to graft on the familiar democratic features of elections to regimes whose tone has in the past often been severely repressive. Finer[3] dismissed them as 'façade democracies', but less unflattering terms include 'limited democracies' and 'authoritarian democracies'.

Good examples are provided by some of the Asian states such as Malaysia and Singapore, in both of which effective, stable government has been provided by regimes that are 'repressive-responsive'. Hague and Harrop quote Egypt, Singapore and Tunisia also, as having systems in which semi-competitive elections are held (there may be some attempt to manipulate the outcome), but in which opposition can also be kept under control by intimidation. There may be 'roughing up' of opponents and harassing of dissidents, as in the Ukranian elections of 2004. Among other abuses in the Ukraine, supporters of the Prime Minister were bussed from place to place, so that they could vote again; people were brought in from Russia to vote for him; and likely voters for opposition candidates were given pens to mark the ballot paper from which the ink disappeared shortly afterwards.

These 'democracies' are far removed from the Western-style ones as exemplified by Britain and the United States. Governmental institutions such as the assembly and the judiciary are liable to be cowed by the dominant force. But the transition to power has been achieved by peaceful means via the process of elections, whether it be in parts of Africa and Latin America, and the bulk of Eastern Europe.

British democracy in practice

Is Britain a working democracy?

For most people, the answer is a resounding 'yes', in that it has the usual characteristics of liberal, representative democracy. Indeed, Hacker[4] felt inspired to describe Britain and the United States as 'the world's two leading democracies'. Traditional features of the democratic way of life have long existed in both countries, including:

- ample opportunities for the free expression of opinions
- elections by secret ballot from a choice of candidates
- government resting on consent and being accountable to the people
- opportunities for people to influence government
- a spirit of tolerance prevailing between the majority and the minority
- a reluctance to coerce recalcitrant minorities, and through free elections the means by which a legitimate and peaceful minority may seek to transform itself into a majority
- the provision for power to change hands peacefully
- limited government and the protection of individual rights
- an independent judiciary
- a free media.

Criticism of the workings of our democracy

A few decades ago, political analysts in many parts of the world were worried about the fragility of democracy. Governments were struggling to cope with new issues that came on to the political agenda, demands, and political institutions were having difficulty adjusting to calls for a more participatory democracy. Several scholars described this situation as a crisis of Western democracy. However, the ending of the Cold War in the late twentieth century has given rise to a new euphoria about democracy and the democratic process, even on the part of some who had earlier trumpeted the warning calls. And yet, as democracy celebrates its triumph over communism, there are continuing signs of public doubts about the vitality of the democratic process. Joseph Nye and his colleagues[5] demonstrated that low levels of political trust among the American public continued into the 1990s. Several subsequent cross-national analyses suggest this is not a distinctly American phenomenon. Indeed, some writers would go further and suggest that there is a 'crisis of democracy'. Fuchs and Klingemann[6] suggest that the public in several democracies have become increasingly alienated from the democratic system, as a result of

- greater centralisation
- its failure to deliver what citizens want
- lower opportunities for participation.

Democracy is more than observance of a particular form of government, based on the existence of free institutions. It is an ideal, something to aspire to. In other words, although the framework may exist, it needs to be maintained in a constant state of good repair. As in other democracies, there are blemishes within the British system.

If such talk may seem unduly alarming or inapplicable in Britain, nonetheless many examples of possible deficiencies within our democracy have been considered elsewhere in this book, among them:

- lack of knowledge, interest and belief in politicians on the part of the electorate
- low levels of political participation and of turnout in elections
- the electoral system, as used at Westminster
- ownership and control of, and trivial content in, the news media
- the denial or erosion of rights, as indicated by Democratic Audit (see Box 10.1) and elsewhere
- the growing importance of money and finance issues in politics, in particular reliance on large donations – be they from unions, business or affluent individuals
- the existence of quangos
- allegations that we have an 'elective dictatorship', in which governments armed with a Commons majority can drive their programme on to the statute book

- the lack of openness in government and of any freedom of information legislation
- the limited use of direct democracy, as a means of engaging people's interest
- the lack of popular control over institutions of the European Union.

Some would question whether these are blemishes upon the British record. Not everyone is convinced that proportional electoral systems are more democratic, or that regular (or any) referendums are a good thing. Others listed, such as the allegedly inadequate protection of rights or the lack of freedom of information, have recently been addressed. The elective dictatorship theory is open to challenge and – in the light of the outcome of the 2005 election – we may be approaching the end of an era of 'presidential government'.

Few countries can claim to have a perfect system. At least British citizens live in a country that has evolved by peaceful change, rather than through violent upheaval. It also has a long attachment to freedom. If in several respects, the reality has fallen short of the democratic ideal, the commitment to democracy has always been apparent and there are always people ready to highlight any lapses from that ideal.

Box 10.1 The findings of Democratic Audit

Democratic Audit, a research body attached to the Human Rights Centre at the University of Essex, seeks to evaluate the quality of democracy and the protection of rights in Britain and around the world. It encourages a critical stance of democratic arrangements in order to facilitate their reform and provide people with the chance to influence and control the countries in which they live.

Democratic Audit recognises that there is no such thing as a perfect democracy. It:

- views democracy as a continuum, so that any democracy may be more or less democratic than another, often more or less democratic in one area than in another
- has done pioneering work on democracy assessment, developing comparative approaches that can be used to assess democracies everywhere

- scores democracies according to several detailed qualitative and quantitative criteria, and sets them against the norms and best practice in European and other modern democracies.

For its 1996 audit of civil and political rights in the UK, Klug et al.[7] developed a Human Rights Index based on the European Convention on Human Rights and other international human rights instruments. Their findings pointed to the lack of adequate protection of fundamental political rights and freedoms in Britain, in comparison with other democracies. They detected a 'weakness at the very heart of Britain's political and constitutional system'. Thereafter this and a further study of democracy were to be used as a baseline for future analyses.

Comparing the state of democracy under the Conservatives to May 1997 and Labour to 2002, the writers of the most recent publication[8] suggest that in every area other than voter turnout, democracy under the Blair government has fared better than its predecessors, although on the 'existence of an honest and responsive media' the two records score the same. However, this does not imply that since 1997, all has been well within the body politic. Indeed, in areas such as accountability to Parliament, devolution (England being described as 'a hole in the heart of devolution'), free and fair elections, open government, responsive government and women in public life, their findings are generally damning.

The conclusion is that although Britain is a liberal democracy, 'parliamentary democracy here is at risk', largely because we live under what Lord Hailsham[9] once referred to as an 'elective dictatorship' and Jack Straw[10] described as 'executive democracy'. Democratic Audit single out two 'obsolete features of our constitutional arrangements' for special criticism: the FPTP electoral system ('notoriously disproportionate') and the largely unchecked power of governments (particularly those with vast majorities) to dominate Parliament.

The attitudes and way of life of British citizens provide a setting in which democratic principles and practices have generally flourished. But as society evolves, so too does our democracy. New situations create a need for new remedies. As more power becomes centralised in the hands of the Executive, so new checks and balances become necessary. Successful adaptation requires that our politicians, media and people have a critical appreciation of our institutions and are vigilant against any abuses of the best democratic practice.

✅ What you should have learnt from reading this chapter

This chapter has distinguished different uses of the term 'democracy' and assessed the way in which democracy is working in Britain. It has examined:

- the widespread approval of the word 'democracy'
- different types of democracy around the world
- the distinction between direct and indirect (representative) democracy
- the characteristics of indirect and liberal democracies
- why Britain qualifies as a democracy
- why some people have doubts about the effectiveness of democracy in Britain and feel that our so-called democratic system has serious limitations.

🔍 Glossary of key terms

Autocracy Government by an individual with unrestricted authority.
Fraternity Bonds of comradeship and sympathy between people who are united in their aims and interests.

❓ Likely examination questions

Are modern forms of democracy truly democratic?

Winston Churchill described democracy as 'the worst form of government except all the others that have been tried from time to time'. How can democracy be defended against this charge?

How well does democracy work in Britain at the present time?

In what ways could British government be made more democratic?

Helpful websites

www.ucl.ac.uk/constitution-unit   The Constitution Unit. For its publications, add/publications

www.democraticaudit.com   Democratic Audit

Suggestions for further reading

A. Arblaster, *Democracy*, Oxford University Press, 1994

B. Crick, *Democracy: A Very Short Introduction*, Oxford University Press, 2002.

D. Beetham, I. Byrne, P. Ngan et al., *Democracy under Blair*, Politico's Publishing, 2003.

C. Bromley, J. Curtice and B. Seyd, *Is Britain Facing a Crisis of Democracy?*, Constitution Unit, 2004.

R. Dahl, *Democracy and its Critics*, Yale University Press, 1989.

References

Chapter 1

1. A. Hanson and M. Walles, *Governing Britain*, Fontana, 1977.
2. A. Birch, *The British System of Government*, Allen & Unwin, 1975.
3. J. Blondel, *Comparative Government: An Introduction*, Prentice Hall, 1995.
4. Lord Stevens, as quoted in *The Guardian*, 13 July 2005.
5. *The Economist*, 23 July 2005.
6. CRE research conducted for *Connections*, Commission for Racial Equality, Winter 2004–5.
7. F. Northedge, *Descent From Power: British Foreign Policy, 1945–73*, Allen & Unwin, 1974.
8. A. Heywood, *Politics*, Macmillan, 1997.
9. H. Cantril, *The Pattern of Human Concerns*, Rutgers University Press, 1965.
10. I. Inglehart, *Culture Shifts in Advanced Industrial Society*, Princeton University Press, 1990.
11. R. Dalton, *Citizen Politics in Western Democracies*, Seen Bridges Press, 2001.
12. G. Almond and S. Verba, *The Civic Culture*, Princeton University Press, 1963.
13. G. Almond and S. Verba, *The Civic Culture Revisited*, Princeton University Press, 1980.
14. G. Parry, G. Moyser and N. Day, *Political Participation and Democracy in Britain*, Cambridge University Press, 1992.
15. J. Curtice and R. Jowell, 'Trust in the Political System', in R. Jowell, J. Curtice, A. Park et al. (eds), *British Social Attitudes: The 14th Report*, Ashgate, 1997.
16. J. Blondel, *Comparative Government: An Introduction*, Prentice Hall, 1995, and R. Punnett, *British Government and Politics*, Gower, 1971.
17. W. Bagehot, *The English Constitution*, Cambridge University Press, 2001 [1867].

Chapter 2

1. A. Heywood, *Politics*, Macmillan, 1997.
2. F. Hayek, *The Constitution of Liberty*, University of Chicago Press, 1960.

3. J. Marais, as quoted in J. Danziger, *Understanding the Political World*, Addison Wesley Longman, 2001.

4. A. Heywood, *Politics*, Macmillan, 1997.

5. K. Wheare, *Federal Government*, Oxford University Press, 1963.

6. A. Dicey, *Introduction to the Study of the Law and the Constitution*, Macmillan, 1885.

7. E. Wade and G. Philips, *Constitutional Law*, Longman, reissued 1998.

8. G. Peele, *Governing the UK*, Blackwell, 2004.

9. A. Hanson and M. Walles, *Governing Britain*, Fontana, 1997.

10. H. Elcock, 'The British Constitution: Broke, but who will fix it?', *Talking Politics*, September 1996.

11. A. Adonis, *Parliament Today*, Manchester University Press, 1993.

12. P. Norton, 'Constitutional Change: A Response to Elcock', in G. Peele, *Governing the UK*, Blackwell, 2004.

13. P. Hennessy, *The Hidden Wiring: Unearthing the British Constitution*, Gollancz, 1995.

14. T. Blair, *The Guardian*, 10 September 1995.

15. T. Blair, as quoted in R. Hazell, *Constitutional Futures: A History of the Next Ten Years*, Oxford University Press, 1999.

16. D. Irvine, as quoted in R. Hazell, *Constitutional Futures: A History of the Next Ten Years*, Oxford University Press, 1999.

17. T. Blair, *The Guardian*, 10 September 1995.

18. G. Peele, 'Introduction', in P. Dunleavy, A. Gamble, R. Hefferman et al. (eds), *Developments in British Politics 7*, Palgrave, 2003.

19. R. Hague and M. Harrop, *Comparative Government and Politics: An Introduction*, Palgrave, 2004.

20. A. Dicey, *Introduction to the Study of the Law and the Constitution*, Macmillan, 1885.

21. F. Klug, K. Starmer and S. Weir, *The Three Pillars of Liberty*, Routledge, 1996.

22. K. Starmer, 'Two Years of the Human Rights Act', *European Human Rights Law Review*, vol. 1, 2003.

23. V. Bogdanor, *The British Constitution in the Twentieth Century*, Clarendon Press, 2003.

24. A. Stevens, *Government and Politics of France*, Palgrave, 2003.

25. L. Hartz, *The Liberal Tradition in America*, Harcourt Brace, 1955.

Chapter 3

1. J. Blondel, *Comparative Government: An Introduction*, Prentice Hall, 1995.
2. R. Hague and M. Harrop, *Comparative Government and Politics: An Introduction*, Palgrave, 2004.
3. Editorial in *The Economist*, 20 January 2000.
4. G. Howe, 'Where next for the Lords?', *Citizenship PA*, January 2004.
5. M. Bragg, as quoted in F. Cooney and P. Fotheringham, *UK Politics Today*, Pulse Publications, 2002 .
6. K. Bartlett, 'The case for an Elected House of Lords', *Citizenship PA*, January 2004.
7. R. Hague and M. Harrop, *Comparative Government and Politics: An Introduction*, Palgrave, 2004.
8. *Shifting the Balance: Select Committees and the Executive*, report of the Commons Liaison Committee, HMSO, 2000.
9. G. Thomas, *Parliament in an Age of Reform*, Politics Association/SHU Press, 2000.
10. A. Mitchell, as quoted in G. Thomas, *Parliament in an Age of Reform*, Politics Association/SHU Press, 2000.
11. Hours survey, as quoted in G. Thomas, *Parliament in an Age of Reform*, Politics Association/SHU Press, 2000.
12. M. Foot, as quoted in A. Heywood, *Politics*, Macmillan, 1997.
13. P. Richards, *Honourable Members*, Faber & Faber, 1964.
14. P. Norton, 'The House of Commons: the half-empty bottle of reform', in B. Jones (ed.), *Political Issues in Britain today*, Manchester University Press, 1999.
15. H. Berrington, 'Political Ethics: The Nolan Report', *Government and Opposition* 30, 1995.
16. J. Lovenduski, 'Whose Secretary Are You, Minister?', as quoted in *The Guardian*, 7 December 2004.
17. I. Budge and K. Newton, *The Politics of the New Europe*, Longman, 1997.
18. M. Holland, *European Integration: From Community to Union*, Pinter, 1994.
19. W. Wilson, *Congressional Government*, Meridian Books, revised edition 1956.
20. J. Blondel, *Comparative Government: An Introduction*, Prentice Hall, 1995.
21. P. Norton, *Does Parliament Matter?*, Harvester Wheatsheaf, 1993.
22. R. Hague and M. Harrop, *Comparative Government and Politics: An Introduction*, Palgrave, 2004.

Chapter 4

1. A. Heywood, *Politics*, Macmillan, 1997.
2. A. Heywood, *Politics*, Macmillan, 1997.
3. I. Jennings, *Cabinet Government*, Cambridge University Press, 1959.
4. P. Gordon Walker, *The Cabinet*, Cape, 1970.
5. A. Hanson and M. Walles, *Governing Britain*, Fontana, 1980.
6. P. Madgwick, *An Introduction to British Politics*, Hutchinson, 1984.
7. P. Norton, *The British Polity*, Longman, 2001.
8. N. Lawson, *The View From No. 11*, Bantam, 1992.
9. M. Burch, 'Prime Minister and Cabinet: An Executive in Transition', in R. Pyper and L. Robins (eds), *Governing the UK in the 1990s*, Macmillan, 1995.
10. R. Crossman, *The Diaries of a Cabinet Minister*, vol. 2, Hamish Hamilton/Jonathan Cape, 1976.
11. M. Heseltine, *The Observer*, 12 January 1986.
12. T. Blair, as quoted in P. Hennessy, *The Prime Minister: The Office and its Holders since 1945*, Allen Lane, 2000.
13. P. Madgwick, *An Introduction to British Politics*, Hutchinson, 1984.
14. R. Crossman, in an introduction to a reissue of W. Bagehot, *The English Constitution*, Fontana, 1963.
15. J. Mackintosh, *The British Cabinet*, Stevens, 1977.
16. M. Foley, *The Rise of the British Presidency*, Manchester University Press, 1993.
17. D. Mayhew, *Divided We Govern*, Yale University Press, 1991.
18. T. Benn, 'The Case for a Constitutional Premiership', in A. King, *The British Prime Minister*, Macmillan, 1985.
19. T. Blair, as quoted in P. Hennessy, *The Prime Minister: The Office and its Holders since 1945*, Allen Lane, 2000.
20. P. Hennessy, *The Prime Minister: The Office and its Holders since 1945*, Allen Lane, 2000.
21. P. Hennessy, as reported in *The Guardian*, 28 February 2005.
22. R. Hague and M. Harrop, *Comparative Government and Politics: An Introduction*, Palgrave, 2004.
23. G. Wasserman, *The Basics of American Politics*, Longman, 1996.
24. R. Neustadt, *Presidential Power: The Politics of Leadership*, Wiley & Sons, 1960.

Chapter 5

1. J. Griffiths, *The Politics of the Judiciary*, Fontana, 1997.
2. Lord Hailsham, House of Lords' judgement, 1997.
3. Lord Taylor, 'The Judiciary in the Nineties', The Dimbleby Lecture, 1992.
4. C. Falconer, as quoted in *Monitor* no. 27 (The Constitution Unit Bulletin), July 2004.
5. A. Sampson, *Who Runs This Place? The Anatomy of Britain in the 21st Century*, John Murray, 2004.
6. J. Griffiths, *The Politics of the Judiciary*, Fontana, 1997.
7. J. Griffiths, *The Politics of the Judiciary*, Fontana, 1997.
8. G. Drewry, 'Judges and Politics in Britain', *Social Studies Review*, November 1986.
9. S. Lee, 'The Law and the Constitution', in A. Seldon and D. Kavanagh (eds), *The Major Effect*, Macmillan, 1994.
10. I. Budge and K. Newton, *The Politics of the New Europe*, Longman, 1997.
11. Lord Taylor, 'The Judiciary in the Nineties', The Dimbleby Lecture, 1992.
12. H. Woolf, *The Guardian*, 18 December 2002.
13. J. Jowell (ed.), *Lord Denning the Judge and the Law*, Sweet & Maxwell, 1984.
14. J. Griffiths, *The Politics of the Judiciary*, Fontana, 1997.
15. H. Woolf, *The Guardian*, 18 December 2002.
16. P. Boateng, as quoted in G. Peele, *Governing the UK*, Blackwell, 2004.
17. R. Hague and M. Harrop, *Comparative Government and Politics: An Introduction*, Palgrave, 2004.
18. K. Ewing and C. Gearty, *Freedom under Thatcher*, Clarendon Press, 1990.
19. Chief Justice Hughes quoted in R. Hague and M. Harrop, *Comparative Government and Politics: An Introduction*, Palgrave, 2004.
20. J. Biskupic, 'Justices want to be known as Jurists, not Activists', *Washington Post*, 9 January 2000.
21. T. Yarbrough, 'The Supreme Court and the Constitution', in G. Peele, C. Bailey, B. Cain and B. Guy Peters, *Developments in American Politics* 4, Palgrave, 2002.
22. J. Blondel, *Comparative Government: An Introduction*, Prentice Hall, 1995.
23. T. Bingham, as quoted in G. Peele, *Governing the UK*, Blackwell, 2004.
24. L. Lloyd, as quoted in P. Norton, 'A Bill of Rights: The Case Against', *Talking Politics*, April 1993.

Chapter 6

1. U. Bullman, 'The Politics of the Third Level', in C. Jeffery (ed.), *The Regional Dimension of the European Union: Towards Third Level in Europe*, Cass, 1997.
2. V. Bogdanor, *Devolution in the United Kingdom*, Oxford University Press, 1999.
3. Poll conducted for *The Scotsman*, 29 June 2001.
4. A. Salmond, *Citizenship* 3:iii, The Politics Association/Perpetuity Press, 2005.
5. V. Bogdanor, *Devolution in the United Kingdom*, Oxford University Press, 1999.
6. B. Coxall and L. Robins, *Contemporary British Politics*, Macmillan, 1998.
7. V. Bogdanor, *Devolution in the United Kingdom*, Oxford University Press, 1999.
8. T. Blair, as quoted in H. Atkinson and S. Wilks-Heeg, *British Local Government since 1979*, Politics Association/SHU Press, 1997.
9. R. Agranoff, 'Federal Evolution in Spain', *International Political Science Review* 17:4, 1996.
10. R. Singh, *Governing Britain: The Politics of a Divided Democracy*, Oxford University Press, 2003.
11. J. Blondel, *Comparative Government: An Introduction*, Prentice Hall, 1995.
12. A. Ward, 'Labour's Strange Constitutional "Design" ', in J. Jowell and D. Oliver (eds), *Britain's Changing Constitution*, Oxford University Press, 2000.

Chapter 7

1. R. Ball, *Modern Government and Politics*, Macmillan, 1993 .
2. R. Punnett, *British Government and Politics*, Gower, 1971.
3. M. Duverger, *Political Parties*, Methuen, 1962.
4. M. Duverger, *Political Parties*, Methuen, 1962.
5. A. Birch, *The British System of Government*, Allen & Unwin, 1967.
6. R. McKenzie, *British Political Parties*, Heinemann, 1963.
7. B. Pimlott, *Contemporary Record*, summer 1989.
8. D. Kavanagh and P. Morris, *Consensus Politics from Attlee to Thatcher*, Blackwell, 1994.
9. S. Finer (ed.), *Adversary Politics and Electoral Reform*, Wigram, 1975.
10. S. Finer (ed.), *Adversary Politics and Electoral Reform*, Wigram, 1975.
11. I. Budge, I. Crewe, D. McKay et al., *The New British Politics*, Longman, 1999.

12. G. Parry, *British Government*, Butterworths, 1969.
13. I. Gilmour, *Inside Right*, Quartet, 1978.
14. C. Crosland, *The Future of Socialism*, Cape, 1977.
15. W. Hutton, *The State We're In*, Vintage, 1996.
16. T. Blair, *The Guardian*, 17 May 1998.
17. A. Giddens, *The Third Way: The Renewal of Social Democracy*, Polity Press, 1998.
18. R. McKenzie, *British Political Parties*, Heinemann, 1963.
19. A. Ranney, as quoted in R. McKenzie, *British Political Parties*, Heinemann, 1963.
20. J. Blondel, *Comparative Government: An Introduction*, Prentice Hall, 1995.
21. I. Budge and K. Newton, *The Politics of the New Europe*, Longman, 1997.
22. A. Stevens, *Government and Politics of France*, Palgrave, 2003.
23. R. Hague and M. Harrop, *Comparative Government and Politics*, Palgrave, 2004.
24. D. Maidment and D. McGrew, *The American Political Process*, Sage/Oxford University Press, 1992.
25. P. Herrnson, *Party Campaigning in the 1980s*, Harvard University Press, 1998.

Chapter 8

1. A. Heywood, *Politics*, Macmillan, 1997.
2. S. Finer, *Anonymous Empire*, Pall Mall, 1967.
3. J. Stewart, *British Pressure Groups*, Oxford University Press, 1958.
4. W. Grant, *Pressure Groups and British Politics*, Palgrave, 2000.
5. R. Hague and M. Harrop, *Comparative Government and Politics: An Introduction*, Palgrave, 2004.
6. T. Matthews, 'Interest Groups', in R. Smith and L. Watson (ed), *Politics in Australia*, Allen & Unwin, 1989.
7. M. Rush, *Parliament and Pressure Groups*, Clarendon, 1990 .
8. R. Baggott, 'The Measurement of Change in Pressure Group Politics', *Talking Politics*, September 1992.
9. R. Baggott, *Pressure Groups and the Policy Process*, Politics Association/SHU Press, 2000.
10. R. Baggott, *Pressure Groups and the Policy Process*, Politics Association/SHU Press, 2000.
11. S. Finer, *Anonymous Empire*, Pall Mall, 1967.

12. A. Stevens, *Government and Politics of France*, Palgrave, 2003.
13. S. Waters, 'New Social Movement Politics in France: The Rise of Civic Forms of Mobilisation', *West European Politics* 21:3, 1998.
14. D. Watts, questionnaire to 15 groups, 2005.

Chapter 9

1. R. Gould and C. Jackson, *A Guide for Election Observers*, Commonwealth Parliamentary Association, 1995.
2. A. Heath, R. Jowell and J. Curtice, *Labour's Last Chance*, Dartmouth, 1994.
3. G. Wallas, *Human Nature in Politics*, Constable, 1908, reissued 1948.
4. W. Fletcher, as quoted in P. Norris, J. Curtice, D. Sanders et al. (eds), *On Message: Communicating the Campaign*, Sage, 1999.
5. L. Bille in S. Bowler and D. Farrell (eds), *Electoral Strategies and Political Marketing*, Macmillan, 1992.
6. D. Farrell and R. Schmitt-Beck (ed.), *Do Political Campaigns Matter?*, Routledge, 2002.
7. A. Rawnsley, 'Box of Political Tricks', *The Guardian*, 9 September 1988.
8. D. Kavanagh, *Election Campaigning: The New Marketing of Politics*, Blackwell, 1993.
9. D. Farrell, *Comparing Electoral Systems*, Harvester Wheatsheaf, 1997.
10. Report of the Plant Committee, *A Working Party on Electoral Reform: Interim Findings*, 1991.
11. *The Report of the Independent Commission on Voting Systems*, chaired by Lord Jenkins, HMSO, 1998.
12. D. Farrell, *Comparing Electoral Systems*, Harvester Wheatsheaf, 1997.
13. *The Report of the Independent Commission on Voting Systems*, chaired by Lord Jenkins, HMSO, 1998.
14. M. Duverger, *Political Parties*, Methuen, 1962.
15. P. Norton, *The Constitution in Flux*, Blackwell, 1982.
16. V. Bogdanor, *The Observer*, 4 April 1992.
17. A. Ball, *Modern Government and Politics*, Macmillan, 1993.
18. R. Hague and M. Harrop, *Comparative Government and Politics: An Introduction*, Palgrave, 2004.
19. R. Punnett, *British Government and Politics*, Gower, 1971.
20. P. Madgwick, *A New Introduction to British Politics*, Thornes, 1994.
21. B. Sarlvik and I. Crewe, *Decade of Dealignment*, Cambridge University Press, 1983.

22. P. Kellner, *The New Society*, 2 June 1983.
23. D. Denver, *Elections and Voters in Britain*, Palgrave, 2003.
24. J. Blumler and D. McQuail, *Television in Politics*, Faber & Faber, 1967.
25. W. Lippman, *Public Opinion*, Macmillan, 1938 .
26. D. Gill and B. Adams, *ABC of Communication Studies*, Nelson, 1998.
27. D. Glover, *The Sociology of the Mass Media*, Causeway Press, 1984.
28. F. Piven and R. Cloward, *Why Americans Don't Vote*, Pantheon Books, 1998.
29. D. Magleby, 'Direct Legislation in the United States', in D. Butler and A. Ranney (eds), *Referendums Around the World*, Macmillan, 1994.
30. R. Hague and M. Harrop, *Comparative Government and Politics: An Introduction*, Palgrave, 2004.
31. Editorial in *The Guardian*, 4 March 1993.
32. R. Hague and M. Harrop, *Comparative Government and Politics: An Introduction*, Palgrave, 2004.
33. A. Stevens, *Government and Politics of France*, Palgrave, 2003.
34. J. Colomer, *Political Institutions in Europe*, Routledge, 1996.

Chapter 10

1. B. Crick, *In Defence of Politics*, Penguin, 1982.
2. R. Hague and M. Harrop, *Comparative Government and Politics: An Introduction*, Palgrave, 2004.
3. S. Finer, *The History of Government from the Earliest Times*, Oxford University Press, 1997.
4. A. Hacker, 'Britain's Political Style Is Not Like Ours', *New York Times Magazine*, September 1964.
5. J. Nye, J. Nye Jr, P. Zelikow and D. King (eds), *Why People Don't Trust Government*, Harvard University Press, 1997.
6. D. Fuchs and H.-D. Klingemann, *Citizen and the State: A Relationship Transformed*, Oxford University Press, 1995.
7. F. Klug, K. Starmer and S. Weir, *The Three Pillars of Liberty*, Routledge, 1996.
8. D. Beetham, I. Byrne, P. Ngan and S. Weir, *Democracy under Blair: A Democratic Audit of the UK*, Politico's Publishing, 2003.
9. Lord Hailsham, *The Elective Dictatorship*, BBC. Publications, 1976.
10. J. Straw, as quoted in D. Beetham, I. Byrne, P. Ngan et al., *Democracy under Blair: A Democratic Audit of the UK*, Politico's Publishing, 2003.

Index

Bold indicates that the term is defined

Veritas, 252
voting behaviour, 349–58
    determinants, 345–6
    embourgeoisement, 352
    Germany, 368–9
    impact of media, 318–19, 356
    social class, 352
    trends, 349–53
    UK, 349–53

Wales
    Act (1998), 194, 202, 203
    Act of Union (1535), 2
    culture/language, 4
    devolved government, 11, 42
    history, 2, 4, 37
    National Assembly, 43, 202–3
    see also devolution re. referendums

war against Iraq (2003), 34, 135, 137,
    149, 150, 249, 250, 251–2, 322,
    346
War Powers Act (1973) (US), 107,
    108
West Lothian (English) question, 44,
    200–2
Westland Affair (1986), 126, 146, 150,
    154
Wilson, Harold, 127, 146, 246
women
    in House of Commons, 95–100,
        337
    in House of Lords, 68, 75, 94
    in national parliaments worldwide,
        92–3
    in Scottish Parliament, 198